Uncertainty

A Guide to Dealing with Uncertainty in
Quantitative Risk and Policy Analysis

Solum certum nihil esse certi
The only certainty is uncertainty

Pliny the Elder, *Historia Naturalis*, Bk ii, 7

Uncertainty

A Guide to Dealing with Uncertainty in Quantitative Risk and Policy Analysis

M. Granger Morgan and Max Henrion

with

a chapter by Mitchell Small

CAMBRIDGE
UNIVERSITY PRESS

Published by the Press Syndicate of the University of Cambridge
The Pitt Building, Trumpington Street, Cambridge CB2 1RP
40 West 20th Street, New York, NY 10011-4211, USA
10 Stamford Road, Oakleigh, Melbourne 3166, Australia

First published 1990
Reprinted 1991
First paperback edition 1992

Printed in the United States of America

Library of Congress Cataloging-in-Publication Data

Morgan, M. Granger (Millett Granger), 1941–
Uncertainty: a guide to dealing with uncertainty in quantitative risk and policy analysis /
M. Granger Morgan and Max Henrion ; with a chapter by Mitchell Small.
p. cm.
ISBN 0-521-36542-2
1. Uncertainty – Mathematical models. 2. Risk – Mathematical models.
3. Policy sciences – Mathematical models. I. Henrion, Max.
II. Small, Mitchell. III. Title.
HB615.M665 1990   89-22404
361.6'1'0151 – dc20   CIP

British Library Cataloguing in Publication Data

Morgan, M. Granger
Uncertainty: a guide to dealing with uncertainty in quantitative risk and policy analysis.
1. Reliability theory
I. Title II. Henrion, Max III. Small, Mitchell
519.5

ISBN 0-521-36542-2 hardback
ISBN 0-521-42744-4 paperback

Contents

Preface

To people trained in the physical sciences dealing with uncertainty is almost second nature. Serious physical scientists would not report an experimental result without an associated estimate of uncertainty, nor would they design a new experiment without giving careful attention to uncertainties. Thus, when we first left the physical sciences and started doing policy analysis, we simply did what came naturally. We worried about uncertainty. It didn't take long to discover that only a handful of other analysts (most of them trained in decision analysis or engineering) shared our concern. It took only a little longer to understand that, with its enormous inherent uncertainties, the field of policy analysis needs to be concerned with the characterization and analysis of uncertainty to an extent that far exceeds the need in the physical sciences. We set out to do such analysis, and along the way to build computer-based tools which would make the job easier. In the process, we discovered that what really matters is the training and philosophy of the analysts who use these tools. Through the doctoral program in the Department of Engineering and Public Policy at Carnegie Mellon University we have invested heavily in such education.

Today, while the adequate treatment of uncertainty in policy analysis is still the exception, not the rule, the exceptions are becoming more frequent. Throughout regulatory agencies, in executive branch staffs, national laboratories, universities, industry, and the halls of Congress, thoughtful people are coming to the same conclusion ... "it really isn't safe to be ignoring all this uncertainty; it may be important to the decisions we must make."

This book is designed for four audiences: practicing analysts who have become persuaded that dealing with uncertainty is important and want to learn how to do it; students who are just getting started in quantitative policy analysis and want to develop good skills and habits; managers or decision makers who are unlikely to ever do much analysis on their own but want to understand the available techniques well enough to know what to request, and how to critique the results; and the growing community of skilled analysts who work on these issues regularly, but do not yet have a general reference text that summarizes the basic ideas and techniques of the field in one convenient place. To all of you we hope that the ideas and pages that follow will give as much enjoyment and challenge as they have given us in their development, synthesis, and writing.

The preparation of this book was assisted by many people, among the most important of whom have been several successive groups of doctoral students in the Graduate Research Methods course of the Department of Engineering and Public Policy at Carnegie Mellon University. We are particularly grateful to Greg

McRae for many useful discussions and ideas; to Sam Morris, who collaborated on much of the research that got us started in this field; to Theresa Mullin, who kindly allowed us to use short excerpts of text from her Ph.D. thesis in portions of Chapters 6 and 7; and to Patti Steranchak, who helped us handle the innumerable details of producing the manuscript. Among the other colleagues, students, and family members who deserve special thanks are: Deborah Amaral, Hal Bamford, Nat Barr, Robyn Dawes, Greg Fischer, Baruch Fischhoff, Bob Hahn, Harald Ibrekk, Jay Kadane, Lester Lave, Victoria Massimino, Tom McCurdey, Betty Morgan, Frederick Morgan, Indira Nair, Warner North, Harvey Richmond, Bill Rish, Paul Slovic, and Maxine Small.

Primary support for the preparation of this book was provided by the U. S. National Science Foundation under grant PRA 8413097/-01. Support for many of the specific results reported has come from a variety of sources including NSF grants IST-8112439, IST-8316890, IST-8514090/-01, PRA-7913070, and SES-8715564; various contracts from the Health and Environmental Risk Assessment Program of the U.S. Department of Energy; the Biomedical and Environmental Assessment Division of Brookhaven National Laboratories; and the Department of Engineering and Public Policy of Carnegie Mellon University. Support for the final preparation of the manuscript was provided by a grant from the Alcoa Foundation.

1   Introduction

To know one's ignorance is the best part of knowledge.
Lao Tzu, *The Tao*, no. 71

Life is full of uncertainties. Most of us have learned to live comfortably with day-to-day uncertainties and to make choices and decisions in their presence. We have evolved cognitive heuristics and developed strategies, technologies, and institutions such as weather reports, pocket-sized raincoats, and insurance to accommodate or compensate for the effects of uncertainty. Looked at with care, these heuristics and strategies do not always perform as well as we would like (Dawes, 1988). When our cognitive processes for dealing with uncertainty introduce error or bias into our judgments we are often unable to detect the fact. When things go seriously wrong we may not be around to learn the lesson – or we may still be unable to detect that the problem came from faulty processing of uncertain information. Thus, we muddle through – often doing quite well, occasionally getting into serious trouble.

Of course, uncertainty is not limited to our private lives. It also occurs in larger and more public situations. Frequently in public discussion, policy analysis, regulatory decision making and other contexts, we proceed as if we understand and can predict the world precisely. While a moment's reflection is sufficient to persuade anyone that this is not true, a number of political, behavioral, and analytical factors combine to promote the continuation of this practice.

This book is about dealing with scientific and technical uncertainty in risk analysis and in other forms of quantitative policy analysis and policy-focused research. Until recently this uncertainty has been treated in much the same way we have dealt with other uncertainties in our private and public lives. However, the past decade has seen a growing recognition that policies that ignore uncertainty about technology, and about the physical world, often lead in the long run to unsatisfactory technical, social, and political outcomes. Recent growth in interest, understanding, and technical skill in the field of risk analysis and assessment has worked to promote this change. By definition, risk involves an "exposure to a *chance* of injury or loss" (Random House, 1966). The fact that risk inherently involves chance or probability leads directly to a need to describe and deal with uncertainty.

The result has been a rapid rise in interest in techniques whose practical application was originally pioneered by workers in decision analysis like Howard Raiffa (Raiffa and Schlaifer, 1961; Raiffa, 1968) at Harvard and Ronald

1

Howard (1966) at Stanford.   Good early examples of applications include
the work of Jack Grayson (1960) on oil wildcatting; work by Ron Howard,
Jim Matheson, and Warner North on controlling the risks posed by hurricanes
(Howard, Matheson, and North, 1972) and work by Warner North and co-
authors on such diverse problems as spacecraft biocontamination of Mars
(North, Judd, and Pezier, 1973) and the risks of wildfires in the Santa Monica
Mountains (North, Offensend, and Smart, 1975). Over the past decade, many
new investigators have begun to work on theoretical and applied problems of
uncertainty. A number of private sector decision makers, including several large
corporations, now routinely employ decision analytic techniques that incorporate
a treatment of uncertainty in their corporate planning and decision making.
Several federal agencies including the U.S. Nuclear Regulatory Commission,
the U.S. Department of Energy, and the U.S. Environmental Protection Agency
have begun to address the problems of incorporating an explicit treatment of
scientific and technical uncertainty in their analysis and regulatory decision
making. Chapter 2 provides three examples of recent milestones in such public
sector applications.

1.1. Does Uncertainty Really Matter?

The examples in the next chapter make it clear that dealing with uncertainty
in policy analysis and policy-focused research has, at the very least, become
"fashionable." On the other hand, for thousands of years our own and other
societies have been muddling along, making decisions with less than complete
attention to the associated uncertainties. Hence it seems only reasonable to ask
whether, despite the current interest, uncertainty actually matters very much. In
Chapter 3 and again in greater technical detail in Chapter 12, we explore this
question at some length and conclude – not surprisingly, given this book's title –
that, for quite a variety of reasons, uncertainty does matter and should not be
ignored.

The detailed arguments can wait for later. Why, in a nutshell – in language
that a casually interested airplane seatmate would understand – does technical
uncertainty in risk assessment and other forms of policy research and analysis
really matter? We could try an argument by analogy. Natural scientists are
expected as a matter of course to include an estimate of the probable error
when they report the value of quantities they have measured. The uncertainties
involved in most quantitative policy analyses are much greater than those
involved in work in the natural sciences. So policy analysts should report
their uncertainties too.

Such an argument would probably satisfy some seatmates. On the other hand,
the perceptive seatmate might insist on more specific arguments. In that case,
we would offer three:

1. A central purpose of policy research and policy analysis is to help identify the important factors and the sources of disagreement in a problem, and to help anticipate the unexpected. An explicit treatment of uncertainty forces us think more carefully about such matters, helps us identify which factors are most and least important, and helps us plan for contingencies or hedge our bets.
2. Increasingly we must rely on experts when we make decisions. It is often hard to be sure we understand exactly what they are telling us. It is harder still to know what to do when different experts appear to be telling us different things. If we insist they tell us about the uncertainty of their judgments, we will be clearer about how much they think they know and whether they really disagree.
3. Rarely is any problem solved once and for all. Problems have a way of resurfacing. The details may change but the basic problems keep coming back again and again. Sometimes we would like to be able to use, or adapt, policy analyses that have been done in the past to help with the problems of the moment. This is much easier to do when the uncertainties of the past work have been carefully described, because then we can have greater confidence that we are using the earlier work in an appropriate way.

The technical details of characterizing and dealing with uncertainty in policy research and analysis can get fairly complicated. It is important to remember that these *are* details and not lose sight of the big picture. Both people who commission and people who perform analysis that deals with uncertainty should from time to time return to the three broad arguments just listed and ask, "Is this really what our analysis is doing?" When the answer is not clearly yes, the time has come for some careful rethinking.

1.2. Outline of the Book

We close this introductory chapter with a brief outline of the balance of the book. For readers unfamiliar with the topic, Chapter 2 motivates the chapters that follow by presenting three recent and visible examples of risk and policy analyses in which uncertainty played an important role. Chapters 3 through 10 cover the central issues of the book. The final two chapters provide more specialized details. Chapter 3 presents a general overview of the subject of quantitative policy research and analysis and explores where and how the issue of uncertainty fits in this broader context. Chapter 4, "The Nature and Sources of Uncertainty," discusses various sources of uncertainty in some detail and then develops a general taxonomy of the kinds of quantities that can enter in policy analysis and the way in which to treat uncertainty about these quantities. There is a standard set of techniques for dealing with uncertainty in situations in which large amounts of relevant historical data, such as test results and time series, are available. Chapter 5, "Probability Distributions and Statistical Estimation," briefly surveys many of these techniques. This chapter, written principally by our colleague Mitchell Small, should serve to refresh the memory of those who have studied such techniques in the past. Mathematically knowledgeable readers who have had little or no training in probability and statistics should find this chapter a useful overview of key portions of the field. However, before taking action on the basis of this overview, readers without previous training in probability and statistics are urged to reflect seriously on the adage that "a little knowledge can be a dangerous thing."

Although it is important to make use of whatever good evidence is available, for many problems addressed by policy analysis the evidence available is insufficient to allow for the application of classical statistical techniques of the kind reviewed in Chapter 5. In these circumstances, about all one can do is resort to the use of "expert judgment," as explored in Chapters 6 and 7. The past fifteen years have witnessed very considerable progress in our understanding of the way in which people think about and make judgments in the presence of uncertainty. This literature is reviewed in Chapter 6, and Chapter 7 discusses the actual mechanics of eliciting subjective probabilistic judgments from experts.

Chapter 8, "The Propagation and Analysis of Uncertainty," is a fairly complete discussion of the various techniques for propagating uncertainty through quantitative policy models and for analyzing the implications of uncertainty in such models.

Representing, modeling, and analyzing uncertainty are of limited use if one cannot effectively communicate to other people the results of these efforts. Probably the most efficient means for such communication is through pictures. In Chapter 9, "The Graphic Communication of Uncertainty," we explore this subject both from the perspective of communication to technical people and from the perspective of communication to semitechnical and nontechnical people.

Most techniques discussed in Chapter 8 require the use of a computer. Not all computers are equally helpful in quantitative policy analysis. Conventional computer environments that support standard procedural languages such as FORTRAN often do not make it possible to engage in many of the activities identified in Chapter 3 as being important in "good" policy analysis. Chapter 10 describes an experimental computer environment that we have constructed, discusses the various evaluative experiments we have run, and outlines some of the more general insights we have gained while performing this research.

The final two chapters are more specialized. Chapter 11 explores a number of problems related to very large models. Chapter 12 is a decision theoretic discussion of the value of including uncertainty in an analysis.

References

Dawes, R. W. (1988). *Rational Choice in an Uncertain World*, Harcourt Brace & Jovanovich, New York.

Grayson, C. J. (1960). *Decisions Under Uncertainty: Drilling Decisions by Oil and Gas Operators*, Harvard Business School, Plimpton Press, Cambridge, Mass.

Howard, R. A. (1966). "Decision Analysis: Applied Decision Theory," *Proceedings of the Fourth International Conference on Operational Research*, ed. D. B. Hertz and J. Melese, pp. 55–71, Wiley-Interscience, New York.

Howard, R. A., Matheson, J. E., and North, D. W. (1972). The Decision to Seed Hurricanes, *Science*, 176, (February 23):1191–1202.

North, D. W., Judd, B. R., and Pezier, J. P. (1973). "New Methodology for Assessing the Probability of Contaminating Mars," paper presented to the XVII meeting of COSPAR, São Paulo, Brazil, (COSPAR Identification V.4.3).

North, D. W., Offensend, F. L. and Smart, C. N. (1975). "Planning Wildfire Protection for the Santa Monica Mountains," *Fire Journal* (January).

Raiffa, H. (1968). *Decision Analysis: Introductory Lectures on Choices Under Uncertainty*, Addison-Wesley, Reading, Mass.

Raiffa, H., and Schlaifer, R. O. (1961). *Applied Statistical Decision Theory*, Harvard Business School, Cambridge, Mass.

Random House (1966). *The Random House Dictionary of the English Language*, ed. Jess Stein, Random House, New York.

2   Recent Milestones

Probabilities direct the conduct of the wise man.
Cicero, *De Natura Deorum*,
Book 1, chap. 5, sec. 12

Although a considerable theoretical literature and a number of small scale applications of techniques for dealing with uncertainty in policy analysis and policy focused research have been around for a couple of decades, larger applications to major policy problems are a more recent phenomenon. Because many of the ideas and techniques involved are new, even to members of the technical community, their introduction into policy circles has been uneven and accompanied by a variety of mistakes and false starts. Nevertheless, there have now been a number of important applications, and several U.S. federal agencies have become seriously committed to the continued development and use of these techniques. For readers unfamiliar with these developments we briefly motivate the discussions that follow with three case examples that involve techniques for incorporating an explicit treatment of uncertainty in (1) estimates of the safety of light-water nuclear reactors; (2) the regulatory analysis of common ("criteria") air pollutants; and (3) estimates of the probable impacts on the ozone layer of continued release of chlorofluorocarbons.

2.1. Reactor Safety

One of the earliest large-scale studies to employ a formal treatment of uncertainty was the Reactor Safety Study, NUREG-75/014 (WASH-1400), generally known as the "Rasmussen report" (Rasmussen et al., 1975). In the early 1970s what was then the U.S. Atomic Energy Commission (AEC) asked Norman C. Rasmussen, a professor of nuclear engineering at the Massachusetts Institute of Technology, to undertake a quantitative study of the safety of light-water reactors. In order to make the task concrete, two specific commercial light-water power reactors, one a pressurized water reactor and one a boiling water reactor, were selected for study. Rasmussen assembled a team of roughly sixty people, who undertook to identify and formally describe, in terms of event trees, the various scenarios they believed might lead to major accidents in each of the two reactors studied. Fault trees were developed to estimate the probabilities of the various events. A combination of historical evidence from the nuclear and other industries, together with expert judgment, were used to construct the probability estimates, most of which were taken to be log-normally distributed. The probabilities of the various accident scenarios were then estimated through stochastic simulation. To assess the consequence of these accidents, models of exposure process for released radioactive contaminants were employed. Models of effects processes were added to assess the immediate and delayed health consequences to populations exposed to the releases. These exposure and effects models did not incorporate as much attention to the treatment of uncertainty as did the reactor accident models. Finally, an attempt was made to compare the resulting risks with a variety of natural and other man-made hazards. In summary:

The Rasmussen group estimated the overall probability of a sequence of events leading to a core melt as one chance in 20,000 reactor-years of operation; they found the average core melt would itself not present a major threat to the public health and safety, and they concluded (in a widely quoted and much criticized statement) that the likelihood of an average citizen's being killed in a reactor accident is about the same as the chance of his being killed by a falling meteorite. (Lewis, 1980)

The Rasmussen report was greeted with both great interest and substantial criticism. Some of the criticisms involved valid technical concerns, some were adversarial reactions motivated by opposition to nuclear power. To obtain an independent evaluation and deal with the criticisms the U.S. Nuclear Regulatory Commission (NRC) appointed a second committee, the Risk Assessment Review Group under the chairmanship of another academic, Harold W. Lewis, a professor of physics at the University of California at Santa Barbara. The resulting "Lewis report" (Lewis et al., 1975) confirmed many of the technical criticisms of the Rasmussen report, including criticisms about the treatment of multiple failures resulting from a common cause, and the ways in which uncertainties were represented, propagated, and interpreted. It drew attention to the difficulties of incorporating various human elements such as human adaptability during accidents; to the pervasive regulatory influence in the choice of uncertain parameters; to the "inscrutable" nature of the written report; and to the fact that the executive summary did not provide a good description of the contents of the report. However, despite such concerns about the details, the report concluded that the techniques developed and demonstrated in the Rasmussen study were, in Lewis's words,

extremely valuable and should be far more widely applied in the process of regulating the nuclear industry. Such probabilistic techniques, which provide guidance on the important issues in reactor safety, would be helpful in determining the priorities of the NRC both in its safety-research program and in the deployment of its regulatory and inspection resources. (Lewis, 1980)

At about the same time, the American Physical Study released a study of light-water reactor safety that they had conducted under National Science Foundation (NSF) and AEC support[1] (APS, 1975). Although this latter study was not undertaken as a specific evaluation of the Rasmussen report, the APS group did

---

1. There was considerable overlap in membership of this study group and the Risk Assessment Review Group. Lewis was chairman of both groups.

review the Rasmussen report in considerable detail. On the validity of such studies they observed:

It is difficult to quantify accurately the probabilities that any accident-initiating event might occur. Many aspects need to be better understood through experience and research before such calculations are tractable ... we recognize that the event-tree and fault-tree approach can have merit in highlighting *relative* strengths and weaknesses of reactor systems, particularly through comparisons of different sequences of reactor behavior. However, based on our experience with problems of this nature involving very low probabilities, we do not now have confidence in the presently calculated absolute values of the probabilities of the various branches. (APS, 1975)

Despite these reservations, the conclusions of the APS group call for significantly expanded research on probabilistic techniques including checks against empirically observed rates for small accidents and "parametric studies of phenomena which are ill understood in the identified sequences" and the adoption of quantitatively stated safety goals for reactor performance. (APS, 1975)

Although it had various shortcomings, the Rasmussen report got many things right. For example, it concluded that transients, small loss-of-coolant accidents, and human errors are important contributors to the overall risks of nuclear power. Lewis points out that "these three items ... were the central features of the Three Mile Island accident" (Lewis, 1980). While they have continued to undergo refinement, the general techniques pioneered in the Rasmussen report are now used widely and routinely in a variety of applications by the NRC, by the atomic energy agencies of many other nations, and by the nuclear industry, including applications such as the design of new reactors (Gonzalez et al., 1987).

The Rasmussen study, and the several dozen probabilistic reactor safety studies that have followed it, played a substantial role in stimulating the Nuclear Regulatory Commission to develop probabilistic "safety objectives" in addition to their traditional "qualitative safety goals." After a series of workshops, staff studies, and public comments, in August 1986 the NRC promulgated the following specific objectives:

- The risks to an average individual in the vicinity of a nuclear power plant of prompt fatalities that might result from reactor accidents should not exceed one-tenth of one percent (0.1 percent) of the sum of prompt fatalities resulting from other accidents to which members of the U.S. population are generally exposed.
- The risk to the population in the area near a nuclear power plant of cancer fatalities that might result from nuclear power plant operation should not exceed one-tenth of one percent (0.1 percent) of the sum of cancer fatality risks resulting from all other causes (NRC, 1986).

Although they did not promulgate it, they also indicated their intention to consider a quantitative objective for accident rates:

Consistent with the traditional defense-in-depth approach and the accident mitigation philosophy requiring reliable performance of containment systems, the overall mean frequency of a large release of radioactive materials to the environment from a reactor accident should be less than 1 in 1,000,000 per year of reactor operation (NRC, 1986).

The commission recognized the probabilistic nature of any such estimates. In the context of the safety objectives they explained that:

The Commission is aware that uncertainties are not caused by the use of quantitative methodology in decision making but are merely highlighted through use of the quantification process. Confidence in the use of probabilistic and risk assessment techniques has steadily improved .... In fact, through the quantitative techniques, important uncertainties have been and continue to be brought into better focus and may even be reduced compared with those that would remain with a sole reliance on deterministic decision making. To the extent practicable the Commission intends to ensure that the quantitative techniques used for regulatory decision making take into account the potential uncertainties that exist so that an estimate can be made on the confidence level to be ascribed to the quantitative results (NRC, 1986).

The commission goes on to explain that for the purposes of implementing their quantitative safety objectives, they intend to use mean values, but that they intend to remain alert to the ranges associated with the estimates and with the phenomenology that produces these ranges.

The process of implementing these objectives, of developing benefit–cost techniques to evaluate proposed changes, and of adopting the proposed accident rate guideline has proceeded slowly and has stimulated all kinds of activity and controversy (Cave, 1987). The proposal has been made to require all U.S. nuclear plants to provide a probabilistic risk assessment that shows their expected performance with respect to the quantitative safety objectives. Because the commission developed the objectives with existing assessments in mind, it is perhaps not surprising that assessments completed to date of a number of U.S. plants show the objectives being met (Cave, 1987). Of course, most of these assessments contain significant model assumptions, some of whose consequences have not yet been sufficiently explored. As alternative model assumptions are made in future assessments, compliance may not always be so automatic.

Although these and other activities related to the design and regulation of nuclear power have substantially stimulated the development and wider use of techniques for dealing with uncertainty in quantitative policy studies, they have certainly not resolved the basic dilemmas that the nuclear industry faces. That, of course, is because these dilemmas involve issues far more fundamental than accurately describing uncertain accident rates and consequences.

2.2. Air Pollution

The Clean Air Act requires the U.S. Environmental Protection Agency to establish, and periodically revise, national ambient air quality standards for a number of ubiquitous or "criteria" air pollutants. Until the late 1970s the EPA approached this task by first reviewing the relevant atmospheric and biological literature and then applying what was basically a seat-of-the-pants approach that relied on agency personnel to make judgments regarding complex health issues.

Later this approach was expanded to include expert advice from outside scientific review panels. This process mixed scientific, economic, and value judgments without differentiating them, and many of the participants were unaware they were being made. Understandably, the EPA's Office of Air Quality Planning and Standards (OAQPS) was uncomfortable with these procedures. Thus, in 1977 when OAQPS began the process of reevaluating the ambient standard for ozone, they opted to pursue a dual strategy. In addition to their traditional approach the office put Thomas Feagans and William Biller to work on developing a formal decision analytic approach that would incorporate the very considerable scientific uncertainties through the use of elicited expert subjective judgments (Feagans and Biller, 1978, 1981).

The Feagans–Biller work suffered from a number of serious problems in both its conception and its execution. The process of promulgating any new national ambient air quality standard is contentious, and the ozone standard proved particularly controversial. In the course of this controversy the Feagans–Biller work was severely criticized by both outside groups, such as the American Petroleum Institute (API, 1978), and by several EPA advisory panels. Although it had initially tried to use the Feagans–Biller work as part of the process of setting the new ozone standard, in the face of this criticism the EPA backed off and subsequently argued that the Feagans–Biller work had been only experimental in nature. A more detailed, if not entirely balanced, history of this rocky beginning can be found in Marraro (1982). In the aftermath of this fight, a special subcommittee of the EPA Science Advisory Board, the Committee on Health Risk Assessment, was established to assist OAQPS in developing a satisfactory approach.[2] Following advice from this committee the agency gradually abandoned its earlier formulation of the problem and turned to the community of experienced decision analysts for ideas and advice. In April 1980, OAQPS convened a "brainstorming" session at which a number of these experts presented concept papers they had developed under a series of small contracts.[3] At about the same time, a contract was let with Thomas Wallsten of the University of North Carolina to undertake a review of the psychological literature on expert elicitation (Wallsten and Bendescu, 1980, 1983). After reviewing the results of the brainstorming session, larger follow-up contracts were let to two groups – the first under the general leadership of Miley Merkhofer at SRI International (Smith, McNamee, and Merkhofer, 1982) and the second under the joint leadership of Rakesh Sarin of UCLA,

---

2. One of us, Granger Morgan, served on this committee and the several subsequent EPA/SAB committees that have overseen OAQPS's work in this area.

3. Authors who contributed to this process included Howard Raiffa and Richard Zeckhauser; Richard de Neufville and Marie-Elizabeth Pate (Cornell); Chris Whipple and Baruch Fischhoff; Kenneth Manton, H. O. Hartley, and Max Woodbury; Robert Winkler and Rakesh Sarin; and Miley Merkhofer. For a summary, see EPA (1981).

Robert Wenkler of Indiana University, and Ralph Keeney of Woodward-Clyde (Keeney et al., 1982) – to perform pilot studies. Because the office was engaged in revising the carbon monoxide standard, they used this problem as a test bed. However, they were careful to avoid making use of their exploratory analysis in the regulatory decision process. When in the mid-1980s OAQPS undertook the revision of the ambient standard for airborne lead, they decided they had made enough progress to try once again to use elicited expert subjective judgment and associated techniques as part of the regulatory decision process. Thomas Wallsten, together with Ronald Whitfield of Argonne National Laboratories, undertook to assess expert opinions on the effect of lead exposure on lead-induced hemoglobin decrements, elevated levels of erythrocyte protoporphyrin (EP), and IQ decrements (Wallsten and Whitfield, 1986).[4] The resulting distributions were incorporated in the "staff paper" (EPA, 1986) in which OAQPS provides its advice to the administrator on a recommended range of standards. The elicitation work on lead received favorable review by the agency's Clean Air Scientific Advisory Committee.

The next criterion pollutant up for revision after lead was again ozone. On the basis of the considerable experience gained during the intervening years, EPA has chosen to make substantial use of techniques for characterizing and dealing with uncertainty in expert scientific judgments in the course of this and all subsequent revisions of ambient air quality standards. Choosing not to rush the process, the EPA has so far performed only limited analysis that uses the elicited distributions it has been obtaining. Such analysis can probably be expected to grow in sophistication and complexity in the future.[5]

2.3. Ozone and Chlorofluorocarbons

A third example is provided by a series of U.S. National Academy of Sciences studies of the depletion of stratospheric ozone by chlorofluorocarbons. The first was conducted in 1975 in the context of the controversy over whether to build the SST (NAS, 1975). Since then there have been a number of follow-up studies and reports (NAS, 1976a, 1976b, 1979a, 1979b, 1982), each one refining and elaborating the conclusions of those that preceded. The basic concern of all of these studies has been the possibility that the release through human activity of various gaseous air pollutants – in particular chlorofluorocarbons such as F-11 and F-12 – could contribute to the depletion of the thin layer of ozone in the

---

4. For a detailed discussion of the elicitation protocols and procedures employed in this work, see section 7.3.

5. Judging from previous experience, this process may not be without complications. However, OAQPS has now established quite a good record of learning from their mistakes so that the prospects of long-term success are probably good. For a discussion of the evolution of the use of probabilistic assessment at OAQPS from an EPA perspective, see Richmond (1987).

stratosphere which protects living things from the sun's ultraviolet radiation. The uncertainties involved in this problem include an incomplete understanding of the relevant processes of atmospheric transport, chemistry, and loss; uncertainty about the rate constants that are associated with these various processes; and uncertainty about the existence and nature of the relationship between exposure to UV radiation and biological effects, especially various kinds of human skin cancers.

While all of these studies have adopted a largely qualitative approach to the biology, the 1976 study did attempt an approximate characterization of the uncertainties associated with the seven reaction rates believed to be most critical in controlling ozone concentration. Then, under the chairmanship of John Tukey, the Impacts Committee of the 1979 study (NAS, 1979a, 1979b) undertook a more elaborate analysis of uncertainties. The authors observe that in the 1976 report

no attempt was made to estimate the systematic errors in evaluating rates or omission of chemical processes. Without such estimates, decision makers are free to make their own judgments ranging from uncritical acceptance of the current models to complete skepticism as to their having any likelihood of being correct. (NAS, 1979b)

In the 1979 study uncertainties in the various rate coefficients of the one-dimensional model used were assumed to be log-normally distributed and the necessary coefficient values for each distribution were estimated. A Monte Carlo simulation was then run to obtain a distribution for the predicted overall ozone depletion. The panel went on to discuss several newly identified reactions, such as the reaction of ClO with BrO, which were not included in their model. They constructed subjective estimates of how much the results of their model should be adjusted to include these new considerations. They performed similar adjustments to incorporate uncertainty introduced by the one-dimensional transport parameterization used and by the way in which averages were taken in that model. The latter was done by comparing the results of the one-dimensional model with results obtained with a two-dimensional model. Finally consideration was given to possible tropospheric sinks, not included in the model. Having completed these arguments the panel concluded:

Our best estimate of ozone depletion at steady state and for sustained 1977 emission rates is 16.5 percent. There is a quantifiable uncertainty due to known uncertainties in reaction rate of about ±8 percent. We obtain a total uncertainty of ±11.5 percent. (NAS, 1979b)

By using the adjusted distributions, the committee was then able to report in their nontechnical summary that their best estimate of the amount of ozone depletion that would occur if the worldwide release of chlorofluorocarbons continues at 1977 levels is about 16% and that there is "a roughly even chance that the eventual depletion ... would lie between 10 and 23 percent" (NAS, 1979a). They reported that they were "quite confident (19 chances in 20) that it would lie between 5 and 28 percent" and that "there is 1 chance in 40 that ozone depletion will be less than 5% and 1 chance in 40 that it will be greater than 28%" (NAS, 1979a).

Many scientists feel far less comfortable about uncertainty estimates of the kind just discussed than with what they might term the "objective uncertainties" associated with the results of specific scientific experiments.[6] This discomfort is well reflected in the 1982 academy report on ozone, which did not have the benefit of John Tukey's persuasive presence. In that report we find the following interesting discussion:

Our opinions are divided on whether there are sufficient scientific grounds to estimate the effects of resolving one of the discrepancies, that of ClO in the upper stratosphere, on calculations of ozone reduction. We agree that we do not know enough at this time to make a quantitative judgment of the uncertainty associated with other major discrepancies, NO_2 at high latitudes and lifetime of CFCs in the stratosphere above 20 km.

Those of us who believe there are grounds to judge the effect of resolving the ClO issue conclude that our estimate of ozone reduction from CFC emissions should not change by more than a factor of 2.

Those of us unwilling to offer quantitative estimates of uncertainty hold the conviction that no rigorous scientific basis exists for such statements. We are concerned by the implications of the discrepancies noted earlier. These discrepancies should be resolved in the next few years by orderly application of the scientific method with appropriate interaction between theory and observation. We see no reason to prejudge the result of this process. (NAS, 1982)

The tensions reflected in this discussion are a recurring theme to which we will return several times in the later chapters of this book. Despite this disagreement, the panel did reach a consensus conclusion:

Our current understanding indicates that if production of CFCs continue into the future at the rate existing in 1977, the steady state reduction in total ozone, in the absence of other perturbations, would be between 5 percent and 9 percent. Previous estimates fluctuate between roughly 5 percent and 20 percent, with those current in 1979 ranging from 15 to 18 percent. (NAS, 1982)

Although some of the academy's ozone studies illustrate the application of a variety of formal techniques for dealing with uncertainty, together their greatest value as an example lies elsewhere. The successful treatment of uncertainty involves more than describing the uncertainties in individual variables and then propagating them through a model. Often, as with ozone, the difficulties of understanding the problem itself and the limitations and uncertainties in our current models are far more important. The process of *iterative analysis*, which is reflected in the *set* of studies the academy has conducted on the problem of stratospheric ozone, offers an excellent illustration of how to handle scientific uncertainty in a complex evolving policy problem. The process has resulted

6. In Chapter 6 we will see that in fact many of these "objective" uncertainties often show systematic tendencies toward overconfidence and thus might arguably be considered to be as "subjective" as any other.

in careful examination of important uncertainties and a periodic review and identification of the research needed to resolve these uncertainties. Some of this research has been done and the results have allowed later panels to refine their assessments. The U.S. Interagency Ozone Trends Panel reported in 1988 that ozone has decreased more rapidly at some times and places than previously predicted (Kerr, 1988a). New evidence on clorine dioxide and ozone depletion in Arctic as well as in Antarctic regions (Kerr, 1988b) also suggests that the time is approaching for yet another iteration in the assessment cycle.

References

API (1978). An evaluation of the Environmental Protection Agency's risk assessment methodology as applied to photochemical oxidants (ozone), coordinated by William M. Ollison, American Petroleum Institute.

APS (1975). "Report to the American Physical Society of the Study Group on Light-water Reactor Safety," *Reviews of Modern Physics*, supplement no. 1.

Cave, L. (1987). "United States Makes Slow Progress Towards Implementing Its Safety Goals," *Nuclear Engineering International*, (May): 22–23.

EPA (1981, May). *Conceptual Approaches to Health Risk Assessment for Alternative NAAQS*, Strategies and Air Standards Division, Office of Air Quality and Standards, U.S. Environmental Protection Agency, Research Triangle Park, N.C.

EPA (1986). "Review of the National Ambient Air Quality Standards for Lead: Assessment of Scientific and Technical Information," OAQPS Staff Paper, Strategies and Air Standards Division, U.S. Environmental Protection Agency, Research Triangle Park, N.C.

Feagans, T. B., and Biller, W. F. (1978, July). *A Method for Assessing the Health Risks Associated with Air Quality Standards*, Strategies and Air Standards Division, Office of Air Quality and Standards, U. S. Environmental Protection Agency, Research Triangle Park, N.C.

Feagans, T. B., and Biller, W. F. (1981). "Risk Assessment: Describing the Protection Provided by Ambient Air Quality Standards," *The Environmental Professional*, 3:235–247.

Gonzalez, A. J., Frischengruber, K., Recalde, J. A., Solanilla, R. B., and Vanzulli, R. C. (1987). "Argentina Offers a 380 MWe PHWR with Enhanced Safety Features," *Nuclear Engineering International*, May: 24–34.

Keeney, R. L., Keller, L. R., Sarin, R. K., Sicherman, A., and Wenkler, R. L. (1982). *Development and Application of a Risk Assessment Methodology to Study Alternative National Ambient Carbon Monoxide Standards*, Woodward-Clyde Associates, San Francisco.

Kerr, R. A. (1988a). "Stratospheric Ozone is Decreasing," Research News, *Science*, 239:1489–1491.

Kerr, R. A. (1988b). "Evidence of Arctic Oxone Destruction," Research News, *Science*, 240:1144–1145.

Lewis, H. W. (1980). "The Safety of Fission Reactors," *Scientific American*, March: 53–65.

Lewis, H. W., Budnitz, R. J., Kouts, H. J. C., von Hippel, F., Lowenstein, W., and Zachariasen, F. (1975). *Risk Assessment Group Report to the U.S. Nuclear Regulatory Commission*, U.S. Nuclear Regulatory Commission, Washington, D.C.

Marraro, C. H. (1982). Chapter 3, "Revising the Ozone Standard," in *Quantitative Risk Assessment in Regulation*, ed. Lester B. Lave, pp. 55–97, Brookings Institution, Washington, D.C.

NAS (U.S. National Academy of Sciences) (1975). *Environmental Impact of Stratospheric Flight: Biological and Climate Effects of Aircraft Emissions in the Stratosphere*, report of a committee of the National Research Council, Washington, D.C.

NAS (1976a). *Halocarbons: Environmental Effects of Chlorofluoromethane Release*, report of a committee of the National Research Council, Washington, D.C.

NAS (1976b). *Halocarbons: Effects on Stratospheric Ozone*, report of a committee of the National Research Council, Washington, D.C.

NAS (1979a). *Protection Against Depletion of Stratospheric Ozone by Chlorofluorocarbons*, report by the Committee on Impacts of Stratospheric Change and the Committee on Alternatives for the Reduction of Chlorofluorocarbon Emissions, National Research Council, Washington, D.C.

NAS (1979b). *Stratospheric Ozone Depletion by Halocarbons: Chemistry and Transport*, report of a committee of the National Research Council, Washington, D.C.

NAS (1982). *Causes and Effects of Stratospheric Ozone Reduction: An Update*, report by the Committee on Chemistry and Physics of Ozone Depletion, and the Committee on Biological Effects of Increased Solar Ultraviolet Radiation, Environmental Health Sciences Board, National Research Council, Washington, D.C.

NRC (U.S. Nuclear Regulatory Commission) (1986). "Safety Goals for the Operation of Nuclear Power Plants; Policy Statement," *Federal Register*, 51 (August 4): 28044–28049.

Rasmussen et al. (1975). *Reactor Safety Study: An Assessment of Accident Risks in U. S. Commercial Nuclear Power Plants*, Nuclear Regulatory Commission, NUREG-75/014 (WASH-1400), Washington, D.C.

Richmond, H. M. (1987). "Development of Probabilistic Health Risk Assessment for National Ambient Air Quality Standards," paper presented at the APCA International Specialty Conference on Regulatory Approaches for Control of Air Pollutants, February, Atlanta, Ga.

Smith, A. E., McNamee, P. C., and Merkhofer, M. W. (1982). *Development of Decision Analysis Methodology for Health Risk Assessment*, SRI International, Menlo Park, Calif.

Wallsten, T. S., and Budescu, D. V. (1980). "Encoding Subjective Probabilities: A Psychological and Psychometric Review," EPA Strategy and Standards Division, Research Triangle Park, N.C.

Wallsten, T. S., and Budescu, D. V. (1983). "Encoding Subjective Probabilities: A Psychological and Psychometric Review," *Management Science*, 29:151–173.

Wallsten, T. S., and Whitfield, R. G. (1986). "Estimating the Risks of Lead-Induced Health Effects," ANL/AA-32, Argonne National Laboratory, Chicago, Ill.

3 An Overview of Quantitative Policy Analysis

> Modest doubt is called the beacon of the wise.
> William Shakespeare,
> *Troilus and Cressida*, II, ii, 56

There is something wonderfully absorbing about the details of policy analysis and policy-focused research. Indeed, the balance of this book will be devoted to a discussion of just one set of details, those related to the characterization and treatment of uncertainty. But, before proceeding, we should explore some broader issues. We need to clarify what we mean by *policy analysis* and *policy research*, and we must ask "What constitutes good policy analysis?" We first do this indirectly by comparing policy analysis to scientific research. Then we explore the role of analysis in the process of developing and choosing policy alternatives, examine a variety of alternative philosophical frameworks within which analysis may be undertaken, and explore some of the problems of choosing the boundaries for a policy analysis. Finally, we return to the problem of identifying the attributes of "good" policy analysis. This time our approach is more direct. We examine the motivations people have in commissioning and undertaking analysis and work from these motivations to develop what we term "ten commandments" for good policy analysis, one of which involves being explicit about uncertainties. The chapter concludes with a discussion of when and why policy analysis should deal with uncertainty.

3.1. Policy Research and Policy Analysis

Throughout the preceding chapters we have referred to policy research and analysis, sometimes using the even more awkward phrase "policy analysis and policy-focused research." For convenience we and many others often lump the two activities together and use the single phrase "policy analysis" to refer to both. They are different, and the distinction is important. In its narrow sense, policy analysis is analytical activity undertaken in direct support of specific public or private[1] sector decision makers who are faced with a decision that must be made or a problem that must be resolved. As one of us has argued, the objective of policy analysis "is to evaluate, order and structure incomplete knowledge so as to allow decisions to be made with as complete an understanding as possible

---

1. Some would limit the phrase "policy analysis" to public sector problems and actors. Although we limit our usage to issues involving general social concerns, it seems clear to us that both the problems and the actors may involve the private sector.

16

of the current state of knowledge, its limitations and its implications" (Morgan, 1978). In the narrow sense of the phrase, policy analysis is inherently a short-term activity. Somebody needs to make a decision. "The analyst is called on to use the tools and understanding that are readily available to try to provide analytical insight that can illuminate, and hence perhaps improve, the decision" (Morgan, 1985).

Although much of the literature on policy analysis is framed in terms of clearly identified decision makers who make definitive decisions at well-specified times, the real world is generally more complex. Issues are frequently not resolved in a permanent way but periodically cycle back onto the policy agenda. Indeed, in some cases, such as the regular periodic review that the U.S. Environmental Protection Agency (EPA) makes of its ambient standards for criteria air pollutants, this iterative process has been formalized (Gage, 1980). When decisions *are* made, or reached, the decision processes are frequently far more convoluted than the simple model of a single decision maker would suggest. They often involve a series of complex interactions between a variety of actors in a number of different organizations. For these reasons the traditional do-the-best-with-what-you've-got-now model is not the only role that work on policy problems can play. There is often a need for longer term, more fundamental policy-focused research that improves the basic quality of our understanding of major problems. Through such research a gradual improvement can take place in the understanding that is available each time a problem cycles back onto policy agendas. Policy research can also contribute by developing and demonstrating improved analytical techniques and tools that are appropriate for use in the policy environment.

We particularly emphasize policy research that involves problems in which scientific and engineering issues are important to the policy questions – that is, on policy problems in which the scientific and technical issues cannot be treated as a "black box." A traditional view holds that the science and engineering community should lay out the "facts," making it clear what is known and what is not known. Then the politicians can take over and decide what to do. This, for example, appears to be the basic model that underlies the science court proposals that have been advanced by Arthur Kantrowitz (1975). But in many problems successful policy development requires more than a list of what we do and don't know. Careful analysis, synthesis, and interpretation is required if the policy-making process is going to use the available science adequately. Usually such activities cannot be done quickly. They take the same time, care, and iteration that are required in more conventional research. They also require people who combine the necessary technical knowledge with the necessary policy insights and skills (Bereiter, 1983). In the discussions that follow, we distinguish between policy analysis and policy-focused research when it is especially important. However, in much of our discussion we follow the common practice of using the single phrase "policy analysis," or sometimes just the word "analysis," to refer to both.

3.2. Policy Research and Analysis versus Natural Science

What are the attributes of good policy research and analysis? Later in this chapter we approach the question more directly. But first it is illustrative to compare the immature norms of policy analysis with the more established norms of research in the natural sciences.[2] There is ongoing debate about what exactly constitutes the scientific method, but there is general agreement about a number of desiderata. These include the critical role of empirical testing; documentation and the reproducibility of results; explicit reporting of uncertainty; peer review; and open debate about alternative theories. Let us consider each aspect in turn for the perspective it provides on policy research and analysis.

3.2.1. Empirical Testing

Policy analysis often involves the development of models for which empirical validation is difficult or impossible. For example, models may be required to forecast the implications of decisions for years and sometimes decades into the future. If it is possible at all, direct testing of the predictive validity of such models often cannot be carried out until long after the analysis is required. Models can sometimes be calibrated against historical data, but there can be no guarantee that past relationships will continue to hold in the future. Recall the fate of energy demand predictions made in the early 1970s. Relevant technical and scientific data may exist (such as failure rates for the components of nuclear reactors, or the results from animal studies of the carcinogenic effects of a chemical pollutant); but the analyst must employ further assumptions to produce policy-relevant results from them, assumptions that are untestable within the scope of the study (such as the incidence of common mode failures among reactor components, or biological issues involved in extrapolating carcinogenic potency from mouse to man).

If the policy model is intended not only to forecast but also to produce decision recommendations, then the problem of validation becomes even stickier (Fischhoff, 1980). A decision analysis must use some model of human preferences, such as a multi-attribute utility function, to select among alternative choices. In principle, models of human preference can be tested empirically by observing how people actually choose, but the practical difficulties are legion.

Although one should not understate the importance of limited empirical validation where it is possible, nor the need for developing better validation methods, adequate empirical validation is clearly not possible for most policy

---

2. The discussion in this section is based directly on a paper by Max Henrion (1984).

analysis. This unfortunate, but unavoidable, situation places a greater burden on policy analysts to observe the other conventions of scientific procedure, which have evolved to encourage its practitioners to be diligent and honest. However, it seems these conventions are not yet as well accepted among policy analysts as they are among natural scientists.

3.2.2. Documentation and Reproducibility

An essential principle of scientific research is that reports should provide sufficient description of procedures and assumptions that other scientists can verify all calculations and, if necessary, have enough information to undertake a replication of the results. In many cases policy models are formulated as large computer programs. A number of surveys of such models have concluded that all too commonly the program, the assumptions, and the data used are not documented well enough to make such replication practical. For example, Greenberger, Grensen, and Crissey (1976), on the basis of case studies of the use of policy models in the U.S. government, concluded:

Professional standards for model building are non-existent. The documentation of model and source data is in an unbelievably primitive state. This goes even (and sometimes especially) for models actively consulted by policy makers. Poor documentation makes it next to impossible for anyone but the modeler to reproduce the modeling results and to probe the effects of changes to the model. Sometimes a model is kept proprietary by its builder for commercial reasons. The customer is allowed to see only the results, not the assumptions.

In some cases, the problem has not been the physical *lack* of documentation but rather the vast mass of it, rendered indigestible by poor organization and cross-referencing. This was a criticism by the Risk Assessment Review Group (Lewis, 1978) of the Reactor Safety Study (Rasmussen, 1975).

Accounts of such policy models are frequently not published in the open literature. Even if they were, many such models are so large and complex that they could not be completely described within a single article – though we believe a reasonable job could usually be done of describing the more important details and assumptions. In the natural sciences, experimental equipment and procedures are also frequently too complex to be completely described in a single article; but within a specific discipline there is sufficient standardization that there is no need to go into details except where novel equipment or procedures are used. Hence, the conduct of research can be adequately communicated to someone versed in the discipline within an article of manageable size. Unfortunately, such standardization of methods and tools (especially modeling software) is not nearly so advanced in most fields of policy analysis, nor are there yet generally agreed-upon conventions about what form and level of detail to report them in.

3.2.3. Reporting Uncertainty

In the experimental sciences, it is standard practice to report estimates of random and systematic error in measurements (Henrion and Fischhoff, 1986). This provides an explicit statement by the researchers of the uncertainty they ascribe to their results and allows one to determine the significance of divergence between different measurements and theories. In many cases, analysis assuming a "best value" for each uncertain value will produce a quite different result from one incorporating an explicit probabilistic analysis (see Chapter 8). Decision analysts have developed practical techniques for encoding expert judgment about uncertain quantities in terms of subjective probability distributions and for probabilistic analysis of decision models (see Chapters 7 and 8). But despite, or perhaps because of, the vast uncertainties inherent in most policy models, it is still not standard practice to treat uncertainties in an explicit probabilistic fashion, outside the relatively small fraternity of decision analysts. The examples mentioned in Chapter 2 are noteworthy exceptions.

3.2.4. Peer Review

In traditional fields of science, peer review takes place largely through the mechanisms of refereeing and publication of research reports. Most of this work is done on an unpaid basis as an integral part of the work of a scientist. For a complex policy model, a thorough review can be an extremely arduous and time-consuming business, even if adequate documentation exists. Such review is far from standard practice (von Hippel, 1981). Peer review is especially problematic for analysis based on large complex models. In Chapter 11 we argue that such models are often inappropriate and unnecessary in policy analysis, but there is no denying they are common.

There is increasing interest in the problems and practice of model assessment (NBS, 1980). It has been suggested (GAO, 1979) that model assessment should include examination of all data, assumptions, and computer code, with additional runs of the model to examine sensitivities. Models are often assembled by a team of specialists from several different disciplines (e.g., economists, natural scientists, engineers, statisticians, computer specialists, etc.). It is unrealistic to expect a reviewer to be able to perform a complete assessment, unpaid and single-handed. In the case of large models, a proper external assessment will require a multidisciplinary team, and a significant budget.

As yet, this kind of review process is rare in most areas, although in a few notable exceptions, sponsors of policy research have initiated ongoing groups for model assessment. One is the independent Professional Audit Review Team (PART) established by the U.S. Congress to review analyses by the Energy Information Administration (PART, 1979), and another is the Energy Modeling Forum (Weyant, 1981) set up by industry and U.S. government agencies to provide in-depth assessments of energy policy models. In a few areas, such as environmental policy, citizen groups and industry lobbyists now often perform detailed external critiques of government analyses that will be the basis for regulatory action. Because of the adversarial nature of the environments in which this takes place, such reviews are often not balanced, but they can nevertheless be an important vehicle for identifying problems in agency analysis.

Many practitioners in policy analysis have argued that peer reviewed pub-lication is not appropriate to the field, an argument sometimes made even in the case of modest analyses that do not involve large complex models. The claim is that peer review is not feasible because of the time urgent nature of the work. Although in some circumstance this may be true, we believe that for virtually all policy-focused research, and for a substantial fraction of policy analysis, it is *not* true. Further, we believe that a lack of focus on peer reviewed publication has contributed to the limited attention that has been paid to standards of good analytic practice, and to the slow rate of convergence on such standards, as well as to a failure to focus sufficiently on extracting generalizable insights from specific analyses. Historically there have been problems in finding appropriate publication outlets for peer reviewed publication of policy analysis, but with the growth of journals such as *Risk Analysis*, *Environmental Science and Technology*, *Telecommunications Policy*, and *Issues in Science and Technology*, and with the growing interest in policy matters in a variety of traditional journals including *Science* and several publications of the various engineering societies, appropriate publication outlets can usually now be found.

3.2.5. Debate

Almost by definition, policy analysis deals with problem situations that are ill defined and that have been termed "messy" (Ackoff, 1974) and "wicked" (Rittel and Webber, 1973). Any model used in analysis is at best an approximation to the real world. So the question is not whether a model is true but, rather, whether it is the best among contending models. "Best" has to do with explaining more, more simply, but is dependent on the purpose of the model and is a matter of judgment. Kuhn has pointed out that, within an established scientific discipline, there are norms about how to conduct experiments, about what kinds of theories are permissible and what questions are interesting (Kuhn, 1962). These constitute its prevailing *paradigm*, and they provide a context for choosing among theories. If one tries to apply this concept to policy analysis, in most areas there seems to be no single paradigm clearly prevailing, but rather a number of different criteria and methodologies contending, including benefit–cost analysis, decision analysis, systems dynamics, econometric modeling, rights-based analysis, and others. Thus, in policy analysis, the lack of agreement

Table 3.1. *A comparison of features of science with those of policy research and analysis*

Features of science	Features of policy analysis
Empirical testing	Testing often impractical
Full documentation	Documentation typically inadequate
Reporting of uncertainty	Uncertainty usually incomplete or missing
Peer review	Review not standard and in some cases arduous
Open debate	Debate hindered by the above problems

on paradigm, and the prevalence of messy, wicked problems, make the selection of a criterion for what is "best" especially difficult.

The philosopher of science Paul Feyerabend proposes that even in the traditional sciences the choice of paradigm and hence the choice of theory is a matter of judgment, and suggests that progress arises mainly from debate between partisans of alternative theories (Feyerabend, 1978). Hence he has stressed the importance of proposing *counter-theories* that offer alternative explanations and provide maximal challenges to a theory, and so stimulate constructive debate. In wrestling with these problems in policy analysis, Mason and Mitroff (Mason, 1969; Mitroff and Mason, 1980) have made similar suggestions about the importance of finding *counter-models* which provide alternative explanations of the situation, and offer concrete references for the assessment of a given model. They suggest policy analysis as a dialectical process, in which a model is proposed, and one or more counter-models are offered in response. Debate ensues about the relative merits and failings of the alternatives, and, with luck, an improved model can be constructed from a synthesis of the initial ones. The process may then be repeated.

This can take place at two levels: first, *within* a particular study, the model development should involve iterative exploration of alternative formulations, which are proposed and critiqued by members of the project team. Second, *among* studies on a particular topic, each project should, of course, start by examining accounts and critiques of previous models and hence synthesize the most useful elements into the new model. The Energy Modeling Forum (Weyant, 1981) was set up to foster precisely this kind of process. But as yet in many areas such review and debate are unusual, hampered by the problems of inadequate documentation and publication, inadequate treatment of uncertainty, and the lack of peer review.

Table 3.1 summarizes the characteristics of science that we have discussed and our evaluation of how policy research and analysis stacks up against these criteria. This table offers one useful starting place when later in the chapter we develop arguments about the attributes of good policy analysis.

3.3. Which Comes First: Goals or Analysis?

Policy research and analysis is undertaken with a variety of motivations, but for the moment let's assume it is motivated by a desire to obtain better insight and understanding about the problem at hand. In thinking about such analysis, the conceptualization that most beginning practitioners adopt involves clearly identified and authorized decision makers who have well-defined goals and employ analysis to determine how best to achieve these goals. In some cases the alternative policy options are also clearly established and the point of analysis is to assist the decision maker in choosing among a discrete or continuous set of options – that is, to find "the answer." In other cases the possible alternatives are not clearly defined and analysis is used to help the decision maker to identify and explore possible alternatives as well as to choose among them. Without endorsing it, James G. March has summarized this model concisely as follows:

Human beings make choices. If done properly choices are made by evaluating alternatives in terms of goals on the basis of information currently available. The alternative that is most attractive in terms of the goals is chosen. The process of making choices can be improved by using the technology of choice. Through the paraphernalia of modern techniques, we can improve the quality of the search for alternatives, the quality of information, and the quality of the analysis used to evaluate alternatives. Although actual choice may fall short of the ideal in various ways, it is an attractive model of how choices should be made by individuals, organizations, and social systems. (March, 1976)

In contrast to this dominant conceptualization, a number of observers have argued that people do not have fixed goals, and that one of the primary objectives of analysis should be to provide what Henry S. Rowen (1976) terms a "heuristic aid" to assist in the systematic exploration of alternative possible goals. Analysis, he argues, should be used to "provide a conceptual framework (or several) for relating means to ends, for thinking about ends" as well as for "identifying the existing technical alternatives, and for inventing new ones."

March has asserted that "the argument that goal development and choice are independent behaviorally seems clearly false. It seems ... perfectly obvious that a description that assumes that goals come first and action comes later is frequently radically wrong. Human choice behavior is at least as much a process of discovering goals as of acting on them" (March, 1976). He argues that although "the prior specification of criteria and the prior specification of evaluational procedures that depend on such criteria, are common presumptions in contemporary social policy making ... they are presumptions that inhibit the serendipitous discovery of new criteria. Experience should be used explicitly as an occasion for evaluating our values as well as our actions" (March, 1976).

In this spirit Rowen has defined policy analysis as "a set of procedures for inventing, exploring and comparing alternatives available for achieving certain social goals – and for inventing, exploring and comparing the alternative ends themselves – in a world limited in knowledge, in resources, and in rationality" (Rowen, 1976). We agree. At the same time, it is clearly inappropriate to launch into a fundamental reassessment of the agency's philosophical approach to risk management every time the Food and Drug Administration considers a new drug for market approval or every time the EPA revises its ambient standards for one of the criteria air pollutants. In many situations such as these, the goals *are* well established and unlikely to change on the time scale of the analysis. In others, the ambiguity about goals is limited, and at most a bit of fine tuning is required. In such circumstances analysts can safely pursue the conventional "fixed goals various means" model. However, even in these circumstances we should be careful not to let the goals that govern the decisions go unexamined for too long. In situations that are less routine, or that involve new or unusual elements, we should be careful not to engage in "means-oriented" analysis until we have asked whether analysis is also needed to help us in clarifying, understanding, and agreeing on goals.

A second problem with the dominant conceptualization of policy analysis is more apparent and requires less discussion. There are circumstances that involve a single clearly identified and authorized decision maker. However, they are the exception. Most policy decisions involve complex political and organizational interactions with a variety of individual and institutional actors. In such cases a "single decision maker" model is not a very good description of reality. In such circumstances, substance-focused policy analysis is likely to be more effective if it is undertaken so as to be useful to a variety of the actors who are involved.

The phrase "policy analysis" is misleading because it suggests that the goal is simply to understand and analyze the situation. In practice, the generation of alternative options and the construction of an appropriate model for evaluating them can be very much a creative act. When policy analysis is most successful, the result is not simply to accurately reflect the existing situation but rather to transform the situation by creating one or several more productive interpretations of it.

3.4. Philosophical Frameworks for Analysis

Policy analysis is generally performed within some broader philosophical framework, but it is easy to forget this and assume that analytical procedures, such as the maximization of expected net benefit, reflect some universal social truth. They do not. They reflect normative choices, and these choices carry important implications for the nature of society. In the subsections that follow we briefly review some of the decision-making criteria commonly used in risk management and give a number of examples of common risk management policy strategies.

We have chosen to focus our discussion to make it more concrete. Similar examples could be developed in other application areas.

3.4.1. Criteria for Decision Making

A wide variety of decision criteria for risk management decision making have been discussed in the literature (Schulze, 1980; Goldstein, 1981; Lave, 1981; Stone, 1974; Schulze and Kneese, 1981). Not all of these discussions are consistent. In Table 3.2 we summarize a set of decision criteria that we believe capture most of the major philosophical alternatives in use today. A very similar table could be constructed for most other policy making contexts.

We term the first set of criteria in Table 3.2 *utility-based* criteria because they all involve decisions that are based on the valuation of outcomes. The first two involve a balancing of benefits and costs, either in conventional *deterministic benefit–cost* analysis (Mishan, 1973) or, when uncertainty has been incorporated, in *probabilistic benefit–cost* analysis. Using techniques of decision analysis the latter estimates the expected value of the net benefits.

If the value of benefits cannot be estimated but a choice between a number of alternatives must be made, a *cost effectiveness* criterion may be used. A desired and obtainable objective is selected, perhaps on noneconomic grounds. One then chooses the alternative that will achieve this objective at the lowest cost, all other things being kept more or less equal. Implicit in this approach is an assumption that the investments needed to get to the stated objective are worthwhile but a formal cost–benefit criterion is not applied.

The *bounded cost* criterion is sometimes also termed the "regulatory budget" approach. This strategy sets a maximum budget that society can afford to devote to risk management activity, and then tries to allocate resources in a way that maximizes the amount of risk reduction (or other social good) achieved within the budgetary constraint. Although the bounded cost approach may not set the budget constraint at the socially optimal level, within that constraint it does at least provide an incentive for local efficiency in the allocation of resources.

The most general formulation of utility based criteria is in terms of *maximizing a multi-attribute utility function* (Keeney and Raiffa, 1976). Most decisions involve choices between options involving collections of attributes that are incommensurate. On rare occasion it may be feasible, but in general it is not appropriate just to convert the level of each attribute to an equivalent monetary value and sum to get the total value of an option. Multi-attribute utility theory provides a theoretically appealing way to avoid this dilemma. Although conceptually simple, the approach can become operationally complex, and thus opaque to many people. Unless great care is taken, the resulting decision models and associated manipulations may appear mysterious and hence suspect to lay users.

Table 3.2. *Examples of some of the alternative decision criteria that may be applied in policy analysis for risk management*

Utility-based criteria

- *Deterministic benefit–cost*: Estimate the benefits and costs of the alternatives in economic terms and choose the one with the highest net benefit.
- *Probabilistic benefit–cost*: Same as deterministic benefit–cost but incorporate uncertainties and use expected value of resulting uncertain net benefit.
- *Cost effectiveness*: Select a desired performance level, perhaps on noneconomic grounds. Then choose the option that achieves the desired level at the lowest cost.
- *Bounded cost*: Do the best you can within the constraints of a budget that is the maximum budget society is prepared to devote to the activity.
- *Maximize multi-attribute utility*: This is the most general form of utility based criterion. Rather than use monetary value as the evaluation measure, MAU involves specifying a utility function that evaluates outcomes in terms of all their important attributes (including uncertainties and risks). The alternative with maximum utility is selected.
- *Minimize chance of worst possible outcome ... maximize chance of best possible outcome, etc.*: Political and behavioral considerations frequently dictate the use of such criteria.

Rights-base criteria

- *Zero risk*: Independent of the benefits and costs, and of how big the risks are, eliminate the risks, or do not allow their introduction.
- *Bounded or constrained risk*: Independent of the costs and benefits, constrain the level of risk so that it does not exceed a specific level or, more generally, so that it meets a set of specified criteria.
- *Approval/compensation*: Allow risks to be imposed only on people who have voluntarily given consent, perhaps after compensation.
- *Approved process*: Not strictly a decision criterion for analysis, but widely applied in risk management decision making. See discussion in text.

Technology-based criteria

- *Best available technology*: Do the best job of reducing the risk that is possible with "current" or "best available" technology. Because, to a significant extent, the meaning of words like "current" or "best available" is economically determined, in practice technology-based criteria are often modified forms of utility-based criteria.

Hybrid criteria
Hybrids of utility- and rights-based criteria are sometimes used. For example, an upper bound on risk may be established (rights-based) below which a benefit–cost (utility-based) criterion is applied.

Expected utility or expected gain or loss are not the only things that can be maximized or minimized. For example, one can choose to *minimize the chance of the worst possible outcome* or *maximize the chance of the best possible outcome*. There may be unusual circumstance in which society wants to do this. More typically, however, political and behavioral considerations dictate the use of such criteria. For example, a risk management decision maker may be willing to accept, and may be able to get by with, more than the expected level of undesirable outcomes on a day-to-day basis. He may be prepared to do this if it will reduce the chance of the worst possible outcome's occurring, an event that would lead to a major investigation and have serious political consequences. As a result, society as a whole may be worse off. Of course, examples like this can be viewed as equivalent to maximizing a multi-attribute utility function that includes both society's objectives and the decision maker's personal objectives, but operationally this is not done.

In contrast to the utility-based criteria, *rights-based criteria* are not primarily concerned with outcomes. Their concern is with process and allowed action or activities. The *zero risk* criterion says: Independent of the benefits and costs, and of how big the risks are, eliminate, or do not allow the introduction of, the risk. Although this is not feasible for naturally occurring risks and some "old" risks imposed by human activity, it certainly is feasible for many "new" human risks. There is no reason why every technology that is feasible should be implemented. This criterion recognizes that not all human activities that impose new risks must inevitably be accepted ... independent of how great the individual or collective benefits. They can be forbidden in the same way that individuals in free societies are forbidden, independent of the benefits involved, to do certain things infringing on others' basic individual rights and freedoms.

If zero risk is too stringent, one can *bound* or *constrain* the level of risk that will be accepted. Thus, one might require that independent of the costs and benefits, the risk will not be allowed to exceed a specific level or, more generally, that it must meet a set of specified criteria. Many concepts in the common law, such as nuisance and reckless endangerment are based on criteria of this sort.

Another rights-based approach, particularly popular in some libertarian formulations (Howard, 1980), might be called the *approval–compensation* criterion. Under this approach one allows risks (or other costs) to be imposed only on people who have voluntarily given consent, perhaps after agreeing to some level of compensation for their inconvenience or possible loss.

All these decision criteria can be applied in risk management decision making. However, the most widely used rights-based approach (*approved process*) is not strictly a decision criterion for analysis. Loosely, it says: Insist that all the relevant parties observe a specified set of procedures, such as some legally defined notion of due process. Then any decision reached will by definition be acceptable. Different actors in such a process are likely to frame the problem in different ways and apply very different, possibly conflicting, decision criteria. The decision criteria of some of the official participants may be stipulated by legislation. In such circumstances it makes little sense to talk of a single social "decision criterion." The vocabulary of decision analysis is simply not appropriate to such a social process.

Technology-based criteria such as requiring the use of *best available technology* are widely used in environmental regulation. This criterion says: Do the best job of reducing the risk that is possible with "current" technological capability. In practice, the criterion is almost never applied as a pure strategy. Rather, some "feasibility–affordability" criterion is added, making it a mixed criterion or perhaps even a pure cost-effectiveness criterion. The approach has the further complication that technology frequently changes. Thus, for example, environmental control requirements based on detectable levels have generally proved to be infeasible because modern measurement techniques have rapidly outpaced our ability to control.

Often *hybrids* of utility and rights-based criteria are applied. For example, a bounded risk criterion may be used to set an upper limit that, for ethical reasons, cannot be exceeded and a benefit–cost criterion may be applied below that level. Depending upon how the objective is chosen, some cost-effectiveness approaches might be considered hybrid approaches.

3.4.2. General Policy Strategies

In addition to the problem of selecting the decision criterion that will be employed, a variety of choices among broad policy strategies or philosophies are usually required. Again, to make our discussion concrete, we focus on two examples drawn from risk management decision making. Very similar issues arise in other policy domains. It is common in risk management decision making in the United States, particularly at the federal level, to seek generic, one-time solutions. In contrast, William C. Clark (1980) has called for what he terms "adaptive design" in the development of risk management strategies. He argues that because problems often vary considerably from one specific circumstance to another it can be unwise to try to impose a single solution across all contexts. In addition, he argues, we rarely know enough about a problem to solve it definitively, and that for this reason it is a good idea to seek solutions that can be adaptive over time, that can be modified and improved as our understanding is refined. He places considerable emphasis on the importance of learning from mistakes, something many organizations find very hard to do.

In the context of environmental risk management decision making, Clark's arguments translate to a call for more site-specific solutions, and the more frequent adoption of "adaptive look-ahead" management strategies (NRC, 1986). They also argue for the development of institutional arrangements that will allow us to understand and learn from mistakes without losing the insights in a mad scramble to assign blame. An excellent illustration of an institution able to do this in a nonenvironmental context is the National Transportation Safety Board, which investigates and learns from aircraft accidents in the United States.

This is not the place for a protracted discussion of the relative merits of "one time" and "adaptive look-ahead" or of "generic" and "site-specific" solutions to environmental problems. Clearly, in some contexts counter arguments based on issues such as simplicity and political feasibility can be raised to Clark's proposals. The point is that just as one can get into serious difficulties by embarking on analysis without taking some time to reflect on the decision criteria that apply to the problem at hand, one can also get into serious trouble by failing to think carefully about the alternative policy strategies available within the context of such criteria.

The process of choosing decision criteria and policy strategies may not involve a single decision and may not precede all analysis. Until a problem has been subjected to some analysis, one may not understand it well enough to make reasonable choices. Indeed, even while different parties are arguing that a problem should be framed in terms of different decision criteria and policy strategies, it is sometimes possible to perform an analysis that can accommodate and allow a comparison among these alternatives (Goldstein, 1981).

3.4.3. Being Consistent about Criteria and Strategies

All too frequently, individuals and organizations undertake analysis without explicitly choosing the decision criteria and policy strategies they will use. Of course in some circumstances this is not a problem. For example:

- The analysis may be addressing a specific set of technical issues that are important in the context of a broader policy problem. Examples might include an estimate of population exposure to an environmental pollutant, or an examination of the implications of using a variety of alternative atmospheric chemical reactions to describe an air pollution problem. However, even when one is working on such apparently technical questions, one must be certain that important assumptions about decision criteria or policy strategies are not being implicitly made.
- The criteria and strategies may already be clearly established either by legal frameworks (e.g., the Clean Air Act) or by prior practice (e.g., many design problems in geotechnical engineering), with the result that answers to questions about decision criteria and policy strategies are well prescribed.

However, even in these situations it is a good idea to reflect a bit on the issues of decision criteria and policy strategies before getting very far into analysis.

In a surprisingly large number of situations, people get into trouble by embarking on analysis without first sorting out what decision criterion and strategies will be used. Indeed, without realizing it, they frequently apply different criteria or strategies in different parts of the same analysis. The result is often an inconsistent mess. An excellent illustration of this problem is the approach the EPA took in 1983 to the regulation of possible health risks from uranium mill tailings (EPA, 1983a; 1983b). A discussion of this case can be found in the report of a National Academy study in which one of us participated (NRC, 1986).

As just noted, many social decisions are not made on the basis of analyses that use clear decision criteria. Rather they are made by following a prescribed process. One might assume that the process will include analysis as one of its elements but this is often not true. When process considerations are dominant, and many different actors with different objectives and interests are involved, it may become difficult or impossible to apply a single coherent formulation and decision criterion to a decision process. Some problems lend themselves comfortably to such politically negotiated solutions. Others, particularly those involving large coupled physical systems, do not.

John G. Kemeny (1980) has written about these latter cases. He suggests that expert groups should be charged with developing coherent alternative options, where coherent clearly includes a consistent application of decision criteria. He argues that although he trusts politicians operating through democratic institutions to choose among such options, he does not consider it reasonable to have them design the options. Suppose, he argues, "that Congress designed an airplane, with each committee designing one component of it and an eleventh-hour conference committee deciding how the various pieces should be put together?" Obviously, he continues, no rational person would fly on such an airplane. Yet, Kemeny argues, this is precisely the way in which polices directed at many large coupled interactive systems are now developed.

3.4.4. Choosing Explicitly

The message of this section is simple. At an early stage in the process of performing a policy analysis the available choices for decision criteria and policy strategies must be identified, seriously considered, and a selection made. If this is not done, the result can be an analytical muddle that no amount of sophisticated analysis of uncertainty, of the kind discussed in the balance of this book, can help to unscramble.

3.5. Setting the Boundaries

In addition to choosing the general philosophical framework within which an analysis will be performed, the boundaries of that analysis must also be chosen. If we accept that the development of "insight and understanding" should be the principal objective of quantitative policy analysis, then a careful examination of where to set the boundaries becomes an important part of the process of analysis. In the following discussion we stress the importance of adopting an iterative approach to refining the formulation of the analysis, and clarifying the questions being addressed. One of the most important parts of this iterative process involves looking at the implications of alternative choices of boundaries. At any given time it may be possible to do this in only an approximate way, because to do it completely may require a much wider analysis than is feasible, given available resources and scientific understanding. Nevertheless, it is important to try and also to communicate to others what bounding assumptions have been made, how carefully they and various alternatives have been considered and the choice justified, and how the boundaries that have been selected may limit or otherwise affect the nature of the insights and understanding the analysis may yield.

The choice of what to include and what to leave out is one of the most fundamental and difficult problems in quantitative policy analysis. E. S. Quade argues that: "Good policy analysis should seek to establish the boundaries of the issue under investigation where thought and analysis show them to be and not where off-the-cuff decisions or convention, whether established by government jurisdiction, academic tradition, or industrial practice, would have them" (Quade, 1975). Good advice, but often not easily followed. Of course, some systems and problems involve tight coupling between a handful of factors and rather loose coupling to the broader world. In these cases, once you have understood the system, boundaries may suggest themselves rather naturally. But more typically, systems and problems are interconnected with the broader world in what appears as a seamless web of associations and dependencies. Where should you cut the connections? What should you model and what should you treat as exogenous, that is, as external to the problem?

We can offer no simple recipes. Careful study may help, but professional taste and judgment must play a significant role in most cases. If factors that may be important cannot be modeled, then parametric or other sensitivity studies may at least make it possible to identify their potential importance. Clear communication of what was done, why it was done, and what the analyst believes are the consequences, are probably as important as anything.

Quade's warning against letting convention or fiat be the basis for setting boundaries is well taken. In addition to the more obvious forms this can assume, analysts must also guard against the boundaries that can be imposed by the adoption of particular analytical tools or techniques. For example, in a consideration of the use of cost–benefit analysis in support of decisions about large civil engineering projects such as dams, Socolow (1976) has argued that even ideal cost–benefit analysis suffers from serious boundary-related problems, and that cost–benefit analysis as actually practiced often runs roughshod over questions of choosing system boundaries. He writes:

Discussions of the limitations of cost–benefit analysis nearly always emphasize uncertainties about the discount rate and contain caveats about the lack of sensitivity regarding who gets what. Only rarely do they call attention to the problem of drawing a boundary around the system being studied. As in idealized thermodynamics, the cost–benefit theory presupposes a system coupled with its surroundings in such a simple way that one can change the system without perceptibly affecting the surroundings. To do a sensible cost–benefit comparison of two alternative futures, one has to include in the "system" all the activities with which are associated large differences depending on which future is being considered. (Socolow, 1976)

To simplify these problems in "actual" or routine analysis, Socolow argues that professions and organizations tend to develop arbitrary "golden rules":

Golden rules have been developed that shelter the practitioner of benefit–cost analysis from the uncertainty about boundaries. The analysis becomes stylized, like the folk art of an isolated village. Those costs and benefits which it is permissible to include in the analysis become codified, as do many of the procedures for evaluating their dollar magnitudes. The warping effect on discourse is substantial. (Socolow, 1976)

While benefit–cost calculations performed by the U.S. Corps of Engineers may be an extreme example of this phenomenon, they are by no means an exception. Similar, if slightly more subtle, imposition of boundaries by convention or fiat is found in many if not the majority of applied analyses undertaken in support of government decision making.[3]

Often the motivation of such implicit bounding by fiat is to make tractable, and perhaps routine, what would otherwise be a very difficult analytical task. Such arbitrarily imposed bounds often severely limit, or eliminate, one's ability to derive real "insight and understanding" about the problem from the analytical results. Of course, viewed from a perspective of bureaucratic behavior, the desire to routinize a difficult task is understandable. Although it may not be explicitly understood as a consequence, eliminating the complications and surprise that new insight and understanding can bring, may often also be a bureaucratically desirable consequence.

Clear communication about the boundaries, their rationale and implications, can also be important in setting future research and policy agendas. Consider the case of "acid rain." The problem was initially framed as a problem of sulfur pollution from large point sources such as power plants and smelters. Various scientific and policy studies were undertaken within the boundaries of this framing. However, as these studies progressed it became clear that such a choice of boundaries might be inappropriate. Field studies suggested a more complex set of sources and relationships between sources and receptors. Studies in atmospheric chemistry began to make it clear that various other chemical constituents were important in controlling such factors as the rate at which sulfur dioxide is oxidized into sulfate aerosols. Although some of these chemical constituents also come from large point sources, more dispersed sources such as automobiles are very important. Thus the set of actors who needed to be considered in the policy question was widened. Studies in atmospheric chemistry in turn led to the understanding that sulfur was not the only, and sometimes not even the primary, source of acid deposition. Studies under

---

3. For example, in the context of the EPA, consider the practice, maintained until quite recently, of always dealing with particulates in terms of TSP, a total mass measure that often ignores or underestimates particulates in the submicron respirable size range. Or consider the practice of arbitrarily specifying what will be considered "the most sensitive population" in order to simplify health impact assessment studies.

way today suggest there may be significant nonlinear coupling between the production of undesired pollutant end products, such as acid deposition, and the levels of the various atmospheric constituents. It now appears that under some circumstances reductions in the level of some constituents can lead to increases rather decreases in the levels of final pollutant products. At the same time, there is growing evidence that some of the environmental damage of greatest concern, such as damage to forests, may not result from acid deposition but rather from exposure to other air pollutants such as oxidants.

It is clear from this evolution in understanding – both of the science and of the policy problems and questions – that there is no way that a quantitative policy analysis of the general topic of acid rain, undertaken a number of years ago, could have explored and dealt with all these issues in the process of setting its boundaries. Too much relevant science was simply not known. What it might have been able to do was alert policymakers to the many scientific uncertainties, offer warnings against imposing "one time solution strategies" and instead argue for "adaptive" strategies that can respond appropriately as improved scientific understanding becomes available, and identify a number of scientific and policy questions that warrant careful further study.

In short, although it is important to adopt an iterative process within the confines of any given policy analysis, it is equally important to adopt such a process more generally when dealing with policy focused research. We should always be working to refine both the questions, and our answers. Thinking carefully about the boundaries to the analyses is one excellent strategy for doing this.

3.6. Motivations for Undertaking Policy Analysis

Until now we have been assuming that policy analysis is undertaken to provide better insight and understanding about a problem. In fact, people commission or perform policy research and analysis with a variety of motivations. The attributes of a good analysis might be expected to depend, at least in part, on the particular motivation. Table 3.3 lists a number of motivations, broken down into four broad classes. Under the first, *substance-focused* motivations, the interest is the substance of the problem itself. At the simplest level the objective may be to get "the answer" to a specifically formulated policy question. Once obtained, this answer will then be implemented without further consideration or interpretation. Such applications are rare in broad policy contexts but not unusual in the detailed implementation of policies. For example, a model may be used as the sole basis for deciding who is eligible to participate in a program. Data on applicants are fed to the model and the results are accepted as the decision on eligibility.

More generally, analysis may be used to develop insight and understanding

Table 3.3. *Summary of some of the motivations that people and organizations have in undertaking quantitative policy-focused research and analysis*

Substance-focused motivations

1. To obtain an "answer" to a specifically formulated policy question that will be directly implemented without further consideration or interpretation.
2. To develop insight and understanding that will be useful to one or several policymakers who are faced with making decisions on a specific well defined set of policy issues or options.
3. To illuminate and provide insight on a general area of policy concern for a variety of interested parties.

Position-focused motivations

4. To provide substantiation and arguments to support one's views in an adversarial procedure.
5. To generate an answer in situations in which one is expected to justify the action taken on the basis of the scientific and technical specifics of the problem.

Process-focused motivations

6. To persuade others that one has got things under control, knows what he or she is doing, and should be trusted.
7. Because the law says one must.
8. Because other people expect it.
9. Because it is not clear what else to do and the political reality of the situation requires that one do something.

Analyst-focused motivations

10. To derive enjoyment and professional recognition and rewards.
11. To use a specific problem context as a vehicle to demonstrate, test, refine, or develop new analytical techniques and tools.
12. Because it is the analyst's job.
13. Because it is the only thing the analyst knows how to do.

that will be useful to one or several policymakers who are faced with deciding on a specific well defined set of policy issues or options. In this case the policy questions under consideration are well-specified and analysis is used simply as a tool to get some, if not all, of the insights, data, or answers that are needed to make a decision on the previously formulated problem.

Finally, a substance-focused motivation may lead to analysis or research undertaken to illuminate and provide insight on a general area of policy concern for a variety of interested parties. In this formulation, analysis serves not just as a tool for obtaining data and answers related to specifically formulated questions but as a vehicle for the broad iterative exploration of how to frame and state the policy questions and alternatives that should be addressed.

When the motivation is *substance-focused*, the specifics of the results,

including the insights and understanding gained while performing the analysis, are of primary importance. The results are also important in analysis undertaken with *position-focused* motivations. But although all results are allowed and considered in the first context, only results that meet some external standard of acceptability – for example, that provide support for a previously selected policy position – are allowed in analysis undertaken with this second motivation. Position-focused analysis may be undertaken to provide substantiation and arguments to support someone's views in an adversarial procedure. This is a very common model of the role of analysis. It is the paradigm adopted by most lawyers and political scientists, but its use is by no means restricted to these professions. Position-focused analysis is also undertaken to generate an answer in situations in which someone is expected to justify the action taken on the basis of the scientific and technical specifics of the problem. This is different from the three substance-focused motivations in Table 3.3. With the latter, one is interested in the analytic formulation and in refining it to obtain the best result possible. With a position-focused motivation one is far less interested in the analytic formulation and will settle for any analysis that is minimally defensible and yields an acceptable result.

In analysis that is undertaken with a *process-focused* motivation, the specific contents of the analysis and the results obtained are essentially irrelevant so long as they don't become a source of embarrassment. What matters is that one has gone through the act of performing the analysis. A common reason for such a motivation is to persuade others that one has got things under control, knows what he or she is doing, and should be trusted. Performing quantitative policy analysis can sometimes achieve this end because it draws on the tools and images of science and social science and the paradigm of "rational decision making." Alternatively, one may adopt a process-focused motivation because the law says an analysis must be done, as, for example, in environmental impact statements; because other people expect it; or because it is not clear what else to do and the political reality of the situation requires that one do something. This last situation might be termed the "commission a study and buy time" syndrome.

Finally, it is important to remember that some analysis gets done with *analyst-focused* motivations. For example, people like us derive enjoyment and professional recognition and rewards from doing policy research and analysis. Sometimes we use a specific problem context as a vehicle to demonstrate, test, refine, or develop new analytical techniques and tools. It is probably also true that some analysis gets done simply because it is the analyst's job or because it is the only thing the analyst knows how to do.

In any real situation, the motivations for performing a particular piece of policy research or analysis usually do not fit any single category listed in Table 3.3 but involve some combination of several.

3.7. All Motivations Require Some Focus on Substance

Given the wide range of motivations listed in Table 3.3, it is tempting to conclude that the identification of a general set of "attributes of good policy analysis" is a hopeless task. However, although people and organizations undertake research and analysis with a wide set of motivations, if it is to serve its purpose analysis must be able to pass, at least to some minimal extent, as having been undertaken with a substance-focused motivation. For example, for a piece of analysis undertaken with a position-focused motivation to be effective, others must be prepared to treat it as substance-focused. If one can readily demonstrate that the inputs for the analysis were artfully chosen to get the desired answer, the effectiveness of the analysis as an adversarial tool is greatly diminished.

Similarly, if it is to serve its purpose, research or analysis undertaken with a process-motivation must be able to pass as substance-motivated work. Consider motivation 6 in Table 3.3. Performing analysis may be an effective way for an agency to persuade others that it knows what it is doing, because they assume that the analysis is being undertaken to get answers to policy questions or to provide general policy illumination. Since the policy-making process is often too convoluted for outside observers to follow, people's perceptions of what the agency is doing may be quite unaffected by the fact that none of the quantitative analysis that is performed ever has any impact on, or perhaps even significance for, the policy decisions being made. But, if the agency were ever to admit publicly that this is what is going on, then, of course, the process of performing the analysis is no longer of value. To retain its value, the fiction must be maintained that the analysis is being undertaken with substance-focused motivations.

Thus we come to an interesting conclusion: We can identify a wide variety of motivations for commissioning or performing policy research and analysis, but for it to be effective, all such work must meet some minimal standards as successful substance-focused work. If we produce a list of the attributes of good substance-focused policy research and analysis, all work will have to meet these criteria to at least some extent. As people become more sophisticated about critiquing policy analysis, the minimum standards of acceptable work can be expected to rise. Thus, although the motivations for undertaking the work may be very mixed, the quality of policy research and analysis, when measured against a substance-focused criteria, should be expected to improve with time. For those of us who believe that good substance-focused policy research and analysis can make important contributions to improving the quality of the policy-making process, this is good news indeed.

3.8. Ten Commandments for Good Policy Analysis

What then, are the attributes characterizing "good" substance-focused policy research and analysis? In order to make it clear that it is normative, we offer

Table 3.4. *"Ten commandments" for good policy analysis*

====

1.   Do your homework with literature, experts, and users.
2.   Let the problem drive the analysis.
3.   Make the analysis as simple as possible, but no simpler.
4.   Identify all significant assumptions.
5.   Be explicit about decision criteria and policy strategies.
6.   Be explicit about uncertainties.
7.   Perform systematic sensitivity and uncertainty analysis.
8.   Iteratively refine the problem statement and the analysis.
9.   Document clearly and completely.
10. Expose the work to peer review.

====

our answer in Table 3.4 in the form of "ten commandments." We know of no analysis, including any of our own, that satisfactorily meets all of these commandments. Some may object that if the commandments are unachievable, they should be abandoned. We disagree. Most Christians consider a life without sin unachievable. Nevertheless, they have found it to be a useful guiding objective. The point is to try to get as close to the ideal as possible. We argue that for policy analysts the "commandments" in Table 3.4 should serve a similar role.

3.8.1. Do Your Homework with Literature, Experts, and Users

The practical implications of our first commandment vary across applications. If you are doing policy analysis for a client, you should place heavy emphasis on understanding his needs and on making sure that the problem he has stated is the problem he actually faces and wants you to solve. Typically this cannot be accomplished in one shot but requires a number of iterations over the course of the analysis. It is also important not to let the client's problem statement and needs be your only consideration. Sometimes an analyst's greatest contribution can be in helping a client to reframe his problem. To do that, you need to do your homework on the problem and the field.

If you are doing policy-focused research, there may be no clearly identified client or user. However, the commandment still applies in the sense that before going very far you should work hard to understand the policy context and the perspectives of practitioners, experts, and others involved with the problem.

3.8.2. Let the Problem Drive the Analysis

This is a very straightforward commandment that means exactly what it says. What you do and the models you build should be driven by the specifics of the problem you are working on and not by such extraneous factors as what tools you like to use or what software you already have built.

3.8.3. Make the Analysis as Simple as Possible, but No Simpler

Simplicity is desirable in policy analysis for several reasons: it makes the analysis easier to understand and easier to describe to other analysts or users, it makes it more "transparent," and this means people are more likely to have faith in the conclusions that are reached. "Simple" is, of course, a relative concept. It depends on the policy questions being asked. What is simple in one context may be very complex in another. If a policy model is being built with various general purpose applications in mind, some extra complexity may be the inevitable price of generality. However, be careful. The need for generality is an argument for complexity that is much overused.

The admonition "no simpler" is equally important. If an analysis uses assumptions or models that are too simple, important aspects of the problem may be missed, or incorrectly handled, and the conclusions reached may be wrong.

The process of identifying the correct level of detail requires iteration, both with the analysis and with the problem statement. Our discussion on choosing boundaries (Section 3.5) is especially relevant to this commandment.

3.8.4. Identify All Significant Assumptions

"Significant assumptions" are those that may significantly affect the conclusions of the analysis. They include assumptions about:

- the main *policy concerns, issues,* or *decisions* that prompted the analysis (for example, whether a new chemical poses a risk to public health, or whether and how much to regulate emissions of a particular pollutant);
- the *evaluation criteria* to be used to define issues of concern or options (for example, the nature, magnitude, and number of human health effects, the cost of emission control technologies, or the effects of a policy on industrial innovation);
- the *scope* and *boundaries* of the analysis and the way in which alternative selections might be expected to influence the conclusions reached (for example, the geographic boundaries, the types of costs and benefits considered);
- *soft* or *intangible* issues that are ignored or inadequately dealt with in the quantitative analysis (for example, the issue of personal-freedom in the context of mandatory-seat-belt or helmet laws, the intrinsic value of wilderness, equity of distribution of costs and benefits, or "commons" problems);
- approximations introduced by the *level of aggregation or of detail* in models (for example, the number of time periods used, the spatial resolution of a geographic model, the number of terms retained in a series expansion, or whether to include dependency on things like age and sex in a health effects model);
- *value judgments and tradeoffs* (for example, discount rate for social welfare, attitude toward risk, or investment rates to prevent expected mortality and morbidity);
- the *objective function(s)* used, including methods of combining ratings on multiple criteria, for evaluating decisions or issues of concern (e.g., maximize the minimum expected utility, minimize the maximum regret, or simply report scores against criteria in an uncombined form).

3.8.5. Be Explicit about Decision Criteria and Policy Strategies

Decision criteria and policy strategies are, of course, significant assumptions. We call them out for special attention because, as explained in Sections 3.4.1 and 3.4.2, they are especially important and are too frequently overlooked or taken for granted.

3.8.6. Be Explicit about Uncertainties

Uncertainties about which an analyst should be explicit include:

- *uncertainty about* technical, scientific, economic, and political *quantities* (for example, uncertainty about chemical rate constants in atmospheric pollutants, uncertainty about what the price of oil or the inflation rate will be next year, uncertainty about how much clean-up will be required by a regulatory agency after a chemical spill occurs);
- *uncertainty about* the appropriate *functional form* of technical, scientific, economic, and political models (for example, uncertainty about whether a chemical reaction can be treated as first-order, or uncertainty about the functional form of a cancer dose-response model);
- *disagreements* among experts about the value of quantities or the functional form of models (for example, different atmospheric scientists may use different chemical rate constants to define an air pollution process, different health experts may use different functional models of dose-response).

We postpone a justification of the commandment on uncertainty to Section 3.9.

3.8.7. Perform Systematic Sensitivity and Uncertainty Analysis

It is usually not immediately obvious which assumptions and uncertainties may significantly affect the conclusions. The purpose of sensitivity and uncertainty analysis is to find this out. *Sensitivity analysis* is the computation of the effect of changes in input values or assumptions (including boundaries and model functional form) on the outputs. *Uncertainty analysis* is the computation of the total uncertainty induced in the output by quantified uncertainty in the inputs and models, and the attributes of the relative importance of the input uncertainties in terms of their contributions. Failure to engage in systematic sensitivity and uncertainty analysis leaves both analysts and users unable to judge the adequacy of the analysis, and the conclusions reached.

Techniques used in sensitivity and uncertainty analysis may include:

- deterministic, one-at-a-time analysis of each factor holding all others constant at nominal values;
- deterministic joint analysis, changing the value of more than one factor at a time;
- parametric analysis, moving one or a few inputs across reasonably selected ranges such as from low to high values in order to examine the shape of the response;
- probabilistic analysis, using correlation, rank correlation, regression, or other means to examine how much of the uncertainty in conclusions is attributable to which inputs.

These are discussed in detail in Chapter 8.

3.8.8. Iteratively Refine the Problem Statement and the Analysis

As the analyst begins to identify the issues that are important in the problem, new data or other information may be sought to *iteratively refine* the analysis through:

- *elaboration* (or addition) of those aspects of the analysis that have been shown to be important and where greater detail may improve the quality of the analysis, and
- *simplification* (or elimination) of those aspects of the analysis that have been shown to be unimportant to the questions of concern.

The objective should be to keep the analysis as simple, clear, and understandable as possible, consistent with the objectives and questions that are of concern. To this end the analyst should work to avoid analytic and other complexity for its own sake.

As argued in Section 3.5, in addition to refining the analytic formulation of the problem within the given problem statement, the analyst should also use the process of sensitivity analysis and iteration to refine, and if necessary redefine, the broader policy objective of the analysis.

In our experience (Henrion, Morgan, Nair, and Wiecha, 1986), the majority of analysts, especially inexperienced analysts, do not take this kind of iterative approach to policy analysis. Instead, they approach their task in a linear way. They conceptualize the analysis they think is needed; construct the analytical tools they believe are required; apply them; obtain answers; perhaps perform some sensitivity analysis on those answers; and then write up the results. The process is illustrated in Figure 3.1.

Without exception, all of the very good analysts we know take something like the very different approach illustrated in Figure 3.2. They view the process of analysis as a process of learning and discovery. They let the policy questions and the structure of the problem drive the analysis, but they take neither for granted and they frequently refine or even redefine both. After dealings with large numbers of inexperienced and mediocre analysts, and many beginning policy-oriented graduate students, we cannot overemphasize the importance of the difference between this iterative conceptualization of the process of policy analysis and the simple linear approach represented by Figure 3.1.

3.8.9. Document Clearly and Completely

The next-to-last ingredient in the process of performing good policy analysis is *documentation*. Documentation is needed to help the analyst himself keep track of what he has done, to help other analysts who may use or modify the analysis, and to provide users with a basis for evaluating the results. Documentation is not something that can be done effectively if it is left until the end. It must proceed as an integral part of the process of sensitivity analysis and iterative refinement.

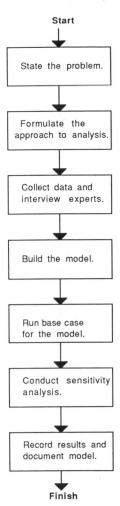

Figure 3.1. Example of the linear approach to analysis adopted by many, especially inexperienced, analysts.

All of the activities we have outlined should be clearly and comprehensively reported on. In particular, the documentation should:

- identify all components and assumptions of the analysis, including a clear representation of uncertainties;
- identify the results of sensitivity analysis to show which uncertainties, disagreements, omissions, scope and modeling decisions had most effect and to justify the choices that were made;
- report on major alternative model formulations that were explored, including sensitivity of the conclusions to alternative technical and value assumptions;
- provide sufficiently complete documentation of the final model that all modeling and calculations could be reproduced from it;

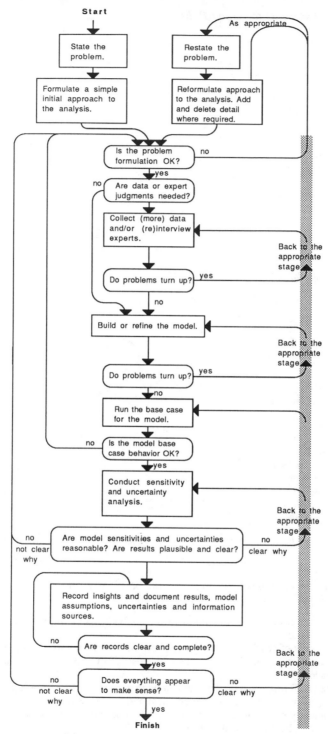

Figure 3.2. Illustration of the process of "good" policy analysis as discussed in the text. Note the heavy emphasis on iterative refinement.

- list all main limitations of the analysis;
- summarize all main conclusions, limitations, and insights in one easily accessible place.

3.8.10. Expose to Peer Review

In Section 3.2.4 we discussed the importance of open debate by peers in the natural sciences and argued that such debate could be even more beneficial in policy analysis. We argued further that, despite occasional claims to the contrary, peer review is becoming increasingly feasible for policy analysis. Thus, our final commandment is that all policy research and analysis should be subjected to careful critical peer review.

3.9. Why Consider Uncertainty?

Because this book is about uncertainty we devote the final section of this overview chapter to a more detailed justification of our commandment to "be explicit about uncertainties."

Historically, the most common approach to uncertainty in policy analysis has been to ignore it. Quade has characterized this strategy as "a chronic disease of planners" (Quade, 1975). But if we have been ignoring it for years and surviving, why is it important to worry about characterizing and dealing with uncertainty when performing policy research and analysis? Indeed, some might argue that since decision theory shows that a decision maker who wishes to maximize the expected utility of an outcome can often achieve his ends by using the mean values of a model's output variables, there is frequently no need for him to concern himself with anything but "best estimates."

Of course, decision theory does demonstrate that it is important to worry about uncertainty:

- when one is performing an analysis in which people's attitude toward risk is likely to be important, for example, when people display significant risk aversion;
- when one is performing an analysis in which uncertain information from different sources must be combined. The precision of each source should help determine its weighting in the combination;
- when a decision must be made about whether to expend resources to acquire additional information. In general, the greater the uncertainty, the greater the expected value of additional information.

In addition to these standard arguments, in his doctoral dissertation Max Henrion (1982) advanced a fourth decision theoretic reason for explicitly dealing with uncertainty. He argued that such treatment is important:

- when the loss function in the analysis has a significant element that has third order dependency on the uncertain quantity and decision variable, and in particular when losses are asymmetric around the optimal decision. To quantify such situations Henrion defined a measure called the *expected value of including uncertainty* or EVIU.

A general discussion of the EVIU and a comparison of this measure with the more familiar measure of expected value of perfect information (EVPI) is provided in Chapter 12 on "the value of knowing how little you know."

Although decision theory has helped to focus attention on uncertainty, it does not capture everything that is important in real policy problems. There are a number of other reasons why it may be important to characterize and deal with uncertainty in an analysis, even when the EVIU appears small or zero:

• There is considerable empirical evidence to suggest that, because of the limitations of the human thought process, cognitive biases may give rise to "best estimates" that are not actually very good. A number of these heuristics and the biases they produce are discussed at some length in Chapter 6. Even if all that is needed is a "best estimate" answer, the quality of that answer may be significantly improved by an analysis that forces people to think about the full range of uncertainty associated with the problem.
• Model building is necessarily an iterative process and an art. Analysis of sources of uncertainty can guide the design and refinement of a model to help select the appropriate level of detail for each component.
• Many real-world "decisions" are not made by a single person at a discrete time. More typically, a decision process may involve multiple actors making explicit and implicit decisions over an extended period. A piece of analysis will be more useful if it treats the uncertainty explicitly allowing users to evaluate its conclusions and limitations better in the changing context of the ongoing decision process.
• Many problems in technology and public policy involve complex mixtures of disagreements over issues of value and of fact. Analytical procedures that explicitly characterize and deal with technical uncertainty (and parameterize or otherwise deal explicitly with issues of value) can help to produce a clearer separation of the two. This *may* help to lead to a more open and rational decision process.
• Policy analysts have a professional and ethical responsibility to present not just "answers" but also a clear and explicit statement of the implications and limitations of their work. Attempts to fully characterize and deal with important associated uncertainties help them to execute this responsibility better.

References

Ackoff, R. L. (1974). *Redesigning the Future*, Wiley, New York.

Bereiter, S. (1983). "Engineers with a Difference," *IEEE Spectrum*, (February): 63–66.

Clark, W. C. (1980). "Witches, Floods, and Wonder Drugs: Historical Perspectives on Risk Managment," in *Societal Risk Assessment: How Safe is Safe Enough*, ed. R. C. Schwing and W. A. Albers, Plenum, New York.

EPA (1983a). "Potential Health and Environmental Hazards of Uranium Mine Wastes, Vols. I, II and III," EPA 520/1-83-007.

EPA (1983b). "Final Environmental Impact Statement for Standards for the Control of Byproduct Materials from Uranium Ore Processing (40 CFR Part 192), Vols. I and II," EPA 520/1-83-008-1.

Feyerabend, P. (1978). "Against Method: Outline of an Anarchist Theory of Knowledge," Verso Editions, London.

Fischhoff, B. (1980). "Clinical Decision Analysis," *Operational Research*, 28, no. 1: 28–43.

Gage, S. J. (1980). Testimony in the "oversight hearings to examine how the Clean Air Act is working to control air pollution throughout the country," Subcommittee on Health and the Environment of the Committee on Interstate and Foreign Commerce, U.S. House of

Representatives, 96th Cong., 1st ses., July-November 1979, U.S. Government Printing Office, (Serial no. 96-110): 236–282, Washington, D.C.

GAO (1979). "Guidelines for Model Evaluation," Tech. Report PAD-79-17, U.S. General Accounting Office, Washington, D.C.

Goldstein, S. N. (1981). "Uncertainty in Life Cycle Demand and the Preference Between Flexible and Dedicated Mass-Production Systems," Ph.D. diss., Department of Engineering and Public Policy, Carnegie Mellon University. See esp. Chapter 2, section on "Applying Decision Rules."

Greenberger, M., Grensen, M., and Crissey, B. (1976). "Models in the Policy Process: Public Decision-Making in the Computer Era," Russell Sage Foundation, New York.

Henrion, M. (1982). "The Value of Knowing How Little You Know: The Advantages of a Probabilistic Treatment of Uncertainty in Policy Analysis," Ph.D. diss., Carnegie Mellon University, Pittsburgh.

Henrion, M. (1984). "Computer Aids for the Dialectical Design of Policy Models," *Design Policy: Design and Information Technology*, pp. 53–61, The Design Council, London.

Henrion, M., and Fischhoff, B. (1986). "Assessing Uncertainty in Physical Constants," *American Journal of Physics*, 54:791–798.

Henrion, M., Morgan, M. G., Nair, I., and Wiecha, C. (1986). "Evaluating an Information System for Policy Modeling and Uncertainty Analysis," *Journal of the American Society for Information Science*, 37, no. 5:319–330.

Howard, R. A. (1980). "On Making Life and Death Decisions," in *Societal Risk Assessment: How Safe is Safe Enough?*, ed. Richard C. Schwing and Walter A. Albers, pp. 88–113, Plenum, New York.

Kantrowitz, A. (1975). "Controlling Technology Democratically," *American Scientist*, 63 (September-October): 505–509.

Keeney, R. L., and Raiffa, H. (1976). "Decisions with Multiple Objectives: Preferences and Value Tradeoffs," Wiley, New York.

Kemeny, J. G. (1980). "Saving American Democracy: The Lessons of Three Mile Island," *Technology Review*, 83 (June-July): 64–75.

Kuhn, T. S. (1962). "The Structure of Scientific Revolutions," University of Chicago Press.

Lave, L. B. (1981). *The Strategy of Social Regulation: Decision Frameworks for Policy*, The Brookings Institution, Washington, D.C.

Lewis, H. (1978). "Report of the Risk Assessment Review Group," NUREG/CR-0400, U.S. Nuclear Regulatory Commission, Washington, D.C.

March, G. (1976). Chapter 5: "The technology of foolishness," in *Ambiguity and Choice in Organizations*, ed. J. G. March and J. P. Olsen, pp. 69–81, Universitetsforlaget, Oslo, Norway.

Mason, R. O. (1969). "A Dialectical Approach to Strategic Planning," *Management Science*, 21:B403–14.

Mishan, E. J. (1973). *Economics for Social Decisions: Elements of Cost–Benefit Analysis*, Praeger, New York.

Mitroff, I. I., and Mason, R. O. (1980). "On Structuring Ill-Structured Policy Issues: Further Explorations in a Methodology for Messy Problems," *Strategic Management*, 1:331–42.

Morgan, M. G. (1978). "Bad Science and Good Policy Analysis," editorial, *Science*, 201 (September 15): 971.

Morgan, M. G. (1985). "New NSF Role in Technical Policy Research is Needed," *IEEE, The Institute*, 9 (June): 2.

NBS (1980). *Validations and Assessment Issues of Energy Models*, ed. S. I. Gass, proceedings of a workshop held at the National Bureau of Standards, Washington, D.C., (NBS Special Publication 569).

NRC (1986). *Scientific Basis for Risk Assessment and Management of Uranium Mill Tailings*, report of the Uranium Mill Tailings Study Panel, M. Granger Morgan, Chairman, National Research Council, National Academy Press, Washington, D.C.

PART (1979). "Activities of the Energy Information Administration," *Professional Audit Review Team*, U.S. General Accounting Office, Washington, D.C.

Quade, E. S. (1975). *Analysis for Public Decisions*, Elsevier, New York.

Rasmussen et al. (1975). *Reactor Safety Study: An Assessment of Accident Risks in U.S. Commercial Nuclear Power Plants*, Nuclear Regulatory Commission, NUREG-75/014 (WASH-1400), Washington, D.C.

Rittel, H., and Webber, M. (1973). "Dilemmas in a General Theory of Planning," *Policy Science*, 4:155–69.

Rowen, H. S. (1976). "Policy Analysis as Heuristic Aid: The Design of Means, Ends, and Institutions," in *When Values Conflict: Essays on Environmental Analysis, Discourse and Decision*, ed. L. H. Tribe, C. S. Schelling, and J. Voss, pp. 137–152, Ballinger, Cambridge, Mass.

Schulze, W. D. (1980). "Ethics, Economics and Value of Safety," in *Societal Risk Assessment: How Safe is Safe Enough?*, ed. R. C. Schwing and W. A. Albers, pp. 217–231, Plenum, New York.

Schulze, W. D., and Kneese, A. V. (1981). "Risk in benefit-cost analysis," *Risk Analysis*, 1:81–88.

Socolow, R. H. (1976). "Chapter 1: Failures of Discourse," in *Boundaries of Analysis: An Inquiry into the Tocks Island Dam Controversy*, ed. H. A. Feiveson, F. W. Sinden, and R. H. Socolow, Ballinger, Cambridge, Mass.

Stone, C. D. (1974). *Should Trees Have Standing: Toward Legal Rights for Natural Objects*, William Kaufmann, Los Altos, Calif, p. 102.

von Hippel, F. (1981). "The Emperor's New Clothes–1981," *Physics Today*, 34:34–41.

Weyant, J. P. (1981). "Modeling for Insights, Not Numbers: The Experiences of the Energy Modeling Forum," Tech. Report Occasional Paper EMF OP 5.1, Energy Modeling Forum, Palo Alto, Calif.

4   The Nature and Sources of Uncertainty

> Probability does not exist.
> Bruno de Finetti, preface,
> *The Theory of Probability*

4.1. Introduction

"Uncertainty" is a capacious term, used to encompass a multiplicity of concepts. Uncertainty may arise because of incomplete information – what will be the U.S. defense budget in the year 2050? – or because of disagreement between information sources – what was the 1987 Soviet defense budget? Uncertainty may arise from linguistic imprecision – what exactly is meant by "The river is wide"? It may refer to variability – what is the flow rate of the Ohio River? Uncertainty may be about a quantity – the slope of a linear dose-response function – or about the structure of a model – the shape of a dose-response function. Even where we have complete information in principle, we may be uncertain because of simplifications and approximations introduced to make analyzing the information cognitively or computationally more tractable. As well as being uncertain about what is the case in the external world, we may be uncertain about what we like, that is about our preferences, and uncertain about what to do about it, that is, about our decisions. Very possibly, we may even be uncertain about our degree of uncertainty. The variety of types and sources of uncertainty, along with the lack of agreed terminology, can generate considerable confusion. Probability is often used as the measure of uncertain belief, and the conceptual confusions are often compounded by the controversy about the nature of probability. We think it important to distinguish clearly between the different types and sources of uncertainty, since they need to be treated in different ways. In particular, we will argue that probability is an appropriate way to express some of these kinds of uncertainty but not others.

We start this chapter with a discussion of probability, and our reasons for adopting a subjectivist or Bayesian view of probability. In the light of this, we try to clarify the distinctions among the different kinds of uncertainty, based on their different sources. We then present a taxonomy of the different kinds of quantities and variables used in quantitative policy and risk analysis models, and present our views on how best to treat their uncertainties. This is followed by a discussion of uncertainties about the form and structure of models. Finally, we examine the question of which quantities should be considered inputs and which outputs, and present a view of the goal of analysis as finding mutually compatible sets of beliefs, values, models, and decisions.

47

Although parts of this discussion raise some rather deep philosophical questions, we touch on them only to the degree necessary for our specific goals: namely, how to treat uncertainty for effective and justifiable policy analysis. Fortunately, since our goals here are practical rather than philosophical, our rather pragmatic orientation and carefully chosen distinctions, it turns out, allow us to sidestep many of the controversies that this topic can engender.

4.2. The Nature of Probability

Probability is certainly the best-known and most widely used formalism for quantifying uncertainty. However, there is often confusion and controversy about what kind of notion it is. So we commence by discussing of two views of probability, the frequentist, or classical, and the subjectivist, or Bayesian, and explain why we incline toward the latter in this book. Here we provide only an introduction to some of the issues. More detailed discussions are found, for example, in Savage (1954); Lindley (1973); de Finetti (1974); and Hacking (1975).

An uncertain quantity may be discrete, such as the outcome of the flip of a coin or throw of dice, or continuous, such as total 1988 U.S. atmospheric emissions of carbon dioxide in millions of tons. An important class of two-valued discrete quantities is logical variables or propositions, with value true or false. In the following discussion, to keep things simple we will consider two-valued uncertain quantities or trials, such as the toss of a coin, in which an event, such as the coin's coming up heads, may occur or not. In later sections we will generalize this to multivalued and continuous quantities.

4.2.1. The Frequentist View

The classical or frequentist view of probability defines the probability of an event's occurring in a particular trial as the *frequency* with which it occurs in a long sequence of similar trials. More precisely, the probability is the value to which the long-run frequency converges as the number of trials increases. In this view, the probability is actually a property of a theoretically infinite sequence of trials rather than of a single event. It is sometimes thought of as a property or "propensity" of the physical system that generates the events, such as the coin or dice. With such an event as the toss of a coin, it is easy to think of the sequence of trials of which it is a member, and natural to judge that this particular trial is typical of all trials. (More technically, it may be judged to be *exchangeable* with other trials in the sequence.)

The problem is that for most events of interest for real-world decision making, it is not clear what the relevant population of trials of similar events should be. If one is trying to estimate the probability that a particular chemical under current review is carcinogenic, what is the relevant parent population against which to compare it? The population of all known chemicals? All chemicals reviewed for carcinogenicity? All chemicals tested for carcinogenicity? All chemicals with a similar molecular substructure? What about an event that is unique, such as the probability judged in 1988 that room temperature superconductors will be identified before the year 2000?

One traditional response has been to distinguish events whose probabilities are "knowable," which have an obvious parent population, and those whose probabilities are "unknowable," which do not. An early influential text on decision making distinguished these as situations of "risk" and "uncertainty," respectively (Luce and Raiffa, 1957). The problem with this view, which still has some adherents (not including Luce and Raiffa), is that it renders the theory of probability virtually inapplicable to real-world decision making, outside games of chance involving dice or cards. Thus, we find this distinction unhelpful.

4.2.2. The Personalist or Bayesian View

Instead we will adopt the personalistic view of probability, also known as subjectivist or Bayesian. In this view a probability of an event is the degree of belief that a person has that it will occur, given all the relevant information currently known to that person. Thus the probability is a function not only of the event, but of the state of information. It is common to write it as a function of two arguments, $P(X \mid e)$, where X is the uncertain event, and e is the person's state of information on which it is conditioned.

Since different people may have different information relevant to an event, and the same person may acquire new information as time progresses, there is strictly no such thing as "the" probability of an event. Different people or one person at different times may legitimately assign different probabilities to the same event. In this view, a probability is fundamentally unlike objectively measurable physical properties, such as mass or length in Newtonian physics, in that it depends in an essential way on the observer. This is the sense underlying de Finetti's assertion that "probability does not exist." Of course, in the light of relativity and quantum mechanics, the modern physicist might retort that actually physical properties are similarly dependent on the observer. Be that as it may, to remind ourselves of this, we will often refer to "your" probability or "the expert's" probability, rather than "the" probability.

Does this subjectivist view mean that your probability assignments can be completely arbitrary? No, because if they are legitimate probabilities, they must be consistent with the axioms of probability. For example, if you assign probability p that an event X will occur, you should assign probability $1 - p$ to its complement, that X doesn't occur. The probability that one of a set of mutually exclusive events occurs should be the sum of their probabilities. In fact, subjective probabilities should obey the same axioms as objective or frequentist probabilities, otherwise they are not probabilities. Bayes' theorem is a simple consequence of these axioms, and so is just as true for frequentist as for subjective probabilities.

Moreover, if you believe that all trials in a sequence of trials are exchangeable with each other (as in all tosses of the same coin), then your probability for the coin's coming up heads should converge to the long run frequency of heads, as you observe more and more trials. This implies that where there is sufficient empirical data for the frequentist to estimate a probability, the subjectivist's assessment of "his" or "her" probability will converge to the frequentist's estimate of "the" probability of the event. In other words, they will tend to agree. The difference is that if there are no data, say in assessing the probability of heads for a newly bent coin that has never been tossed before, the subjectivist would still be able to assess a probability, where the frequentist would not.

4.2.3. The Clarity Test

Even from the personalist or subjectivist view, an event or quantity must be well-specified for a meaningful probability distribution to be assessable. By *well-specified*, we mean that given complete information, people would agree whether or not the event had occurred. Similarly, a well-specified quantity is one with a single true value, which would be empirically measurable, at least in principle. R. A. Howard (Howard and Matheson, 1984) has suggested the *clarity test* as a conceptual way to sharpen up the notion of well-specifiedness. Imagine a clairvoyante who could know all facts about the universe, past, present, and future. Given the description of the event or quantity, could she say unambiguously whether the event will occur (or had occurred), or could she give the exact numerical value of the quantity? If so, it is well-specified.

Thus, "the price of gasoline" would not pass the clarity test. The clairvoyante would want to know what kind of gasoline, sold where and when, before she could give its exact value. An adequate specification of the quantity might be "the average retail price of regular unleaded gasoline in dollars per gallon observed at service stations in the northeastern United States on January 1, 1990." Without such precision, vagueness about what the parameter represents is liable to get confounded with uncertainty about its true value.

4.3. Types of Quantity

We have suggested that subjective probability distributions are often a good way to express uncertainty, but we should emphasize that they are appropriate only for certain types of quantities. These we will term *empirical* or *chance* quantities, representing properties or states of the world. However, a policy model may also contain a variety of other types of quantities playing different roles within the analysis, including decision variables, value parameters, and

Table 4.1. *Summary of types of quantity in policy models*

Type of quantity	Examples	Treatment of uncertainty
Empirical parameter or chance variable	Thermal efficiency, oxidation rate, fuel price	Probabilistic, parametric, or switchover
Defined constant	Atomic weight, π, joules per kilowatt-hr	Certain by definition
Decision variable	Plant size (utility), emissions cap (EPA)	Parametric or switchover
Value parameter	Discount rate, "value of life," risk tolerance	Parametric or switchover
Index variable	Longitude and latitude, height, time period	Certain by definition
Model domain parameter	Geographic region, time horizon, time increment	Parametric or switchover
Outcome criterion	Net present value, utility	Determined by treatment of its inputs

others. We will argue that it is generally inappropriate to represent uncertainty about decision variables and value parameters by probability distributions. But it is often useful to conduct a parametric sensitivity analysis on these quantities, that is to examine the effect on the output of deterministic changes to the uncertain quantity. A variety of other approaches to representing and analyzing uncertainties is possible and is discussed in greater detail in Chapter 8.

The main types of quantity we find it useful to distinguish are listed in Table 4.1. Because the way in which one treats the uncertainty should depend on the type of quantity, it is important to distinguish among the various types. The following sections discuss each in some detail.

4.3.1. Empirical Quantities

Empirical quantities represent measurable properties of the real-world systems being modeled. They include quantities in the domains of natural science and engineering, such as the oxidation rates of atmospheric pollutants, the thermal efficiency of a power plant, the failure rate of a valve, or the carcinogenic potency of a chemical, and quantities in the domain of the social sciences, such as demand elasticities or prices in economics, or judgmental biases in psychology. To be empirical, variables must be measurable, at least in principle, either now or at some time in the past or future.

They should be sufficiently well-specified so that they can pass the clarity test. Thus, it is permissible to express uncertainty about an empirical quantity in the form of a probability distribution. Indeed, we suggest that the *only* type of quantity whose uncertainty may appropriately be represented in probabilistic terms are empirical quantities. This is because they are the only type of quantity that is both uncertain and can be said to have a *true*, as opposed to an *appropriate* or *good*, value.

In the decision analysis literature, uncertain empirical quantities are generally termed *chance nodes*, *chance variables*, or *nature's choices* in discussions of decision trees and influence diagrams. In principle, all empirical quantities are uncertain. There is never absolute certainty about the truth of any empirical proposition or about the exact value of any continuous empirical quantity. No matter how great its precision, no experiment can measure a real-valued quantity with zero error. However, it is common that the uncertainty, for practical purposes, is negligible in many of the empirical quantities and so they may be treated as certain in the model.

4.3.2. Defined Constants

The fundamental physical constants, such as the gravitational constant, the charge of the electron, or Planck's constant are actually empirical quantities to be measured and therefore inherently uncertain, if only to a small degree. However, some quantities are certain by definition, and these we call "defined constants." Examples are the number of days in December, the numbers of joules in a kilowatt-hour, or the atomic number of oxygen, or mathematical constants such as π. This is the one category of quantities about whose uncertainty we never have to worry. Its only importance in the current context is its distinction from empirical quantities.

4.3.3. Decision Variables

Decision variables are quantities over which the decision maker exercises direct control. They are sometimes also referred to as *control variables* or *policy variables*. For example, in a risk assessment model designed to help an EPA decision maker set a standard for a particular air pollutant, the permitted maximum ambient level or total quantity of pollutant emitted might be a decision variable. For a utility company, the type and specifications for the pollution control equipment may be decision variables. One may very well be uncertain about the "best" value for a decision variable – otherwise why would we be constructing a policy model in the first place? But it does not make sense to be uncertain about its "true" value. If it is a decision variable, then by definition it has no true value. It is up to the decision maker to select its value.

Some policy models, particularly in policy-oriented research, do not have any explicit decision variables. However, it is desirable that, to the extent possible, policy models should be directed at possible decisions, at least implicitly; the process of developing and assessing a model can be more focused if these decisions are made explicit.

The question of whether a specific quantity is a decision variable, an empirical quantity, or some other type of quantity depends on the context and intent of the model, and particularly who the decision maker is. Thus, the government standard for the maximum permissible level of mercury in fish may be a decision variable from the viewpoint of a regulatory agency (the EPA), but it may be an empirical quantity from the viewpoint of the fisherman or fishmonger. Before the agency has promulgated its decision on this standard, the quantity may be a highly uncertain empirical quantity, appropriately modeled by a probability distribution, from the point of view of the latter.

4.3.4. Value Parameters

Value parameters represent aspects of the preferences of the decision makers or the people they represent. One common example is the discount rate applied for combining costs and benefits accruing at different times. Another, often used in decision analysis, is the risk tolerance, a parameter sometimes used to specify the degree of risk aversion when comparing uncertain outcomes. A third and often controversial value parameter is the "value of life," sometimes better stated as the rate of investment per statistical death averted that is deemed appropriate for a safety program, such as safer highway construction standards or civil aviation regulations.

It is not unusual for a value parameter to be treated as an empirical quantity, but it is usually a serious mistake. For example, an empirically observable discount rate or interest rate from some other institution may be used to set the discount rate for a decision. Certainly consideration of evidence about discount and interest rates may be helpful in selecting a discount rate for a cost–benefit analysis, but the quantity finally selected for one's own decision is unavoidably a value judgment and should be explicitly treated as such.

Whether the value assumed by value parameters can be appropriately treated as probabilistic is debatable. One could argue that if you are not sure what you prefer, you could deal with this by treating your own value parameters as probabilistically uncertain (Cyert and DeGroot, 1987). In our view this is rarely helpful in policy modeling and can lead to confusion. If you are not sure of your values, it is generally better to vary your value coefficients parametrically. That is, you should repeat the analysis for a range of possible values of the value parameter(s). In this way you can learn whether changes in the parameter's value produce changes in outcomes that you care about.

We have two reasons for this view. First, value parameters tend to be among those quantities people are most unsure about, and that contribute most to uncertainty about what decision is best. Probabilistic treatment of the uncertainty may hide the impact of this uncertainty, and decision makers may never have an opportunity to see the implications of their possible alternative value choices. If they are treated parametrically, it is likely to provide more insight into the situation. Second, as argued in Chapter 3, we do not view selection of values as necessarily preceding analysis. It is often an important purpose of analysis to help people to choose or clarify their values. If an analysis indicates that current uncertainty about values does not affect the conclusions that are reached, the decision maker and analyst need not invest the effort to refine his values further (Fischer, 1980). If, on the other hand, the conclusions are found to vary substantially across the range of uncertainty about values, this suggests that careful thought and refinement will be worthwhile, perhaps using results from the model as one consideration in the refinement process.

As with decision variables, classification of a quantity as a value parameter is context-dependent. If the quantity models the values and preferences of the decision maker or those represented in making the decision, it should be treated as a value parameter. If, however, it describes the values of some other person or group whose preferences are being modeled to help predict their responses, as in a gaming situation, it should probably be classified as an empirical parameter. For example, an oil company executive trying to design a pricing strategy needs to model his company's objectives with value parameters. But in forecasting the responses of customers and competitors, the preferences of these other parties should be treated as empirical parameters, and might be estimated by market research and econometric analysis. Thus, the difference between a value parameter and an empirical parameter is also a matter of intent and perspective.

4.3.5. Index Variables

Index variables are used to identify a location or cell in the spatial or temporal domain of a model, for example, a particular year in a multi-year model, or a geographic grid square within a geographic model. Index variables also may be used to specify a member of a set of elements, such as one of the states of the United States, or one of a set of possible species of chemical pollutant for models disaggregated by state or chemical species, respectively. Some discussions of modeling, particularly in dynamic simulation, refer to these as *independent variables*. We avoid this term because of the potential confusion with the usage of this same term with a somewhat different meaning in statistical analysis and econometric modeling.

It does not make sense to be uncertain about the value of an index variable. Of course, this does not mean that one can never be uncertain about quantities like space and time. Again it is a matter of the context of use. For example, it makes sense to be uncertain about the distance at which a ball tossed in the air will hit the ground if distance is a computed quantity, and not an index variable (that is, not independent). On the other hand, if the model computes the height of the ball above ground as a function of distance, then distance is an index variable and not uncertain. In this case the height of the ball at a given distance may be uncertain.

4.3.6. Model Domain Parameters

Model domain parameters specify the domain or scope of the system being modeled, generally by specifying the range and increments for index variables. For example, in an analysis of a multi-year investment project, the horizon year (last year modeled) is a domain parameter delimiting the temporal extent of the model. Or in models of the transport of atmospheric pollution, the spatial extent of the model may be controlled by domain parameters specifying the "ceiling height," and minimum and maximum longitude and latitude. Domain parameters are also used to define the level of detail or granularity of the model. Temporal granularity is controlled by the time increment defining periods for analysis, as a month, quarter, or year. Spatial detail may be controlled by division into horizontal layers, and the geographic grid spacing. Domain parameters may also define *base line* properties. For example, in performing a generic analysis of the risks of alternative types of power plant, the analyst may arbitrarily select the size of the plants for modeling at 1000 Mw_e for purposes of comparison.

Model domain parameters are quantities that are often ignored during uncertainty analysis, despite having very considerable potential impact. It is the finite domain of analysis and finite degree of detail that give rise to approximation uncertainty. They control both the precision of the representation and the computational complexity. Model domain parameters should be chosen so that the model deals adequately with the full range of the system of interest, to avoid undue approximation without excessive computation costs. Choosing these parameters to make a balanced trade-off is one of the most important and most difficult aspects of model design. It is usual to be uncertain about what values are *appropriate* for them. But, as for decision variables or value parameters, you cannot be uncertain about what the "true" values of model domain parameters are – they have no "true" values, except perhaps that the potentially relevant temporal and spatial domain is infinitely large and infinitely detailed. The choice of value is up to the modeler. It would be inappropriate, and usually impractical, to represent uncertainty about a model domain parameter by a subjective probability distribution. But it is often an excellent idea – and too rarely done – to vary them parametrically to examine how they affect the results of the analysis. Such a sensitivity analysis can allow a more informed choice of model domain parameters in subsequent modeling.

4.3.7. State Variables

In a dynamic model, state variables are members of a minimal subset of all variables from whose values, given at any time during the course of a model's execution, it is possible to compute the values of *all* the model's variables at the same and future times. Whether state variables are treated as certain or as uncertain in value depends on the way in which input parameters have been specified. Although constituting an important concept in dynamic modeling, the notion of state variables is not particularly helpful in the present discussion of uncertainty and so will not be elaborated further.

4.3.8. Outcome Criteria

By outcome criteria we mean the variables used to rank or measure the desirability of possible outcomes. Different traditions among policy analysts have predilections for different outcome criteria. Some commonly used criteria are net profit, cost–benefit ratio, the internal rate of return, net present value, and utility. These quantities will be deterministic or probabilistic according to whether any of the input quantities on which they depend are probabilistic. For the decision analysis fraternity the defining criterion is expected utility.

4.4. Sources of Uncertainty in Empirical Quantities

There have been several attempts to create taxonomies of different kinds of uncertainty. Most of these have concentrated on uncertainty in empirical quantities, which generally constitute the majority of quantities in models for policy and risk analysis. Uncertainties in empirical quantities can arise from a variety of different kinds of sources. The appropriate method to characterize the uncertainty, and the appropriate method for trying to reduce it, generally depend on the particular kind of source. Hence, we have found it helpful to classify uncertainty in empirical quantities in terms of the different kinds of source from which it can arise. These include the following:

- Statistical variation
- Subjective judgment
- Linguistic imprecision
- Variability
- Inherent randomness
- Disagreement
- Approximation

In the following section we will distinguish and discuss each source of uncertainty in turn.

4.4.1. Random Error and Statistical Variation

The most-studied and best-understood kind of uncertainty arises from random error in direct measurements of a quantity. No measurement of an empirical quantity, such as the speed of light, can be absolutely exact. Imperfections in the measuring instrument and observational technique will inevitably give rise to variations from one observation to the next. This is as true of the complex apparatus used to measure the speed of light, even though it may have an accuracy of 1 part in 10^{12}, as it is of a wooden yardstick used by a carpenter with an accuracy of 1 in 1,000. It is just the relative size of the errors that may be different. The resulting uncertainty depends on the size of the variations between observations and the number of observations taken. The armamentarium of statistics provides a variety of well-known techniques for quantifying this uncertainty, such as standard deviation, confidence intervals, and others. A number of these are discussed in Chapter 5.

4.4.2. Systematic Error and Subjective Judgment

Any measurement involves not only random error but also systematic error. Systematic error is defined as the difference between the true value of the quantity of interest and the value to which the mean of the measurements converges as more measurements are taken. Systematic errors arise from biases in the measuring apparatus and experimental procedure. They may be due to imprecise calibration, faulty reading of the scale, and inaccuracies in the assumptions used to infer the actual quantity from the observable readings.

The task of the scientist making the measurement is to try to reduce the systematic error to a minimum. This may be done by careful design and calibration of the measurement apparatus and procedure, and careful analysis of the assumptions in the calculations. However, there will always be an irreducible residual systematic error. Because a good investigator will adjust for all the sources of bias that are known, the remaining sources of systematic error are therefore those that are unknown or merely suspected. Thus, estimating their possible magnitude is extremely difficult and of necessity involves a large element of subjective judgment.

This is true even of highly precise measurements of fundamental physical constants, such as the speed of light or the mass of the electron. In most such measurements, once the apparatus is set up and calibrated, it is relatively easy to take numerous observations. Thus, the random error due to variability of the observations about their mean can be reduced arbitrarily simply by taking sufficient observations. However, the systematic error is not reduced by additional observations, and so generally comes to dominate the overall error.

Anyone who doubts that the estimation of systematic error is a subjective process may look at the reported error in historical measurements of physical constants and compare them with more recent and accurate values. In Figure 4.1 we reproduce a figure from Henrion and Fischhoff (1986) showing historical

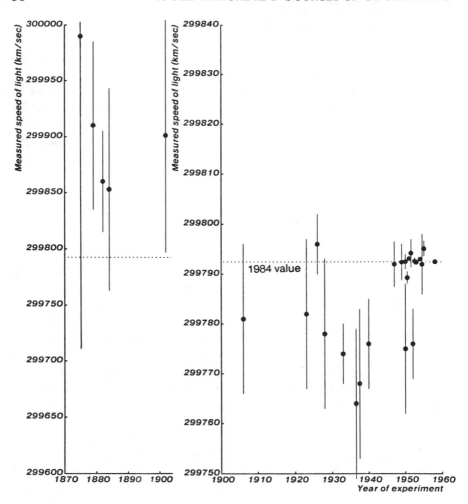

Figure 4.1. Experimental measurements of the speed of light between 1875 and 1960. Vertical bars show reported uncertainty as standard error. Horizontal dashed line represents currently accepted value. Less than 50% of the error bars enclose the accepted value, instead of the expected 70%. From Henrion and Fischoff, 1986.

measurements of the speed of light. The vertical error bars represent the estimate of the total error in the measurement as originally reported, as plus or minus one standard deviation. The currently accepted value is shown as the dashed horizontal line. If well calibrated, this value should be within the error bars in about 70 percent of the cases. Actually, it is between the error bars less than 50 percent of the cases.

It turns out there is a consistent tendency to underestimate the systematic error. This tendency has been found to be almost universal in all measurements of physical quantities that have been looked at. Perhaps this should not be surprising, given the difficulty in making subjective estimates about errors that are essentially unknown at the time. When quantifying uncertainties, it is much easier to underestimate the existence or effect of little-known sources of error than to overestimate them. Given the inevitability of subjectivity in estimating uncertainty in the extraordinarily precise measurements of fundamental physical constants, it should be no surprise that subjective judgment is just as unavoidable in estimates of uncertainty in the generally far less precisely known quantities of interest in policy and risk analysis.

The systematic error is the difference between the quantity being measured and the quantity of interest, which are virtually never quite the same. Sometimes the differences are slight, as in measurements of the speed of light in a near vacuum to estimate its speed in a perfect vacuum. Or they may be considerable, as in measurements of the carcinogenic potency of a chemical for huge doses in mice to obtain estimates of the effect of small doses in humans. Typically, in risk and policy analysis the difference is large, and consequently the role of subjective judgment is especially critical.

Unfortunately, it is not unusual to ignore the fact that the measured quantity and the quantity of interest are different, and so ignore the systematic error when assessing the overall uncertainty. In such cases the mean value and uncertainty of the quantity of interest are estimated directly as the mean and random error of the measurements. For example, the carcinogenic potency of a large dose of a chemical in mice may be assumed to be the same as its low-dose carcinogenic potency in humans, normalized to a common dose of chemical per unit body weight (milligrams per kilogram). This may well be a reasonable first order approximation in the absence of other information, and a useful way to estimate the mean of the quantity. But it is important to remember that this relies on several significant assumptions, for example, that the effect is similar in mice and men as a function of average concentration, and that the dose-response rate is linear from low to high doses. Both these common assumptions introduce very considerable additional uncertainty, and are based largely on subjective judgment. It is not the use of subjective judgment that is a mistake. That is generally unavoidable. The mistake is to ignore it, and hence overlook the introduction of major additional sources of uncertainty.

Another situation in which judgmental elements often get smuggled in, and the concomitant increase in uncertainty gets forgotten, is in using the results of a regression analysis of past data for forecasting future performance. The standard deviations and R-squared values represent random error or degree of fit of the model to the past data. In extrapolating from the past to future forecasts, there is not only uncertainty from the imperfect fit to past data, but also uncertainty about how much the future will be like the past. In some cases, expert judgment may suggest adjustment of the trend lines from the past, up or down according to knowledge of circumstances not built into the model. But even if the median assumption is that the trend line continues as before, there is likely to be additional uncertainty. In most cases, this judgmental uncertainty about how much the future will be like the past will be considerably larger than the uncertainty due to imperfect fit to the past.

It is common in discussions of uncertainty to distinguish between estimates based on empirical measurement – such as the maximum temperature at which a given material exhibits superconductivity – and estimates based entirely on subjective judgment – such as the date, if any, estimated in 1988, at which room temperature superconductivity will first be demonstrated. Our discussion of systematic error suggests this distinction is not absolute but rather one of degree. Careful examination of what is involved in measuring physical constants and assessing their uncertainty, reveals that even here, there is an irreducible component of subjective judgment. At the other extreme, even estimates of the date of an "unprecedented" innovation, though largely a matter of judgment, should not be entirely innocent of empirical data. Evidence about the current state of the art in superconducting materials and the recent rate of progress will presumably help to inform such an estimate. Empirical study of past technological breakthroughs, especially of the time lag between recognition of the possibility and its achievement (or nonachievement) may also be helpful. Even when there seems to be virtually no empirical information about the likely value of a quantity, there is often good evidence to provide bounds on it. For example, the carcinogenic potency of an untested chemical to which people are widely exposed may have a lower bound of zero, and an approximate upper bound may be determined by the observation that exposed people are not dropping like flies. Although we should not overstate the degree to which all estimation can be empirically based, the key point is that there is a continuum between empirical and subjective estimates.

4.4.3. Linguistic Imprecision

In everyday conversation, we often refer to events or quantities with imprecise language, which would not pass the clarity test. Indeed, we do the same in professional writing. For example, the proposition that "Pat is tall" is ill specified. Would it be true if Pat was five feet nine inches? To assign a probability to it, we need a greater precision, for example, the proposition "Pat is taller than six feet." "The water-flow rate in the Ohio river" is an ill-specified quantity. More specifics are needed before a probability distribution would be applicable, for example, "The net water flow rate in the Ohio out of Pittsburgh at noon on January 1, 1988."

The orthodox Bayesian view is that linguistic imprecision should simply be eliminated by providing a careful specification of all events and quantities so that they can pass the clarity test. This is regarded as an important part of the task of the decision analyst. An alternative view is fuzzy set theory (Zadeh, 1984) that sees linguistic imprecision as an unavoidable aspect of human discourse which should be explicitly handled by a formal system for reasoning. A conventional "crisp" set is defined by a membership function, which specifies for every object whether or not it is a member of the set. In contrast, a fuzzy set is defined by a fuzzy membership function, which allows degrees of membership intermediate between 0 and 1. For example, Pat at five feet nine inches might have degree of membership of about 0.5 in the fuzzy set of tall people. Fuzzy set theory defines operations for the union, intersection, and complement of fuzzy sets, as simple generalizations of the corresponding crisp set operations.

For some purposes it may be very useful to be able to represent linguistic imprecision explicitly in aids for inference and decision making. This is particularly so when a formal model must be constructed from judgments of those who are unable or unwilling to produce well-specified quantities. The idea of a decision aid that can handle inputs in linguistic form, and can present and explain results in similar form, is certainly appealing. Unfortunately, we know of no strong reasons, either theoretical or empirical, for believing that the fuzzy set operations are good representations of human reasoning with linguistic imprecision. What little experimental evidence there is (Oden, 1977) suggests that they are not.

There has been considerable research on the correspondence between numerical probabilities and probabilities expressed by verbal phrases, such as "quite likely," "highly improbable," and the like. (Beyth-Marom, 1982; Wallsten et al., 1986). Most people seem more comfortable with such phrases than with the numbers. Unfortunately, there is considerable variation in the way different people interpret the phrases, and their interpretation is very context dependent. Saying that rain is "fairly likely" tomorrow means something rather different in London than in Tucson, Arizona. Similarly, the quantitative implications of "Pat is tall" are greatly affected by knowledge of whether Pat is male or female, adult or child. There is still considerable room for research on developing more empirically based models of linguistic imprecision and qualitative reasoning under uncertainty, but these examples suggest that simple mappings between words and numbers are unlikely to be adequate.

For the moment, at least, in policy and risk analysis it seems wiser to seek clear specifications of the events and quantities to be used in models, and, as far as possible, to avoid linguistic imprecision as a source of uncertainty. Whereas many sources of uncertainty, including lack of information and computational limitations, are often expensive or impossible to eliminate, uncertainty due to linguistic imprecision is usually relatively easy to remove with a bit of clear thinking. In the rest of this book, we will assume this approach.

4.4.4. Variability

Many quantities are variable over time or space. Some examples are the aforementioned flow of the Ohio River at Pittsburgh during this year, the weight of newborn infants in Washington, D.C., during the same period, or the retail price of regular unleaded gasoline in the United States in ten years' time. None of these quantities, as described, would pass the clarity test, since all leave crucial dimensions unspecified: for example, the exact date, the identity of the infant, or the location in the United States of the filling station. To be precise, these descriptions are not of particular quantities but of populations of quantities. However, these populations are reasonably well-specified and could each be described by a frequency distribution.

Frequency distributions are sometimes called probability distributions and, indeed, have the same formal properties. However, it helps to keep the two concepts distinct. It is possible to have a high degree of certainty about a frequency distribution. For example, it is not hard to imagine obtaining the statistics on the weights of all newborns in Washington, D.C., during a year, and compiling a precise frequency distribution. On the other hand, one may be quite uncertain about a frequency distribution, for example, for gasoline prices in ten years' time. Uncertainty about a frequency distribution may be represented by probability distributions about its various parameters, such as its mean, standard deviation, median, or other percentiles. It is not hard to think about uncertainty about *frequency distributions*, represented probabilistically. But uncertainty about *probability distributions* is more problematic.

Suppose we are interested in modeling the uncertainty about an individual sampled at random from a given population with known frequency distribution. Then it is appropriate to represent our uncertainty about the quantity for this individual by a probability distribution with the same parameters as its parent frequency distribution. For instance, our uncertainty about the weight of a randomly selected newborn from the Washington, D.C., population might appropriately be modeled by a probability distribution corresponding to the frequency distribution. However, if we are also uncertain about the frequency distribution it is drawn from, our uncertainty about the weight of the specific infant has two components, derived from this uncertainty as well as the uncertainty from sampling from the distribution. Statistical methods for handling such concepts are discussed in Chapter 5. The key point here is the distinction between uncertainty and variability.

A common mistake is failure to distinguish between variability due to sampling from a frequency distribution and empirical uncertainty that arises from incomplete scientific or technical knowledge. For example, in considering the effect of the acidification of the aquatic environment on fish viability, there may be variability in sensitivity to pH among fish species, and there may also be scientific uncertainty about the actual sensitivity of any one species. The uncertainty due to the variability can be reduced by disaggregation, computing the impact on each species separately, whereas the scientific uncertainty can be reduced only by further research on the impacts of acidity on fish survival by species. Examination of the first kind of uncertainty can tell you how much disaggregation is worthwhile in performing the assessment. Examination of the second kind of uncertainty may tell you about the relative importance of carrying out more fish research. But this sort of uncertainty analysis is impossible unless the two kinds of uncertainty are carefully distinguished.

4.4.5. Randomness and Unpredictability

Inherent randomness is sometimes distinguished from other kinds of uncertainty, in being irreducible even in principle. The dominant paradigm in quantum mechanics views Heisenberg indeterminacy as a kind of inherent randomness in this sense. The position and velocity of a particle are not simultaneously determinable with complete accuracy, even in principle. Of course, there are still a few physicists who subscribe to Einstein's dictum, that "God does not play dice." In other words, the indeterminacy is not a matter of principle but simply a result of our limited understanding of the world. There may be hidden variables and causal mechanisms that, if only we understood them, would resolve the apparent indeterminacy.

Whatever the merits of the alternative views of quantum mechanics, the practical issue for analysis at the macrolevels of concern to the rest of us is whether uncertain quantities are predictable *in practice*. Even if there were actually a well-defined pattern that could enable us to predict values in principle, to do so in practice requires knowledge of the pattern. This leads us to a personalist view of randomness: You see a quantity as random if you do not know of any pattern or model that can account for its variation. In this view, randomness, like probability, is a function of the knowledge available to the assessor. A quantity may legitimately be random to one person, but deterministic to another who knows its underlying generating process. In this view the *pseudo* in the phrase *pseudo-random numbers* as generated by computer random number algorithms, is redundant. The numbers may be completely determined if you know the algorithm, but if you don't, they are indeed random as far as you are concerned.

Even if the physical laws governing a system are well understood, its behavior may be unpredictable because of modeling and computational limitations. In recent decades, it has become apparent that many non-linear systems exhibit extreme sensitivity to initial conditions. For example, it has been shown with meteorological models that tiny differences in initial conditions lead to vast changes in the course of subsequent weather. This is sometimes labeled the "butterfly effect": the notion that the beating of a butterfly's wing in Beijing may influence the course of a storm in New York next month. Since representation of initial conditions is limited by lack of both data and the computational limitations of accuracy and detail with even the largest supercomputers, this phenomenon explains the difficulty in weather prediction of more than a week ahead and, in fact, suggests that long-range weather prediction may be practically impossible. This principle of sensitivity to initial conditions is exploited in devices intended to exhibit random behavior, such as coin tossing, dice, and roulette wheels. It is not that we believe these devices are immune to the standard physical laws, but rather that very slight, unmeasurable differences in the initial orientation, position, or velocity lead to large differences in the outcome.[1]

Interesting though these issues of inherent randomness and the limits of predictability may be, they do not seem to pose practical difficulties for uncertainty in risk analysis and other quantitative policy analysis. The main objective in this context is to distinguish uncertainty that might be reducible by further research or more detailed modeling from uncertainty that is unlikely to be reducible, whether because of "inherent randomness" or because of practical unpredictability. For example, in predicting the environmental impact of an accidental radioactive release from a nuclear power plant, the wind speed and direction at the time will be crucial. The best we can do is model the variability based on wind-rose data, that is empirical frequency distributions of wind velocity. Even if we could know the exact date in the future of the release, the inherent unpredictability of the wind would prevent us from reducing the uncertainty from this source.

4.4.6. Disagreement

The activity of science, including gathering evidence and comparing of alternative theories, usually generates an eventual consensus among scientists about the values of scientific measurable quantities, at least in the long run. However, where data are hard to obtain, such as measurements of the health effects of environmental contaminants that are widely dispersed and at low concentrations, the long run may be very long indeed. Policy decisions may need to be made long before the disagreements are resolved. Thus, in practice, such disagreements between scientific experts are often an important source of uncertainty in risk and other policy analysis.

Although much disagreement arises simply from different technical interpretations of the same available scientific evidence, it is often substantially

---

1. See Gleick (1987) for an excellent exposition of these ideas for the general reader.

complicated by the fact that people view the problem from very different perspectives. Inhalation toxicologists, clinical practitioners, lung physiologists, and epidemiologists have very different perspectives on the impact of specific air pollutants on health. In addition, people frequently hold direct or indirect stakes in the outcome to the question and thus their judgments may be influenced by motivational bias, consciously or unconsciously.[2] In some cases these stakes may be quite clear, for example, the outcome may affect their employment or income. In others they may be rather more subtle, for example, the expert may have staked some of his or her reputation on a particular view.'

Although there are differences of opinion about some uncertain empirical quantity among informed experts, a common approach is to combine the opinions using weights. A variety of approaches is used to assign these weights. They may be derived from self-ratings by the experts, or from ratings by the experts of each other, or they may be derived from the uncertainty expressed in the distributions. They may be assigned directly by the analyst on the basis of his or her information about the relative knowledge, reliability, and calibration of the experts. A Bayesian decision maker or analyst may regard the opinion of each expert as data, supplemented by any evidence or judgments about the quality of judgment by the various experts. These data and evidence may be used by the analyst to update his or her own opinion and arrive at a single posterior probability distribution operating directly either on the weights, or on the results after applying them in a model. Thus, the final distribution essentially represents the best judgment of the analyst based on the experts.

A variety of sophisticated Bayesian assessment and combination techniques have been suggested for performing this (Genest and Zidek, 1986). In practice, these approaches tend to be rather difficult to apply, requiring complex judgments of the dependence among the experts. A simpler approach, compatible with some Bayesian formulations, is combining the expert distributions using a weighted average of the probability mass or density for each value.

If there appear to be differences of opinion between informed experts about a particular quantity, it is important to examine first whether these differences are significant relative to the uncertainty acknowledged by each expert. An important advantage of asking experts to express their best judgment about an uncertain quantity in the form of a subjective probability distribution is that it makes this question relatively easy to answer. Whether the differences matter will, in general, depend on the question being asked. If the disagreement between experts appears at all substantial, it is usually best first to carry out a sensitivity analysis to examine the effects of each opinion on the conclusions of the analysis. If the differences of opinion have little impact on the results, any reasonable combination scheme may be used: for example, equal weighting.

---

2. See Chapters 6 and 7 for a more detailed discussions of bias in expert judgment.

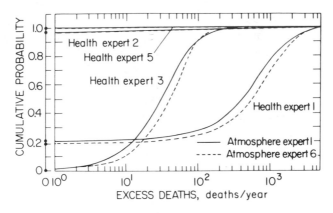

Figure 4.2. Assessment, in the form of cumulative distribution functions, of the average annual health impact in excess deaths from exposure to sulfate air pollution from a new 1 Gw$_e$ FGD-equipped, coal-fired power plant in Pittsburgh, Pa. Results are shown for the health effects models of four different health experts, and the atmospheric models of the two most different of seven different atmospheric science experts (Morgan et al., 1984). In this example, the use of one average model to represent the atmospheric science part of the problem would be justified because of the very limited sensitivity of the outcome to the range of opinions of atmospheric scientists. Averaging the views of the set of health effects experts before running the assessment model would clearly not be justified because this would lead to very different, and quite misleading, results.

If, on the other hand, they have significant impact, then it may be unwise to combine them at all. Instead, the results of the analysis may be reported for each expert or each significantly different class of opinion. If the results depend on which expert you believe, this is a crucial insight from the analysis and should be prominently communicated.

An illustration may help clarify this point. In analyzing of the possible health impacts from the long-range transport of sulfur air pollution from coal-fired power plants in the Ohio River basin, we built separate assessment models to represent the views of each of a number of atmospheric scientists and air pollution health effects experts (Morgan et al., 1984). Figure 4.2 compares the resulting probabilistic estimates of the annual number of excess deaths resulting from a 1000 Mw$_e$ FGD scrubbed plant in Pittsburgh, Pennsylvania. These estimates are based on probability distributions representing the expert judgment about the human health effects of atmospheric sulfates by four health experts, and expert judgments about sulfur oxidation rates according to the two most different of seven different atmospheric chemists. Although in this example, producing one average model to represent the atmospheric science part of the problem is justified because of the very limited sensitivity of the outcome to the range of opinions of atmospheric scientists, averaging across the views of the health effects experts before running the assessment model would clearly lead to very different, and quite misleading, results.

4.4.7. Approximations

Approximation uncertainty arises because the model is only a simplified version of the real-world system being modeled. The domain parameters specify the model's scope in terms of its spatial and temporal domains, and also control the model's level of resolution for the index variables, such as the time intervals and grid size used in modeling temporally or spatially varying values. Approximations are also introduced by the use of discrete probability distributions to represent continuous distributions, or the finite number of runs used in a Monte Carlo simulation. Each approximation represents a trade-off between the precision of the representation and the computational costs of the model.

It is often hard to know how much uncertainty is produced by a given approximation. In a few cases, simple theoretical arguments can be advanced in choosing the necessary resolution. For example, information theory tells us that the spatial and temporal resolution of a model must be at least twice the wavelength of the highest spatial frequency or temporal variation that is to be modeled. As we shall see later, statistical estimation of the uncertainty introduced by a given Monte Carlo sample size is fairly straightforward. However, in many contexts the only feasible approach in estimating the approximation uncertainty is to increase the resolution or scope, for example, reducing the grid size or time steps to examine the effects on the results. With many computer models this requires fundamental reprogramming, and so it is relatively rare that modelers carry out such examination in a systematic way. This is unfortunate because a comparison of uncertainty introduced by model implementation and simulation with other sources of uncertainty can help analysts select an appropriate level of model detail. "Appropriate" here means neither so complex that the computational burden is overwhelming, nor so simple that approximation uncertainty dominates all other sources.

4.5. Uncertainty about Model Form

Hitherto we have considered uncertainty about quantities or parameters of a model, but not about the form or structure of the model itself. Uncertainty about the form of a model is generally harder to think about than uncertainty about the value of a quantity. But experienced analysts often argue that uncertainty about structure is usually more important, and more likely to have a substantial effect on the results of the analysis. However, there has been relatively little research into situations in which there is uncertainty or disagreement about what form of model to use, for either facts or values; and much that remains to be done in developing methods of dealing with them. In fact, the distinction between uncertainty about model structure and uncertainty about quantity values is rather slippery. Suppose one has two or more possible model structures. One approach sometimes suggested is to assign probabilities to the different models and combine their results accordingly. This approach has a fundamental problem that is often not appreciated. Any model is unavoidably a simplification of reality. Any real-world system contains phenomena or behaviors that cannot be produced by even the most detailed model. Even if a model is a good approximation to a particular real-world system and usually gives accurate results, it can never be completely exact. Careful thought leads us to the following disturbing conclusion: *Every model is definitely false.* Although we may be able to say that one model is *better* than another, in the sense that it produces more accurate predictions, we cannot say it is more probable. Therefore, it is inappropriate to try to assign probabilities to models.

We may compare the predictions of different model structures, but it seems we cannot legitimately employ probabilities to express our belief in their validities. Fortunately, there is often a way out, by assimilating the models into a single *metamodel*, which contains the models as special cases, according to a value of one or more index parameters. For example, consider a dose-response function with uncertain form: it may have a threshold or not, and it may be linear or exponential. It is straightforward to define a dose-response function with a threshold parameter and dose exponent parameter, which will also reproduce non-threshold models (if the threshold parameter is zero) and linear models (if the exponent is one).

In this way, uncertainty about the model form can be converted into uncertainty about these parameter values. If the uncertainty about functional form concerns a matter of scientific fact, as in the case of the dose-response function, it may be viewed as uncertainty about an empirical quantity, and it may be appropriate to express it a subjective probability distribution. This approach often simplifies the analysis. It allows probability distributions to be assessed over the appropriate model structure, reinterpreted as a model parameter. It also makes it easier to compare the impact of uncertainty about the model form with other uncertainties.

However, uncertainty about model form frequently reflects disagreements between experts about the underlying scientific or technical mechanism. When it gives rise to significant differences, as it often does, it may be more appropriate to examine it parametrically rather than attempt to assess a probability distribution over the alternative forms or weighting the opinions of different experts, as we have already argued with respect to disagreements about empirical quantities.

It is also possible, indeed common, to be uncertain about the form of utility functions, particularly when they involve multiple attributes. This might include uncertainty about the class of risk attitude (e.g., risk aversion) and the form of the multi-attribute function, for example, whether attributes should be considered utility independent, and so whether an additive or multiplicative model is appropriate. There may also be questions about how to combine preference functions of different people, or uncertainty about whether nonutilitarian ethical formulations might be more appropriate, such as the Pareto criterion or various rights-based criteria.

In such cases, it may also be possible to convert the uncertainty about the form of preference functions into an uncertain parameter in a higher-order preference function that encompasses the alternative forms. For example, if one adopts the view that no person or organization has the right to impose an increased risk of death on another person, then in principle one could simply use an enormous number to weight external mortality risks within a multi-attribute utility function to model this value system. However, the questions of what kind of ethical approach to employ and how to discover and combine preferences of different stakeholders are extremely knotty. Beyond the discussion in Chapter 3 we will not address them further in this book.

As argued previously about value parameters, we believe it is generally not appropriate to model uncertainty about this probabilistically. If these issues are especially acute for a particular analysis – for example, if a project raises equity issues, or if there are major ethical controversies involved – the prudent analyst will leave their resolution to the users of the analysis. The study may list the various different kinds of impact on the different groups of people, without attempting to judge whether these impacts are commensurable and if so how. Those who wish to make use of the results can then combine them or not as they see fit.

4.6. Inputs, Outputs, and Model Solution Methods

Thus far we have purposely avoided referring to the various types of quantity we have discussed as "inputs" or "outputs," since their role in a model can vary. In a *predictive* policy model, it is usual for uncertain empirical quantities (X), decisions (D), value parameters (V), and domain parameters (M) to be specified as inputs, and some criterion quantity, such as net present value or utility (U) to be the main output of interest. As we noted in the preceding section, conclusions reached about U may also be affected by uncertainty about the form of the functional relationship f, where f incorporates both the factual and value structure of the model being employed. We can diagram the flow of information in a predictive model thus:

$$f(X, D, V, M) \rightarrow U$$

In what we call *classical decision analysis*, the goal is to discover the optimal decision ($D*$) from the empirical quantities (X), with our uncertainty over them expressed as probability distributions, and the value and domain parameters (V) and (M). The axioms of decision theory prescribe that optimal decisions (or Bayes' decisions) are ones that maximize expected utility (MEU). Including

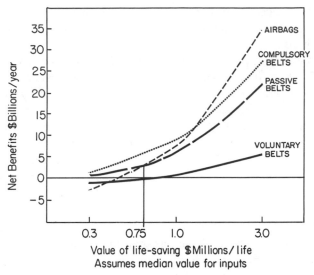

Figure 4.3. Illustration of a switchover analysis for net benefits from various strategies for motor vehicle occupant crash restraints performed as a function of the rate of investment in lifesaving. From Graham and Henrion (1984).

this criterion as a kind of input to the analysis, we may diagram the flow of information in classical decision analysis thus:

$$f(X, V, M, \text{MEU}) \rightarrow D*$$

From this view a decision is an output rather than an input of the modelling process. The methods of operations research provide a wide variety of other optimizing and satisficing solution methods, which likewise produce an optimal or satisficing decision $D*$ given the specified quantities, values, and model.

A third approach is what one might call *reverse analysis*, or *policy region analysis* (Watson and Buede, 1987). To avoid having to specify explicitly the value or range of one or two particularly uncertain empirical quantities (X') or value parameters (V'), we may examine what sets of values correspond to which decisions (D) being optimal. This only works when the decision variable(s) are discrete. One example is *switchover analysis*, where the model is examined, analytically or numerically, to discover the value(s) of a specified uncertain input at which the optimal decision changes. An illustration from our own work is shown in Figure 4.3. More generally the space defined by the uncertain quantities $(X'$ or $V')$ is mapped into policy regions over which the optimal decision is the same. This kind of analysis may be represented thus:

$$f(X, V, M, \text{MEU}) \rightarrow (D*, X')$$

$$f(X, V, M, \text{MEU}) \rightarrow (D*, V')$$

The result of the analysis is a simplified model $(D*, X')$ or $(D*, V')$ that specifies sets of decisions and values of uncertain quantities that are compatible with one another. Such results may be used in two ways: either to discover what decision is implied by what value of X' or V', or what value of X' or V' is implied by which decision. If there are a variety of alternative models f_i to be explored, a similar strategy may be employed across a range of functional forms specified by a *model form* parameter i.

From the "classical policy analysis" point of view such reverse analysis may be regarded as ethically suspect. It allows the "decision maker" to ask the question: What input and model assumptions do I need to justify the decision I want to make (for unstated and perhaps nefarious reasons)? However, if one takes the view that the primary purpose of the analysis is insight into the interrelationships of all the various components, and their mutual implications, then this reverse or policy region analysis may be entirely appropriate. In this latter view, all the quantities including empirical quantities and probabilities distributions over the latter, value parameters, model domain, parameters, decisions, and criteria may be uncertain or undetermined. The goal of analysis may be seen as identifying a set of mutually compatible and plausible beliefs, values, decisions, and models.

One might view the questions of what form of analysis to use, whether a model should be predictive, satisficing, or optimizing, and what kind of solution techniques to use, as additional sources of uncertainty. It would even be possible to construct a *model analysis parameter* that specifies the solution technique and analytic methods to be employed in "solving" the model. It is easiest to think of such parameters as indices that select the specific techniques that will be employed from across the set of techniques that might be employed. It is, of course, rare that any actual analysis explicitly contains such a parameter. Rather, the choice is made before the model is constructed. It is, however, important to recognize the existence of the choice, and in many cases to examine the sensitivity of this choice.

References

Beyth-Marom, R. (1982). "How Probable Is Probable? A Numerical Translation of Verbal Probability Expressions," *Journal of Forecasting*, 1:257–269.

Cyert, R. M., and DeGroot M. H. (1987). *Bayesian Analysis and Uncertainty in Economic Theory*, Rowman & Littlefield, Totowa, N.J.

de Finetti, N. (1974). *Theory of Probability*, 2 vols., Wiley, New York.

Fischer, G. (1980). "A Constructive Approach to Utility Assessment: Assessing Preferences That Are Ill-defined or Uncertain," paper presented to the TIMS/ORSA Joint National Meeting, May, Washington, D.C., Copy available from author at Carnegie Mellon University, Pittsburgh.

Genest, C., and Zidek, J. (1986). "Combining Probability Distributions: A Critique and Annotated Bibliography," *Statistical Science*, 1, no. 1:114–148.

Gleick, J. (1987). *Chaos: Making a New Science*, Viking (Penguin), New York.

Graham, J. D., and Henrion, M. (1984). "A Probabilistic Analysis of the Passive-restraint Question," *Risk Analysis*, 4:25–40.

Hacking, I. (1975). *The Emergence of Probability*, Cambridge University Press, Cambridge.

Henrion, M., and Fischhoff, B. (1986). "Assessing Uncertainty in Physical Constants," *American Journal of Physics*, 54, no. 9 (September): 791–798.

Howard, R. A. (1988). "Uncertainty About Probability: A Decision Analysis Perspective," *Risk Analysis*, 8, no. 1 (March): 91–98.

Howard, R. A., and Matheson, J.'E. (1984). *Readings in the Principles and Practice of Decision Analysis*, Strategic Decision Systems: Menlo Park, Calif.

Lindley, D. V. (1973). *Making Decisions*, Wiley, New York.

Luce, R. D., and Raiffa, H. (1957). *Games and Decisions*, Wiley, New York.

Morgan, M. G., Morris, S. C., Henrion, M., Amaral, D. A. L., and Rish, William R. (1984). "Technical Uncertainty in Quantitative Policy Analysis: A Sulfur Air Pollution Example," *Risk Analysis*, 4 (September): 201–216.

Oden, G. C. (1977). "Integration of Fuzzy Logical Information," *Journal of Experimental Psychology: Human Perception and Performance*, 4, no. 3:565–575.

Raiffa, H. (1968). *Decision Analysis: Introductory Lectures on Choice Under Uncertainty*, Addison-Wesley: Reading, Mass.

Savage, L. J. (1954). *The Foundations of Statistics*, Wiley, New York.

Wallsten, T. S., Budescu, D. V., Rapoport, A., Zwick, R., and Forsyth, B. (1986). "Measuring the Vague Meanings of Probability Terms," *Journal of Experimental Psychology: General*, 115:348–365.

Watson, S. R., and Buede, D. M. (1987). *Decision Synthesis: The Principles and Practice of Decision Analysis*, Cambridge University Press, New York.

Zadeh, L. A. (1984). "Making Computers Think Like People," *IEEE Spectrum* (August).

5   Probability Distributions and Statistical Estimation

> The theory of probability is at the bottom nothing
> but common sense reduced to calculus.
> Pierre de Laplace,
> *Théorie Analytique de Probabilités*,
> introduction, 1812–20

5.1. Introduction

Suppose you wish to represent uncertainty about an empirical quantity by a probability distribution. If you have some empirical data directly relevant to the quantity, you may want to use statistical methods to help select a distribution and estimate its parameters. If you feel you know little or nothing about the quantity before seeing the observations, you may want to use standard classical statistical methods. If you feel you do have some prior opinions about the quantity, based on whatever knowledge and reasoning, you may want to combine these prior opinions with the observed evidence and use Bayesian updating methods to obtain posterior distributions. If you have no directly relevant observations of the quantity, then you may wish to express your opinion directly by a subjective probability distribution. We discuss methods for doing this Chapters 6 and 7, but before getting to them it will be useful to review some of the basic properties of probability distributions.

The methods presented in this chapter cover a range of useful procedures in probability and statistics. The discussion is provided as a review and a compact reference and is not intended to replace a full course or text on the subject, many of which are available (e.g., Benjamin and Cornell, 1970; Ang and Tang, 1975; DeGroot, 1975). A good foundation in the basic ideas of probability and statistics is absolutely essential to the adequate treatment of uncertainty in most quantitative policy analyses including risk assessments. Those without such a grounding may find the discussion in this chapter to be a useful overview, but it would be dangerous to treat this as a sufficient foundation by itself.

The major focus of this chapter is the properties of probability distributions. We describe a range of standard distribution functions, and methods for estimating their parameters. We also outline procedures for generating sample values from different distributions for use in subsequent uncertainty analysis.

The principal author of this chapter is Mitchell Small.

5.2. Characterizing Probability Distributions

There is a variety of different ways of representing probability distributions, either in their entirety as cumulative distribution functions or probability density functions, or by selected parameters, such as their fractiles or moments. The following descriptions are phrased in terms of their application to subjective probability distributions, but they apply just as well to any other conception of probability distributions, including objective frequency distributions for a specific population.

5.2.1. Cumulative Distribution Functions

Suppose X is a *random variable*, that is, an empirical quantity about whose value we are uncertain. Uncertain belief about the relative likelihood of the variable having different possible values is represented by a *probability distribution*. Let x be a particular possible value that X might have. We use the convention that uppercase letters refer to variables and lowercase letters refer to specific values they may take. The probability distribution for X may be represented by its *cumulative distribution function* (CDF). This function gives the probability that X will be less than or equal each possible value x:

$$F(X) \equiv P[X \leq x]$$

It is called "cumulative" because it represents the cumulative probability that X will have any value less than or equal to x. An example is illustrated in Figure 5.1(a). As x increases from its smallest to its largest values, $F(x)$ increases monotonically, that is, has non-negative slope. Because it represents a probability, it must go from 0 to 1 as x goes from its least to greatest possible value.[1]

5.2.2. Fractiles

The *median* of a random variable is a value such that there is a 0.5 probability that the actual value of the variable is less than that value. If we denote the median of X as $X_{0.5}$, then by definition:

$$P[X \leq X_{0.5}] \equiv 0.5$$

The median is the 0.5 *fractile* (or *quantile*) of a distribution. More generally, the p fractile, X_p, of a distribution is a value such that there is a probability p that the actual value of the random variable will be less than that value:

$$P[X \leq X_p] \equiv p$$

---

1.   Not all distributions are across finite intervals. Some may extend to infinity in either or both directions.

If the probability is expressed in percent, then the fractile value is referred to as a *percentile*. Thus the median is the 50th percentile. The 0.25 and 0.75 fractiles are often termed *quartiles* of the distribution, and the range $[X_{0.25}, X_{0.75}]$ is known as the *interquartile range*. It is a useful measure of the dispersion of the distribution (the degree of uncertainty about the quantity). These are illustrated in Figure 5.1(a).

The probability distribution for X may also be represented by its *probability density function* (PDF), which is the derivative of the CDF:

$$f(X) = \frac{dF(x)}{dX}$$

The PDF represents the density of probability, so that $f(x)\Delta x$ is the probability that X is within the range $x - \Delta x/2$ to $x + \Delta x/2$, for some small increment Δx. Figure 5.1(b) illustrates the PDF corresponding to the CDF of Figure 5.1(a). The *mode* or modes are the values of X that have maximum probability density. The PDF has units of X^{-1}. Thus, if X is the weight of a particular elephant in kilograms, and the probability density function $f(x)$ represents the opinion of an expert judge of elephants, then its units are in probability per kilogram interval.

When X is a discrete random variable with possible values $(x_1, x_2, \dots x_n)$, the PDF is replaced by a *probability mass function* (PMF). This gives the probability that X has each possible value x_i:

$$p(x_i) = P[X = x_i]$$

The CDF is defined as before, but takes step jumps at the discrete values of X where $p(x_i) > 0$.

5.2.3. Moments

Probability distribution functions are often characterized by their *moments*. The best known is the first moment, the *mean* or *expected value* of the distribution. This is defined for a continuous and discrete variable, respectively as:

$$\mu = \int_X x\,f(x)\,dx$$

$$\mu = \sum_{i=1}^{n} x_i\,p(x_i)$$

The expected value is sometimes known as the *first central moment*. More generally, *central moments* are defined as the expectation of the nth power of the difference between X and its mean. Thus the nth central moment of X is

$$\mu_n = \int_X (x - \mu)^n\,f(x)\,dx$$

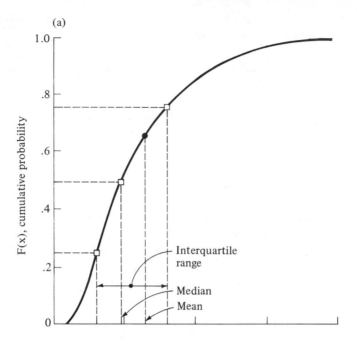

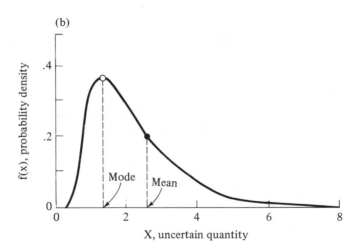

Figure 5.1. (a) A cumulative distribution function (CDF), with median and quartiles marked, above (b) the corresponding probability density function (PDF), with mode marked. Also shown is the mean. Although in this example the mean lies inside the interquartile range, for highly skewed distributions the mean may lie well outside this range.

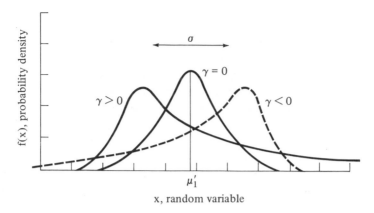

Figure 5.2. Probability density functions with negative, zero, and positive coefficients of skewness.

or, for discrete distributions,

$$\mu_n = \sum_X (x - \mu)^n p(x)$$

The second central moment, μ_2, is more commonly known as the *variance* and denoted as σ^2. Its square root, σ, is the *standard deviation*. The standard deviation and variance reflect the amount of spread or dispersion in the distribution.

It is sometimes useful to characterize the shape of a distribution with a dimensionless measure of spread known as the *coefficient of variation*. This is the ratio of the standard deviation to the mean:

$$\nu = \frac{\sigma}{\mu}$$

It is also often useful to characterize and classify distributions using dimensionless measures based on the third and fourth central moments. These are generally presented as the *coefficient of skewness*,

$$\gamma_1 = \frac{\mu_3}{\sigma_3}$$

and the *coefficient of kurtosis*:

$$\gamma_2 = \frac{\mu_4}{\sigma_4}$$

The skewness coefficient is zero for a symmetric distribution. Examples of distributions with positive and negative skew are illustrated in Figure 5.2. The mean and standard deviation are also indicated for these distributions. Positive skew is commonly observed with highly variable quantities that can take on only positive values. The kurtosis indicates the degree to which the distribution is flat (like a uniform distribution) as opposed to having a high central peak.

5.3. Estimation

Suppose we have a sample of observations of some random variable. How can we use these to infer the properties, such as the fractiles or moments, of the probability distribution from which they are drawn? This is the general problem of estimation, and the focus of the field of statistics. In the context of uncertainty analysis for a model, we may need to perform estimation in two kinds of situation: first, when we try to characterize the probability distribution of some input quantity to a model for which we have some empirical observations; second, when we try to characterize the probability distribution for an uncertain quantity that is output by the model. In Chapter 8, we describe Monte Carlo sampling and other replication techniques for propagating uncertainty through a model. In these techniques, the model is run multiple times, each run or "realization" producing a sample value for each output. Thus, we need to estimate the properties of the actual probability distribution induced over the outputs from the specific sample of actual output values.

Because we have only a finite number of values to work from, estimates will always be only approximate. There are a variety of different ways to obtain an estimate and a number of criteria for evaluating the quality of estimates. In particular, the frequentist or classical view of probability can lead to a different approach to estimation than the subjectivist or Bayesian one. We first outline some classical criteria and estimation methods because these are most widely taught and used. We conclude the section with a brief discussion of the Bayesian view of estimation.

5.3.1. Classical Estimation

An *estimator* is a function of the observed sample values that provides an estimate of a parameter of the parent population distribution, such as a fractile or moment. The classical viewpoint maintains that because each parameter has a single, true, if unknown, value, parameters should not be treated as random variables. Classical statistics is concerned with the *sampling distribution* for each estimator, that is, the distribution of possible estimated parameter values generated by applying the estimator to a sample. Given the sample estimate of the parameter, we can use the sampling distribution of the statistic to infer the likelihood that the sample was drawn from a particular population with a particular parameter value. Inferences on the distribution of the true (population) parameter, however, are generally beyond the scope of classical statistics.

In presenting classical methods for parameter estimation we often speak of particular characteristics of estimators that make them "good." These generally relate to the shape and spread of the sampling distribution around the true parameter values.

A good estimator should be

1. *Consistent*: It should converge to the population value as the number of observations increases.
2. *Unbiased*: The average value of the parameter estimator should equal the population value.
3. *Efficient*: The variance of the sampling distribution should be minimized to ensure closeness to the population value (assuming an unbiased estimator).
4. *Sufficient*: It should make maximum use of the information contained in the data.
5. *Robust*: It should be relatively insensitive to departure from the assumed, underlying distribution.
6. *Practical*: It should strike a balance between the need for the above characteristics and computational effort.

Item 6 is not normally included in lists of classical statistical criteria, but is always considered by the practicing analyst.

To derive estimators, a number of well-established procedures are available. The most widely used are the method of matching moments, the method of least squares, and the method of maximum likelihood. In the method of *matching moments*, the parameters of the probability distribution are selected to match the moments of the observed data. The number of moments used corresponds to the number of parameters to be estimated. This procedure is usually quite straightforward to implement, but it does not always satisfy the criteria just listed.

The method of *least squares* involves the selection of parameter estimates to minimize the sum of the squares of the difference between the observed data and the assumed estimates. This method is most commonly used in conditional models where the distribution of a random variable is predicted, given the value of other variables, as in regression analysis.

The method of *maximum likelihood* involves the selection of parameter values most likely to yield the observed data set. A likelihood function is defined, which for independent samples is simply the product of the PDF (or PMF) evaluated at each of the observation values. The values of the parameters that maximize this function (or, equivalently, the log of this function, which is easier to work with because the product function is transformed to a summation) are determined using standard techniques of calculus. That is, the first derivatives of the (log) likelihood function taken with respect to the parameters are set equal to zero. Maximum likelihood estimators do quite well in terms of the first five criteria for statistical estimation listed previously, and are generally the method of choice when available. However, they are difficult to identify and calculate for certain distributions.

5.3.2. Estimating Moments

In the following we use the standard notation of a "hat" to distinguish an estimate, say $\hat{\mu}$ from the parameter it is estimating, μ. The most straightforward approach to estimating moments of a distribution is simply to match the moments of the sample. Given m observations x_i of the random variable X, the estimator for the mean and variance are:

$$\bar{x} \equiv \hat{\mu}n = \frac{1}{m} \sum_{i=1}^{m} x_i$$

$$S_*^2 \equiv \hat{\sigma}^2 = \frac{1}{m} \sum_{i=1}^{m} (x_i - \bar{x})^2 \tag{1}$$

The above estimator for the variance generally leads to an efficient estimate of σ^2, but it is biased to the low side. This is because the value of $\bar{x}$ used in the equation is itself only an estimate. The bias is removed with the adjusted formula:

$$S^2 = \frac{1}{m-1} \sum_{i=1}^{m} (x_i - \bar{x})^2$$

For this reason the latter is generally preferred, although for large values of m, the difference in the estimates is negligible.

How uncertain are the values of the moments estimated from observed data sets? Assuming the observations are independent, the sampling variance of the mean is given by:

$$Var[\bar{x}] = \frac{\sigma^2}{m} \tag{2}$$

The sampling distribution for $\bar{x}$ depends on the underlying distribution of X. If X is normally distributed, $\bar{x}$ is described by a t *distribution*. The t distribution converges to a normal distribution as m becomes large. In fact, one of the most far-reaching results in all of statistics is that no matter what the underlying distribution of X, the sampling distribution of $\bar{x}$ converges to the normal distribution as m becomes large. This is a result of the *central limit theorem*. In most applications, a value of $m = 30$ is sufficient for the approximation to be accurate, unless the underlying distribution has a very unusual, asymmetric shape. If the underlying distribution is similar to a normal, a much smaller sample size is sufficient.

The central limit theorem allows a normal distribution with a mean $\bar{x}$ and a variance given by Equation 2 to be used to represent the uncertainty in the estimated mean of X. In this case we can estimate the standard deviation of the sample mean using the estimate of the standard deviation, S,

$$S_m = \frac{S}{\sqrt{m}} \tag{3}$$

We can use this to estimate an α *confidence interval* for the mean. Suppose Φ is a random variable with unit normal distribution. Let c be the corresponding deviation such that the range $(-c, c)$ encloses α probability, that is,

$$P(-c < \Phi < c) = \alpha$$

Then the α confidence interval for μ, the mean of x, is

$$\left(\bar{x} - c\frac{S}{\sqrt{m}}, \bar{x} + c\frac{S}{\sqrt{m}} \right) \tag{4}$$

Note that this should *not* be interpreted as saying that the true mean has a probability α of being within this range. That would mean treating the true mean as a random variable, which is incompatible with the classical view. Instead we note, before observing the sample, that the two quantities enclosing the interval are random variables (functions of the fixed but unknown mean and variance), and that they have an *alpha* probability of enclosing the mean. In the Bayesian approach, on the other hand, it *is* permissible to treat the mean (and other parameters) as uncertain random variables, as discussed in the following sections.

5.3.3. Estimating Fractiles

It is often useful in uncertainty analysis to be able to estimate fractiles from a sample of values. Suppose we wish to estimate the pth fractile X_p from a sample of m values x_i.

It is convenient to have the sample of m values of x in increasing order. Without loss of generality, we relabel them in this order so that we have:

$$x_1 \leq x_2 \leq \cdots x_m$$

(These may be termed the *order statistics* of the sample.)

A simple way to estimate the pth fractile X_p is as the corresponding sample value x_j, where $j = mp$. This assumes that mp is a whole number. If it is not, one can simply round to the nearest sample value.

This will give x_m as the estimate of the maximum value, that is, $X_{1.0}$. This will be biased too small for continuous variables, because the true maximum is almost certain to be larger than the observed maximum. A still simple, but slightly better, approach is to interpret the x_i observed value as the $i/(m + 1)$ fractile, that is,

$$\hat{X}_{i/(m+1)} = x_i \tag{5}$$

Other plotting position formulas are available for the observed CDF, but involve only minor adjustments to the suggested estimators.

It is also possible to calculate the probability that two statistics will enclose a specified fractile of a distribution. Hence, we can estimate a confidence interval for the fractile. By definition, the probability that a random sample value x is less than its pth fractile is p:

$$P[x \leq X_p] = p$$

Therefore, given a random sample of m values of x, the probability that exactly j of them are less than or equal to fractile X_p is:

$$\binom{m}{j} p^j (1 - p)^{m-j}$$

$$\text{where} \quad \binom{m}{j} = \frac{m!}{j!(m-j)!}$$

So, in general the number j_p of sample values less than X_p has a binomial distribution with parameters p and m.

If we choose two order statistics x_i, x_k, where $x_i \leq x_k$, then the probability that they will enclose fractile X_p is:

$$P[x_i \leq X_p \leq x_k] = \sum_{j=1}^{k} \binom{m}{j} p^j (1 - p)^{m-j}$$

We can evaluate this sum using standard statistical tables for the binomial distribution, and hence obtain confidence intervals for X_p. For example, if the number of samples $m = 15$, and we are interested in the 0.2 fractile, so $p = 0.2$. From tables of the binomial distribution we find that

$$P[x_1 \leq X_{0.2} \leq x_6] = 0.90$$

In other words, the interval between the smallest observation x_1 and sixth smallest observation x_6 forms a confidence interval for the 0.2 fractile with confidence 0.90.

If the number, j_p, of sample values less than X_p is reasonably large, we can approximate its binomial distribution with a normal distribution with mean mp and variance $\sigma^2 = mp(1 - p)$. This makes computing confidence intervals and other statistics somewhat easier. Suppose we are interested in a confidence interval with confidence α. Suppose Φ is a random variable with unit normal distribution. Again, let c be the corresponding deviation such that,

$$P[-c < \Phi < c] = \alpha$$

Then an interval with confidence of α containing j_p is approximately,

$$(mp - c\sigma, mp + c\sigma)$$

The number of ordered sample values in this interval is therefore

$$2c\sigma = 2c\sqrt{mp(1-p)} \tag{6}$$

Note that the value of p for which this number is largest is 0.5. In other words, for a given m, the fractile we are most uncertain about is the median, as measured by the number of sample values. This does not imply that the median is the most uncertain fractile in terms of the value of the variable; this uncertainty is often greatest at the tails of the distribution, depending on the distribution shape. The uncertainty in the value of the fractile is determined by the particular values of the sample over the interval (i, k) defined below.

Let us define the order numbers (ranks) defining the uncertain interval thus:

$$i = \left\lfloor mp - c\sqrt{mp(1-p)} \right\rfloor,$$

$$k = \left\lceil mp + c\sqrt{mp(1-p)} \right\rceil \tag{7}$$

Where the notation $\lfloor\ \rfloor$ and $\lceil\ \rceil$ indicates that we round these two quantities down and up respectively to the nearest whole numbers. The corresponding values from the ordered sample provide an approximate confidence interval for fractile X_p:

$$(x_i, x_k) \tag{8}$$

As an example, suppose we have a sample size $m = 100$, and wish to obtain a 95% confidence interval for the median, so $c \approx 2$, $p = 0.5$. From (7) we calculate:

$$i = \left\lfloor 100 \times 0.5 - 2\sqrt{100 \times 0.5 \times 0.5} \right\rfloor = 40$$

$$k = \left\lceil 100 \times 0.5 + 2\sqrt{100 \times 0.5 \times 0.5} \right\rceil = 60$$

So (x_{40}, x_{60}) gives an approximate 95% confidence interval for the median.

5.3.4. Bayesian Estimation

In classical estimation, a parameter of a probability distribution, even if unknown, is considered to be fixed with a single true value, and it is considered inappropriate to treat it as a random variable. Hence, for example, an α

confidence interval for parameter r should not be interpreted as specifying a range in which r lies with probability α, no matter how tempting this may seem. In Bayesian estimation, on the other hand, we may indeed treat a parameter as a random variable. The probability distribution over a parameter (or set of parameters) expresses our knowledge and uncertainty about the true value of the parameter. We can use the probability distribution to obtain an α *credible interval* for the parameter, being an interval that has probability α of containing the true value of the parameter.

In the Bayesian approach, we start with an initial *prior* distribution for the parameter, r. This is based on whatever relevant information, e, is known to the analyst or expert before observing the data. We denote this prior distribution as $f(r \mid e)$. We denote the sample observations as $\underline{x} = (x_1, x_2, \ldots x_m)$. After observing this sample data, we update the prior to obtain the *posterior* distribution $f(r \mid \underline{x}, e)$. If we can express our knowledge of the dependence of the observations $\underline{x}$ on the parameter r in terms of a *likelihood function*, $f(\underline{x} \mid r, e)$, then we can employ Bayes' rule to calculate the posterior:

$$f(r \mid \underline{x}, e) \equiv \frac{f(r, \underline{x} \mid e)}{f(\underline{x} \mid e)} = \frac{f(\underline{x} \mid r, e) \times f(r \mid e)}{\int f(\underline{x} \mid r, e) \times f(r \mid e) \, dr} \tag{9}$$

Note that the expected value of r may change. Typically, but not always, the spread or variance of the distribution tends to reduce with increasing information. An example is illustrated in Figure 5.3, showing series of Bayesian updates as more and more data become available.

The likelihood function here is the same as the likelihood function used in maximum likelihood estimation. For continuous distributions, computation of the posterior from the prior and likelihood is often difficult. In a few cases, however, the form of the prior on the uncertain quantity and the prior on the parameter(s) is such that the posterior on the uncertainty quantity ends up from the same family as the prior. In this case, observing new data changes only the parameters of the prior, but not the form of the distribution. This makes analysis relatively straightforward. When this happens, the families of the prior on the quantity and the family of the prior parameter are known as *conjugate pairs*. One example is when the prior on the quantity is a Bernoulli distribution, and the prior on its parameter p is a beta distribution. Another example is when the quantity is normal, and the prior on the mean is also normal, and the prior on its variance is a gamma distribution. More detailed discussion of the topic of conjugate priors is beyond the scope of this book, and interested readers are referred to DeGroot (1970).

The most common objection to the Bayesian approach is the need to assess prior distributions for the quantity and its parameters, no matter how little is known about them. The classical approach has no need to assess priors, or any

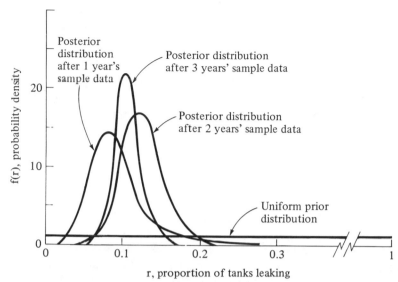

Figure 5.3. Example of a prior and posterior distribution in Bayesian estimation of a parameter. In this case the fraction of underground tanks that are leaking in a large population of underground tanks is being estimated on the basis of annual sample data. Starting with no knowledge of the fraction (uniform prior), each year more data are collected and Bayes' rule is applied to update the estimate. Over time, with increasing information, the spread or variance of the distribution is reduced. It is assumed here that there is no systematic increase (or decrease) in the proportion of tanks leaking over the three-year period, so the true proportion is the same throughout, but is unknown.

judgmental distributions. While the classical, or frequentist, and Bayesian, or personalist, approaches to estimation are quite different in their fundamentals, they turn out to be sometimes (but by no means always) rather similar in practice. For example, in estimating the mean of a distribution, it turns out that if the prior distributions for the mean and variance are fairly smooth and do not assign high probability to any particular small set of values, and if m is large, then the confidence coefficient assigned to any interval will be approximately equal to the posterior probability assigned to that interval by the Bayesian analysis (DeGroot, 1970). If very little is known, it is possible to use *diffuse* priors, which are very flat and wide, in the limits, being uniform over the real line, for example. The practical issues in assessing informative priors are addressed in the chapters that follow.

5.4. Common and Useful Probability Distribution Functions

Probability distribution functions often arise from the fundamental properties of the quantities we are attempting to represent. Quantities formed from adding many uncertain quantities tend to be normally distributed, and quantities formed from multiplying uncertain quantities tend to be lognormal. Events that occur randomly in time lead to exponential and Poisson distributions. Often, however, distributions are selected on an empirical basis – they provide a reasonable representation of the observed data.

This section provides an outline of the properties and use of a number of the most common and useful distribution functions. Formulas are given for the PDF (or PMF for discrete random variables), and the CDF where simple, closed-form solutions are available. Equations are given for computing the moments of the distribution in terms of its parameters. Methods for estimating distribution parameters from observed data are given and the uncertainty in these estimates is discussed. Methods for generating random samples from the distributions for use in Monte Carlo analysis are also presented. In each case, it is assumed that a pseudo-random number generator is available to generate independent, uniformly distributed variates on the range zero to one, denoted by the symbol U. Graphs of the probability density or mass function for the distributions considered are presented in Figure 5.4a–i. In each case, the expected value is 10, except for the beta distribution, which is shown over the range zero to one. Representative values of the coefficient of variation are presented.

The results in the following sections represent concise summaries of distribution functions. More detailed information is available in Johnson and Kotz (1969, 1970a,b) and Hastings and Peacock (1974). More detailed presentations of methods for generating random variables are given in Bratley, Fox, and Schrage (1983).

5.4.1. Normal Distribution

The normal, or Gaussian, distribution arises in many applications, in part because of the central limit theorem, which results in a normal distribution for additive quantities, and in part because of its well studied and frequent use in classical statistics. The normal distribution is commonly employed to represent uncertainty resulting from unbiased measurement errors, for example, in the measured weights of elephants.

The major features of the normal distribution are summarized in Table 5.1. The normally distributed random variable takes on values over the entire range of real numbers. Evaluation of the CDF requires numerical approximation of the integral of the PDF, but solutions are commonly found in statistical tables and available computer subroutines. The parameters of the distribution are directly related to the first and second moments, and the skewness coefficient is zero due to the symmetry of the distribution.

The parameters of the distribution are estimated from the sample mean and standard deviation. These estimates satisfy the method of moments criteria and are maximum likelihood. As with the variance, however, the estimate of $\hat{\sigma} = S_*$ is biased, and the adjusted version given by $\hat{\sigma} = S$ is generally preferable.

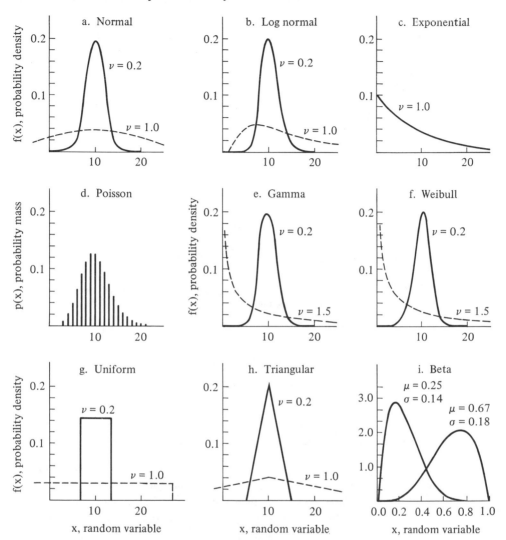

Figure 5.4. Plots of common probability distributions discussed in the text: a. Normal, b. Lognormal, c. Exponential, d. Poisson, e. Gamma, f. Weibull, g. Uniform, h. Triangular, i. Beta.

As indicated in Section D of Table 5.1, various methods for generating random normal variates are available. The traditional summation method is based on the central limit theorem and the moment properties of the zero–one random variate. The Box–Muller method is based on a two-dimensional polar transformation, and generally requires less computer time than the traditional method.

Many of the distributions described in the following sections converge to a normal distribution as their coefficients of variation become small. For many

Table 5.1. *Normal distribution*

A. *Functional representation*

PDF: $f(x) = \dfrac{1}{(2\pi)^{1/2}\sigma} \exp\left(-\dfrac{(x-\mu)^2}{2\sigma^2}\right);\qquad \infty \geq x \geq -\infty$

CDF: There is no closed-form representation. Tables and numerical methods exist.

B. *Moments*

Mean and standard deviation given by parameters of the distribution, μ and σ, respectively.

$\gamma_1 = 0,\quad \gamma_2 = 3$

C. *Parameter estimation*

Method of moments, maximum likelihood

$\hat{\mu} = \overline{X},\quad \hat{\sigma} = S \quad (\hat{\sigma} = S_* \text{ for maximum likelihood})$

D. *Generation of random samples*

$X_i = X_s \sigma + \mu$

where X_s is normally distributed with mean zero, variance one, and can be generated by:

Summation method:

$$X_s = \left(\sum_{i=1}^{12} U_i\right) - 6$$

or in pairs by the Box–Muller method:

$$X_{S,i} = \left(-2\ln U_i\right)^{1/2} \cos\left(2\pi U_{i+1}\right)$$
$$X_{S,i+1} = \left(-2\ln U_i\right)^{1/2} \sin\left(2\pi U_{i+1}\right)$$

---

quantities (lengths, weights, concentrations, etc.), the normal distribution is theoretically inappropriate because negative values are allowed. So long as the coefficient of variation is less than about 0.2, this problem can be safely ignored in most applications, as the probability of obtaining observations more than five standard deviations away from the mean is quite small. Indeed, with the summation method for random number generation it is impossible to obtain observations more than six standard deviations removed from the mean.

5.4.2. Lognormal Distribution

The lognormal distribution results when the logarithm of the random variable is described by a normal distribution. That is, if X is lognormally distributed, then $Y = \ln X$ is normally distributed. The properties of the lognormal distribution follow directly, and probability computations are made on the normal variable Y, with subsequent transformation to the corresponding value of $X = \exp Y$. The

Table 5.2. *Lognormal distribution*

A. *Functional representation*

PDF: $f(x) = \dfrac{1}{\phi x (2\pi)^{1/2}} \exp\left(-\dfrac{[\ln x - \xi]^2}{2\phi^2}\right)$; $0 \le x \le \infty$

where ξ and ϕ are the parameters of the distribution

CDF: Computed from normal distribution of $\ln x$.

B. *Moments*

Define $\omega = \exp(\phi^2)$

$\mu = \exp(\xi + \phi^2/2)$ $\qquad \sigma^2 = \omega(\omega - 1)\exp(2\xi)$

$\gamma_1 = (\omega - 1)^{1/2}(\omega + 2)$ $\qquad \gamma_2 = \omega^4 + 2\omega^3 + 2\omega^2 - 3$

C. *Parameter estimation*

    i. Maximum likelihood

$$\hat{\xi} = \overline{\ln X} = \frac{1}{n}\sum_{i=1}^{n}\ln x_i$$

$$\hat{\phi} = S_{*\ln X} = \left(\frac{1}{n}\sum_{i=1}^{n}(\ln x_i - \hat{\xi})^2\right)^{1/2}$$

D. *Generation of random samples*

    i. Generate $Y = \ln X$ as a normal variate with mean ξ and standard deviation ϕ as specified in Table 5.1.

    ii. Compute $X_i = \exp\left(Y_i\right)$

---

lognormal distribution applies as the limiting case for multiplicative quantities due to the approach to normality of the sum of the logs.

The lognormal distribution is often found to provide a good representation for physical quantities that are constrained to being non-negative, and are positively skewed, such as pollutant concentrations, stream flows, or accident event magnitudes (e.g., spill quantity or explosion intensity). The lognormal distribution is particularly appropriate for representing large uncertainties that are expressed on a multiplicative or order-of-magnitude basis. For example, when one hears that the quantity X is known to within a factor of 2, or to within an order-of-magnitude (factor of 10), a lognormal distribution is probably appropriate for its representation.

The properties of the lognormal distribution are presented in Table 5.2. The parameters of the distribution are equivalent to the mean and standard deviation of $Y = \ln X$, and this provides the maximum likelihood procedure for estimating the parameters of the distribution. The parameters of the distribution may also be estimated by the method of moments, using inverted forms of the moments

Table 5.3. *Exponential distribution*

A. *Functional representation*

  PDF: $f(x) = \lambda \exp(-\lambda x); \qquad 0 \le x \le \infty$
            where λ is the parameter of the distribution

  CDF: $F(x) = 1 - \exp(-\lambda x)$

B. *Moments*

$$\mu = 1/\lambda \qquad \sigma^2 = 1/\lambda^2$$
$$\gamma_1 = 2 \qquad \gamma_2 = 9$$

C. *Parameter estimation*
  i. Method of moments, maximum likelihood
$$\hat{\lambda} = 1/\overline{X}$$

D. *Generation of random samples*
$$X_i = -\frac{1}{\lambda} \ln U_i$$

---

expressions in Table 5.2, but the maximum likelihood estimates are generally superior.

A three-parameter, or shifted lognormal, distribution can be formulated with the third parameter representing the minimum possible observation. This parameter, referred to as the "location parameter," is equal to zero for the two-parameter case. The use of a nonzero location parameter shifts the expected value of the distribution by the corresponding amount, with no change in the variance or coefficients of skewness and kurtosis. Effective methods for estimating the parameters of a three-parameter lognormal distribution are presented by Stedinger (1980).

5.4.3. *Exponential Distribution*

When events (e.g., accidents) are purely random, the times between successive events are described by an exponential distribution. The parameter of the distribution, λ, is equal to one divided by the average time between events, and is thus equivalent to the occurrence rate of the process. We then say that events occur as a purely random (Poisson) process, at the rate of λ events per unit time. The properties of the exponential distribution are summarized in Table 5.3.

Other quantities may be described by an exponential distribution, such as storm event durations, spill sizes, and the like. However, because the distribution has only one parameter to determine scale, and a fixed shape, more flexibility is obtained using distributions that are more general in form. As indicated in Sections 5.4.5 and 5.4.6, the gamma and Weibull distributions provide this flexibility.

As shown in Figure 5.4c, the mode of the exponential distribution is at zero, and the probability of occurrence continuously decreases with increased values. The coefficient of variation is equal to one, and the skewness and kurtosis are also fixed, consistent with the fixed shape of the distribution.

The method of moments and maximum likelihood estimators for λ are equivalent. The sampling distribution of $\hat{\lambda}$ may be determined by noting that the sampling distribution of $\bar{x} = 1/\hat{\lambda}$ has a chi-squared distribution, which is a particular case of the gamma distribution.

The procedure for generating random exponential variates is an inverse transformation method. This method is based on the result that for $U \sim U(0, 1)$,

$$Y = F^{-1}(U)$$

is distributed as $F(y)$. Here $F^{-1}(.)$ denotes the inverse function of the CDF. The equation is solved by setting U equal to $F(y)$, and solving for y in terms of U. The method is theoretically applicable to any probability distribution function, but the inverse function can be solved in closed form for only a few distributions. The exponential is one such distribution.

5.4.4. Poisson Distribution

When event occurrences are described by the Poisson process discussed in the previous section, the number of events that occur in a time period of fixed length T follows a Poisson distribution. The parameter of the distribution α is equal to the average number of events expected over the interval, which is λT. Inferences about the sampling distribution or Bayes' distribution of α thus may be made directly from the corresponding distribution of λ in the exponential distribution. The number of events is, of course, discrete, and constrained to non-negative integers. The Poisson distribution may be used to represent other discrete quantities, but it is limited in flexibility as it contains only a single parameter. The Poisson distribution is summarized in Table 5.4.

Direct computation with the Poisson distribution is difficult when the parameter α is large. In this case, the discrete Poisson distribution may be approximated by a continuous normal distribution with the same mean and variance. That is, for large α, X is approximately normal with $\mu_x = \alpha$ and $\sigma_x = \alpha^{1/2}$. This does not imply that the probability mass at a particular value of X is equal to the probability density computed with the normal approximation (indeed, the probability mass is dimensionless, whereas the probability density has units of X^{-1}. Rather, the probability mass over intervals of X are nearly equivalent, so direct comparisons are possible using the normal CDF to approximate the Poisson CDF (for large α).

Table 5.4. *Poisson distribution*

A. *Functional representation*

PMF: $p(x) = \dfrac{\alpha^x \exp(-\alpha)}{x!};$ $x = 0, 1, 2, 3 \ldots$

where α is the parameter of the distribution

CDF: $F(x) = \displaystyle\sum_{k=0}^{x} \dfrac{\alpha^k \exp(-\alpha)}{k!}$

B. *Moments*

$\mu = \alpha$ $\sigma^2 = \alpha$

$\gamma_1 = 1/\alpha^{1/2}$ $\gamma_2 = 3 + 1/\alpha$

C. *Parameter estimation*

Method of moments, maximum likelihood

$\hat{\alpha} = \overline{X}$

D. *Generation of random samples*

Multiply successive U_i until the product is less than or equal to $\exp(-\alpha)$. If $i = N$ when this occurs, that is:

$$\prod_{i=1}^{N} U_i \leq \exp(-\alpha) < \prod_{i=1}^{N-1} U_i$$

then, $X_j = N - 1$

The method for generating Poisson variates given in Table 5.4 derives from the relationship between the exponential and Poisson distributions described in Section 5.4.4. A normal random variate may be generated to approximate the distribution when α is large.

5.4.5. Gamma Distribution

Given a random Poisson process, the gamma distribution describes the time required for the occurrence of k events. As indicated in Table 5.5, k is the shape parameter of the distribution, while λ is the scale parameter, again corresponding to the rate of the Poisson process. For $k = 1$, the distribution is equivalent to the exponential distribution with parameter λ.

The gamma distribution is widely applicable to many physical quantities. It is similar to the lognormal, although it is less positively skewed and less "tail-heavy." As such, it generally prescribes a lower probability to extreme values (on the tail of the distribution) than does the lognormal. The gamma distribution has been used to represent precipitation quantities, pollutant concentrations, and the time between event occurrences when the event process is not purely random (e.g., there is event clustering). Evaluation of the PDF requires a value for the

Table 5.5. *Gamma distribution*

A. *Functional representation*

PDF: $f(x) = \dfrac{\lambda^k x^{k-1} \exp(-\lambda x)}{\Gamma(k)};$ $0 \le x \le \infty$

where λ and k are the parameters (scale and shape, respectively) of the distribution

CDF: There is no closed-form representation. Tables and numerical methods exist

B. *Moments*

$$\mu = k/\lambda \qquad \sigma^2 = k/\lambda^2$$
$$\gamma_1 = 2/k^{1/2} \qquad \gamma_2 = 3 + \tfrac{6}{k}$$

C. *Parameter estimation*

   i. Method of moments

   $$\hat{k} = \overline{X}^2/S^2$$
   $$\hat{\lambda} = \overline{X}/S^2$$

D. *Generation of random samples*

   i. For integer values of k:

   $$X_i = -\frac{1}{\lambda} \sum_{i=1}^{k} \ln U_i$$

   ii. For noninteger $k < 1$:

   1. Generate U_{i1}, U_{i2}, U_{i3}
   2. Check if $U_{i1}^{1/k} + U_{i2}^{1/(1-k)} \le 1$
      If yes, continue; otherwise return to step 1
   3. $X_i = \dfrac{1}{\lambda}(-\ln U_{i3}) \dfrac{U_{i1}^{1/k}}{U_{i1}^{1/k} + U_{i2}^{1/(1-k)}}$

   iii. For noninteger $k > 1$:
   Use result that if X_1 is gamma distributed with λ and k_1, and X_2 is gamma distributed with λ and k_2, then $X = X_1 + X_2$ is gamma distributed with λ and $k = k_1 + k_2$. That is, add appropriate X_1 and X_2 generated from i. and ii. above.

---

gamma function $\Gamma(k)$, which for integer values of k equals $(k-1)!$. For noninteger k, tables or numerical routines for the gamma function are required. Evaluation of the CDF requires additional numerical analyses or tables.

The moments of the gamma distribution are easily calculated, and as indicated in Table 5.5, this provides a straightforward method for estimating the parameters. These estimates are not maximum likelihood, and superior estimates (i.e., more efficient) can be obtained with numerical approximations to the maximum likelihood estimates (e.g., Johnson and Kotz, 1970a). However, the added complexity of these methods is such that they may be

Table 5.6. *Weibull distribution*

A. *Functional representation*

PDF: $f(x) = \dfrac{k}{c}(x/c)^{k-1} \exp[-(x/c)^k];$ $0 \le x \le \infty$

where c and k are the parameters (scale and shape, respectively) of the distribution

CDF: $F(x) = 1 - \exp[-(x/c)^k]$

B. *Moments*

$$\mu = c\Gamma(1 + \frac{1}{k}) \qquad \sigma^2 = c^2 \left(\Gamma(1 + \frac{2}{k}) + \Gamma^2(1 + \frac{1}{k}) \right)$$

C. *Parameter estimation*

Rearrange expression for CDF to obtain:

$Z = mY + b$

where $Z = \ln\{-\ln[1 - F(x)]\}$ and $Y = \ln x$

Then $\hat{k} = m$ and $\hat{c} = \exp(-b/m)$

That is, using the observed values of x and $F(x)$, compute Z and Y for each observation, and plot or regress Z vs. Y. The resulting regression parameters, m (the slope) and b (the intercept), are used to estimate k and c.

D. *Generation of random samples*

$$X_i = c(-\ln U_i)^{1/k}$$

appropriate only when very accurate estimates of the gamma parameters are needed.

The generation of random gamma variates is complicated, particularly for noninteger k. When k is equal to an integer, values are generated using the property that a gamma variate is equal to the sum of k exponential variates with the same parameter λ. For noninteger k, the methods outlined in Table 5.5 (Ang and Tang, 1984) can be used, requiring the use of at least three values of U for each value of X, and the incorporation of the indicated acceptance–rejection tests.

5.4.6. Weibull Distribution

The Weibull, another distribution applicable to non-negative physical quantities, is often used to represent distributions of failure time in reliability models, as well as other physical quantities such as wind speed. It is similar in shape to the gamma distribution, and like the gamma, collapses to an exponential distribution when the shape parameter (k) equals one. However, it tends to be less skewed and tail-heavy than the gamma distribution, and even exhibits a small negative skew when the shape parameter becomes large (greater than 3.6). It has the advantage that both the PDF and CDF are expressed in a functional form that is easy to calculate, although the expressions for the moments are complicated.

Table 5.7. *Uniform distribution*

A. *Functional representation*

PDF: $f(x) = \dfrac{1}{b-a};\qquad a \leq x \leq b$

where a and b are the parameters of the distribution

CDF: $F(x) = \dfrac{x-a}{b-a}$

B. *Moments*

$$\mu = \frac{a+b}{2} \qquad \sigma^2 = \frac{(b-a)^2}{12}$$

$$\gamma_1 = 0 \qquad \gamma_2 = 1.8$$

C. *Parameter estimation*

  i. Method of moments:

$$\hat{a} = \overline{X} - 3S$$
$$\hat{b} = \overline{X} + 3S$$

D. *Generation of random samples*

$$X_i = a + (b-a)U_i$$

Estimation of the parameters of the Weibull distribution can be based on the method of moments or a maximum likelihood procedure, although both require numerical iteration. An alternative procedure is presented in Table 5.6, whereby the expression for the CDF is transformed and linearized. The observed data and CDF are similarly transformed, and graphical or regression techniques are applied to estimate k and c. The inverse method is used for random number generation.

5.4.7. Uniform Distribution

The uniform distribution provides one of the simplest means of representing our uncertainty in a model input. Its use is appropriate when we are able and willing to identify a range of possible values, but unable to decide which values within this range are more likely to occur than others. Examples of physical situations where the uniform distribution may be appropriate include the location of a leak or failure along a section of pipe given that a leak has occurred, or the direction from which high winds or elephants may approach a building.

The characteristics of the uniform distribution are summarized in Table 5.7. Parameters may be estimated from observed data using the method of moments, but are often determined using physical or subjective reasoning to determine minimum and maximum possible values for the random variable. Random variate generation is quite straightforward.

Table 5.8. *Triangular distribution*

A. *Functional representation*

PDF: $f(x) = \dfrac{b - |x - a|}{b^2}$; $a - b \le x \le a + b$

where a and b are the parameters of the distribution

CDF: $F(x) = \dfrac{1}{2} + \dfrac{1}{b^2}\left(\dfrac{1}{2}(x^2 - a^2) + (b - a)(x - a)\right)$; $a - b \le x \le a$

$\quad\quad\quad = 1 + \dfrac{1}{b^2}\left(-\dfrac{1}{2}(x^2 + [a + b]^2) + (a + b)x\right)$; $a \le x \le a + b$

B. *Moments*

$\mu = a$ $\qquad\qquad \sigma^2 = \dfrac{b^2}{6}$

$\gamma_1 = 0$ $\qquad\qquad \gamma_2 = 2.4$

C. *Parameter estimation*

i. Method of moments

$\hat{a} = \overline{X}$

$\hat{b} = \sqrt{6}S$

D. *Generation of random samples*

$X_i = a - b + b\left(2U_i\right)^{1/2}$; $0 \le U_i \le 0.5$

$\quad = a + b\left(2 - 2U_i\right)^{1/2}$; $0.5 \le U_i \le 1.0$

5.4.8. Triangular Distribution

For certain model input parameters, values toward the middle of the range of possible values are considered more likely to occur than values near either extreme. When this is the case, the triangular distribution provides a convenient means of representing uncertainty. Table 5.8 summarizes the properties of a symmetric triangular distribution.

When uncertainties are large and asymmetric, both the uniform and triangular distributions can be modified to yield loguniform or logtriangular distributions, in which $Y = \ln X$ is assumed to have the indicated distribution. Computations and parameter estimation are based on Y, with subsequent transformation to the desired random variable by $X = \exp(Y)$.

In addition to being simple, the apparently arbitrary shape and "sharp corners" of the uniform and triangular distributions can, in some contexts, be a convenient way to telegraph the message that the details of the shape of the distributions of variables in a model are not precisely known. This may help to prevent overinterpretation of results or a false sense of confidence in subtle details of model results.

Table 5.9. *Beta distribution*

A. *Functional representation*

PDF: $f(x) = \dfrac{1}{B(c,d)} x^{c-1}(1-x)^{d-1};\qquad 0 \le x \le 1$

where $B(c,d) = \dfrac{\Gamma(c)\Gamma(d)}{\Gamma(c+d)}$

and c and d are the parameters of the distribution

CDF: There is no closed-form representation. Tables and numerical methods exist.

B. *Moments*

$$\mu = c/(c+d) \qquad\qquad \sigma^2 = \frac{cd}{(c+d)^2(c+d+1)}$$

$$\gamma_1 = \frac{2(d-c)(c+d+1)^{1/2}}{(c+d+2)(cd)^{1/2}} \qquad \gamma_2 = \frac{3(c+d+1)[2(c+d)^2+cd(c+d-6)]}{cd(c+d+2)(c+d+3)}$$

C. *Parameter estimation*

  i. Methods of moments

$$\hat{c} = \left(\overline{X}^2 - \overline{X}^3 - S^2\overline{X}\right)/S^2$$

$$\hat{d} = \left[\overline{X}\left(1-\overline{X}\right)^2 - S^2\left(1-\overline{X}\right)\right]/S^2$$

D. *Generation of random samples*

  1. Generate U_{i1} and U_{i2}

  2. Check if $U_{i1}^{1/c} + U_{i2}^{1/d} \le 1$

  If yes, continue; otherwise return to step 1.

  3. $X_i = \dfrac{U_{i1}^{1/c}}{U_{i1}^{1/c} + U_{i2}^{1/d}}$

5.4.9. Beta Distribution

As indicated in Figure 5.4i, the beta distribution provides a very flexible means of representing variability over a fixed range. With the two-parameter form given in Figure 5.4(i) and Table 5.9, the range is from zero to one. The distribution can be readily transformed to a four-parameter form in which the additional parameters represent the range endpoints. The flexibility of the distribution encourages its empirical use in a wide range of applications.

A particularly important use for the beta distribution arises in its application as a conjugate distribution for the parameter of a Bernoulli distribution. In this application, the beta distribution is used to represent the uncertainty in the probability of occurrence of an event, and can be linked to observed records of event occurrence in previous trials or experiments.

The moments of the beta distribution are relatively easy to calculate, and the method of moments is commonly used to estimate parameters. Random variate generation involves an acceptance–rejection calculation, similar to that used for the gamma distribution.

5.4.10. Probability of an Event: The Bernoulli Distribution

One of the most fundamental issues in risk assessment is the determination of the probability of an event. Often the event of concern is an accident, either natural or technologically induced. It could involve the determination of whether an exposure is likely to cause harm, as in the assessment of a carcinogen. Probability assessments may be required for low probability, high consequence events. By the very nature of these events, historical data on which to base such assessments are sparse.

The starting point for the representation of event probabilities is the discrete, zero–one random variable. Such a random variable, X, is said to follow a *Bernoulli distribution* with probability mass function:

$$p(x) = \begin{cases} 1 - p, & \text{if } X = 0; \\ p, & \text{if } X = 1; \\ 0, & \text{otherwise.} \end{cases}$$

where p is the parameter of the distribution. The outcome $x = 1$ denotes the occurrence of the event; that is, the accident, positive test result, exceedance of a given level in another random variable, and so on. The outcome $x = 0$ denotes the non–occurrence of the event.

The Bernoulli random variable is fully characterized by its parameter, p, has an expected value of p and a variance of $p(1 - p)$. It is easy to simulate with a random number generator:

$$x_i = \begin{cases} 0, & \text{if } U_i > p; \\ 1, & \text{if } U_i < p. \end{cases}$$

5.4.11. Binomial Distribution

The sampling distribution of a Bernoulli random variable is derived by considering independent, multiple samples or trials. In practice, these observations are obtained by gathering historical occurrence records for the event of concern. If n independent trials or occurrence periods are considered, the probability of obtaining x events is given by the binomial distribution:

$$p(x) = \binom{n}{x} p^x (1 - p)^{n-x} \quad \text{where } x = 0, 1, 2, 3, \ldots$$

The mean and variance of the binomial distribution are:

$$\mu = np, \qquad \sigma^2 = np(1 - p)$$

The CDF of a binomial random variable, that is, the probability of obtaining less than or equal to X events in n independent trials, is given by

$$F(X) = \sum_{x=0}^{X} p(x)$$

The binomial distribution can be approximated by a normal distribution with $\mu = np$ and $\sigma^2 = np(1 - p)$ when the mean np is large.

The binomial distribution is useful for determining the probability of a given number of event occurrences when the parameter p is known. As the sampling distribution for p, it is used to determine classical confidence intervals for p from experimental trials, as we saw in the earlier discussion of estimating fractiles. However, it is not appropriate for use in determining the distribution of an unknown event probability. For this purpose, a Bayesian perspective is required, and the beta distribution is often used.

5.5. Multivariate Distributions

So far we have discussed only univariate distributions, that is, probability distributions over single-dimensional quantities, discrete or continuous. If two or more quantities are probabilistically dependent, then it may be desirable to model their uncertainty with a multivariate distribution. For example, a set of correlated quantities may be modeled by a *multivariate normal distribution*. This implies that the marginal distribution for each quantity X_i alone will be a simple univariate normal, with mean μ_i. The dependencies are specified by a matrix of covariances, σ_{ij}^2 between each pair of variables, X_i and X_j. The multivariate normal is the most widely used distribution for dependent continuous variables. There are also multivariate discrete distributions, such as the multinomial, as a multidimensional version of the binomial. Interested readers should consult one of the many standard statistics texts, such as DeGroot (1975). The question of how to generate samples from normal and other multivariate distributions is discussed in Chapter 8.

5.6. Evaluating the Fit of a Distribution

We have briefly discussed methods of estimating the parameters of a distribution to best fit a set of observations. This assumes we already know what family of distributions we believe the observations are generated by, and the only question is the value of the mean, variance, or other parameters. Of course, if we are interested only in fractiles of the distribution without making assumptions about the overall shape, we can estimate the fractiles of the generating distribution (and their uncertainty) as already described in Section 5.3.3. However, if we choose to represent the data with a standard parametric distribution (i.e., normal, beta, or whatever), we may want to know how good the fit is.

There are three standard approaches to testing whether a set of data is consistent with a proposed distribution:

1. the chi-squared test;
2. the Kolmogorov–Smirnov test; and
3. probability plots and correlation tests.

The chi-squared test compares the number of sample observations found in discrete classes to that predicted by the proposed model. The chi-squared test is best suited for discrete random variables and discrete classes (e.g., Hollander and Wolfe, 1973). For continuous random variables, the Kolmogorov–Smirnov test provides a simpler procedure for comparison, although corrections to the standard test statistic are required when the parameters of the proposed distribution are estimated from the sample, and these corrections are difficult to determine (e.g., Crutcher, 1975). The test statistic is given by the maximum difference between the observed and proposed CDF's. A third approach for examining distribution fits is based on probability plot correlation tests. Probability plots involve graphical transformations of the CDF such that a given distribution plots as a straight line (Benjamin and Cornell, 1970). For example, so-called probability paper and log-probability paper is available with scales transformed in such a way that a CDF of a normal or log-normal distribution, respectively, will appear as a straight line. The degree of fit of the proposed model is measured by the straightness of the relationships obtained by plotting the sample CDF. Procedures are available for evaluating the normal and other selected distributions (Filliben, 1975; Vogel, 1986).

The statistical procedures described above test the hypothesis that the observed sample was drawn from the proposed distributions. With large, empirical data sets, it is likely that the tests will reject any parametric distribution function, even if it provides a reasonable approximation to the observed distribution. In this case, it is preferable to compute a "goodness of fit" of the proposed distribution (e.g., D'Agustino and Stephens, 1986) and use this as a basis for selecting between alternative distributions.

References

Ang, A. H-S., and Tang, W. (1975). *Probability Concepts in Engineering Planning and Design, Volume 1 – Basic Principles*, Wiley, New York.

Ang, A. H-S., and Tang, W. (1984). *Probability Concepts in Engineering Planning and Design, Volume 2 – Decision, Risk, and Reliability*, Wiley, New York.

Benjamin, J. R., and Cornell, A. (1970). *Probability, Statistics, and Decision for Civil Engineers*, McGraw-Hill, New York.

Bratley, P., Fox, B. L., and Schrage, L. E. (1983). *A Guide to Simulation*, Springer-Verlag, New York.

Crutcher, H. L. (1975). "A Note on the Possible Misuse of the Kolmogorov–Smirnov Test," *Journal of Applied Meteorology*, 14:1600–1603.

D'Agustino, R. B., and Stephens, M. A. (1986). *Goodness-of-Fit Techniques*, M. Dekker, New York.

DeGroot, M. H. (1970). *Optimal Statistical Decision*, McGraw-Hill, New York.

DeGroot, M. H. (1975). *Probability and Statistics*, Addison-Wesley, Reading, Mass.

Filliben, J. J. (1975). "The Probability Plot Correlation Coefficient Test for Normality," *Technometrics*, 17, no. 1.

Hastings, N. A. J., and Peacock, J. B. (1974). *Statistical Distributions: A Handbook for Students and Practitioners*, Wiley, New York.

Hollander, M., and Wolf, D. A. (1973). *Nonparametric Statistical Methods*, Wiley, New York.

Johnson, N. L., and Kotz, S. (1969). *Discrete Distributions*, Wiley, New York.

Johnson, N. L., and Kotz, S. (1970a). *Continuous Univariate Distributions – 1: Distributions in Statistics*, Wiley, New York.

Johnson, N. L., and Kotz, S. (1970b). *Distributions in Statistics: Continuous Univariate Distributions – 2*, Wiley, New York.

Stedinger, J. R. (1980). "Fitting Lognormal Distributions to Hydrologic Data," *Water Resources Research*, 16:481–490.

Vogel, R. M. (1986). "The Probability Plot Correlation Coefficient Test for Normal, Lognormal and Gumbel Distributional Hypothesis," *Water Resources Research*, 22, no. 4:587–590.

6   Human Judgment about and with Uncertainty

We dance around in a ring and suppose,
But the secret sits in the middle and knows.
                                        Robert Frost

When the value of an uncertain quantity is needed in policy analysis, and limits in data or understanding preclude the use of conventional statistical techniques to produce probabilistic estimates, about the only remaining option is to ask experts for their best professional judgment. The past twenty years have witnessed remarkable progress in the development of understanding of how both experts and laypersons make judgments that involve uncertainty. Much of this new knowledge is directly relevant to problems encountered in quantitative policy analysis, especially to the elicitation of subjective probability distributions from experts.

We begin this chapter with a brief look at the psychology of judgment under uncertainty. We then turn to a somewhat more detailed review of experimental findings on the psychology, and some of the mechanics, of probability assessment. Most findings reported involve "encyclopedia"-type questions posed to nonexpert subjects. We close the chapter by examining the question "are experts different?" We defer until Chapter 7 a discussion of practical protocols for probability assessment.

6.1. The Psychology of Judgment under Uncertainty

When, as experts or laypersons, we think about and make judgments in the presence of uncertainty, we make use of a set of heuristic procedures. These procedures serve us well in many circumstances (Nisbett and Ross, 1980). However, because these are at best only approximate procedures, they can sometimes lead to biased outcomes, or even outright errors. In this section we briefly summarize three of these heuristics. Interested readers will find that an anthology edited by Daniel Kahneman, Paul Slovic, and Amos Tversky offers a good starting place for a more thorough exploration of this subject (Kahneman et al., 1982).[1] In assessing the frequency of a class of events or objects, or the

---

Portions of the discussion in this chapter are based directly on earlier reviews by the authors and by our doctoral student Theresa Mullin (1986).

1. This literature is not without its detractors. L. Jonathan Cohen (1981) has advanced a variety of criticisms. Although the details of several are interesting, as criticisms of the basic body of work, we do not find them compelling.

probability of occurrence of a specific event, people often resort to the heuristic procedure of *availability*. That is, their probability judgment is driven by the ease with which they can think of previous occurrences of the event, or the ease with which they can imagine the event occurring. For problems with which one has a large amount of direct personal experience this heuristic is likely to perform rather well. For example, if someone were to estimate the likelihood of encountering a highway patrolman during their commute to work tomorrow by thinking about how often they have encountered patrolmen during this same daily drive over the past ten years, they would typically produce quite a good estimate. Barring unusual events, the ease with which they are able to think of previous encounters with patrolmen is likely to be fairly well correlated with the actual frequency with which patrolmen occur along that route.

However, a variety of factors can introduce bias when this heuristic is used. For example, some events or items may be much easier to recall than others. Tversky and Kahneman (1973) report one example from an experiment in which subjects listened to recorded lists of the names of 39 people, some of whom could be described only as well known, the remainder of whom could be described as famous. Some lists included 19 women and more famous women than famous men, some included 19 men and more famous men than famous women. Eighty of 99 subjects ($p < .001$ by sign test) when asked whether men or women predominated on the list they had heard, chose the sex that involved the larger number of famous individuals. Similar results are reported by Estes (1976) in studies of multiple-cue probability learning tasks, which found that while subjects' predictions of the probability of events closely corresponded to actual relative frequency when the different cues occurred equally often, their judgments of probability appeared to be based on the absolute frequency of a cue rather than relative frequency. When these parameters conflicted, judgments of probability were biased toward cues with the greatest absolute frequency. Estes concludes that if one accepts the idea that probability learning is based on acquisition of information about frequency of various individual events in a probabilistic situation, then two general conditions must be met if the learning process is to lead to unbiased estimates of probability by the learner: First, the alternative events involved in a situation must have roughly equal opportunities of occurrence; and second, the learner must attend to and encode occurrences of all the alternative events with equal uniformity or efficiency (Estes, 1976).

A compelling practical example of the operation of the heuristic of availability is provided in an experiment conducted by S. Lichtenstein, P. Slovic, B. Fischhoff, M. Layman, and B. Combs in which several groups of well-educated Americans (N about 40) were told that roughly 50,000 people die each year in traffic accidents in the United States and were then asked to estimate the number of deaths that occur each year in the United States from a variety of

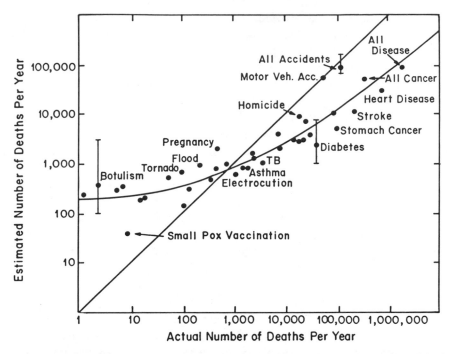

Figure 6.1. Plot showing the geometric mean of people's estimates of the annual numbers of deaths from a variety of causes (vertical axis) versus the actual numbers of deaths (horizontal axis). In general, the occurrence of frequent causes of deaths is underestimated and that of less frequent causes is overestimated. The operation of bias from the heuristic of availability is clearly illustrated by the points for stroke and botulism. Much of the "scatter" of the points is not noise but can be reproduced. The figure is redrawn from Lichtenstein et al. (1978).

other causes (Lichtenstein et al., 1978). If the availability heuristic is operating, one would expect to see some systematic biases in the responses. For example, deaths from botulism are quite rare but Americans learn through the press about virtually every one that occurs. On the other hand, deaths by stroke are fairly common but Americans typically learn about them only when a friend, relative, or famous person is involved.

Figure 6.1 shows the results obtained, with the geometric mean of the estimated number of deaths plotted vertically and the actuarially determined incidence rates plotted horizontally. Note that, as the availability heuristic would suggest, the incidence rate of causes such as botulism is overestimated and that of risks such as stroke is underestimated. We have performed a replication of this study and obtained very similar results (EPP, 1983).

Bias through the use of availability can also arise because of variations in the ease with which an event can be imagined. This is especially true in the context of scenarios, in which people often assess the probability of occurrence of a story that links several events in sequence to be greater than the probability of occurrence of the individual events that make up the scenario (Tversky and Kahneman, 1973; Dawes, 1987). Again, the reason appears to be a dependence on availability. Linked events in a scenario are easier to imagine than the individual events in isolation.

In summary, use of the availability heuristic will yield reasonable results when a person's experience and memory of observed events corresponds fairly well with actual event frequencies; is likely to lead to overestimates if recall or imagination is enhanced (e.g., recent experience, dramatic or salient events, plausible scenario, etc.); and is likely to lead to underestimates if recall or imagination is difficult (e.g., no recent experience, concept is abstract, not encoded in memory, etc.).

Representativeness is a second heuristic procedure often used in judgments about uncertain events. In judging the likelihood that a specific object belongs to a particular class of objects, or that an event is generated by a particular process, people expect the fine structure or details of the object or event to reflect the larger class or process. For example, people judge the string of coin tosses HTHTTH to be more likely than either the string HHHTTT or the string HTHTHT because they know that the *process* of coin tossing is random. Although of course, all three sequences are equally likely to occur, the first string *looks* more random than the other two outcomes (Kahneman and Tversky, 1972). This phenomenon, of expecting in the small behavior that which one knows exists in the large, gives rise to what Tversky and Kahneman have termed "belief in the law of small numbers" (Tversky and Kahneman, 1971) and is frequently evidenced even among technical people with substantial formal statistical training (Tversky and Kahneman, 1971; Kahneman and Tversky, 1972).

Another consequence of representativeness is that people often pay too much attention to specific details (which may or may not contain information) while ignoring or paying insufficient attention to background information such as base rates. Thus, for example, Kahneman and Tversky gave subjects the following problem: "A panel of psychologists have interviewed and administered personality tests to 30 engineers and 70 lawyers, all successful in their respective fields. On the basis of this information, thumbnail descriptions of the 30 engineers and 70 lawyers have been written ... For each description, please indicate your probability that the person is an engineer, on a scale from 0 to 100." They found that responses were based on how much the described person was judged to sound like an engineer or lawyer without regard for the 30:70 ratio (Kahneman and Tversky, 1973). For example, the description "Jack is a 45-year old man. He is married and has four children. He is generally conservative, careful, and ambitious. He shows no interest in political and social issues and spends most of his free time on his many hobbies which include home carpentry, sailing, and mathematical puzzles" was judged with very high probability to involve an engineer, while the description "Dick is a 30-year old man. He is married with no children. A man of high ability and high motivation, he promises to be quite successful in his field. He is well liked by his colleagues" was judged at 50:50, *not* 30:70, because subjects clearly recognized that the description said nothing relevant about a lawyer–engineer distinction and appeared to forget the base rate information. However, when asked "Suppose now that you are given no information whatsoever about an individual chosen at random from the sample?," subjects correctly gave 30:70 odds indicating they did know how to use the base rate information. "Evidently," Kahneman and Tversky conclude, "people respond differently when given no specific evidence and when given worthless evidence. When no specific evidence is given, the prior probabilities are properly utilized; when worthless specific evidence is given, prior probabilities are ignored" (Kahneman and Tversky, 1973).

There do appear to be some circumstances in which subjects are sensitive to changes in base rates and the stated accuracy of the source of information. Fischhoff, Slovic, and Lichtenstein (1979) have reported experiments in which subjects shifted their judgments in the proper direction in correspondence to changes in these factors, although the magnitude of judgments shifts was too conservative. Subjects in this study were insensitive to changes in predictive ability that result from changes in sample size information; however, Bar-Hillel (1979) has reported a study in which subjects' perception of sample accuracy increased with sample size. These judgments appeared to reflect a sensitivity to the sample-to-population ratio rather than absolute sample size.

One other frequently used heuristic is *anchoring and adjustment*. Under this heuristic, a natural starting point, or anchor, is selected as a first approximation to the value of the quantity being estimated and then this value is adjusted to reflect supplementary information. Typically the adjustment is insufficient and the result is biased toward the anchor. For example, in estimating a 90% credible interval for an uncertain quantity, one may first estimate a most likely value, and then adjust this up and down to enclose the interval. If the adjustment is too small, the implied probability distribution will be too narrow. This has been suggested as an explanation for the overconfidence regularly observed when continuous distributions are assessed (see Section 6.4.2). Kahneman and Tversky report a number of experimental demonstrations of anchoring and adjustment (Kahneman and Tversky, 1973). In one particularly clear demonstration, subjects were told the objective was to estimate a quantity, Q, in percent (e.g., the percentage of African countries in the UN). A "wheel of fortune" was spun for the subject to produce a quantity A, $1 \leq A \leq 100$. Subjects were led to believe that the result was a random number between 0 and 100, although in fact the wheel always yielded either 10 or 65. After obtaining A, subjects were asked if Q was greater than or less than A. Subjects

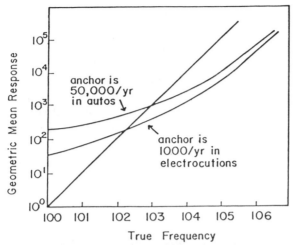

Figure 6.2. Comparison of the best fit quadratic curve for the data from the experiment in Figure 6.1 in which subjects were told that roughly 50,000 people die each year in traffic accidents in the United States to the results from an identical experiment in which different subjects were told that roughly 1,000 people die each year in the United States from accidental electrocutions. The downward shift in the mean response is an illustration of the bias produced by the operation of the heuristic of anchoring and adjustment. The figure is based on data from Lichtenstein et al. (1978).

were then asked to estimate Q by adjusting their response up or down from A. For the African UN membership question, when A was 10, the median estimate of Q was 25, but when A was 65, the median estimate of Q was 45.

Another striking illustration of this heuristic was provided when Lichtenstein et al. (1978) repeated the experiment reported in Figure 6.1 with the one difference that rather than tell their subjects that roughly 50,000 people die each year in the United States from motor vehicle accidents, they told their new subjects that about 1,000 people die each year in the United States from accidental electrocutions. The operation of the heuristic of anchoring and adjustment is clearly illustrated by a systematic downward shift in all the resulting estimates. Figure 6.2 shows the results. Note that the entire mean response has moved down as a result of the lower anchor.

6.2. The Psychology of Probability Assessment

There exists a considerable and growing literature on the assessment of probabilities, including several reviews. Hampton, Moore, and Thomas (Hampton et al., 1973) provide an early survey of methods, for both individuals and groups of experts, with the emphasis on business applications. A book on decision analysis by Brown, Kahr, and Peterson (Brown et al., 1974) contains a review with practical recommendations. Spetzler and Staël von Holstein (1975) describe the experience of the Decision Analysis Group at Stanford Research

Institute, who have been among the pioneers in the application of probability encoding techniques to real-world decision problems. Beach (1975) reviews expert judgment under uncertainty in a number of realistic settings, including applications in the military, in weather forecasting, in medicine, and in business. Hogarth (1975) considers the assessment of subjective probabilities in the light of the psychological evidence on our cognitive limitations. Lichtenstein, Fischhoff, and Phillips (1982) survey studies of the empirical evaluation of probability assessments in terms of calibration. More recently, rather comprehensive reviews of the literature relevant to the elicitation of subjective probabilistic judgments have been completed by Henrion (1980), Wallsten and Budescu (1980), and Mullin (1986).

6.3. Evaluating Subjective Probability Judgments

As we discussed in Section 4.2.2, according to the *personalistic* or *subjectivist* school of probability, the probability of an event is a measure of a person's degree of belief that it will occur. Probability is not a property inherent to the event but is a statement of an observer's judgment that it will occur. Of course, subjective "degrees of belief" are not directly amenable to inspection by others, but the concept of personal probability may be operationalized in terms of the kinds of bets the person is prepared to base on them.

Early discussions of the use of subjective probability in decision and policy analysis tended to take the perspective that these constructs existed in the heads of subjects. The process of eliciting probabilities or probability distributions was thus viewed as involving extracting or eliciting these existing constructs. More recently it has become apparent that in most cases experts and laypersons do not carry fully formed probability values and distributions around in their heads, but must synthesize or construct them when an analyst asks for them. Because the kinds of heuristics we have briefly just discussed can be expected to operate during this construction or synthesis process, the question of how to minimize bias and systematic error in elicitation has grown increasingly important over the years.

A set of personal probabilities assessed in quantitative terms are said to be *coherent* if they conform with the axioms of probability theory. They are coherent if, and only if, it is impossible to use them to make a "Dutch Book" against the assessor, that is, a series of bets that he or she will be certain to lose (de Finetti, 1974). In this formulation a probability may legitimately vary from one assessor to another depending on what information they have. The question therefore arises as to what constitute good probability assessments, beyond the basic criterion of coherence. Winkler and Murphy (1968) distinguish two kinds of "goodness": *Substantive expertise* refers to the knowledge that the assessor has about the quantity to be assessed; and *normative expertise* refers to the skill of the assessor in expressing his or her beliefs in probabilistic form. For example, a meteorologist might have substantive expertise in forecasting the probability of rain tomorrow, but a decision theorist might be expected to have more normative expertise (although, as we shall see, the latter expectation may be in vain). As a practical matter the most important thing is to find someone with some substantive expertise. If your expert doesn't actually know anything about the topic in question, you will never extract anything useful no matter how well calibrated he or she is, and no matter what elicitation technique you use.

Substantive expertise can be measured by how well a set of assessments predicts the actual outcomes; a substantive expert should on the average assign high probabilities to those events that turn out to occur, and low ones to those that do not. The most popular measure of normative expertise is *calibration*, also known as *reliability*. An assessor is said to be well calibrated if the assessed probability of events corresponds with their empirical frequency of occurrence. For example, for a large set of events to each of which the assessor assigns a probability of 0.8, about 80% should actually occur if the assessor is well calibrated.

6.3.1. Scoring Rules

A set of probability assessments may be evaluated by a *scoring rule*, which is a function of the difference between the actual outcomes and the assessed probability distributions. Scoring rules may be used as a basis for rewarding assessors in order to motivate them. A scoring rule is said to be *proper* if assessors maximize their expected score by reporting their true opinions. Many functions have been found that satisfy this condition (e.g., Savage, 1971; Murphy, 1972; Matheson and Winkler, 1976).

A widely used proper scoring rule for the discrete case is the *Brier score* (Brier, 1950), which is a quadratic function of the differences between the assessed probability of events and the fraction that occur. This has been applied by a number of investigators including Murphy (1974), for evaluating the performance of meteorologists forecasting the probability of rain, and by Lichtenstein and Fischhoff (1977; 1980) for a series of psychological studies of probability assessment. The Brier score may be partitioned into three terms to separate components of the assessor's performance. The first reflects ability to predict the correct outcome, that is, the assessor's *knowledge* in the task domain. The second is a measure of *calibration*, the degree to which assessed probabilities match empirical frequency. The third measures *resolution*, which reflects the power to discriminate between different levels of probability.

Matheson and Winkler (1976) have proposed two families of proper scoring rules for the assessment of continuous probability distributions. These incorporate weighting functions to express the fact that the elicitor might be more interested in precise specifications of the probability distribution at certain ranges than at others. The domain of the weighting functions may be probability space (e.g., more weight in the tails of the distribution) or value space (e.g., more weight for values between 10 and 20 units). Pearl (1978) suggests that the choice of scoring rule should depend on the decision problem for which the probability assessments are required. In this case, one might argue that scoring rules should reflect the payoff function of the decision maker so that expert assessors will be motivated similarly to the person who is consulting them. Pearl shows how various standard scoring rules are appropriate to particular payoff functions.

Hogarth (1975) acknowledges the conceptual elegance of scoring rules but criticizes them on practical grounds. He is skeptical about whether assessors have the cognitive capacity to determine the "optimal" response, which would maximize their expected reward based on a proper scoring rule, and so doubts that they much affect an expert's performance. Von Winterfeldt and Edwards (1973) show that scoring rules are inevitably insensitive to small departures from the optimum strategy. Hogarth also doubts whether human assessors can be said to possess a "true underlying probability distribution" at all, which also undermines their rationale as a tool to encourage honesty. But even if scoring rules are not directly effective in promoting accurate reporting, they are nevertheless important for evaluating the performance of assessors.

6.3.2. Measuring Calibration

The overwhelming emphasis of empirical studies of people's abilities as probability assessors has been on their calibration. Calibration can be measured empirically in experiments that involve many assessments of quantities about which assessors have some relevant but imperfect knowledge, and whose true value can be found by the experimenter. Typically in these experiments subjects are asked about their degree of uncertainty about such things as the populations of countries, dates of historical events, or meanings of words, which can be looked up in an almanac or dictionary.

To measure calibration for a set of assessments of discrete probabilities, they are partitioned into subsets with the same or similar assessed probabilities. These probabilities are then plotted against the actual fraction of each subset that is true, forming a *calibration curve* (see Figure 6.3). For a well-calibrated judge the curve should be near the diagonal. For an underconfident judge the assessed probabilities are nearer 0.5 than they should be; more typically, judges are overconfident and the probabilities are assessed too near certainty (0 or 1). An analogous calibration curve can be compiled for assessments of continuous distributions for unknown quantities. For each item the fractile of

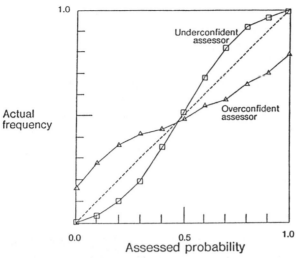

Figure 6.3. Calibration curves from assessments of discrete probabilities.

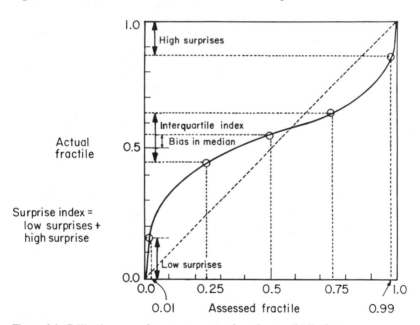

Figure 6.4. Calibration curve from assessments of continuous distributions.

the assessed distribution at which the true value occurs is recorded. These fractiles form a distribution of values between 0 and 1, and the cumulative of this distribution is also a calibration curve (see Figure 6.4). Again the curve of a well-calibrated assessor would be the diagonal. Systematic bias in the median is indicated if the curve does not intersect the diagonal at (0.5,0.5).

Two commonly used measures of calibration on unknown quantities compare the predicted probability of falling within a particular interval with the actual number of values inside it. The *interquartile index* is the proportion of values that turn out to fall between the assessed quartiles, that is, the 0.25 and 0.75 fractiles. The *surprise index* is usually defined as the proportion of values falling outside a 98% credible interval, that is, less than the .01 fractile or greater than the 0.99 fractile. A perfectly calibrated assessor would have an interquartile index of about 50% and a surprise index of about 2% (the complement of the 98% interval). Later sections report experimental calibration results for a variety of alternative approaches to eliciting judgments involving both discrete and continuous probabilities.

6.4. Techniques for Encoding Probabilities

It is convenient to subdivide discussions of probability assessment into methods for eliciting discrete probabilities and methods for eliciting continuous probability distributions. In practice most techniques for eliciting continuous distributions rely on a series of discrete assessments (e.g., of the form "What is the probability that the value of the unknown quantity is less than x?"). These are subsequently used for the interpolation of a continuous distribution. So even if one's primary interest is in unknown quantities, it is still necessary to consider the elicitation of discrete probabilities. Moreover, although both processes may involve questions that have the same logical form, they may appear different psychologically. Thus one should be cautious in drawing conclusions about one from experimental findings on the other.

6.4.1. Encoding Discrete Probabilities

A concern of early research was to compare different response modes for the direct expression of probabilities. Should answers be expressed as probabilities, percentages, or odds? Should they be expressed verbally, in writing, or by indicating a point on a labeled scale? Should the metric of such a scale be probability, odds, or log-odds? Since odds and log-odds scales stretch out the extreme ends of the scale relative to the probability scale, it was conjectured that they would encourage more extreme responses. This would combat *conservatism*, that is, the tendency to unwarranted degrees of uncertainty (too near 0.5), which had been found in some early studies of human performance in Bayesian inference tasks (Edwards, 1968); and, indeed, initial evidence on discrete probabilities confirmed this.

It is now apparent from studies of calibration that much more often the problem is *overconfidence*, that is, judgments tend to be too extreme (too near 0 or 1). Some examples of empirical calibration curves are shown in Figures 6.5 and 6.6. The weather forecasters studied by Murphy and Winkler (1977) do

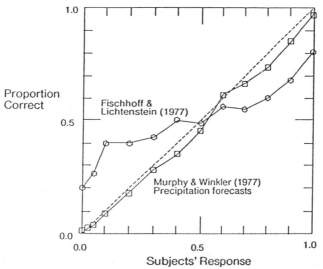

Figure 6.5. Two empirical calibration curves for discrete probabilities.

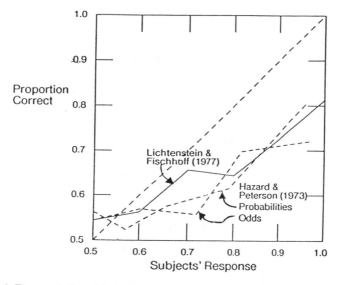

Figure 6.6. Three typical empirical calibration curves for half-range tasks.

show good calibration in their probabilistic forecasts of precipitation; their calibration curve closely follows the diagonal. But these are exceptional and the other curves in Figures 6.5 and 6.6 are more typical of what has been found. Results in Figure 6.6 are from *half-range* studies, in which subjects are asked to assess their degree of belief in the most likely of two complementary alternatives, and so assessed probabilities cannot be less than 0.5. For propositions assessed as having a 0.8 chance of being correct, experimental studies such as those of Fischhoff and Lichtenstein report the actual fraction true is typically 0.55 to 0.7.

In any case, whether the problem is overconfidence or underconfidence, more recent studies have found little difference in the calibration of results from using probability or odds response (Hazard and Peterson, 1973; Seaver, Winterfield, and Edwards, 1978). Probably a more important criterion is the suitability of the response mode to the cognitive style, skills, and preferences of the assessor; some people are used to odds, others may prefer probabilities. For rare events (e.g., 50 to 1) odds may be easier for many people because they avoid small decimals or negative exponents.

6.4.2. Encoding Continuous Distributions

The most frequently used methods for encoding continuous distributions rely on a series of questions to establish points on the cumulative distribution function (CDF) or the probability density function (PDF). Spetzler and Staël von Holstein (1975) distinguish methods depending on whether they elicit values or probabilities: With *fixed value* methods the probability that the quantity lies in a specified range of values is assessed. In *fixed probability* methods values of the quantity that bound specified fractiles or confidence intervals are assessed. A typical question might be "Give a value x such that you think the unknown quantity has a 25% chance of being less than x." Commonly used fractiles are the median (0.5), tertiles (0.33, 0.67), quartiles (0.25, 0.75), octiles (0.125, 0.875), and extremes such as (0.01, 0.99). In the *bisection* or *interval* method the median is assessed first, followed by the median of each half-range (quartiles), the median of each quarter-range (octiles), and so on. At one time this was a relatively popular approach but it has been criticized as producing cumulative errors and extreme overconfidence (Spetzler and Staël von Holstein, 1975; Ludke, Strauss, and Gustafson, 1977).

Fixed value methods usually involve dividing up the range of the variable into equal intervals. The assessor judges either the probabilities that the value lies in each interval, approximating the PDF, or the probabilities that the quantity is less than a selection of given values, approximating the CDF. Raiffa (1968) and Schlaifer (1969) suggested that the CDF might be intuitively easier to deal with than the PDF. The probabilities are larger and there is ample evidence that people have trouble with small probabilities. On the other hand certain properties of distributions, such as symmetry and the location of the mode(s), are much easier to see on the PDF (see our discussion in Chapter 9). Some experimental studies (Winkler, 1967; Schaefer and Borcherding, 1973) have reported that subjects found the PDF easier to deal with than the CDF, but this is likely to depend on education and experience.

In comparing fixed value methods with fixed probability methods (fractiles), there is now mounting evidence that the former produce distributions that are more diffuse and hence usually better calibrated (Winkler, 1967; Pitz, 1974; Ludke et al., 1977; Seaver et al., 1978). For example Seaver et al. (1978) found 5% surprises with PDF techniques compared to 24% to 34% surprises with fractile methods. An exception is a study by Murphy and Winkler (1974) of a small sample of weather forecasters who produced somewhat better calibrated results from fractiles than from a fixed value method; however, these subjects were exceptionally well-calibrated with either method.

A variant on the PDF fixed value method asks assessors not to assign absolute probabilities to the intervals on the value scale, but only to rank them by probability and then to rank the first differences between them. The actual probabilities are then quantified by a procedure suggested by Smith (1967), based on psychometric scaling techniques. Hampton et al. (1973) give details of this method but comment that "this method involving the ranking of differences will be psychologically and intuitively meaningless to the decision-maker and ... is likely to tax the latter's patience." Notwithstanding, Ludke et al. (1977) studied it experimentally and found it more accurate and more reliable (i.e., consistent between two sessions three weeks apart) than other methods, including bisection and standard PDF. However, the diffuseness of the distributions assessed by ranking is partly controlled by Smith's computational procedure rather than by the assessor (a point not mentioned by the authors). Thus, it amounts to a recalibration of the subjective distribution. In this study it may have compensated for the normal overconfidence of the subjects, but this might not be the case in general.

The most direct method for encoding continuous distributions is simply for the assessor to draw points on the distribution curve, either the PDF or the CDF. The response medium may be pencil and paper, or a lightpen or joystick with interactive computer graphics. In the latter case the program can fit distribution curves automatically to a few points for immediate verification and possible revision (Schlaifer, 1971; Barclay and Randall, 1975; Mullin, 1986). There seems to be little direct experimental evidence on the calibration of distributions so produced. In one set of elicitations of experts we have conducted we obtained significantly narrower distributions from the one expert who insisted on directly drawing PDFs than we did from six other experts elicited with a combination of fixed value and fixed probability techniques (Morgan et al., 1984).

If one has prior knowledge about the family of distributions to which the assessed distribution should belong, then probably the simplest method from the elicitor's point of view is to ask the assessor to estimate the parameters directly. However, assessors rarely have the requisite statistical expertise and thus require thorough training in the relationship between the parameters and the shape of the distributions (Seaver, 1978). Two methods introduced by Winkler (1967) are directed at eliciting the parameters of subjective beta distributions for answering questions like "What proportion of students at the University of Chicago wear glasses?" With the *equivalent prior sample* (EPS) method you assess quantities r and n such that your current opinion on the proportion p would be equivalent to the opinion you would have obtained from finding that r wore glasses from a sample of n students. The ratio r/n should be what you assess as the most likely value for p (its mode), and the sample size n indicates your confidence in your opinion.[2] In the related *hypothetical future samples* (HFS) method you assess what effect it would have on your opinion of p to observe a new sample, for instance, "Suppose you encounter a new group of forty students of whom twenty-five wear glasses; how much would this change your prior opinion on the proportion?"

Winkler (1967) and Schaefer and Borcherding (1973) report that assessors found considerable difficulty in learning to use these techniques (EPS and HFS) compared to fractiles or PDF techniques, although surprisingly, after training, Winkler's subjects rated them as better on clarity and ease of use. Both these studies and also Seaver (1978), who used a similar method, obtained distributions that were far too tight, implying considerable overconfidence, more so than those obtained by other methods. However, Schaefer and Borcherding (1973) did find that their subjects could be trained to produce much more diffuse distributions using EPS. On the whole these techniques involving direct assessment of parameters do not seem very promising, being apparently harder to learn and understand than the other techniques discussed and even more conducive to overconfidence.

The one consistent finding across all elicitation techniques that have been examined is a strong and consistent tendency to overconfidence. Table 6.1 gives a summary of the interquartile and surprise indices from a wide range of studies of the assessment of continuous distributions. Interquartile indices are typically between 20% and 40%, instead of the 50% one would obtain with a well-calibrated assessor. The surprise index is almost always far too large, from 5% to 40%, instead of 2%.

6.4.3. Disaggregation

It has become something of an article of faith in the decision analysis community that disaggregation of an elicitation problem holds the potential for significantly improved performance on many elicitation tasks. For example, North and Merkhofer (Morgan, Henrion, and Morris, 1980) have described a training exercise used in the now defunct SRI Decision Analysis Group in which participants were first asked to directly estimate the hog population of the United States and then asked to estimate it as the product (U.S. population)(annual

---

2. These quantities are simply related to the more traditional parameters of the beta distribution: $\alpha = r + 1, \beta = n - r + 1$.

Table 6.1. *Summary of calibration indices for continuous distributions*

	Number of assessments N	Interquartile index (ideal 50%)	Surprise index (ideal 2%)
Alpert & Raiffa (1969)			
Group 1-A	880	33	46
Group 2 & 3	1,670	33	39
Group 4	600	36	21
Hession & McCarthy (1974)			
Fractiles	2,035	25	47
Selvidge (1975)			
Five fractiles	400	56	10
Seven fractiles	520	50	7
Schaefer & Borcherding (1973)			
Fractiles	396	23	39
Hypothetical sample	396	16	50
Pickhardt & Wallace (1974)			
Group 1	?	39	32
Group 2	?	30	46
Seaver, von Winterfeldt, & Edwards (1978)			
Fractiles	160	42	34
Odds-fractiles	160	53	24
Probabilities	180	57	5
Odds	180	47	5
Log-odds	140	31	20
Stael von Holstein (1971)			
Fixed intervals	1,269	27	30
Murphy & Winkler (1974 & 1977)			
Fixed intervals	132	45	27 (ideal 25)
Fractiles	432	54	21 (ideal 25)
Schaefer (1976)			
Fixed interval	660	27	25
Lichtenstein & Fischhoff (1978)			
Fractiles	924	33	41
Seaver (1978)			
Parameters of beta dist.	3,200	29	25

These results are for subjects without feedback training. They are partly taken from Lichtenstein, Fischhoff, and Phillips (1982), with additional data for more recent studies.

average bacon consumption per capita)(average amount of bacon per hog). Although no formal studies were apparently ever done, the informal reports are that the latter approach produced much better estimates. In structuring elicitation problems, experienced analysts routinely try to find the level of aggregation and the specific quantities with which the expert is most familiar and comfortable. While we view this strategy as very wise, and clearly supported by general psychological arguments, the few attempts to document the utility of disaggregation in elicitation tasks have yielded mixed results.

Gettys et al. (1973) found that decomposition of posterior probability judgments into a series of conditional probability judgments later combined using a modified version of Bayes' rule tended to produce judgments closer to the theoretically prescribed values than were direct assessments of posterior probability. On the other hand, the results of a study by Burns and Pearl (1981) question both the value of decomposition and the often assumed superiority of decompositions of probability judgments into causal rather than diagnostic inferences. Judgments based on causal inferences were no more valid than those based on diagnostic inferences, and the synthesized estimates were neither uniformly nor greatly superior to direct estimates.

In a study by Armstrong, Denniston, and Gordon (1975) subjects' estimates of general knowledge quantities were found to be more accurate if based on decompositions than if made directly. The decompositions used in this study were made by the experimenters. Henrion, Fischer, and Mullin (1989; see also Mullin, 1986) conducted a study of the impact of disaggregation on the performance of undergraduates answering almanac-type questions. Three treatments, involving no decomposition, decompositions provided by the investigators, and subject's own disaggregations were employed. Assessments based on decomposition models were found to be no more accurate or better calibrated than estimates made directly. This might have been due to the limited validity of such models for the tasks at hand, as well as the possibility that though subjects found the subquantities generally easier to estimate, they actually knew little more about them than they knew about the overall quantity. However, use of the simple multiplicative decomposition models significantly altered the direction of the bias in subjects' judgments, from systematic underestimation to overestimation of the unknown quantities. This result demonstrates the powerful effect that problem structuring can have on the actual estimation. A particular model specification may affect estimates by its basic mathematical properties and by the limits it tends to impose on the processes that are considered and thus the information and sources of uncertainty that will be incorporated into an assessment.

6.4.4. The Use of Reasons and Disconfirming Information

In Section 6.1 we saw that people sometimes fail to make good use of disconfirming information. In probabilistic estimation this has the effect of promoting overconfidence in one's judgments (Einhorn and Hogarth, 1978). In several experimental studies in which subjects were forced to consider disconfirming information, assessed overconfidence was significantly reduced.

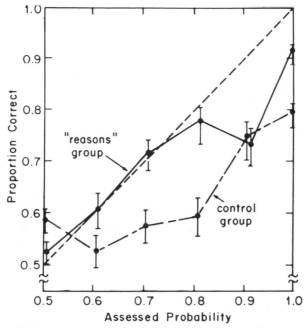

Figure 6.7. Koriat, Lichtenstein, and Fischhoff (1980) found an improvement in the calibration of assessors when they were required to list reasons for and against the judgments they made.

One manifestation of overconfidence comes in the form of "hindsight bias" (Slovic and Fischhoff, 1977). Subjects were found to exaggerate the predictability of reported outcomes, apparently because they failed to think about how things could have turned out differently. When, in experiments that involved only two possible outcomes, Slovic and Fischhoff had subjects specifically consider why the unreported outcome might have occurred, the subjects' bias toward overestimation of the reported outcome's probability was significantly reduced, though not eliminated (Slovic and Fischhoff, 1977).

Getting experts to think carefully about the substantive details of each judgment they make is very important. Koriat, Lichtenstein, and Fischhoff (1980) report a significant improvement in calibration when they asked assessors to provide lists of reasons justifying their judgments as opposed to just providing the judgment (Figure 6.7). In another case subjects were required to either list one reason for their response; or list one reason against their response; or list one reason for and one against. Of these three tactics, only the one in which subjects listed one reason against their choice of response was overconfidence significantly reduced. Fischhoff and MacGregor (1982) tested the effectiveness of using disconfirming information in three studies involving university students' responses to two-alternative outcome predictions concerning local elections, sporting events, and other events whose outcomes would be determined within a month of the experiment. The calibration results of the three cases indicated that asking subjects for reasons for or reasons against their choice of response had produced a consistent but rather small reduction in assessed overconfidence. The rather low overall accuracy achieved by subjects' forecasts indicated that the prediction of these events was fairly difficult for them, a fact that may contribute to the small effect. Hoch (1984) investigated the effect of generating reasons in a study involving student assessments of the probability of possible future events. Events involved both world affairs (another OPEC embargo) and personal choices (future purchase of a VCR). Hoch found that subjects' probability judgments were greatly affected by being asked for reasons. The greatest effect was found for reasons against subject's future purchase of a VCR in the next three years, the event for which subjects could probably generate reasons for or against most easily. Hoch also found that asking for one sort of reason would interfere with subjects' subsequent ability to supply the other sort of reason. Judgments were influenced by the type of reason asked for first. If there was a delay between asking for reasons of one kind and the other, the interference effect would disappear but judgments would then be influenced by the type of reasons asked for last. Hoch concludes that subjects' predictions were malleable because many of the predictions concerned issues that were novel or ambiguous to the subjects. This suggests that debiasing by asking for reasons may have more impact on judgment tasks for which the expert has limited experience than for tasks with which he or she is intimately familiar.

6.4.5. Training in Calibration

It is not clear whether training elicitors on trial tasks, such as encyclopedia questions, will improve actual performance. Alpert and Raiffa (1969) tried to reduce the overconfidence observed in their studies by giving their subjects an extensive report and explanation of their performance with exhortations to "spread those extreme fractiles!" After this initial training experience the increase in interquartile index and reduction in surprise index was only moderate (see Table 6.2). Similar results have been obtained by others, including Pickhardt and Wallace (1974) and Schaefer (1976), who, even after extended feedback including calibration scores for five and six sessions, did not get the surprise index below 20% and 14%, respectively.

On the other hand in a study with discrete assessment tasks, Lichtenstein and Fischhoff (1979) found considerable improvement in calibration after a single session of two hundred items with comprehensive feedback. The learned calibration on two-alternative tasks generalized to other discrete choice tasks differing in difficulty, content, and response mode (four-alternative tasks); but learning on discrete tasks did not seem to generalize to assessing continuous

Table 6.2. *Calibration results showing the effect of training on assessment of unknown quantities*

	Number of assessed distributions N	Interquartile index (ideal = 50) before	Interquartile index (ideal = 50) after	Surprise index (ideal = 2) before	Surprise index (ideal = 2) after
Alpert & Raiffa (1969)					
Groups 2 & 3	1,670	33	44	39	23
Group 4	600	36	43	21	9
Schaefer & Borcherding (1973)					
Fractiles	396	23	38	39	12
HFS	396	16	48	50	6
Pickardt & Wallace (1974)					
Group 1 (5 sessions)	?	39	49	32	20
Group 2 (6 sessions)	?	30	45	46	24
Schaefer (1976)					
(5 sessions)	660	27	34	25	14
Lichtenstein & Fischhoff (1980)					
(Training on discrete tasks)	924	33	37	41	40

distributions, for which there was almost no improvement (see Lichtenstein and Fischhoff entry in Table 6.2).

The nature of the feedback is of great importance. Unclear feedback can make things worse (Hession and McCarthy, 1974). Indeed, Einhorn and Hogarth (1978) propose that it is reinforcement by biased feedback that is partly responsible for our overconfidence in the first place. Hogarth (1975) suggests that *task structure* feedback about the relationships between available information and the tasks is more effective than pure *outcome feedback* such as provided by scoring rules. It may also be important that feedback include personal discussion of results, since this may be less easy to dismiss than a written numerical summary (Lichtenstein and Fischhoff, 1979).

Currently there are only the beginnings of ideas about what an effective training program for assessors should be like. Lichtenstein, Fischhoff, and Phillips (1982) point out that it requires around two hundred assessments to get a reasonably reliable measure of a person's calibration, and so it may be necessary to get several times this number to learn to be consistently well calibrated. Since learning may not be generalizable between different types of tasks, another difficulty may be compiling enough test questions with answers knowable to the trainers, which are similar to the questions of interest (which presumably involve unknown answers). Indeed, for many elicitations required in policy analysis, producing "similar" questions for use in training may be virtually impossible. Compounding the problem is that it remains unclear what the important dimensions of similarity are when dealing with calibration, although we know that difficulty is an important factor. It appears training may be inevitably a rather lengthy and arduous process, and may be specific for particular topics. In the meantime, if we find the situation a little discouraging, we may do well to recall that there is at least one field, namely, weather forecasting, in which, given a well-defined task with regular feedback, practitioners have learn to become excellently calibrated assessors of probability (Murphy and Winkler, 1974, 1977).

6.4.6. Covariation and Dependence

Given the experimental results reported in previous sections, it should be no surprise that there is a significant experimental literature suggesting that people are generally not very good at dealing with correlation structures. Nisbett and Ross (1980) have given the following concise summary of this literature:

The evidence shows that people are poor at detecting many sorts of covariation.... Perception of covariation in the social domain is largely a function of preexisting theories and only very secondarily a function of true covariation. In the absence of theories, people's covariation detection capacities are extremely limited. Though the conditioning literature shows that both animals and humans are extremely accurate covariation detectors under some circumstances, these circumstances are very limited and constrained. The existing literature provides no reason to believe that ... humans would be able to detect relatively weak covariations among stimuli that are relatively indistinctive, subtle and irrelevant motivationally and, most importantly, among stimuli when the presentation interval is very large.

Given this situation, one clearly must be modest in attempts to assess probabilistic dependencies between uncertain parameters. It is often easier to do this with discrete distributions than with continuous ones: If x_1 and x_2 are dependent, one may specify the marginal probabilities for outcomes of x_1, and then the conditional probabilities on x_2 for each value of x_2:

$$P[x_1], P[x_2 \mid x_1]$$

It is often easiest to assess the conditional probabilities in a different sequence from the sequence in which uncertainties will be resolved, which is used in the decision tree. For example, it may be easier to assess the probability of an event conditional on another event that can cause it, rather than vice versa. But if, say, the cause is a disease, and the effect is a test outcome, in a decision analysis one generally wants to reverse the conditioning, obtaining the probability of the disease given the test is positive or negative. Bayes' rule allows the other version to be computed easily:

$$P[x_1 \mid x_2] = \frac{P[x_2 \mid x_1]P[x_1]}{P[x_2 \mid x_1]P[x_1] + P[x_2 \mid \overline{x_1}]P[\overline{x_1}]}$$

For example, it may be easier to assess the probability of each possible outcome of an experiment conditional on the truth of alternative hypotheses, but for the probability tree, the probabilities should be arranged in the sequence with which the information will become known, first the experiment, then the truth. Analogous changing of sequence is useful when there are more than two dependent events. In more complex cases the number of possible sequences for assessing the probabilities becomes large, and matching the way the assessor views the problem is essential. *Influence diagrams* offer a useful formalism for understanding and manipulating these (Howard and Matheson, 1981).

Dependence among continuous quantities is often specified in terms of correlation. Dependence among many continuous quantities may require specification of the correlation (or covariance) matrix. Assessing a correlation matrix, regular or rank order, by subjective judgment is hard to do at best. Most people have only a hazy idea of the meaning of correlation of covariance. One approach to assessment is provided in the PROSA-2 code (Vaurio, 1980): The uncertain parameters are divided into two categories: primary parameters, which are all independent of each other, and secondary parameters, which are dependent on arbitrary combinations of primary ones. The dependence is specified in terms of the conditional expectation of the secondary parameter given a particular (+1 sigma value) of the primary ones on which it depends.

Experimental studies of people's abilities to assess correlations have shown them to be mixed, at best. In some studies, subjects who were asked to judge directly the degree of covariation accurately judged it, but in others they systematically misjudged it (Alloy & Tabachnik, 1984). Accuracy appears to depend on several factors, such as whether the contingency is positive (occurs) or negative (doesn't occur) in dichotomous events, on prior experience with contingent event relationships, and on prior knowledge of whether randomness (no dependency) is a plausible hypothesis.

In practical modeling, very often it is best to try to avoid the problem of asking for direct quantitative assessments of correlations by explicitly modeling the cause of the dependency: For example, if the future unit capital cost of a coal-power plant is considered correlated with that for a nuclear plant, the reason may be that they both depend on inflation in construction costs. In that case it may be easiest to add this as an extra parameter to the model, on which both coal and nuclear costs depend, which makes the task of assessing the input distributions easier and simplifies the computational tasks.

6.4.7. *Multivariate Distributions*

Winkler, Smith, and Kulkarni (1978) describe a method for eliciting multivariate subjective distribution about the coefficients and normal error term of a conventional linear model,

$$y = \Sigma_i \beta_i x_i + \epsilon$$

where the β_i are coefficients and ϵ is a normally distributed error. The coefficients and variance of the error are assumed to have a multivariate normal-gamma distribution being the natural conjugate prior of such a linear model (e.g., see DeGroot, 1970). They assume, quite plausibly, that even assessors who have much experience of particular values of y and the x_i will have little intuition about the linear coefficients, let alone the parameters of the conjugate prior. However, the latter may be estimated by eliciting the simple univariate predictive distributions of the model. Thus, the assessor is faced only with assessing distributions of the dependent y, given a vector of plausible values for the independents x_i. Kadane et al. (1978) describe an interactive computer system that conducts the elicitation using questions about fractiles of the predictive distributions. It monitors the consistency of the answers and can submit any answers that are apparently inconsistent to the assessor for reconsideration. This technique has been applied in eliciting a model of the lifetime of asphalt highway surfaces from experienced highway engineers; but no validation experiments have yet been conducted.

6.4.8. Aids in Elicitation

Most people find it easiest to express probabilities qualitatively, using words and phrases such as "credible," "likely," or "extremely improbable." But there is evidence that different people associate markedly different numerical probabilities with these phrases (Lichtenstein and Newman, 1967). It also appears that for each person the probability associated with each word or phrase varies with the semantic context in which it is used. Hence, in most cases such words and phrases are unreliable as a response mode for probability assessments.

As an aid to conceptualizing probabilities, Raiffa (1968) has suggested that assessors visualize an urn containing colored balls in proportions that approximate the required probabilities. Although such receptacles frequent the pages of statistics textbooks and psychological experiments, it is not clear that they help most people relate probability to their everyday experience.

Savage (1954), accepting that most people do not have clear intuitions about probabilities, argued in favor of *indirect* response modes in which the assessor need only make a choice between bets and so can avoid explicit mention of probabilities. Hampton et al. (1973) point out that "special gambling behavior will be involved in betting situations [involving] risk attitudes and propensity to gamble," which may also confound assessments. However, there exists an indirect response method originally suggested by de Finetti (1974), which, in theory, obviates such difficulties from attitudes to gambling. This "reference

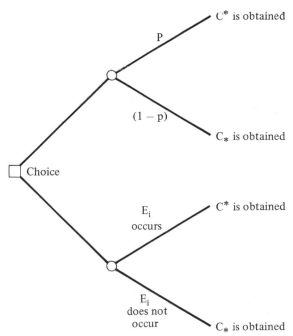

Figure 6.8. Reference lottery formulation of the problem of expert elicitation of the probability that an event E_i will occur. The respondent is asked to choose between a lottery (above) that has a probability p of yielding a desired outcome C^* and a probability $(1 - p)$ of receiving a less desired outcome C_* and a lottery (below) that yields C^* if E_i occurs and yields C_* if E_i does not occur. The value of p is adjusted until the respondent is indifferent in his choice between the two lotteries. The resulting value of p is taken to be the respondent's assessed probability that E_i will occur.

lottery" approach has now become the standard approach in most decision analysis textbooks.

In assessing the probability that a discrete event, E_i will occur, the subject is presented with a choice between two lotteries such as that shown in Figure 6.8. In the first lottery, with probability p a desired outcome, C^* (e.g., a large cash prize of fixed size) will be obtained, and, with a probability $(1-p)$ a less desired outcome C_* (e.g., no prize) will be obtained. In the second lottery, the desired outcome, C^*, will be obtained if E_i occurs and the less desired outcome C_* will be obtained if E_i does not occur. Subjects are asked to adjust the value of p until they are indifferent between the two lotteries. The resulting probability p is then taken as the probability that E_i will occur. Because the reward is the same for each bet, any "special gambling behavior" effects should cancel out. The procedure can be extended to the elicitation of the CDF of a continuous variable x by letting the event E_i be the probability that $x > a_i$, and then varying i in order to obtain evaluations of a variety of values of $\int_{-\infty}^{a_i} f(x)\,dx$, where $f(x)$ is the probability density function. In this way one can trace out the CDF, and through differentiation obtain the PDF.

Although the reference lottery formulation has theoretical appeal, and may have some practical appeal in eliciting people who have no experience with probabilistic thinking, many practicing analysts find it cumbersome, and if they use it at all outside the textbook and classroom, use it only during the early explanatory stages of an elicitation.

Shafer and Tversky (1985) have expressed views on this matter that are worth quoting at length:

The betting semantics has a generality that the frequency and propensity semantics lack. We can always ask ourselves about our attitude towards a bet, quite irrespective of the structure of our evidence. But this lack of connection with the evidence is also a weakness of the betting semantics.

In evaluating the betting semantics, one must distinguish logical from psychological and practical considerations. Ramsey (1931), Savage (1954), and their followers have made an important contribution to the logical analysis of subjective probability by showing that it can be derived from coherent preferences between bets. This logical argument, however, does not imply psychological precedence. Introspection suggests that people typically act on the basis of their beliefs, rather than form beliefs on the basis of their acts. The gambler bets on Team A rather than on Team B because he believes that A is more likely to win. He does not usually infer such a belief from his betting preferences.

It is sometimes argued that the prospect of monetary loss tends to concentrate the mind and thus permits a more honest and acute assessment of the strength of evidence than that obtained by thinking about that evidence directly. There is very little empirical evidence to support this claim. Although incentives can sometimes reduce careless responses, monetary payoffs are neither necessary nor sufficient for careful judgment. In fact, there is evidence showing that people are sometimes willing to incur monetary losses in order to report what they believe (Lieblich and Lieblich, 1969). Personally, we find that questions about betting do not help us think about the evidence; instead they divert our minds to extraneous questions: our attitudes towards the monetary and social consequences of winning or losing a bet, our assessment of the ability and knowledge of our opponent, etc.

Whether or not one employs a betting formulation, physical aids to help in visualizing probability can be very useful even for subjects with rather considerable experience. By far the most successful of the devices that have been tried is the probability wheel, various versions of which are now widely used in practical elicitation. Imagine an orange-colored wheel, part of which is covered by a pie shaped wedge of blue material, the size of which can be adjusted (Figures 6.9 and 6.10). Set the size of the blue wedge so that it covers p of the entire surface. If we add a pointer and arrange to spin the wheel (or the pointer) like a carnival wheel of fortune, there is a probability p that when the wheel stops the pointer will be pointing to blue and a probability $(1 - p)$ that when it stops the pointer will be pointing to orange. In an elicitation, the subject can be asked to vary the proportion of the wheel that is blue until the probability that the pointer will end up on blue is the same as the probability

Figure 6.9. A plastic probability wheel used as an aide in expert elicitation. (Photo courtesy of M. Merkhofer)

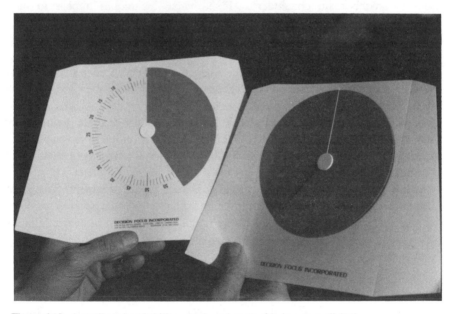

Figure 6.10. A cardboard probability wheel used as an aide in expert elicitation.

that the event E_i will occur. If a reference lottery formulation is to be used one can ask questions such as "Would you rather bet a thousand dollars on the uncertain quantity being less than fifty units or bet a thousand dollars on the pointer stopping in the blue sector?" The sector is adjusted back and forth until the assessor's indifference point is reached, at which time the size of the blue sector should equal the judged probability.

Figure 6.9 shows a plastic probability wheel designed to actually be spun. More typically, one dispenses with the spinning and uses a simple cardboard wheel of the sort shown in Figure 6.10.

We are unaware of any systematic experimental evaluations of the reference lottery technique or of the use of the probability wheel.

6.4.9. Is Any Technique "Best"?

The results of the considerable number of empirical comparisons of various encoding techniques do not show great consistency, and the articles reviewed provide little consensus about which to recommend. Certainly the choice of method should depend on the nature of the task and the experience and preferences of the assessor and the elicitor. Techniques such as ranking and equivalent prior samples have a number of practical shortcomings, one of the more important being that they are hard to explain. In terms of ease of understanding and administration, fixed value and fixed probability methods seem to be the main contenders. Fixed value techniques appear to have emerged as the principal approach used by most practicing analysts. These are typically supplemented by fractiles and other methods for subsequent verification.

The most unequivocal result of experimental studies of probability encoding has been that assessors are poorly calibrated; in most cases they are overconfident, assigning probabilities that are nearer certainty than is warranted by their revealed knowledge. Typical calibration results for discrete probabilities were shown in Figures 6.5 and 6.6. Table 6.1 summarizes the interquartile and surprise indices from a wide range of studies of the assessment of continuous distributions.

Asking subjects to give reasons and to construct careful arguments in support of their judgments appears to improve the quality of assessments in some circumstances. However, such a strategy is not a cure-all. Whatever elicitation procedure is adopted, subjective judgments are inherently prone to bias and must be treated with care.

6.5. Are Experts Different?

Most experimental results discussed in this chapter have come from experiments using groups of undergraduate students and members of organizations such as the League of Women Voters. In most cases the questions asked and the judgment tasks posed have involved general knowledge or "encyclopedia" questions, such as "Which is longer, the Panama Canal or the Suez Canal? In terms of a probability score running from .5 to 1, how sure are you of your answer?" There has been relatively little attention paid to the question of how well, and to what extent, the findings obtained in these studies apply to the subjective probabilistic judgments that experts make about values that clearly lie in their area of expertise.

Differences in real-world decision makers, as well as the decision environment, have been cited in discounting the results of many laboratory studies of judgment behavior. Hogarth (1975) and Edwards (Sjoberg, 1982) have been critical of the pervasive use of students and nonimportant, nonexpert decision tasks in the experimental studies of judgment. The performance of these subjects, in terms of overconfidence, for example, could be quite different from that of experts in applied settings. It has been suggested (Pitz, 1974), and demonstrated in at least one study (Lichtenstein, Fischhoff, and Phillips, 1982), that the more information subjects have about an unknown quantity, the less likely they are to exhibit overconfidence. A further indication of potentially significant differences between the two types of decision makers is offered by the results of a survey by Christensen-Szalanski and Beach (1984). In their survey of professions in the area of judgment and decision, all of the examples of poor performance cited by the eighty respondents involved laboratory studies typically using university students, whereas more than half of the cited work demonstrating good performance was done in applied settings and/or used experts as subjects.

In a few studies, researchers have identified experts' use of an availability heuristic, but found in each case that the operation of this heuristic differed somewhat from the description by Kahneman and Tversky. According to Kahneman and Tversky, event probability judgments based on availability are influenced by the ease with which instances or examples of the event can be recalled. This in turn is affected by the familiarity, recency, salience, drama, and relevance of the event (Kahneman, Slovic, and Tversky, 1982). In a study by Billings and Schaalman, school administrators who made judgments about five possible outcomes of school desegregation, and judgments about various characteristics of past instances of these outcomes related to school desegregation, appeared to differ from nonexperts in their use of availability (Billings and Schaalman, 1980). Although there was a reliance on several variables such as the relative frequency, relevance, and number of past events, there was little use of less valid variables, such as familiarity, recency, or drama. In a study of diagnostic reasoning, Fox (1980) measured availability in terms of probability judgment or diagnosis response times. He considered two components of availability whose roles could be distinguished in this judgment context: the reliability of a cue and the salience of a cue. He found that response time was related to the reliability of disease–symptom associations, but not to any measure of salience (Fox, 1980). Fox also found that for this group of experts, confirming information was retrieved no more easily than disconfirming information. This finding is at variance with the results of several experiments involving general knowledge judgments, where subjects appear reluctant to use negative information (Schustack and Sternberg, 1981), or fail to search for disconfirming information when they make probabilistic judgments (Einhorn and Hogarth, 1978; Koriat et al., 1980).

Although most studies of expert judgment do not offer calibration measures, several have reported experts' judgments that tend to be well calibrated or underconfident rather than overconfident. Wallsten and Budescu (1980) have produced a very nice review of studies in several fields including weather forecasting and medical diagnosis. On weather forecasting, they summarize as follows:

... probability of precipitation forecasts, which have been routine (in the United States) since 1965, are both extremely well calibrated and more informative than climatological forecasts. Indeed these results may be taken as an existence demonstration – there do exist conditions under which experts can provide subjective probability estimates which are relatively free of bias and are highly valid in the sense of being well calibrated. Experience and feedback are probably factors, since calibration is less impressive, although still good, for the less familiar task of assessing probability distributions of high and low temperatures or of severe weather.... Although the probability encoding biases frequently shown in laboratory experiments has not been demonstrated with weather forecasters, there does seem to be a slight bias toward overprediction of weather events.

In light of the excellent calibration, it may not be surprising to note that the probability of precipitation forecasts are also internally consistent. (Wallsten and Budescu, 1980)

Although judgments by physicians can be sensitive to "factors which inappropriately direct the physician's attention to specific diagnoses," there are circumstances in which "physicians can be very well calibrated, although there may be a tendency to overestimate the probabilities of serious diseases" (Wallsten and Budescu, 1980).

In a recent study of the bidding behavior of expert and amateur contract bridge players in the realistic setting of a tournament, Keren (1986) found that expert players were almost perfectly calibrated. By contrast, the amateurs' preplay bidding reflected a bias toward overconfidence. Keren attributed the superior performance of experts to both their greater ability to assess plausibility and uncertainty through construction of more appropriate models of the problem and to a greater ability to translate their subjective assessment into numerical estimates. Thus, the normal task of an expert bridge player affords opportunities for on-the-job training in calibration similar to those enjoyed by weather forecasters. In addition to the acquisition of substantive expertise through their professional experience, the probabilistic form in which they grow accustomed to expressing their beliefs and receiving feedback also allows these judges to gain normative expertise. Tomassini et al. elicited prior probability distributions for financial statement account balances from thirty-two practicing auditors and found a tendency toward underconfidence in their assessments. The authors suggest that this may be partly because of the nature of the audit process and the legal liability climate that surrounds it, and the training of auditors, which makes them particularly cautious and risk averse in making decisions (Tomassini et al., 1982). In other fields where experts may feel moral and professional responsibility, if not legal liability, for the consequences of their subjective judgments, one might expect to find a tendency to be conservative, or underconfident, in their assessments. A possible example of this mixing of probaaility assessments with consequences or objective functions is provided by a study in which physicians tended to overestimate and treat for the possibility of pneumonia (Christensen-Szalanski and Bushyhead, 1981). In the assessment literature such effects are referred to as "motivational bias."

Clinical psychology is one field where there is now substantial experimental evidence of over confidence in expert judgments. Goldberg (1959) found that clinical psychologists were no better than their secretaries at diagnosing brain damage from the results of the commonly used Bender Gestalt test. Oskamp (1982) asked subjects with no training and varying amounts of training in clinical psychology to study a detailed real case study and then choose one of five alternative responses of the individual in subsequent situations which had actually occurred. No significant variation in accuracy was observed across the subjects. On the basis of a review of these and a substantial number of similar studies, Faust (1985) concludes that there is little evidence to support the case that experience and expertise in clinical psychology improves performance on a wide range of such tasks, and that there is significant experimental evidence that they do not. Further, he concludes that significant evidence shows that clinical psychologists do not perform as well as simple actuarial analysis and that they do not, as they often claim, improve their performance by synthesizing a wide variety of separate pieces of evidence. In most cases their judgments can be predicted with very simple models. Dawes (1988) has found similar results in judgment tasks in other fields.

In addition to the significant number of studies in psychology there have been a handful of studies of expert judgments in the areas of business and military intelligence (Wallsten and Budescu, 1980) that show mixed but generally unimpressive performance.

Given the fairly dismal nature of performance of many experts on judgment tasks involving uncertainty, one could easily conclude that the judgments of experts are in general no better than those of nonexperts. This would be overly harsh. Discussing the findings for psychologists, Faust argues:

The problem is that psychologists must deal with an extraordinarily complex subject matter without the aid of a mature science. In branches or areas in which accurate judgments are possible, and these are fewer than most people believe, this success is not based on some unusual judgment power on the part of practitioners. Rather, success is primarily based on the availability of a well-developed science that provides established theory, precise measurements techniques, and prespecified procedures and judgment guidelines. Thus, less strain is placed on cognitive capacities, and one is far less often required to make the large inferential leaps common to psychology. These practitioners are correct more often not because of some intrinsic superiority in their cognitive abilities, but because their science makes it less necessary to exercise such abilities to achieve accurate judgments. (Faust, 1985)

We agree.

A good illustration of how such cognitive limitations can be reflected in even the most classical of hard sciences is provided by work one of us recently completed with Baruch Fischhoff. We examined the performance of physicists in assessing the uncertainty due to possible systematic errors in measurements of physical quantities (Henrion and Fischhoff, 1986). Our examination of historical measurements and recommended values for a number of fundamental physical constants revealed a consistent bias toward underestimating the actual errors. Figure 6.11 shows how the recommended values for the velocity of light have changed between 1929 and 1973. Examination of the individually reported experimental data yield an interquartile index of 41% for the entire time period 1875–1958, and a surprise index of 11% for the same time period, using the 1984 value as the "correct" value. Figure 6.12 shows similar time series for the recommended values for five other physical constants. All show a tendency to overconfidence.

In her Ph.D. thesis Theresa Mullin (1986) reported on a series of verbal protocol studies that she conducted using experts in the areas of electromagnetic field theory and ground water flows who answered technical questions in their own area of expertise, technical questions in the other area in which they were not expert, and a set of general knowledge almanac questions. The technical questions involved the elicitation of full subjective probability distributions and included both advance textbook-type questions as well as less structured "policy-type" questions. For example, the electromagnetic field experts were asked: "What is the *average* level of radio frequency power one would measure at the driver's seat of a tractor-trailer equipped with a transmitter CB radio in mW/cm^2?" Because they involved difficult tasks that could take experts many tens of minutes to work out, verbal protocols were collected for only six experts. Even then, analysis of the protocols presented a formidable task. The results of Mullin's analysis suggest there may be significant differences in the approaches to probabilistic estimation used by experts and nonexperts. She reports that the subjects, as experts, were far more serious and cautious about the tasks than as nonexperts. She found that experts tended to work forward from the estimation problem specification, elaborating on what is generally known or assumed about the quantity and the processes that determined its value. This often detailed discussion would include the identification of significant sources of uncertainty. Experts generally relied on their knowledge of the processes that would actually generate values for the quantity of interest in order to specify sophisticated process models used to compute values for the quantity. In contrast, nonexperts typically worked backward from quantities specified to

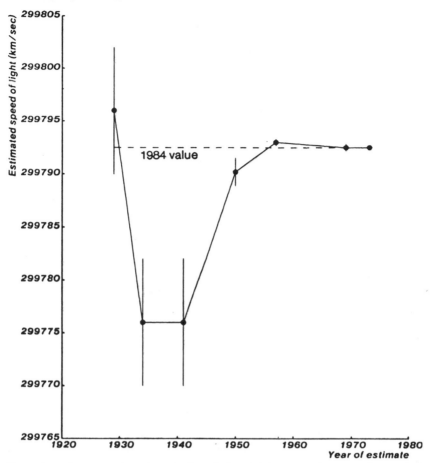

Figure 6.11. Recommended values for the velocity of light, along with reported uncertainties for the period 1929–1973 (Henrion and Fischhoff, 1986).

quantities they knew something about and could better estimate. If the more familiar quantities served to approximate values only at a more disaggregated level, the assessor would typically make use of a decomposition model. A best guess for the specified quantity would thus be produced by working from best guesses for a handful of simpler and more familiar quantities. This difference between expert and nonexpert estimation (by people who are experienced in the techniques of analysis) is reminiscent of differences reported by Larkin et al., (1980) and by Anderson (1982) in studies of expert and novice problem solvers. Even more extreme differences might be anticipated between experts and people who are not experienced in techniques of quantitative analysis such as problem decomposition.

Mullin found that both expert and nonexpert estimation of subjective probabil-

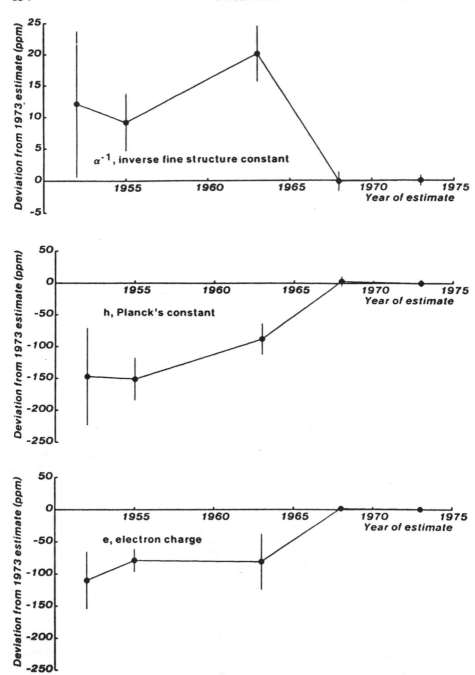

Figure 6.12.   Recommended values for five standard physical constants, along with reported uncertainties for the period 1952–1973 (Henrion and Fischhoff, 1986).

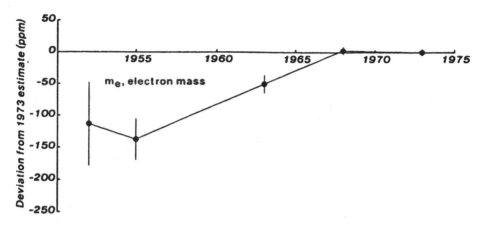

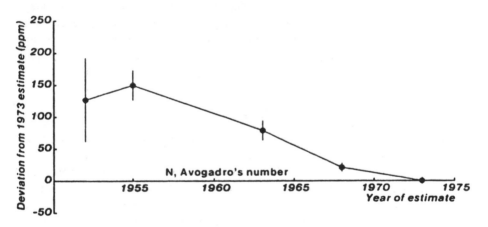

Figure 6.12. (cont.)

ity distributions involved using of the heuristic of anchoring and adjustment, but some of the applications made were quite different. Experts' adjustments from anchors to obtain quartile estimates appeared to involve as little deliberation as nonexperts' adjustments to obtain quartile values. In contrast, when anchoring and adjustment were used by experts to obtain extreme values, the amount of the adjustment was generally guided by their knowledge of the specified quantity, and other critically related factors. Mullin concluded that the significant difference she found between expert and nonexpert estimation behavior indicated that there are real limits to the extent to which one can make inferences about the probabilistic estimation behavior, including the response to debiasing, of experts based on the estimation behavior of nonexperts answering "general knowledge" questions.

How much assessors know about the quantity appears to affect not only the basic approach they take to estimation and the use of anchoring and adjustment, but also whether there may be a tendency to over- or underconfidence. Mullin reports that the effectiveness of debiasing questions in getting the assessor to reconsider his upper and lower bound estimates appeared to depend on the relevance of the question to the assessor's approach to estimating these extremes. Information seeking strategies such as asking why the value might be even higher, or asking for a scenario that might lead to more extreme values, appeared to work best when an information-based, or expert approach to estimation was being used. A counter-heuristic strategy, such as warning about surprises when anchoring and adjustment are used, appeared to be the most effective means of helping assessors using a minimal information, or nonexpert, approach to estimation of extremes. Mullin believes that in contrast to most nonexperts, expert assessors may not always have a tendency to overconfidence and that indiscriminate application of debiasing aimed at overconfidence may not be appropriate. On the other hand, it probably never hurts to encourage experts to think about alternative scenarios, although often they do so without encouragement. Nor, she concludes, is it ever likely to hurt to warn experts to be cautious in their use of anchoring and adjustment.

6.6. Conclusions

This chapter has made it clear that human judgments about uncertainty, or judgments made in the presence of uncertainty, frequently rely on a number of simple cognitive heuristics. Although in many circumstances these heuristics serve us well, they can also be the source of significant bias or even outright error. How significant these problems are is a strong but largely unknown function of both the subject area and the particular judgment tasks required. Although the experimental literature is not sufficiently refined to allow accurate predictions, problems appear more likely to arise in fields involving complex tasks with limited empirically validated theory. There is some evidence that asking for carefully articulated justification and reasons for and against judgments may improve the quality of judgments.

On the question of whether experts are different from nonexperts the situation is also unclear. The findings we have reviewed show that at least in some circumstances they can be. But what those circumstances are and how experts differ from nonexperts is far from clear. The experimental evidence provides no basis for believing that the problems of cognitive bias that can arise in the elicitation of expert subjective judgment are necessarily any less serious than those that have been documented with nonexpert subjects. The experiments we have reviewed clearly show the need for and importance of further studies of expert elicitation involving complex technical judgments of the sort regularly required in engineering–economic policy analysis. Until these studies are performed, one can only proceed with care, simultaneously remembering that elicited expert judgments may be seriously flawed, but are often the only game in town.

References

Alloy, L. B., and Tabachnik, N. (1984). "Assessment of Covariation by Humans and Animals: The Joint Influence of Prior Expectations and Current Statistical Information," *Psychological Review*, 91.

Alpert, M., and Raiffa, H. (1982). "A Progress Report on the Training of Probability Assessors," in Kahneman, Slovic, and Tversky, eds., *Judgment Under Uncertainty: Heuristics and Biases*, Cambridge University Press, New York.

Anderson, J. R. (1982). "Human Information Processing and Artificial Intelligence," lectures given at Carnegie Mellon University, Pittsburgh.

Armstrong, J. S., Denniston, W. B., and Gordon, M. M. (1975). "The Use of the Decomposition Principle in Making Judgments," *Organizational Behavior and Human Performance*, 14.

Bar-Hillel, M. (1979). "The Role of Sample Size in Sample Evaluation," *Organizational Behavior and Human Performance*, 24.

Barclay, S., and Randall, L. S. (1975). *Interactive Decision Analysis Aids for Intelligence Analysis*, Tech. Report Dt/TR 75-4, Decisions and Designs, Inc., McLean, Va.

Beach, B. H. (1975). "Expert Judgement About Uncertainty: Bayesian Decision Making in Realistic Settings," *Organizational Behavior and Human Performance*, 14:10–59.

Billings, R. S., and Schaalman, M. L. (1980). "Administrators' Estimations of the Probability of Outcomes of School Desegregation: A Field Test of the Availability Heuristic," *Organizational Behavior and Human Performance*, 26.

Brier, G. W. (1950). "Verification of forecasts expressed in terms of probability," *Monthly Weather Review*, 78:1–3.

Brown, R. V., Kahr, A. S., and Peterson, C. (1974). *Decision Analysis for the Manager*, Holt, Rinehart & Winston, New York.

Burns, M., and Pearl, J. (1981). "Causal and Diagnostic Inferences: A Comparison of Validity," *Organizational Behavior and Human Performance*, 28.

Christensen-Szalanski, J. J. J., and Beach, L. R. (1984). "The Citation Bias: Fad and Fashion in the Judgment and Decision Literature," *American Psychologist*, 39.

Christensen-Szalanski, J. J. J., and Bushyhead, J. B. (1981). "Physicians' Use of Probabilistic Information in a Real Clinical Setting," *Journal of Experimental Psychology: Human Perception and Performance*, 7, no. 4.

Cohen, J. L. (1981). "Can Human Irrationality be Experimentally Demonstrated?," in *The Behavior and Brain Sciences*, 4:317–370.

Dawes, R. M. (1988). *Rational Choice in an Uncertain World*, Harcourt Brace Jovanovich, San Diego, Calif.

de Finetti, B. (1974). *Theory of Probability*, 2 vols., Wiley, New York (translated from the Italian).

DeGroot, M. (1970). *Optimal Statistical Decisions*, McGraw-Hill, New York.

Edwards, W. (1968). "Conservatism in Human Information Processing," in B. Kleinmuntz, ed., *Formal Representation of Human Judgment*, pp. 17–52, Wiley, New York.

Einhorn, H. J., and Hogarth, R. M. (1978). "Confidence in Judgment: Persistence of the Illusion of Validity," *Psychological Review*, 85 no. 5.

EPP (Engineering and Public Policy)/Carnegie Mellon University Graduate Research Methods Class. (1983). "On Judging the Frequency of Lethal Events: A Replication," *Risk Analysis*, 3:11–16.

Estes, W. K. (1976). "The Cognitive Side of Probability Learning," *Psychological Review*, 83 no. 5.

Faust, D. (1985). "Declarations Versus Investigations: The Case for the Special Reasoning Abilities and Capabilities of the Expert Witness in Psychology/Psychiatry," *Journal of Psychiatry and Law* (Spring-Summer): 33–59.

Fischhoff, B., and MacGregor, D. (1982). "Subjective Confidence in Forecasts," *Journal of Forecasting*, 1.

Fischhoff, B., Slovic, P., and Lichtenstein, S. (1979). "Subjective Sensitivity Analysis," *Organizational Behavior and Human Performance*, 23:339–359.

Fox, J. (1980). "Making Decisions Under the Influence of Memory," *Psychological Review*, 87 no. 2.

Gettys, C., Michel, C., Steiger, J. H., Kelly, C. W., and Peterson, C. R. (1973). "Multiple-Stage Probabilistic Information Processing," *Organizational Behavior and Human Performance*, 10.

Goldberg, L. R. (1959). "The Effectiveness of Clinicians' Judgments: The Diagnosis of Organic Brain Damage from the Bender-Gestalt Test," *Journal of Consulting Psychologists*, 23:23–33.

Hampton, J. M., Moore, P. G., and Thomas, H. (1973). "Subjective Probability and Its Measurement," *Journal of the Royal Statistical Society*, 136.

Hazard, T., and Peterson, C. R. (1973). *Odds Versus Probabilities for Categorical Events*, Tech. Rept. 73-2, Decisions and Designs, Inc., McLean, Va.

Henrion, M. (1980). "Assessing Probabilities: A Review. Appendix 1," in M. G. Morgan, M. Henrion, and S. C. Morris, eds., *Expert Judgments for Policy Analysis*, BNL 51358, Brookhaven National Laboratories, Upton, N.Y.

Henrion, M., Fischer, G. F., and Mullin, T. (1989). "Divide and Conquer? The effect of decomposition on accuracy and calibration," Carnegie Mellon University, Department of Social and Decision Science, Pittsburgh.

Henrion, M., and Fischhoff, B. (1986). "Assessing Uncertainty in Physical Constants," *American Journal of Physics*.

Hession, E., and McCarthy, E. (1974). "Human Performance in Assessing Subjective Probability Distributions," University College, Dublin, Ireland.

Hoch, S. J. (1984). "Availability and Interference in Predictive Judgment," *Journal of Experimental Psychology: Learning, Memory and Cognition*, 10 no. 4.

Hogarth, R. M. (1975). "Cognitive Processes and the Assessment of Subjective Probability Distributions," *JASA*, 70 no. 350.

Howard, R. A., and Matheson, J. (1981). "Influence Diagrams," reprinted in Howard and Matheson, eds. (1984), *Readings on the Principles and Applications of Decision Analysis*, Strategic Decision Group, Palo Alto, Calif.

Kadane, J. B., Dickey, J. M., Winkler, R. L., Smith, W. S., and Peters, S. C. (1978). *Interactive Elicitation of Opinion for a Normal Linear Model*, Tech. Rept. 150, Department of Statistics, Carnegie Mellon Univeristy, Pittsburgh.

Kahneman, D., Slovic, P., and Tversky, A., eds. (1982). *Judgment Under Uncertainty: Heuristics and Biases*, Cambridge University Press, New York.

Kahneman, D., and Tversky, A. (1972). "Subjective Probability: A Judgment of Representativeness," *Cognitive Psychology*, 3:430–454.

Kahneman, D., and Tversky, A. (1973). "On the Psychology of Prediction," *Psychological Review*, 80 no. 4:237–251.

Keren, G. (1987). "Facing Uncertainty in the Game of Bridge: A Calibration Study," *Organizational Behavior and Human Decision Processes*, 39:98–114.

Koriat, A., Lichtenstein, S., and Fischhoff, B. (1980). "Reasons for Confidence," *Journal of Experimental Psychology: Human Learning and Memory*, 6 no. 2.

Larkin, J., McDermott, J., Simon, D. P., and Simon, H. A. (1980). "Expert and Novice Performance in Solving Physics Problems," *Science*, 208.

Lichtenstein, S., and Fischhoff, B. (1977). "Do Those Who Know More Also Know More About How Much They Know?," *Organizational Behavior and Human Performance*, 20:159–183.

Lichtenstein, S., and Fischhoff, B. (1980). "Training for Calibration," *Organizational Behavior and Human Performance*, 26:149–171.

Lichtenstein, S., Fischhoff, B., and Phillips, L. D. (1982). "Calibration of Probabilities: The State of the Art to 1980," in Kahneman, Slovic, and Tversky, eds., *Judgment Under Uncertainty: Heuristics and Biases*, Cambridge University Press, New York.

Lichtenstein, S., and Newman, J. R. (1967). "Empirical Scaling of Common Verbal Phrases Associated with Numerical Probabilities," *Psychonomic Science*, 9:563–564.

Lichtenstein, S., Slovic, P., Fischhoff, B., Layman, M., and Combs, B. (1978). "Judged Frequency of Lethal Events," *Journal of Experimental Psychology: Human Learning and Memory*, 4:551–578.

Lieblich, I., and Lieblich, A. (1969). "Effects of Different Pay-off Matrices on Arithmetic Estimation Tasks: An Attempt to Produce 'Rationality'," *Perceptual and Motor Skills*, 29:467–473.

Ludke, R. L., Strauss, F. F., and Gustafson, D. H. (1977). "Comparison of Five Methods for Estimating Subjective Probability Distributions," *Organizational Behavior and Human Performance*, 19:162–179.

Matheson, J. E., and Winkler, R. L. (1976). "Scoring Rules for Continuous Probability Distributions," *Management Science*, 22.

Morgan, M. G., Henrion, M., and Morris, S. C. (1980). *Expert Judgements for Policy Analysis*, Tech. Report prepared for U.S. Department of Energy under contract no. DE-AC02-76CH00016.

Morgan, M. G., Morris, S. C., Henrion, M., Amaral, D. A. L., and Rish, W. B. (1984). "Treating Technical Uncertainty in Policy Analysis: A Sulfur Air Pollution Example," *Risk Analysis*, 4, no. 3:201–216.

Mullin, T. M. (1986). "Understanding and Supporting the Process of Probabilistic Estimation," Ph.D. diss., Carnegie Mellon University, Pittsburgh.

Murphy, A. H. (1972). "Scalar and Vector Partitions of the Probability Score: Part I. Two-state Situation," *Journal of Applied Meteorology*, 11:273–282.

Murphy, A. H. (1974). "A Sample Skill Score for Probability Forecasts," *Monthly Weather Review*, 102:48–55.

Murphy, A. H., and Winkler, R. L. (1974). "Credible Interval Temperature Forecasting: Some Experimental Results," *Monthly Weather Review*, 102:784–794.

Murphy, A. H., and Winkler, R. L. (1977). "Reliability of Subjective Probability Forecasts of Precipitation and Temperature," *Applied Statistics*, 26.

Nisbett, R., and Ross, L. (1980). *Human Inference: Strategies and Shortcomings of Social Judgment*, Prentice Hall, Englewood Cliffs, N.J.

Oskamp, S. (1982). "Overconfidence in Case Study Judgments," in D. Kahneman, P. Slovic, and A. Tversky, eds., *Judgment Under Uncertainty: Heuristics and Biases*, Cambridge University Press, New York.

Pearl, J. (1978). "An Economic Basis for Certain Methods of Evaluating Probabilistic Forecasts," *International Journal of Man-Machine Studies*, 10:175–183.

Pickhardt, R. C., and Wallace, J. B. (1974). "A Study of the Performance of Subjective Probability Assessors," *Decision Sciences*, 5:347–363.

Pitz, G. F. (1974). "Subjective Probability Distributions for Imperfectly Known Quantities," in L. W. Gregg, ed., *Knowledge and Cognition*, Erlbaum, Hillsdale, N.J.

Raiffa, H. (1968). *Decision Analysis: Introductory Lectures on Choice Under Uncertainty*, Addison-Wesley, Reading, Mass.

Ramsey, F. P. (1931). "Truth and probability," in *The Foundations of Mathematics and Other Logical Essays*, R. G. Braithwaite, ed., Routledge & Kegan Paul, London.

Safer, G., and Tversky, A. (1985). "Languages and Designs for Probability Judgment," *Cognitive Science*, 9:309–339.

Savage, L. J. (1954). *The Foundations of Statistics*, Wiley, New York.

Savage, L. J. (1971). "Elicitation of Personal Probabilities and Expectations," *Journal of the American Statistical Association*, 66.

Schaefer, R. E. (1976). "The Evaluation of Individual and Aggregated Subjective Probability Distributions," *Organizational Behavior and Human Performance*, 17:199–210.

Schaefer, R. E., and Borcherding, K. (1973). "The Assessment of Probability Distribution: A Training Experiment," *Acta Psychologica*, 37:117–129.

Schlaifer, R. (1969). *Analysis of Decisions Under Uncertainty*, McGraw-Hill, New York.

Schlaifer, R. (1971). *Computer Programs for Elementary Decision Analysis*, Graduate School of Business Administration, Harvard University, Boston, Mass.

Schustack, M. W., and Sternberg, R. J. (1981). "Evaluation of Evidence in Causal Inference," *Journal of Experimental Psychology: General*, 110 no. 1.

Seaver, D. A. (1978). *Assessing Probabilities with Multiple Individuals: Group Interaction Versus Mathematical Aggregation*, Tech. Report SSRI-78-3, Social Science Research Institute, University of Southern California, Los Angeles.

Seaver, D. A., von Winterfeldt, D. V., and Edwards, W. (1978). "Eliciting Subjective Probability Distributions on Continuous Variables," *Organizational Behavior and Human Performance*, 21:379–391.

Selvidge, J. (1975). *Experimental Comparison of Different Methods of Assessing the Extremes of Probability Distributions by the Fractile Method*, Management Science Report Series, Report 75-B, Graduate School of Business Administration, University of Colorado, Boulder.

Sjoberg, L. (1982). "Aided and Unaided Decision Making: Improving Intuitive Judgment," *Journal of Forecasting*, 1 no. 4:349–363.

Slovic, P., and Fischhoff, B. (1977). "On the Psychology of Experimental Surprises," *Journal of Experimental Psychology: Human Perception and Performance*, 3 no. 4:544–551.

Smith, L. H. (1967). "Ranking Procedures and Subjective Probability Distributions," *Management Science*, 14 no. 4:236–249.

Spetzler, C. S. and Staël von Holstein, C-A. S. (1975). "Probability Encoding in Decision Analysis," *Management Science*, 22:3.

Staël von Holstein, C.-A. S. (1971). "An Experiment in Probabilistic Weather Forecasting," *Journal of Applied Meteorology*, 10:635–645.

Tomassini, L. A., Solomon, I., Romney, M. B., and Krogstad, J. L. (1982). "Calibration of Auditors' Probabilistic Judgments: Some Empirical Evidence," *Organizational Behavior and Human Performance*, 30.

Tversky, A., and Kahneman, D. (1971). "Belief in the Law of Small Numbers," *Psychological Bulletin*, 76 no. 2:105–110.

Tversky, A., and Kahneman, D. (1973). "Availability: A Heuristic for Judging Frequency and Probability," *Cognitive Psychology*, 4:207–232.

Vaurio, J. K. (1980). *PROSA2, and Probabilistic Response Surface Analysis and Simulation Code*, ANL/RAS-80-26, Argonne National Laboratory, Chicago, Ill.

von Winterfeldt, D., and Edwards, W. (1973). *Flat Maxima in Linear Optimization Models*, Tech. Report 011313-4-T, Engineering Psychology Laboratory, University of Michigan, Ann Arbor.

Wallsten, T. S., and Budescu, D. V. (1980). *Encoding Subjective Probabilities: A Psychological and Psychometric Review*, report to the Strategies and Standards Division of the U.S. Environmental Protection Agency, Research Triangle Park, N.C.

Winkler, R. L. (1967). "The Assessment of Prior Distributions in Bayesian Analysis," *Journal of the American Statistical Association*, 62.

Winkler, R L., and Murphy, A. H. (1968). " 'Good' Probability Assessors," *Journal of Applied Meteorology*, 7:751–758.

Winkler, R. L., Smith, W. S., and Kulkarni, R. B. (1978). "Adaptive Forecasting Models Based on Predictive Distributions," *Management Science*, 24 no. 10 (June): 977–986.

7   Performing Probability Assessment

"It sounded quite a sensible voice, but it just said, "Two to the power of one hundred thousand to one against and falling," and that was all.

Ford skidded down a beam of light and spun around but could see nothing he could seriously believe in.

"What was that voice?" shouted Arthur.

"I don't know," yelled Ford, "I don't know. It sounded like a measurement of probability."

"Probability? What do you mean?"

"Probability. You know, like two to one, three to one, five to four against. It said two to the power of one hundred thousand to one against. That's pretty improbable, you know."

A million-gallon vat of custard unended itself over them without warning.

"But what does it mean?" cried Arthur.

"What, the custard?"

"No, the measurement of improbability?'

"I don't know. I don't know at all."

Douglas Adams, *The Hitchhiker's Guide to the Galaxy*
Harmony Books, New York

The preceding chapter has clearly indicated that understanding of human judgment under uncertainty is still very incomplete. Although it is possible to identify some things one should and should not do in eliciting subjective expert judgments, many aspects of the design of an elicitation protocol must be dealt with as a matter of judgment and taste. In order to give readers some appreciation of the range of approaches that analysts have adopted, we begin with a farily detailed description of elicitation procedures that have been developed and used by three different groups working in somewhat different contexts. After examining this range of solutions, we summarize in Section 7.4 what we believe are the attributes of a "good" protocol for expert elicitation. We then investigate: the problem of experts who "can't or won't play the elicitation game"; problems arising from complexity and correlation; and the problem of multiple experts with different opinions. We conclude with a discussion of some of the limitations, problems, and risks we see in the use of elicited expert subjective judgment in quantitative policy analysis.

7.1. The Stanford/SRI Assessment Protocol

Of the various protocols for expert assessment described in the literature, the most influential has almost certainly been that developed by the group of decision analysts who operated in the Department of Engineering–Economic Systems at

141

Stanford University and at the Stanford Research Institute during the 1960s and 1970s. A summary of this protocol can be found in a paper by Carl S. Spetzler and Carl-Axel S. Staël von Holstein (1975). A more recent and detailed version, along with a sample session transcript, is available in an SRI report prepared by Staël von Holstein and James E. Matheson (1979).

The basic Stanford/SRI interview process consists of five phases labeled: motivating, structuring, conditioning, encoding, and verifying. During the *motivating* stage the analyst develops some initial rapport with the expert. The reason for the elicitation is discussed and the basic idea of probabilistic assessment is explained and justified. In a protocol for a DOE application closely modeled on the Stanford/SRI approach, Dean Boyd and Stephen G. Regulinski offer the following text as an abbreviated illustration of the kind of discussion that might take place during this phase of the process:

The fundamental purpose of the encoding task you are beginning is to represent explicitly the uncertainty about how a process with which you are familiar will look when it becomes technically feasible. A single-point or deterministic estimate cannot represent the range of possible outcomes. Yet it is the range, the possibility of good outcomes as well as bad ones, that makes R&D decisions difficult. Ignoring the range by using a single-point estimate does not make the decision easier, since one will be left wondering whether a different decision would have been made if a different single-point estimate had been used. It is not possible to determine what the "right" single-point estimate is. However, the right probability distribution is the one that best represents your state of information. (Boyd and Regulinski, 1979)

A second activity undertaken during the first motivating stage of the elicitation process is a systematic search for motivational bias, that is, an examination of the possibility that, for any of a number of possible reasons, experts may have a motivation to provide the analyst with an assessment that does not fully or accurately reflect their true beliefs. Boyd and Regulinski offer the following illustrations of circumstances that might contribute to motivational bias, using examples based on an R&D assessment task:

1. The person may want to influence a decision. For example ... a R&D manager might try ... to insure the funding of a desired program.
2. The person may perceive that he or she will be evaluated depending on the outcome. A person might overestimate the time to complete a specific research task to reap the credit of bringing it in early.
3. To appear to be knowledgeable or authoritative, a person may suppress uncertainty that is actually believed to be present. This type of motivational bias crops up frequently in the R&D process. Experts in different technologies feel that they should *know* what is happening (have no uncertainty) in their area of expertise. Thus, they consciously or subconsciously suppress uncertainty. (Boyd and Regulinski, 1979)

Finally, there may be motivational biases that arise from the fact that the expert has taken a strong public position on a question and is reluctant or unwilling to modify or undermine that position by producing a distribution that lends credence to alternative views.

If a significant possibility of motivational bias is found, it may be possible to overcome it either by changing the incentive structure the expert faces, or by disaggregating or otherwise restructuring the assessment task in such a way as to require judgments in which the bias is less likely to enter. There are, of course, limits to how much one can accomplish with such procedures. In our experience, the extent to which motivational bias is important varies considerably with problem and field.

The objective of the second phase of the Stanford/SRI protocol involves *structuring* the uncertain quantity to be elicited. The objective is to arrive at an unambiguous definition of the quantity to be assessed, stated in the form in which the expert will most likely be able to provide reliable judgments. It is important to determine whether there are conditioning factors that may significantly influence the value of the quantity, and if there are, to reach agreement on what values they will assume in the elicitation. Spetzler and Staël von Holstein suggest using the clarity test (see Section 4.2.3) to determine whether a quantity has been unambiguously defined by asking "whether a clairvoyant could reveal the value of the quantity by specifying a single number without requesting clarification. For example, it is not meaningful to ask for 'the price of wheat in 1975,' because the clairvoyant would need to know the quantity, kind of wheat, the date, the exchange, and whether you wanted to know the buying or the selling price. However, 'the closing price of 10,000 bushels of durum wheat on June 30, 1975 at the Chicago Commodity Exchange' is a well defined quantity." The problem of identifying conditioning variables or circumstances may often require some careful work. Boyd and Regulinski point out:

Quite often a person's probability assignments are conditional on a set of unstated assumptions. Thus, the conditional probability assignment does not properly reflect that individual's state of information. For example, a cost estimate might be made with the implicit assumptions that the base design will not change. However, the same person, when questioned about the likelihood of the base design's changing, might think such a possibility very likely. As another example, think of how a person's judgment on the likelihood of a nuclear moratorium might be affected by whether or not that individual implicitly assumed that there would not be a major nuclear accident. The typical response of individuals who realize their unstated assumptions are violated is "all bets are off." (Boyd and Regulinski, 1979)

In the process of defining the quantity that will be the focus of the assessment it is also important to choose a form corresponding to the nature of the expert's knowledge. The expert should not need to engage in units conversions or other mental gymnastics to answer the questions that will be posed. Sometimes this may require that the problem be reformulated and the expert's distribution be used as one input to a model in order to get the distribution on the quantity the analyst is actually interested in.

During the *conditioning* phase of the Stanford/SRI protocol the objective is to get the expert "conditioned to think fundamentally about his or her judgment and to avoid cognitive biases" (Spetzler and Staël von Holstein, 1975). The objective here is to get the expert to explain how he will go about making his probability judgments: what data sets and other information he has available and how he plans to make use of this information. Having done this, the expert is encouraged to consider other possible ways of thinking about, or getting insight on, the problem, and the analyst is instructed to look carefully for possible sources of cognitive bias and to plan his elicitation so as to minimize their possible impact. Boyd and Regulinski (1979) suggest one strategy that may be very useful during the conditioning phase of the protocol is to ask the expert to react to, and try to explain, various scenarios that lead to unexpected outcomes, or given such outcomes, to see if they can invent explanatory scenarios.

In the Stanford/SRI protocol there is some ambiguity about how much the expert is specifically told about the issue of judgmental heuristics and the cognitive biases they may produce. In their writings, Spetzler and Staël von Holstein place rather little emphasis on this, but some analysts, such as Warner North and Lee Merkhofer, who have come out of the Stanford/SRI tradition, place considerable importance on putting potential assessors through a series of warm-up exercises with almanac questions to demonstrate to them directly the operation of such cognitive biases as overconfidence (Morgan, Henrion, and Morris, 1980).

The fourth phase of the protocol involves the actual *encoding* of the expert probabilistic judgments. Spetzler and Staël von Holstein offer the following specific guidelines:

Begin by asking the subject for what he considers to be extreme values for an uncertain quantity. Then ask for scenarios that might lead to outcomes outside of these extremes. Also ask for the probabilities of outcomes outside of the extremes. The deliberate use of availability is designed to counteract the central bias that is otherwise likely to occur. Eliciting the scenarios for extreme outcomes makes them available to the subject, and he is thus more likely to assign higher probabilities to extreme outcomes. This has the overall effect of increasing the variability of his assigned distribution for the variable.

Next take a set of values and use the probability wheel to encode the corresponding probability levels. Do not choose the first value in a way that may seem significant to the subject, otherwise you may cause him to anchor on that value. In particular, do not begin by asking for a likely value and then encode the corresponding probability level. Make the first few choices easy for the subject so that he will be comfortable with the task. This means, for example, that you should begin by making the orange sector much smaller than what might actually correspond to the subject's probability. It is then easy for the subject to state which event is most likely and he becomes more comfortable with the procedure. Next, choose a sector that is much too large. After two easy choices there is generally no problem in homing in on the indifference point.

As you question the subject, plot each response as a point on a cumulative distribution and number them sequentially. An example is shown in Figure 7.1. This will point out any inconsistencies and will also indicate gaps in the distribution that need one or more additional points. Do not show the plotted points to the subject at the point in time. Otherwise, he may try to make subsequent responses consistent with the plotted points.

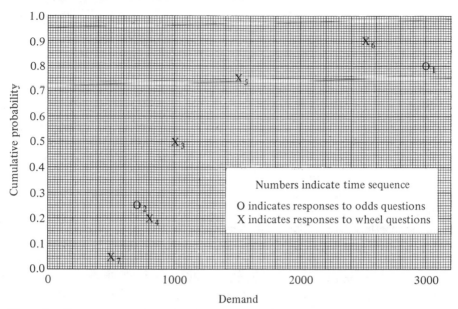

Figure 7.1. Example provided by Spetzler and Staël von Holstein (1975) of points on an elicited distribution.

Next, use the interval technique to generate values for the median and the quartiles. (Spetzler and Staël von Holstein, 1975)

Spetzler and Staël von Holstein are careful to point out that often during the encoding phase a subject's responses may "indicate a need to return to the tasks in the previous three phases. In particular there may be a need for further structuring when the subject's responses and arguments indicate that they are based on different underlying assumptions" (Spetzler and Staël von Holstein, 1975).

During the final *verifying* phase of the protocol the objective is to test the quantitative judgment the expert has provided to see if they in fact correctly reflect his or her beliefs. This can be done in a variety of ways. The results can be plotted both as a CDF and as a PDF and discussed with the expert. Various probabilistic statements can be constructed using the distribution and checked with the expert to see if he agrees. One way to do this is in the form of bets. If disagreement between the expert's views and the elicited distributions are found, one should cycle back through the appropriate phases of the protocol in order to elicit corrections.

While the Stanford/SRI protocol provides a good systematic approach to most of the issues that are important in expert elicitation, it is by no means the only, and in some contexts arguably not always the best, way to approach the problem of expert elicitation. To give some sense of alternative approaches, and suggest that similar ends can be reached through a number of different strategies, Sections 7.2 and 7.3 describe two other carefully designed protocols for expert elicitation that have been employed in large studies of problems involving air pollution health effects.

7.2. A Protocol We Have Used

During the period from 1980 through 1982 the two of us, along with several colleagues, undertook a project designed to demonstrate the use of expert subjective judgment in a real policy problem in which there was a considerable range of different opinions among experts (Morgan et al., 1984). The problem involved estimating the mass balance of sulfur during long-range transport in the plume of large coal-fired power plants located in the Ohio River Valley of the northeastern United States and then estimating the regional health impacts, if any, that might result from human exposure to the sulfur air pollutants. As part of this effort we conducted detailed elicitation sessions with nine leading atmospheric scientists and seven leading health experts. This section provides a description of the protocol we employed. The discussion includes a fair amount of detail about the specific technical issues involved in these elicitations because in this, as in most cases, problem specifics are of great importance and should be allowed to shape the elicitation procedures that are employed. In short, expert elicitation is not an activity that can be antiseptically isolated from the substance and the broader process of policy analysis. Rather, it should be treated as an integral part of that process, being modified and adapted as the needs of the specific problem dictate.[1]

Our interviews with atmospheric science experts were conducted in the summer of 1980. There are two groups of atmospheric scientists with expertise that was relevant to our problems: (1) those involved in the study of sulfur air pollution transport and conversion processes, and (2) those involved in the study of loss processes. The uncertainty in both these areas is important, but until very recently the first had received considerably more attention. We chose to conduct a series of formal interviews with a group of transport/conversion experts first. We decided to construct our own model and subjective distributions for loss process, on the basis of a careful reading of the literature and informal consultation with individual experts, and then to perform sensitivity analysis on our conclusions before deciding whether a round of formal interviews with loss experts would also be necessary.

To prepare for the interviews with the transport–conversion experts we reviewed the technical literature carefully, focusing particularly on the previous five years, and prepared a working paper that consisted of one- or two-page

---

1. Much of the discussion of this section is drawn directly from our paper "Technical Uncertainty in Quantitative Policy Analysis: A Sulfur Air Pollution Example" (Morgan et al., 1984).

summaries of approximately forty of the most important journal articles, along with a simple graphical comparative summary of the results reported in all of these articles. Copies of our review and summaries were mailed to all the experts before we made our visits. On the basis of our reading of the atmospheric chemistry literature and our conversations with selected experts, we chose about a dozen experts who we believed represented the current range of expert opinion. Because we did not plan to combine the experts' opinions or the resulting model outputs in any way, we were concerned only with obtaining a full representation of views and not with the problem of selecting a sample that weighed alternative views in a "representative" fashion. After travel and other schedules had been coordinated, we ended up with a set of nine experts: A. J. Alkezweeny, R. C. Easter, J. Forrest, N. V. Gillani, D. A. Hegg, R. B. Husar, T. V. Larson, L. Newman, and S. E. Schwartz.

In our interviews with sulfur health effects experts, conducted in 1981, we felt it was important to have representation from several different fields. After a similar review of the literature, and a series of consultations with experts, we ended up with a set consisting of two inhalation toxicologists, M. Amdur and R. Frank; two epidemiologists, B. Ferris and F. Speizer; and three researchers who have studied historical mortality records with techniques such as regression: S. Bozzo, L. Lave, and F. Lipfert.

Both the atmospheric science and the health effects experts were assured they would not be identified with individual distributions or results in any of our published work. Accordingly, in all subsequent discussion the experts are referred to by arbitrarily assigned numbers, which do not correspond to alphabetical order.

We felt that for several reasons it was essential to provide our experts with a detailed briefing on the current state of understanding of the processes and problems of human judgment about uncertainty. Accordingly, in consultation with Baruch Fischhoff, we prepared a sixty-page briefing book that allowed us to review this material with our experts in about half an hour (Morgan, Henrion, and Morris, 1980). We doubt that seeing this material had much effect on the responses obtained, but we think the briefing process was important for several reasons. It helped the experts to understand why we approached the actual elicitation process in the way we did. It helped to establish rapport with the experts and indicate that we were trying to do as careful and as complete a job as we could. And it helped us satisfy the obligation we felt as professional colleagues to inform the experts about the problems and pitfalls of elicitation before we got them involved.

Interviews were conducted at the experts' home institutions under circumstances that in most cases allowed full access to files and data. The protocol involved roughly five distinguishable parts. We spent the first ten or twenty minutes explaining the background of our work and describing the analysis in which we were engaged. We then spent approximately a half hour with the briefing book reviewing pertinent psychological literature. Most of our experts showed interest in this material; several got very interested and asked many questions.

The third part of the interview process consisted of an extended technical discussion, which lasted in all cases for at least an hour and often lasted for several hours. We wanted to learn how the expert saw the history and current status of the field, which evidence he viewed as most compelling, and the factors and functional relationships that he felt were important. Discussions often got down to the specific details of individual papers. Two and sometimes three of us took extensive notes. However, in order to promote frank discussion and assure anonymity, the sessions were not recorded.

As the technical discussion began to come to a close we gradually moved into the fourth stage of the interview, which focused on structuring the elicitation. In interviews with atmospheric scientists we explained that most of our health impact estimates would probably be given to us in terms of annual average dose and that hence our interest was in computing annual average exposure. We explained that we were prepared to do this either with a model that used a single annual average oxidation rate or with some more disaggregated model that involved variables such as time of day, amount of sunlight, season, time of flight or distance downwind from the stack, atmospheric characteristics and so on. We were careful to make it clear to each atmospheric expert that we were prepared to build a model that reflected his views and that he should specify the structure with which he felt most comfortable. Thus, for example, while all experts chose to express their views about average oxidation rates in terms of first order rate coefficients, they were explicitly told they need not do so.[2] We explained to health experts that we were interested in whatever short-term or chronic models of mortality and/or morbidity they could supply for sulfur dioxide, primary sulfate, primary combustion aerosols, secondary sulfate, or any combination of these. We were purposely vague about the details of our atmospheric models and indicated a willingness to attempt to construct whatever kind of exposure model their health effects model required. However, as we had anticipated, all the quantitative health effects models obtained were for chronic exposure to total sulfate aerosol measured on an annual average concentration basis.

Once an overall model structure had been established, we began the fifth and final stage of the interview: the actual elicitations. This generally required between one and two hours. From each atmospheric expert we elicited a subjective probability distribution that characterized his views about the fraction

---

2. If this exercise were repeated today, because of the changed state of scientific understanding, several might now adopt more complex models.

of sulfur emitted as primary sulfate particulates. All experts chose to make this judgment on an annual average basis. We then elicited distributions for whatever additional coefficients were necessary to implement the expert's chosen model. The models obtained from health effects experts were considerably more diverse and are discussed in the next section.

In order to overcome the effects of overconfidence brought on by the heuristic of anchoring and adjustment (see Section 6.1), we never began an elicitation by asking for "best value" or other midrange judgments. Rather we began by establishing the maximum and minimum credible values. In each case we asked the expert to justify his response. Then we asked him to pretend that he had been away from the field for several years and that when he returned, he learned that the actual value was known to lie just outside the limit he had given. We asked if he could, on the basis of his current knowledge, invent any plausible explanation for such a finding. After such consideration, an expert sometimes revised his upper or lower value.

Once the range was established we reiterated the details of the specific coefficient under consideration and then elicited cumulative probability values for intermediate points by asking questions such as: "What do you believe is the probability that the average value of this oxidation rate is greater than (or less than) 4% per hour?" Points were chosen in arbitrary order and the experts were asked to try not to think about their previous answers but, to the extent possible, to treat each question independently. The resulting distributions, which the experts were not allowed to see while the elicitation was in progress, showed a remarkable degree of consistency and smoothness. When, on rare occasion, we got inconsistent or noisy results, we would ask additional questions, sometimes shifting to elicitation of values given fixed probabilities. Any remaining inconsistencies in the elicitated distribution were then resolved in subsequent conversation with the expert when we reviewed with him the plot of the results.

To aid experts in their probabilistic judgments we used a standard probability wheel. In the first several elicitations we also used the classic lottery formulations of decision analysis, but abandoned these when it became apparent that our experts, all of whom were well skilled in probability theory, found this to be a confusing and unnecessary encumbrance. After a few tries several people abandoned the probability wheel, preferring to give numbers directly. Atmospheric expert seven insisted that he wanted to draw probability density functions directly, and after some discussion we let him do this. It is interesting that this expert displayed greater confidence (i.e., narrower distributions) than the others. Our protocol was designed to focus on avoiding overconfidence, and the narrower distributions produced by this expert may be due in part to the departure from the protocol. Atmospheric expert nine, while he answered in terms of cumulative distribution functions, restricted his answers to probabilities

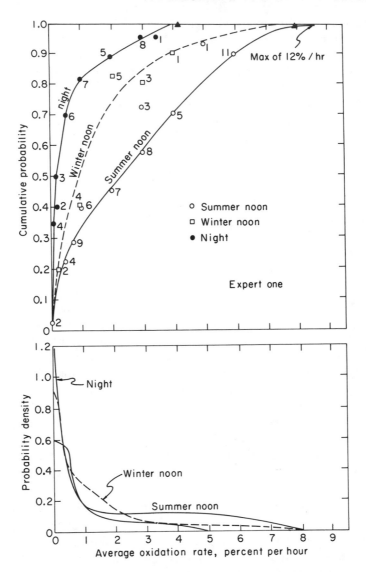

Figure 7.2. Subjective probability density functions (below) and cumulative distributions (above) for average oxidation rates provided by atmospheric expert one. Unlike some other experts this expert specified only one distribution to characterize average night rates for all seasons. He provided additional information on how to handle diurnal and seasonal variation. Points indicated in the upper plot are the original data points, numbered in the order they were elicited. The "scatter" in the points is similar to that for atmospheric experts five and nine, and greater than that for all other atmospheric experts (Morgan et al., 1984).

of 1%, 10%, 25%, 50%, 75%, 90%, and 99% because he didn't believe he was capable of making finer distinctions.

All of the nine atmospheric experts and five of the seven health effects experts gave us some distributions or other quantitative information. Seven of the nine atmospheric experts and four of the seven health effects experts gave us complete usable probabilistic models. The others were, for different reasons, reluctant or unable to supply probabilistic models at the time of our interview, and because their reasons were good, we did not press them. However, although they did not yield full sets of distributions, several of these interviews were among the most technically productive that we held.

After completing all of our interviews, we collectively reviewed our notes. Then each of the five of us took a set of copies of the original data sheets and, while consulting the notes, sketched in a smooth curve for each distribution. The results were compared and the handful of discrepancies were resolved collectively. These curves were then digitized and computer plots of both density functions and cumulative density functions were produced. An example of the full set of plots for average oxidation rates provided by atmospheric expert one is reproduced in Figure 7.2. The upper cumulative distributions also reproduce the original data points. The numbers indicate the order in which the points were elicited. The "scatter" in the elicited data points for this expert is similar to that for three other experts and greater than that for the remaining experts.

Each expert who had produced a complete set of distributions was asked to review the plots of his distributions and to provide various clarifications. In several cases we performed a variety of computations to aid the expert in evaluating the distributions and the model he had specified. After seeing the smoothed plots of their distributions, several experts made minor modifications, which, after face-to-face or telephone consultations, we adopted.

The models that the various experts provided were quite different. In the case of the mass balance portion of the problem we were able to construct a single general model framework that could then be modified to reflect the individual views of each expert. A brief description of this model framework is in Morgan et al. (1984) and more detail is in Morgan et al. (1982). Figure 7.3 summarizes the full set of distributions we obtained from the atmospheric scientists, and Table 7.1 summarizes the ways in which the various models they specified differed. There was far less consistency among the forms of the models proposed by the various health experts, and it turned out to be necessary to construct separate stochastic simulation models to reflect each expert's view. An example of the distributions obtained to implement one of the simpler of these models is shown in Figure 7.4. Others can be found in Amaral (1983) or Morgan et al. (1982).

Because this chapter is concerned with the subject of elicitation we will not discuss here the details of the modeling and stochastic simulation we performed

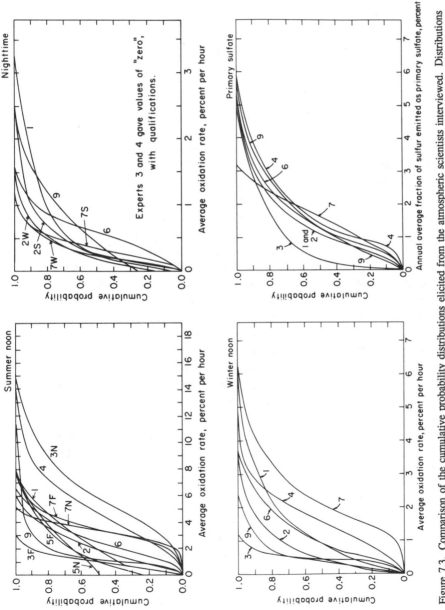

Figure 7.3. Comparison of the cumulative probability distributions elicited from the atmospheric scientists interviewed. Distributions for summer noon, winter noon, and night are for average oxidation rates in percent per hour. Numbers refer to experts. Letters refer to specific conditions and are: N = near, F = far, S = summer, and W = winter. Additional details, such as instructions on how to handle diurnal and seasonal variations, and specifics of range or stability dependencies specified by some experts, are not shown. Distributions of primary sulfate are for the percent of all sulfur emitted by the plant that is emitted as sulfate (Morgan et al., 1984).

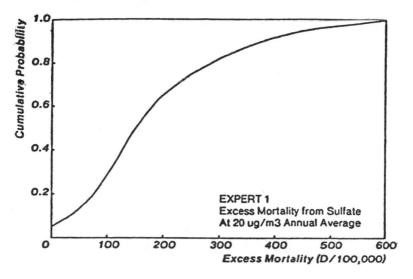

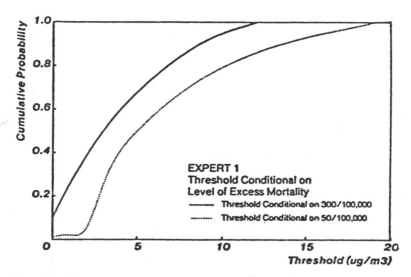

Figure 7.4. Example of elicited distributions obtained to implement health effects functions of one of the sulfur air pollution health effects experts. This particular model involves a linear dose-response function with an uncertain threshold whose distribution is conditional on the uncertain value of the slope. See Amaral (1983) or Morgan et al. (1982) for more detail.

to make use of these distributions. An example of the kinds of results obtained is illustrated in Chapter 4 (see Figure 4.2). Note that in this particular problem the variation in final outcome across the range of opinions of atmosphere scientists is small compared with the variation across the range of health effects experts (Morgan et al., 1984).

Table 7.1. *Summary of the models and subjective distributions supplied by the nine atmospheric science experts interviewed*

			Night Rate		
Expert	Summer noon rate	Winter noon rate	Summer and winter treated separately	Single distribution for all seasons	Notes
1	I	I		I	
2	I	I	I		
3	D	D		"zero"	Summer noon rate varies with flight time. Winter noon rate scales from summer rate.
4	D	D		"zero"	Rates depend on stability class. Night rates are zero unless in-cloud processes occurs.
5	D	–	–	–	
6	I	I		I	
7	D	I	I		Summer noon rate varies with flight time.
8	D	–	–	–	
9	I	I		I	Winter noon rate scaled from summer noon rate.

I = Single distribution. Average value treated as independent of flight time, stability, etc.
D = Multiple distribution. Values given are conditional on flight time and/or stability.
– = Expert was unwilling or unable to provide a distribution.

7.3. The Wallsten/EPA Protocol

As discussed in Section 2.2, the Office of Air Quality Planning and Standards (OAQPS) of the U.S. Environmental Protection Agency has been working on the problem of incorporating uncertainty in expert scientific judgments into their standard setting process for the "criteria" air pollutants. In 1984, in the context of the OAQPS review of the lead standard, Thomas S. Wallsten of the University of North Carolina and Ronald G. Whitfield of Argonne National Laboratory undertook the task of interviewing two sets of health science experts to obtain expert subjective judgments in the form of probability density functions on lead-induced hemoglobin decrements and IQ decrements. A 15 page protocol document (see appendixes in Wallsten and Whitfield, 1986) was developed for the experts to read before the interview began. This document outlines the basic objective of the set of elicitation interviews and describes the kind of information desired, the population at risk, the physiological conditions to be considered, and the set of biological and physical factors the experts should consider while providing their answers. This is followed by a fairly detailed discussion of mental strategies and heuristics and of some of the difficulties these can lead to. The document begins by exploring the fact that people consider information sequentially rather than in parallel and points out that the order of consideration can lead to anchoring and in this way influence conclusions. It explores the effects of memory on judgment, and discusses issues of overconfidence. It warns against the danger of confusing the probability of an event and its severity. Finally, it suggests that when providing estimates that involve rare events or unlikely situations, it is probably best to respond in terms of odds. The discussion concludes as follows:

Although extensive and careful training would be necessary to eliminate all the problems mentioned above, some relatively simple suggestions can help minimize them. Most important is to be aware of one's natural cognitive biases, and try consciously to avoid them. To avoid *sequential effects* keep in mind that the order in which you think of information should not influence your final judgment. It may be helpful to actually note on paper the important facts you are considering and then to reconsider them in two or more sequences. Try to keep an open mind until you have gone through all the evidence, and don't let the early information you consider sway you more than is appropriate.

To avoid *memory effects*, define various classes of information that you deem relevant, and then search your memory for examples of each. Don't restrict your thinking only to items that stand out for specific reasons. Make a special attempt to consider conflicting evidence, and to think of data that may be inconsistent with a particular theory. Also, be careful to concentrate on the given probability judgment and not let your own values (how you would make the decision yourself) affect those judgments.

To accurately *estimate the reliability of information,* pay attention to such matters as sample size and power of statistical tests. Keep in mind that data are probabilistic in nature, subject to elements of random error, imprecise measurements, and subjective evaluation and interpretation. In addition, the further one must extrapolate, or generalize, from a particular study to a situation of interest, the less reliable is the conclusion and the less certainty should be attributed to it. Rely more heavily on information which you consider more reliable, but do not treat it as "absolute truth."

Keep in mind that *the importance of an event or an outcome should not influence its judged probability.* It is rational to let the costliness or severity of an outcome influence the point at which action is taken with respect to it, but not the judgment that is made about the outcomes' likelihood.

Finally, in making probability judgments, think primarily in terms of the measure (probability or odds) with which you feel most comfortable, but sometimes translate to the alternative scale, or even to measures of other events (e.g., the probability of the event not happening). When estimating very small or very large likelihoods, it is usually best to think in terms of odds, which are unbounded, instead of probabilities, which are bounded. For example one can more easily conceptualize odds of 1:200 than a probability of .005. (Wallsten and Whitfield, 1986)

In the final section of the protocol the specific health end point about which judgments will be sought is precisely defined and the process of how the elicitation interview will proceed is outlined in some detail. At several stages the expert is given some choice in the form that his or her responses will take,

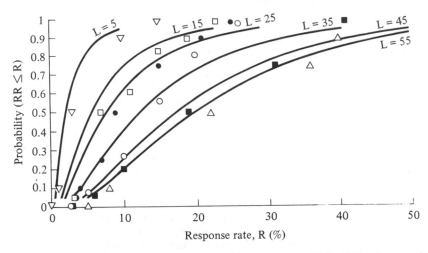

Figure 7.5. Example of an expert's judgments of the percentage of U.S. children between the ages of zero and three who have lead-induced hemoglobin levels that are less than or equal to 9.5 g/dL, conditional on various levels of blood-lead (L) in μg/dL. Distributions were elicited by Wallsten and Whitfield (1986).

but because of the nature of the use that is planned for the results, the questions posed are somewhat more constrained than the questions that we posed to the sulfur health effects experts described in the preceding section.

Five experts on hemoglobin were interviewed: J. Julian Chisolm, Bernard Davidow, Paul Hammond, Sergio Piomelli, and John Rosen. Six experts on IQ were interviewed: Kim Dietrich, Claire Ernhart, Herbert Needleman, Michael Ratter, Gerhard Winneke, and William Yale. In both cases, after the initial session the results were plotted and then presented to the expert in a second session for his consideration and possible revision. The actual elicitations followed much the same procedure as described in Section 7.2. They began each elicitation by obtaining a large, plausible response rate interval, used various methods to quantify judgmental probabilities in that interval, and employed a variety of consistency checks. For each expert a series of distributions was elicited conditional on the blood lead level. Smooth curves were then analytically fit to these. An example is shown in Figure 7.5. After consulting with the expert and obtaining an agreement on this final representation, these analytical representations were then used in all subsequent analyses. Figure 7.6 provides summary plots of all the results obtained for hemoglobin and IQ decrement.

In several EPA/CASAC meetings, Warner North has argued that although excellent, the Wallsten and Whitfield protocol does not place as much emphasis as it might on getting experts to articulate their reasons for the judgments they make, or on documenting these reasons. North has argued that such

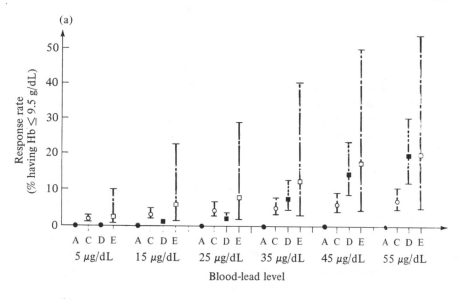

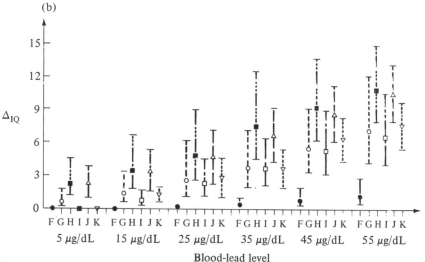

Figure 7.6. (a): Comparison of median and 90% confidence levels on expert judgments about lead-induced hemoglobin effects for children aged zero to three obtained by Wallsten and Whitfield (1986) in elicitations of four of their experts. (b): Similar results obtained from six experts on decrements in IQ as a function of blood-lead level for a population with a low socioeconomic status.

argumentation is important if the full benefits of elicitations are to be available to the standards-setting process, and he has urged that more attention be directed at developing such material in future EPA-sponsored elicitations.

7.4. The Attributes of a "Good" Protocol

Given that there is no single correct protocol for expert elicitations and that somewhat different designs may be better in different specific contexts, how should one choose a protocol when faced with the need to perform expert elicitation? Since there has been relatively little formal empirical evaluation of alternative approaches, in most cases it is not possible to argue that one approach clearly outperforms another in terms of specific objective measures. To a significant degree the choice of the detailed structure of the protocol is a matter of professional judgment. However, such a judgment must be exercised within the bounds of what is now a fairly broad consensus in the professional community about the general attributes – if not the specific details – of a "good" elicitation protocol.

First, and most important, the process of expert elicitation must never be approached as a routine procedure amenable to cookbook solutions. The most important requirement for success is taking things seriously. The elicitor must devote adequate time and attention to careful thought and planning, and must remain alert to potential problems or unusual developments throughout the process. Each elicitation problem considered a special case and should be dealt with carefully on its own terms. In our view there is no surer route to problems than a "quick and dirty" elicitation.

Second, the expert should be given some introduction to the general task of elicitation, and specifically to what is known about the psychology of judgments made in the face of uncertainty. At minimum this should take the form of a brief explanation of the literature on heuristics and cognitive bias and an opportunity to discuss the subject in greater depth if the expert is interested. If it seems appropriate, it may also take the form of some hands-on trial exercises such as warm-up assessments performed with "encyclopedia questions" on some familiar quantity, such as a commute time or the time to get served lunch. This familiarization process is important: one, it helps satisfy the need for "informed consent," so that before they get involved, the experts know something about people's ability to make the kinds of judgments they themselves will be asked to make, and two, it helps explain to the experts why the elicitation process will proceed in the way it does. Finally, if the familiarization with the subject of expert judgment is done well, it can also play the important role of conveying to experts an understanding that the elicitors are serious about the process and are approaching it in a careful professional manner. As seen in Chapter 6, whether practice and trial elicitations also serve the role of improving calibration is in general unclear, and almost certainly depends critically on the elicitation task.

Third, the subject matter about which the expert is to make judgments should be the focal point of the process. The elicitor or one or more members of the eliciting team should themselves have a reasonably complete understanding of this subject matter. The process of elicitation should be viewed as one that helps an expert construct a set of carefully reasoned and considered judgments. This is more likely to succeed if there can be a real technical discussion with pointed give-and-take that allows the expert to sharpen and refine his thinking. It is particularly important to get the expert to lay out the full set of evidence available, explain why he does and does not place confidence in different data and interpretations, and explore and elaborate his perspective and possible biases with respect to the field. When possible, it is best not to define the quantities that will be elicited too precisely *before* the interview process begins. Rather the analyst should explain to the expert roughly what it is that he thinks he needs to learn and enlist the expert's help in refining and giving precise definition to the model and to the quantity that will be elicited. As the discussion proceeds, a variety of the specific techniques, such as "clairvoyant questions," as discussed in preceding sections, may prove useful. It is important that the specific quantity to be elicited be defined in such a way that the expert is able to apply his knowledge as directly and as fully as possible, without intervening mental transformations.

Fourth, once the model and the quantity that is to be elicited are reasonably well defined, it is important to use techniques such as those discussed in preceding sections to:

- refine the definition of the quantity that will be elicited until it is unique and unambiguous,
- examine any unstated assumptions the expert is making,
- look for correlation with, or dependency on, the value of other variables and if it exists deal with it appropriately.

This process, and other critical thinking, should not stop once the actual elicitation has begun. If problems come up during the elicitation, as from time to time they will, the elicitation should be stopped and the problems resolved.

Fifth, the actual elicitation process should follow the general procedures outlined in our description of the three example protocols. To overcome anchoring and overconfidence, one should begin by exploring the upper and lower limits of the values that the quantity of interest can assume. Kahneman and Tversky (1979) have suggested a tactic for avoiding the effects of the overconfidence bias by decomposing the assessment procedure. For many unknown quantities it is possible to distinguish two kinds of information: *Distributional data* give base-rate information about the distribution of the general class of quantities to which the one currently of interest belongs. *Singular data* give diagnostic information that relate to this particular case. When possible they suggest starting from the base distribution and using statistical theory rather than intuition to adjust it for singular data for the particular case.

In eliciting points on the distribution, it is probably best to: randomize the order of the points that are considered; work largely with fixed value questions, switching sometimes to fixed probability, interval, or other questions for clarification and crosschecking; use a probability wheel, at least in the early stages of the process; try to get the expert to consider each point as a separate judgment and for this reason not display the results to the expert during elicitation; when the elicitation is over show the expert the results plotted both as a cumulative distribution function and as a probability density function and go through them systematically together in order to confirm that they correctly reflect the expert's views, and, if they do not, make appropriate revisions. Many techniques already described in this chapter can be helpful in these tasks. However, more important than any of these specifics is the importance of remembering to *think*: Keep the basic objectives and common dangers in mind, use common sense, and be flexible. For example, an expert who is very familiar with subjective probability should be treated differently from one who has little experience. If an expert insists he wants to draw distributions directly, work with him to try to get him to go through the same systematic justifications required in other elicitation procedures.

Instead of trying to induce assessors to be well calibrated by careful elicitation or by training, one might accept poor calibration as a fact of life and attempt to correct for it subsequent to encoding. Calibration curves, which may be compiled from answers to a set of test questions, can be used as functions to map from assessed distributions (discrete or continuous) to well-calibrated ones. Recalibration shares two problems with training for calibration: A considerable number of test questions are needed to draw up a reliable calibration curve, and it may be hard to find test questions similar to the real questions of interest.

A third potential problem is that an intially coherent set of assessments may be rendered incoherent by recalibration. This might be alleviated by the process of *reconciliation* proposed by Lindley, Tversky, and Brown (1979), which uses systematic readjustments to restore coherence to incoherent assessments. Finally, there is the sticky problem that if assessors find out they are being recalibrated – that their opinions are not being taken at "face value" – they are likely to resent it and also may change their calibration, producing a vicious circle of mutual distrust between elicitors and assessors. Perhaps for these reasons we have been unable to find reports of the practical use of recalibration in the decision analysis literature, although we have found examples from particle physics: In experimental determinations of the masses and lifetimes of elementary particles, a degree of overconfidence bias has been empirically demonstrated from the lack of agreement between experiments relative to their reported "standard error." Such reported estimates of standard error are systematically increased by the compilers of particle data tables to adjust for this (Roos et al., 1975).

7.5. Experts Who "Can't or Won't Play the Elicitation Game"

Most analysts who have had substantial experience in expert elicitation have encountered experts who:

1. despite their best efforts, and the best efforts of the analyst to help them, cannot bring themselves to make the judgments needed to perform elicitation, although they agree in principal that such an activity is appropriate, or
2. feel that the quality and nature of the knowledge available is so poor or incomplete that as responsible scientists they do not have an adequate basis upon which to make a judgment.

These two situations are different, but we suspect that, at least in part, similar considerations underlie both. Many scientific experts appear to have fundamental misgivings about whether the kinds of judgments required of them in expert elicitation for policy analysis are consistent with their conception of the norms of proper scientific professional behavior. In their view, good scientists should not take a position on what "the answer" is until they actually have the evidence in hand to make the case unambiguously. There is, however, a very big difference between taking a position on what *the* answer is and identifying the *range* or distribution of answers that might turn out to be correct. Indeed, scientists frequently make judgments of precisely this kind when they decide which theories to develop or which experiments to do next.

Although this argument is logically persuasive, we have found scientists who, while intellectually convinced, found themselves culturally or esthetically unable to put probabilities on things. They understood the arguments in their head, but their gut wasn't persuaded. On the basis of what is really quite a small sample of experiences, we hypothesize that such reactions are more common among professions like biology, toxicology, and medicine that tend to take a more qualitative approach to the world. However, we have also encountered problems among quantitatively skilled physical scientists who were prepared to advance detailed arguments about why all sorts of alternatives might be possible, but who were unwilling or unable to provide any reasonable estimate of the likelihood that any one of them corresponded to actuality. Among engineers we have encountered the least reluctance to play the elicitation game. The culture of engineering places considerable weight on getting the job done with whatever tools are at hand, and so engineers seem to find the need for expert elicitation easier to accept and are more comfortable making the judgments required.

Some of these problems may be diminished if it is possible to provide the expert with anonymity. Since the believability of the results depends on knowing that the experts truly are expert, total anonymity is typically not possible. However, partial anonymity, in the sense of listing the experts but not linking them with their individual distributions, is usually possible. Even in a public sector decision environment, such as analysis by the EPA Office of Air Quality Planning and Standards, in support of the development of U.S. air pollution standards, it has been possible to provide this level of anonymity. Although we believe that such partial anonymity is important to protect the expert and minimize possible peer pressures and motivational biases, it may be of limited usefulness in overcoming the reluctance of experts who feel uncomfortable about participating in elicitation.

Depending on the circumstance of the elicitation there are a number of ways in which, in the words of our Carnegie Mellon colleague Jay Kadane (personal communication, 1987), an analyst can "turn up the heat" on an expert. You can go through a series of arguments to show that answering the questions will not violate the expert's scientific integrity. You can point out that some decisions have to be made before all the scientific facts are in hand, and ask if the expert would really feel better if people with less scientific understanding of the problems than they provided the scientific judgments on which society bases it decisions. You can try to make it clear that in this framework, probability is not a statement about the real world but is, rather, a statement about the expert's belief. You can point out that scientists often informally make such judgments in the pursuit of their own work, and sometimes, as in the case of the Particle Data Group (Rosenfeld, 1975; Henrion and Fischhoff, 1986), make them formally. You can make general arguments about the social responsibilities of professionals and specific arguments about the responsibilities that come with public research support. And you can simply persist until it becomes easier for the expert to cooperate than continue to resist. Despite all such efforts there will probably always be a few who can't or won't play. However, while they may not provide distributions for use in the analysis, they may nevertheless provide rich insights about the nature of the problem that can be of great use in other aspects of the analysis. In our own experience, time spent with experts who did not ultimately produce usable distributions has rarely been time wasted.

Are there problems in which understanding is so inadequate that an approach based on the use of subjective probability is simply not justified? The question can be posed at two levels: at a basic philosophical level and at the level of practical analysis.

A hard-line Bayesian would answer the philosophical question with a resounding no. Others would argue that there are at least a few circumstances in which one is completely ignorant, that is, in which one has no knowledge that can logically be used as the basis for constructing a subjective judgment. Some would further argue that this situation is *not* equivalent to a statement that they assign a uniform probability across all possible states of the world. Instead, they would simply say they don't know.

Much as it may be instructive and fun to argue these philosophical points, the answer one reaches is not particularly important for most of the questions that experts are actually asked to answer in the context of practical policy analyses. With few exceptions, there is at least some limited knowledge relevant to the question at hand. Thus, the real question in performing applied analysis is whether there is some point beyond which the experts' and analysts' efforts to perform an analysis based on subjective probability distributions are no longer worth the insight that the results provide. We believe the answer to this latter question is yes. When the level of understanding is low enough, parametric analysis, simple-order-of-magnitude analysis, or bounding analysis may furnish as much or more insight, with considerably less effort, as a more complex analysis based on distributions elicited from experts. Of course, some limited subjective judgments will still be required if one is going to make choices and take policy action, but such judgments will typically be rather simple. In trying to decide whether a particular problem warrants an approach that makes use of elicited probability distributions, the analyst must make a judgment about how much insight or resolution such an approach is likely to add. Sensitivity analysis can often help make this decision. It is important to remember that the objective is to provide insight and a basis for more informed policy decisions – not flashy-looking complicated results. Analysts must resist the temptation to undertake full probabilistic analysis if the extra effort seems unlikely to lead to significantly better insight or more informed decisions, might needlessly antagonize the community of experts, or might unnecessarily complicate or confuse those who will employ the analytical results.

7.6. Issues of Complexity and Correlation

As we noted in Chapter 6, one of people's important cognitive limitations is an inability to think in a detailed way about correlation without considerable analytical assistance. When an expert's knowledge is sufficiently rich, it is feasible to deal with some limited correlation structures as part of an elicitation problem. For example, a health expert may be able to answer questions about the slope of a linear health effects function conditional on the value that a threshold assumes. Figure 7.4 provides one such set of curves, which we elicited from an expert on the health effects of sulfur air pollution. Some experts may also be able to provide distributions involving a high number of conditioning variables if the value of those variables are all assumed to lie essentially at the values they had in studies the expert or others have conducted. These issues were examined at greater length in Section 6.4.6. The problem of providing expert judgments on the shape of probability distributions over more than one or two dimensions involves very similar cognitive difficulties. Although, as we noted in Section 6.4.7, some work has been done to develop procedures to elicit natural conjugate priors for multivariate normal distributions (Kadane et al., 1978) and for multinomial distributions (Challoner and Duncan, 1987), we doubt that in most situations experts have the cognitive ability to make the required judgments reasonably. The only option we can see in such circumstance is to try to restructure the problem so as to reduce the dimensionality of the assessments required. If the dimensionality of the problem cannot be reduced, you may at least be able to model the correlation structures so that the expert does not have to do this in his or her head.

7.7. Multiple Experts with Different Opinions

What should you do when, more frequently than not, there are a number of experts with different judgments about the same quantity or modeling problem? Many people's immediate reaction is to start looking for ways to combine the judgments. There is a substantial literature addressing the technical issues involved in combining expert judgments. However, before we worry about such technical details, a number of higher level questions should be considered.

If true experts after careful elicitations produce different conclusions, this provides important information about the problem that should not be quickly discarded. The analyst should first try to understand *why* the different experts reach different conclusions. Are there different disciplinary perspectives involved? Do different experts interpret the world with different theoretical models? Are there disagreements about the validity of various experiments or data sets? Have some experts ignored evidence that other experts consider very important? Are their motivational biases operating? Are some (or all) of the experts just not very "expert"? Are the questions being posed simply impossible for human experts to answer? Careful, honest consideration to these questions may lead the analyst to various reformulations of the analysis or back for further consultations with the experts.

Having concluded that there are legitimate differences of opinion among experts, the analyst should then examine the extent to which this range of opinions has important consequences for the results. If the range of opinions has no significant consequences for the model outcome, combining expert opinions to obtain some representative average view is clearly justified and involves no significant loss of information in the analysis. This, for example, was the case for the opinions of atmospheric science experts when drawing conclusions about health impacts in the example presented in Figure 4.1 (for details see Morgan et al., 1984). If, on the other hand, the range of experts' opinions has major consequences for the model outcome, as was the case for the health effects experts in the sulfur air pollution example presented in Section 7.2, then in most cases the experts' opinions should not be combined just to produce some "average" result.

Faced with a diversity of opinions that really matter in terms of their consequences for the results of the analysis, the analyst is faced with the choice of getting the experts to interact to see if the disagreements can be reduced, performing the analysis parametrically across experts, or, if it can be justified, choosing among or combining experts.

Considerable attention has been given to whether to encourage interaction among the group of experts, and, if so, what kind of interaction. Research in social psychology has examined the effect of groups on the formation and modification of individual opinions. There is some evidence that work in groups can provide advantages in creative problem-solving, but also considerable evidence that, for probability assessment, face-to-face interaction between group members can create destructive pressures of various sorts, such as domination by particular individuals for reasons of status or personality unrelated to their ability as probability assessors (Myers and Lamm, 1975).

Many degrees of group interaction have been tried in various group probability assessment techniques. At one end of the spectrum the group meets face-to-face and has unrestricted discussion until it reaches a consensus, as in a jury. At the other end is the so-called *Delphi* method, in which participants do not meet and interaction is restricted to the exchange of anonymous assessments, sometime supplemented by reasons for opinions (Dalkey, 1969; Linstone and Turoff, 1975). The interchange of assessments may be repeated three or four times and usually produces some convergence of opinion. An intermediate method is the *nominal group technique*, in which participants present their initial judgments, independently arrived at, and then discuss them in a structured format designed to prevent anyone's dominating the proceedings (Gustafson et al., 1973). The final assessments are made individually and aggregated mathematically, as in Delphi.

Using primarily almanac-type questions, a number of studies have compared these techniques and variations on them, but have found little or no differences between them, depending partly on the scoring rule used to evaluate the results (Gustafson et al., 1973; Fischer, 1975; Gough, 1975; Seaver, 1978). At least in these experiments, interaction of any kind seems to have increased overconfidence and so worsened calibration. Seaver (1978) found that simple mathematical aggregation with no interaction at all produced the best results, although he points out that the experts have more faith in assessments achieved through face-to-face interaction, which may be of practical importance in persuading them to accept the results of the analysis. One study raises doubts about how far we can safely generalize from these findings using almanac-type questions to real-world tasks. Brockhoff (1975), using bankers as subjects, found that although on almanac questions they did better with Delphi than face-to-face interaction, on questions within their domain of expertise (economics) they did better with face-to-face interaction. As with Mullin's results discussed in Chapter 6, these results raise serious questions about the extrapolation of findings from almanac studies to judgments made by experts. Clearly this issue requires further study.

In some fields, especially in the natural sciences and engineering, experts know all or most of their colleagues and are intimately familiar with their arguments both from published papers and from previous meetings. In such circumstances interactions may produce some modest refinements, and may have the nontrivial consequence of helping the analyst understand much more clearly the nature of the disagreements, but are unlikely to produce major shifts in the experts' theoretical interpretations or their evaluations of available data.

Alternatively, one can simply treat the experts separately and perform the analysis parametrically across experts. When different experts have specified different models as well as different coefficient values, this also entails running a series of alternative models. The set of results will indicate how the model(s) conclusions depend on the range of expert opinions. In performing such an analysis, it is useful to try to obtain the views of a set of experts who in some sense span the full range of serious expert opinion. In choosing such a range there is often the question of how many experts and how to choose them. There is no hard and fast answer. Enough experts are needed to represent the major alternative expert views. Unless one plans to combine the results by treating all experts as having equal weight, and averaging across the resulting model outputs (a procedure we believe is frequently not justified), there is no need to obtain a sample of expert opinions that is representative of the numbers of experts who hold the various views represented.

Keeping experts separate through the analysis allows one to understand the consequences of the range of their opinions for the model outcomes. If, however, one must make a decision, after observing this range, some choices may be necessary. In some cases it may be possible to identify policies that are robust in the sense that they do not display great sensitivity to the range of possible model outcomes. If a choice among probable outcomes must be made, one should still try to identify policies that allow for future flexibility in case it turns out that the choice of expected outcome was not correct.

A Bayesian decision analytic perspective would argue that faced with a variety of experts, a decision maker should assess his own confidence in the judgment of each and then incorporate the alternative model outcomes in a decision analytic framework that weights them by these assessed confidences. Too frequently in the literature it has been assumed that this combining will be done on the *inputs* to models. However, if combining is to be done, this may not always be the proper place to do it. The analyst must look carefully at the underlying assumptions of the experts and the associated model(s) before deciding whether and how to proceed.

In a situation where an analyst has decided that combining judgments can be justified, a large number of alternative procedures might clearly be used. Hogarth (1977) and Seaver (1978) have provided reviews. The simplest approach is the "opinion pool" method which involves forming a weighted arithmetic mean of the component probabilities. The weights may be chosen by the analysts to reflect their opinion of the relative expertise of the assessors, or may be based their self-ratings. Dalkey (1970) reports that self-rating can produce better results than equal rating. Other empirical studies (Winkler, 1971; Seaver, 1978) have found little or no difference in the performance of various differential weighting schemes over simple equal weighting; there are also theoretical reasons for expecting low sensitivity to variations in the weighting schemes for simple linear combinations with nonzero weights (Einhorn and Hogarth, 1975; Wainer, 1976).

Winkler (1968) suggests a Bayesian perspective in which the probabilities assessed by the experts represent new sample evidence for analysts that should be used to update their priors. Morris (1977) generalizes this approach by adding a *calibration function* that represents the analysts' opinions of each assessor's normative expertise. This function is to be used to transform each expert's assessment into a calibrated prior. Analysts then derive a composite posterior simply from the normalized product of the experts' calibrated priors with their own. Although this technique has good conceptual justification, it has not yet found practical application, probably because of the complex judgments it requires. Application is easier if one can assume that the experts' opinions are probabilistically independent, but such a condition is unlikely to be met in real situations because the expert judgments will be influenced by the same sources of information and biases. Future work may reduce these restrictions, but a problem then may be how to assess the forms of dependence among the experts.

Seaver (1978) found that the results of Bayesian aggregation methods were considerably less well calibrated (more overconfident) than the simpler linear averaging schemes, as well as being harder to use. Combining the opinions of multiple experts may not necessarily lead to a better estimation of the uncertainty, depending on the aggregation method used, but there is good reason to believe that the result will be more informative about the central value than using the assessment of a single expert (Winkler, 1971; Seaver, 1976), which is usually more important.

Although in private contexts the formal combination of expert judgments is always possible, if not always appropriate or meaningful, it becomes very awkward in open public sector applications. For example, in the United States, because of the "sunshine laws" agency-standard setting is largely open to public scrutiny. The administrator of the EPA, or his surrogate, is likely to have difficulty publicly saying that he finds Dr. Jones's views six times more credible than Dr. Smith's views, although he or his staff may, of course, think such things. Naturally, weighting of expert opinions and their predicted consequences does occur in public sector decision contexts, but the process tends to be more subtle and verbal in nature. A good example is the EPA's 1981 criteria document on sulfur air pollution (EPA, 1982), which basically dismisses the large epidemiological studies that are based on mortality statistics. No formal weights were assigned, but the effect was the same.

Faced with public decision-making environments in which, for a variety of reasons, the decision makers cannot make formal quantitative evaluations of the alternative expert views or their consequences, the analyst can help by performing parametric analysis that allows the decision maker to work the problem backward, that is, to see the consequences of a range of possible alternative combinations or weightings. Because the public decision maker must often informally factor in a number of other considerations,[3] it is rarely of great practical consequence that a more formal treatment in the combining or weighting of alternative expert views is not possible.

7.8. Limitations, Problems, and Risks

We view the use of expert subjective judgment in quantitative policy analysis as an extremely important tool, which in many cases is clearly preferable to all available alternatives, but some potential limitations and problems with the technique also deserve mention.

First, the use of elicited expert subjective judgment is not a substitute for proper scientific research. Expert judgment can be helpful in policy analysis when decisions must be made before all the necessary science is known. In most cases, however, having made initial decisions on the basis of expert judgment, one should follow up with the appropriate science, to ensure that in the future, policy is more firmly rooted in physical reality. However, quantitative policy analysis based on elicited expert judgments can look very complicated and technical. In environments such as regulatory agencies dominated by nontechnical people more concerned with "answers" than with scientific truth, and in environments where the daily press of agency business results in a short time-constant and in a rather low priority for research, there is a real risk that the widespread adoption of techniques based on subjective expert judgment can reduce pressures to obtain research output, and thus result in a diminished investment in needed research. We do not think the answer lies in limiting the use of expert judgment. Rather, those who use expert judgment have an obligation to link its use continually to the need for research. Several steps to encourage appropriate investments in research can be routinely incorporated into analysis. For example, one can explicitly perform value of information calculations, and explicitly assess research progress that has been

---

3. Some of these considerations, like economic impacts in the case of ambient air quality standards, can be handled only informally because, although they must be considered, the legal decision framework does not allow their consideration. Others must be considered informally because they are politically too touchy to treat explicitly.

made since previous policy analysis activity was undertaken on the problem at hand.

The second issue involves the need for strict quality control. Because the results of full probabilistic analyses using elicited subjective expert judgment can easily get complicated, there is a strong temptation in some policy analytic contexts to use these techniques to produce "snow jobs." In the long run we believe this problem can be adequately handled through the standard processes of peer review. This means, however, that peer review should be more uniformly extended to policy focused research and analysis than it has been in the past. It also means that analysts have an obligation to be critical of work they consider substandard. Failure to exercise appropriate norms of quality control could lead to the techniques' acquiring a bad name in some circles and could significantly impede their wider adoption. As more and more examples of high-quality analysis based on such techniques become available, this risk will diminish.

The third issue involves problems with the experts being elicited. Great care must be taken not to alienate experts, particularly by involving them in slipshod assessments and applications. This especially applies to fields where the number of true experts is quite limited and the level of policy concern very high. Even if not put off by a poor experience, there is a limit to the amount of time an expert wants to spend in elicitation activities. If the first one or two analysts who perform elicitations do not do a good job, or take an overly structured approach, the result could be a refusal by some experts to participate in all future elicitation activities. Although specific arrangements, such as pooled efforts among analysts, may ease this problem in some contexts, in general we see no solution to this potential problem other than the application of high professional standards among practicing analysts. Just as good outdoorsmen don't leave trash behind on their trail, good analysts should try hard not to leave alienated experts behind on their "trail."

Finally, it seems to us important to develop institutions and traditions that protect experts who participate in elicitation from subsequent legal or other entanglements. So far, EPA through its Office of Air Quality Plannning and Standards has set an excellent example by providing partial anonymity to participating experts. Agencies need to continue to pay careful attention to these issues so that experts will not be scared off from participating in this enormously valuable approach to quantitative policy analysis.

References

Amaral, D. A. L. (1983). "Estimating Uncertainty in Policy Analysis: Health Effects from Inhaled Sulfur Oxides," Ph.D. Thesis, Department of Engineering and Public Policy, Carnegie Mellon University, Pittsburgh.

Boyd, D., and Regulinski, S. G. (1979, June). *Characterizing Uncertainty in Technology Cost and Performance*, Project Number 1114, Decision Focus Incorporated, Menlo Park, Calif.

Brockhoff, K. (1975). "The Performance of Forecasting Groups in Computer Dialogue and Face-to-Face Discussion," in *The Delphi Method: Techniques and Applications*, Addison-Wesley, Reading, Mass.

Challoner, K. M., and Duncan, G. (1987). "Some Properties of the Dirichlet Multinomial Distribution and its Use in Prior Elicitation," *Communication in Statistics: Theory and Methods*, 16:511–523.

Dalkey, N. C. (1969). "The Use of Self-Ratings to Improve Group Estimates," *Technological Forecasting* 12:283–291.

Dalkey, N. C. (1970). *The Delphi Method: An Experimental Study of Group Opinion*, Tech. Report RM-5888–PR, Rand Corporation, Santa Monica, Calif.

Einhorn, H. J., and Hogarth, R. M. (1975). "Unit Weighing Schemes for Decision-Making," *Organizational Behavior and Human Performance*, 13:171–192.

EPA (1982, December). *Air Quality Criteria for Particulate Matter and Sulfur Oxides*, Environmental Criteria and Assessment Office, Office of Research and Development, U.S. Environmental Protection Agency, Research Triangle Park, N.C., EPA 600/8-82-029.

Fischer, G. (1975). *An Experimental Study of Four Procedures for Aggregating Subjective Probability Assessments*, Tech. Report 75-7, Decisions and Designs, Inc. Washington, D.C.

Gough, R. (1975). "The Effects of Group Format on Aggregate Subjective Probability Distributions," *Utility, Probability, and Human Decision-Making*, Reidel, Dordrecht, Holland.

Gustafson, D. H., Shukla, R. K., Delbecq, A., and Walster, G. W. (1973). "A Comparative Study of Differences in Subjective Likelihood Estimates Made by Individuals, Interacting Groups, Delphi Groups, and Nominal Groups," *Organizational Behaviour and Human Performance*, 9:200–291.

Henrion, M., and Fischhoff, B. (1986). "Assessing Uncertainty in Physical Constants," *American Journal of Physics*, 54 no. 9 (September): 791–798.

Hogarth, R. M. (1977). "Methods for Aggregating Opinions," Fifth Research Conference on Subjective Probability, Utility, and Decision-Making, Reidel, Dordrecht, Holland.

Kadane, J. B., et al. (1978). *Interactive Elicitation of Opinion for a Normal Linear Model*, Tech. Report 150, Department of Statistics, Carnegie Mellon University, Pittsburgh.

Kahneman, D., and Tversky, A. (1979). "Intuitive Prediction: Biases and Corrective Procedures," *TIMS Studies in Management Sciences*, 12:313–327.

Lindley, D.V., Tversky, A., and Brown, R. V. (1979). "On the Reconciliation of Probability Assessments," *Journal of the Royal Statistical Society Series A V 142, Part 2*, pp. 146–180.

Linstone, H., and Turoff, M. (1975). "The Delphi Method: Techniques and Applications," Addison-Wesley, Reading, Mass.

Morgan, M. G., Amaral, D., Henrion, M., and Morris, S. (1982). *Technological Uncertainty in Policy Analysis*, final report to the NSF Division of Policy Research and Analysis on Grant PRA-7913070, (NTIS document PB83165142).

Morgan, M. G., Henrion, M., and Morris, S. C. (1980). *Expert Judgment for Policy Analysis*, report of an invitational workshop held at Brookhaven National Laboratory, July 8–11 1979, to explore problems and research needs in eliciting and using subjective probabilistic expert judgments for policy analysis involving energy and environmental systems (Brookhaven National Laboratory, BNL 51358).

Morgan, M. G., Morris, S. C., Henrion, M., Amaral, D. A. L., and Rish, W. R. (1984). "Technical Uncertainty in Quantitative Policy Analysis: A Sulfur Air Pollution Example," *Risk Analysis*, 4 (September): 201–216.

Morris, P. A. (1977). "Combining Expert Judgements: A Bayesian Approach," *Management Science*, 23, no. 7:679–693.

Myers, D. G., and Lamm, H. (1975). "The polarizing effect of group discussion," *American Scientist*, 63:297–303.

Roos, M., et al. (1975). "A New Procedure for Averaging Particle Properties," *Physica Fennica*, 10:20–33.

Rosenfeld, A. H. (1975). "The Particle Data Group: Growth and Operations – Eighteen Years of Particle Physics," *Annual Review of Nuclear Science*, 25:555–598.

Seaver, D. A. (1976). *Assessment of Group Preferences and Group Uncertainty for Decision-Making*, Tech. Report 76-4, Social Science Research Institute, University of Southern California, Los Angeles.

Seaver, D. A. (1978). *Assessing Probabilities with Multiple Individuals: Group Interaction vs. Mathematical Aggregation*, Tech. Report SSRI-78-3, Social Science Research Institute, University of Southern California, Los Angeles.

Spetzler, C. S., and Staël von Holstein, C.-A. S. (1975). "Probability Encoding in Decision Analysis," *Management Science*, 22, no. 3.

Staël von Holstein, C.-A. S., and Matheson, J. E. (1979). *A Manual for Encoding Probability Distributions*, SRI International, Palo Alto, Calif.

Wainer, H. (1976). "Estimating Coefficients in Linear Models: It Don't Make No Nevermind," *Psychological Bulletin* 83:213–217.

Winkler, R. L. (1968). "The Consensus of Subjective Probability Distributions," *Management Science*, 15 no. 2: 1105–1120.

Winkler, R. L. (1971). "Probabilistic Prediction: Some Experimental Results," *Journal of American Statistical Association*, 66:675–685.

Wallsten, T. S., and Whitfield, R. G. (1986, December). "Assessing the Risks to Young Children of Three Effects Associated with Elevated Blood-Lead Levels," ANL/AA-32, Argonne National Laboratory, Argonne, Ill.

8　The Propagation and Analysis of Uncertainty

8.1. Introduction

Suppose we have constructed a model to predict the consequences of various possible events and decisions. And suppose further we have identified various uncertainties in the inputs. How can we propagate these uncertainties through the model to discover the uncertainty in the predicted consequences? If the uncertainties are substantial, we may not immediately be able to make definitive recommendations about what decision is "best." But we should be able to obtain useful insights about the relative importance to our conclusions of the various assumptions, decisions, uncertainties, and disagreements in the inputs. These can help us decide whether it is likely to be worthwhile gathering more information, making more careful uncertainty assessments, or refining the model, and which of these could most reduce the uncertainty in the conclusions. In this chapter, we examine various analytic and computational techniques for examining the effects of uncertain inputs within a model. These include:

- methods for computing the effect of changes in inputs on model predictions, i.e., *sensitivity analysis,*
- methods for calculating the uncertainty in the model outputs induced by the uncertainties in its inputs, i.e., *uncertainty propagation,* and
- methods for comparing the importance of the input uncertainties in terms of their relative contributions to uncertainty in the outputs, i.e., *uncertainty analysis.*

A considerable variety of such methods have been developed, with wide differences in conceptual approach, computational effort required, and the power of their results. When developing and analyzing a particular model, it can be difficult to decide which of these methods are most appropriate for the problem at hand. There have been a number of discussions and comparisons of these techniques in the literature (Cox, 1977; Ahmed, Metcalf, and Pegram, 1981; Cox and Baybutt, 1981; Jackson, Hokenbury, and Yeater, 1981; Martz et al., 1983; Fiksel, Cox, and Ojha, 1984; Whitfield and Newsom, 1984; Iman and Helton, 1988). But they seem to have come to dismayingly divergent conclusions about the relative merits of these techniques. This can be at least partly explained by the differences among the kinds of models and problems each study was concerned with. Clearly no one method is always best; the choice should depend on both the nature of the problem and the resources available to the analyst. In this chapter, our objective is to provide an introduction and general review of the principal techniques, an assessment of their relative advantages

172

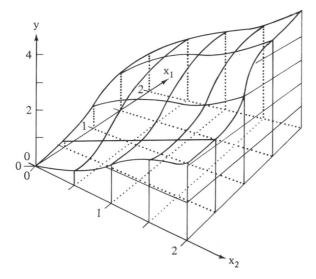

Figure 8.1. An example of a response surface as a function of two inputs, that is, $y = f(x_1, x_2)$.

and disadvantages, and some guidance on how to select techniques appropriate to particular situations.

8.2. Basic Concepts

Before turning to a more detailed review of these techniques, we introduce and illustrate some of the basic concepts using a simple example. Readers who are interested in only an introduction to the general arguments, without the details necessary for actual use, may wish to read this section, then skip to the final section on selecting a method. Students, practitioners, and users of analysis will find details about specific methods in the intervening sections.

Consider a model represented as a function, f, with two uncertain inputs, x_1 and x_2, and one output, y.

$$y = f(x_1, x_2)$$

We will assume both uncertain inputs are empirical quantities, that is, measurable, at least in principle, and so uncertainty about them can legitimately be represented by probability distributions.

Figure 8.1 shows a perspective drawing of such a function. The two inputs are represented by the two horizontal dimensions, and the output is represented by the vertical dimension. The surface displays directly how the value of y changes with variations in the values of its inputs, and is sometimes termed a *response surface*.

A *scenario* is a particular situation, specified by a single value for each input variable. It defines a single point on the response surface. We can describe a scenario as a vector of values for the inputs, for example:

$$X = (x_1, x_2)$$

Let us start by defining a nominal or "base-case" scenario, which consists of a single *nominal value* for each input. These are our initial "best guess" values for the inputs. Each might be the mean, median, or most likely (i.e., mode) values of the full probability distribution. But usually we will choose them before thinking much about the entire range or distribution. Indeed, we may never even get as far as assessing the full distribution.

Let us denote these nominal input values x_1^0 and x_2^0. Together these two input values specify the *nominal scenario*:

$$X^0 = (x_1^0, x_2^0)$$

The corresponding nominal output value is defined as:

$$y^0 = f(x_1^0, x_2^0)$$

The analysis of uncertainty involves measuring the degree to which each input x contributes to uncertainty in the output y. A method to quantify this may be termed a *measure of uncertainty importance*, which we will denote by $U(x, y)$. We will define a number of such measures, roughly in order of increasing sophistication. Perhaps the simplest measure of uncertainty importance is *sensitivity*, that is, the rate of change of the output y with respect to variation in an input x. The two sensitivities in this case are the partial derivatives, of output y with respect to each input. These derivatives are evaluated at the values of the nominal scenario, as indicated by the subscript X^0 after each:

$$\left[\frac{\partial y}{\partial x_1}\right]_{X^0}, \left[\frac{\partial y}{\partial x_2}\right]_{X^0}$$

These sensitivities, illustrated in Figure 8.2, are shown as the slopes of the two tangents to the response surface at the nominal scenario, along the two vertical planes parallel to each of the horizontal axes. Thus, we define simple sensitivity as our first measure of uncertainty importance:

$$U_S(x, y) = \left[\frac{\partial y}{\partial x}\right]_{X^0}$$

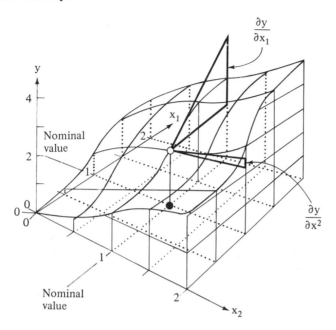

Figure 8.2. Example of a sensitivity analysis using the slopes of y with respect to the inputs x_1 and x_2 evaluated at their nominal values.

One problem with simple sensitivity for comparing the uncertainty importance of different inputs is that it depends on the scale, or units of measurement, of x and y. Sensitivity to an input measured in millimeters will be a thousand times greater than sensitivity to the same input measured in meters. It seems desirable that importance measures should be unaffected by the units of measurement. A simple way to achieve this is to normalize the sensitivity, defining the changes in x and y in relative terms, as a fraction of their nominal values. The *normalized sensitivity* is defined as the ratio of the relative change in y induced by a unit relative change in x (e.g., the percent change in y induced by a 1 percent change in x). This measure of uncertainty importance is sometimes also known as *elasticity*:

$$U_E(x, y) = \left[\frac{\partial y}{\partial x} \right]_{X^0} \times \frac{x^0}{y^0}$$

A drawback of considering only the slopes of the response surface, as do simple sensitivity and elasticity, is that they ignore the degree of uncertainty in each input. An input that has a small sensitivity but a large uncertainty may be just as important as an input with a larger sensitivity but smaller uncertainty. The simplest approach to uncertainty analysis that considers both sensitivity and uncertainty is generally known as first order approximation or, *Gaussian approximation*, after Gauss, who is credited with developing this approach. Let us express the degree of uncertainty in each input x by its *standard deviation*, σ_x. We can then measure its contribution to the output uncertainty, that is, its *uncertainty importance*, as the product of its sensitivity and uncertainty, more specifically as the product of the partial derivative and standard deviation:

$$U_G(x, y) = \left[\frac{\partial y}{\partial x}\right]_{X^0} \sigma_x$$

(Using subscript G for Gauss.)

This is appealing because we can use this measure directly for uncertainty propagation, that is, to estimate the uncertainty of the output. The variance of the output, $\mathrm{Var}[y] \equiv \sigma_y^2$ is estimated as the sum of the squares of the contributions from each input. Denote the variance of each input by $\mathrm{Var}[x_1] \equiv \sigma_1^2$ and $\mathrm{Var}[x_2] \equiv \sigma_2^2$. Then the variance of the output is given by the Gaussian approximation as:

$$\mathrm{Var}[y] \approx \left(\left[\frac{\partial y}{\partial x_1}\right]_{X^0}^2 \mathrm{Var}[x_1]\right) + \left(\left[\frac{\partial y}{\partial x_2}\right]_{X^0}^2 \mathrm{Var}[x_2]\right) \tag{10}$$

Thus the total uncertainty in the output, expressed as variance, is explicitly decomposed as the sum of the contributions from each input. This is the basis for many techniques for error analysis widely used in the physical sciences and engineering.

Gaussian approximation is a *local* approach in that it considers the behavior of the function only in the vicinity of the nominal scenario. Effectively, it assumes that the response surface is a plane over the region of possible input values. This may be fairly accurate for smooth functions and small uncertainties, but it is likely to produce misleading results for complicated or discontinuous functions and for large uncertainties. In such cases we need to use a *global* approach that explicitly evaluates the function for scenarios distant from the nominal scenario.

Suppose we choose a *low* and *high* value for each input, selected to bound its range of plausible variation. They may or may not be symmetrically placed around each input's nominal value. Let us denote these ranges for our two inputs as $[x_1^-, x_1^+]$ and $[x_2^-, x_2^+]$ respectively. The *nominal range sensitivity* method of sensitivity analysis is to compute the effect on the output of varying each input from its low to high value, while keeping the other inputs at their nominal values. For example,

$$U_R(x_1, y) = f(x_1^+, x_2^0) - f(x_1^-, x_2^0)$$

$$U_R(x_2, y) = f(x_1^0, x_2^+) - f(x_1^0, x_2^-)$$

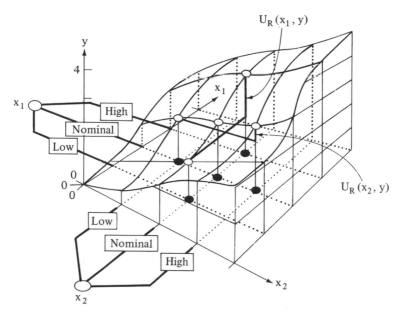

Figure 8.3. An illustration of *nominal range sensitivity*, which is computed as the change in y caused by a change in each input, x_i, from its low to high value, keeping the other inputs at their nominal values.

This is illustrated in Figure 8.3. These effects on the output of the changes in each input are sometimes known as *swing weights*.

The nominal range sensitivity is more than a local measure since it evaluates the model for extreme values of each input; but it is less than global because, when looking at the effect of each input, it holds all the others at their nominal values. For many functions, the effect of one input may depend on the values of other inputs, and so one may want to perform *joint* parametric analysis, graphing the effect of each parameter for several values of the other input(s). More detailed information about the effect of an input may be obtained by *parametric analysis*, that is, evaluating and plotting y for a sequence of different values for each input, holding the others constant. Figure 8.4 shows an example. It gives y as a function of x_1 for a range of different values of x_2. Of course, this is just a projection into two dimensions of some of the lines on the three-dimensional response surface depicted in Figure 8.1 and following figures. The perspective drawings used in these earlier figures are often a good way to display a parametric analysis for two inputs.

We have considered three particular values for each input, labeled low, nominal, and high. To investigate possible interactions between the effects of all the inputs at various levels, we might want to evaluate all possible combinations of each value of each input value with each value of each other input. We term

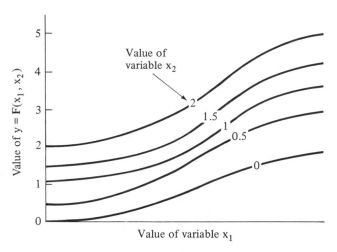

Figure 8.4. An illustration of parametric analysis of y with respect to x_1.

these the *combinatorial scenarios*, as in Figure 8.5. A useful way to represent a set of combinatorial scenarios is as a *scenario tree*, as in Figure 8.6. Each node represents an uncertain quantity or *event*, and each branch from that node, one of its possible outcome values. Each path through the tree from root to terminal represents a sequence of event outcomes determining a specific scenario. The combinatorial scenarios define a rectangular grid of points within the domain of the input space, in this case the two-dimensional rectangle defined by the lower and upper values of the two inputs.

It was easy to compute all combinatorial scenarios for our because function since it has only two inputs each with three levels. If we have, say, ten uncertain variables, each discretized to only three levels, a symmetric tree will have $3^{10} = 59{,}049$ end branches. In other words, the number of scenarios increases exponentially with the number of uncertain inputs. So the computational effort to evaluate the model for every scenario will rapidly become infeasible for more than a dozen or so inputs, even with a powerful computer. And even if the computational burden is acceptable, the results of a parametric analysis with more than three or four dimensions are almost impossible to display in a comprehensible way, and so it is typically of little practical use.[1]

In such situations, it generally makes sense to select only a few scenarios of special interest for examination. For example, in addition to the nominal or "base case" scenario, where every parameter is given its nominal value, we may define a "worst case" scenario, where every parameter is set to its "worst" value, and a "best case" scenario, where each is set to its "best" value. This will often give a very wide range of output values, and we may wonder what the

---

1. In Chapter 9 we discuss graphical techniques for presenting multidimensional information.

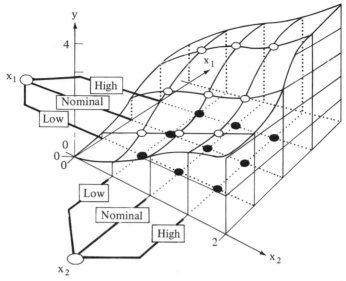

Figure 8.5. An illustration of how a set of combinatorial scenarios might map into the response surface of Figure 8.1.

chances are of such extreme cases actually occurring. If there are more than a few variables, the amount of bad luck for *every* uncertain event simultaneously to turn out for the worst is usually implausible, Murphy's Law notwithstanding! This kind of reasoning suggests trying to assign probabilities to alternative input values so that one can get some idea of the relative probabilities of alternative outcomes.

Lave and Epple (1985) have argued that for problems involving many uncertain variables, the point of doing scenario analysis is primarily to stretch the analyst's thinking by generating unexpected combinations of possible events for consideration, whose implications he or she might otherwise have ignored. This may be very useful, but by itself it is not an adequate mechanism for finding the uncertainty about the outcome.

Given a small number of possible values for each uncertain quantity, you can express the uncertainty as a *discrete probability distribution* over these values. Where there are several quantities it is often convenient to represent the uncertainties by conditional probabilities attached to each branch on the scenario tree, resulting in what is sometimes known as a *probability tree*, as illustrated in Figure 8.7. Each branch is assigned the probability of the quantity represented by that node having that outcome value, conditional on the outcomes of all preceding quantities up to the root of the tree. Each path from the root to a terminal node of the tree represents a feasible scenario whose probability is the product of the conditional probabilities of the branches along that path. By

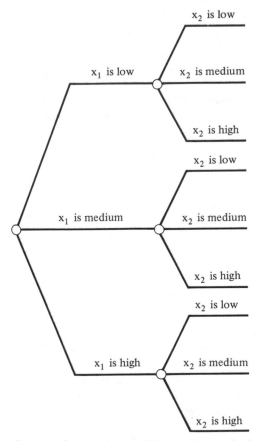

Figure 8.6. Example of a scenario tree which uses three qualitative levels.

calculating the probability and output value for each scenario (terminal node), we can obtain a discrete probability distribution for the output, sometimes known as the *risk profile*, an example of which is shown in Figure 8.7. This is the standard approach used in decision analysis (Raiffa, 1968; Watson and Buede, 1987).

Very often, as in our example, the uncertain quantities are actually continuous rather than discrete. Then it may be more natural to represent the probability distribution over each by a continuous distribution, as either a probability density function or as a cumulative distribution function. The task of uncertainty propagation is then to obtain the continuous probability distribution induced over the output quantity, as illustrated in Figure 8.8. Except in a few very simple cases, which we will mention in Section 8.3, it is hard to obtain analytically the probability distribution of a function of a set of continuous random variables. One approach is to approximate the continuous distributions by discrete ones

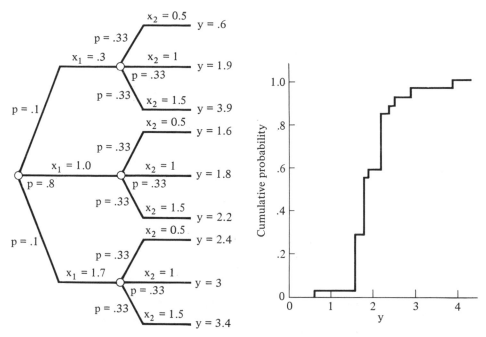

Figure 8.7. Example of a *probability tree* (left), in which the uncertainty in each variable is quantified by attaching conditional probabilities to each branch of the scenario tree of Figure 8.6. The probability of each scenario is computed as the product of the probabilities of the branches that lead to it. The *risk profile* (right) is the cumulative probability distribution for output y, derived from the probabilities and y values for the nine scenarios.

and use the probability tree approach just described. However, if there are more than a few uncertain variables, even if each is approximated by only three discrete values, the combinatorial explosion in the number of terminal nodes is liable to cause severe computational problems.

An alternative approach to enumerating *all* the combinatorial scenarios, is to select a moderate-sized, random *sample* of scenarios for evaluation. In this approach, often called *Monte Carlo simulation*, each scenario is generated by selecting each branch at a node according to its assigned probability. Because the total effort depends on the sample size but not on the number of possible values for each quantity, the branch values may be generated directly from the underlying continuous distribution, without any need for discretization.

The resulting distribution for an output using a sampling approach is inevitably only an approximation to the exact distribution. But so is the result of any probability tree technique that involves discretizing continuous distributions. The accuracy of a Monte Carlo scheme can be increased simply by increasing the sample size. Unlike schemes involving discretizing, the accuracy can easily be estimated using standard statistical techniques. The appropriate sample size

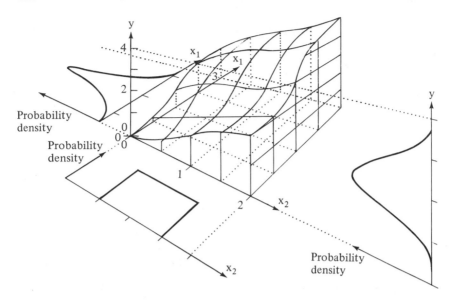

Figure 8.8. An example of the propagation of continuous probability distributions through a model. In this illustration the uncertainty in the value of the inputs is represented by a normal distribution over x_1, and a uniform distribution over x_2.

may be selected to meet the requirements of the application, as we will discuss in Section 8.5.2. For such Monte Carlo schemes, the total computational effort depends on the accuracy required from the results, but for a specified relative precision is only linear in n, the number of uncertain quantities in the model. It is commonly believed that Monte Carlo methods are inherently *more* expensive computationally than probability tree enumeration methods. This may be true for models with few uncertain variables, but in general it is a misconception for larger models. In fact, Monte Carlo methods are usually preferable on purely computational grounds for large models with many uncertain inputs.

It is also sometimes mistakenly asserted that a deficiency of Monte Carlo and other sampling approaches to uncertainty propagation is that they do not provide a simple approach for uncertainty analysis. In fact, there are a variety of measures of uncertainty importance available with such approaches. One such is the correlation of the sample of output values with the corresponding sample of values for each input variable:

$$U_\rho(x, y) = \rho(x, y)$$

This is a truly global measure of uncertainty importance, estimating the effect of uncertainty in x on uncertainty in y, averaged over all possible combinations of values of the other inputs, weighted by their probabilities. In Section 8.5.9

we discuss a variety of related measures, employing correlation and regression coefficients.

We have just introduced a number of basic concepts for sensitivity analysis, uncertainty propagation, and uncertainty analysis. In the rest of the chapter we survey them in more detail, with special attention to the question of how to choose among them.

8.3. Analytic Methods

For all except the simplest cases, such as linear combinations of normal variables, exact analytic methods for propagation of uncertainty are intractable or require elaborate numerical integration (Springer, 1979). However, there are a variety of approximate analytic techniques based on Taylor series expansions of the function (Cheney, 1966). These are sometimes known as the *method of moments*], because they propagate and analyze uncertainty using the mean, variance, and sometimes higher order moments of the probability distributions. We already saw one simple approach, based on the first order or Gaussian approximation, in equation (10). We will now show how this first order approximation for the expectation and variance of a function is derived from the Taylor series, and we will examine its application to a range of important special cases, such as weighted sums and products of powers of uncertain variables. We will also touch on the use of more exact approximations using higher order terms from the Taylor series.

8.3.1. *Approximation from the Taylor Series*

Suppose, instead of just two inputs to function f, as in the example above, we have a vector of n uncertain inputs:

$$X = (x_1, x_2, \ldots x_n)$$

$$y = f(X) \tag{11}$$

We will assume that the nominal value for each input is equal to its expectation:

For $i = 1$ to n, $x_i^0 = E[x_i]$

So the nominal scenario is also the mean scenario, or the expectation of X:

$$X^0 = (x_1^0, x_2^0, \ldots x_n^0) = E[X]$$

The Taylor series expansion provides a way to express deviations of output from its nominal value, $y - y^0$ in terms of deviations of its inputs from their nominal values, $x_i - x_i^0$. Successive terms contain higher order powers of deviations and higher order derivatives of the function with respect to each input. Here is the expansion around the nominal scenario with the first three terms (e.g., see Korn and Korn, 1968):

$$
y - y^0 = \sum_{i=1}^{n} (x_i - x_i^0) \left[\frac{\partial y}{\partial x_i} \right]_{X^0} +
$$

$$
\frac{1}{2} \sum_{i=1}^{n} \sum_{j=1}^{n} (x_i - x_i^0)(x_j - x_j^0) \left[\frac{\partial^2 y}{\partial x_i \, \partial x_j} \right]_{X^0} + \tag{12}
$$

$$
\frac{1}{3!} \sum_{i=1}^{n} \sum_{j=1}^{n} \sum_{k=1}^{n} (x_i - x_i^0)(x_j - x_j^0)(x_k - x_k^0) \left[\frac{\partial^3 y}{\partial x_i \, \partial x_j \, \partial x_k} \right]_{X^0} + \cdots
$$

Note that all derivatives are evaluated at the nominal (i.e., mean) scenario X^0. If the deviations $x_i - x_i^0$ are relatively small, the higher powers will become very small. And if the function is relatively smooth in the region of interest, the higher derivatives will be small. Under these conditions the Taylor series produces a good approximation when the higher order terms are ignored.

For example, let us derive an approximation for the mean of the deviation taking the expectation over equation (12) using terms up to the second order:

$$
E[y - y^0] \approx \sum_{i=1}^{n} E[x_i - x_i^0] \left[\frac{\partial y}{\partial x_i} \right] +
$$

$$
\frac{1}{2} \sum_{i=1}^{n} \sum_{j=1}^{n} E\left[(x_i - x_i^0)(x_j - x_j^0) \right] \left[\frac{\partial^2 y}{\partial x_i \partial x_j} \right]_{X^0} \tag{13}
$$

Since the nominal values of each x_i is equal to its mean, we know $E[x_i - x_i^0] = 0$, so the first term disappears. The covariance between x_i and x_j is given by

$$
\text{Covar}[x_i, x_j] \equiv E\left[(x_i - x_i^0)(x_j - x_j^0) \right]
$$

Substituting this into (13) we obtain:

$$
E[y - y^0] \approx \frac{1}{2} \sum_{i=1}^{n} \sum_{j=1}^{n} \text{Covar}[x_i, x_j] \left[\frac{\partial^2 y}{\partial x_i \partial x_j} \right]_{X^0}
$$

Note that so long as the second derivative terms are nonzero (i.e., the function is nonlinear) the mean output value $E[y]$ is not equal to the nominal output y^0 but is a function of the variances and covariances of the inputs. Put another way, the expected value of the output cannot be computed simply by evaluating the model with all inputs set to their expected values, unless the model is linear.

8.3.2. First Order Approximation

To make things simpler, it is common to take only the first order term. To *first* order, the expected value of the deviation in y is zero, and so the expected value of y *can* be approximated simply by the nominal value:

$$E[y - y^0] \approx 0,$$
$$E[y] \approx y^0 = f(X^0) \tag{14}$$

It is now easy to obtain the general first order approximation for the variance of the output, using only the first order term from equation (12).

$$\text{Var}[y] = E\left[(y - y^0)^2\right] \approx E\left[\left(\sum_{i=1}^{n}(x_i - x_i^0)\left[\frac{\partial y}{\partial x_i}\right]_{X^0}\right)^2\right]$$

$$\text{Var}[y] \approx \sum_{i=1}^{n}\sum_{j=1}^{n} E\left[(x_i - x_i^0)(x_j - x_j^0)\right]\left[\frac{\partial y}{\partial x_i}\right]_{X^0}\left[\frac{\partial y}{\partial x_j}\right]_{X^0}$$

$$\text{Var}[y] \approx \sum_{i=1}^{n}\sum_{j=1}^{n} \text{Covar}[x_i, x_j]\left[\frac{\partial y}{\partial x_i}\right]_{X^0}\left[\frac{\partial y}{\partial x_j}\right]_{X^0}$$

It is often clearer to separate out the variance terms, $\text{Var}[x_i] \equiv \text{Covar}[x_i, x_i]$, from the covariance terms, and, since $\text{Covar}[x_i, x_j] = \text{Covar}[x_j, x_i]$, modify the summation to be over the upper triangle of the matrix (i.e., for $i < j$):

$$\text{Var}[y] \approx \sum_{i=1}^{n} \text{Var}[x_i]\left[\frac{\partial y}{\partial x_i}\right]_{X^0}^2 +$$

$$2\sum_{i=1}^{n}\sum_{j=i+1}^{n} \text{Covar}[x_i, x_j]\left[\frac{\partial y}{\partial x_i}\right]_{X^0}\left[\frac{\partial y}{\partial x_j}\right]_{X^0}$$

If we can assume the inputs are independent, the second term containing the covariances are zero, and this turns into the simple Gaussian approximation formula we saw before with two inputs. The variance of the output is approximately the sum of the squares of the products of the standard deviation and sensitivity of each input:

$$\text{Var}[y] \approx \sum_{i=1}^{n} \text{Var}[x_i]\left[\frac{\partial y}{\partial x_i}\right]_{X^0}^2 \tag{15}$$

These formulas are nice and simple, but it is important to remember that they are only approximations. They replace the actual function by a linear one, that is, a hyperplane, tangent to the response surface at the nominal scenario. Provided the uncertainties are small, and the function is smooth (i.e., small second and higher derivatives) in the range of variation of the inputs, then this may be reasonable.

8.3.3. Weighted Sums

If the function actually *is* linear, the Gaussian formulas are exact. The weighted sum is a very simple but useful example of such a model:

$$y = \sum_{i=1}^{n} a_i x_i$$

We assume the weights a_i are not uncertain. Applying (14) and (15) we obtain the following expressions for the mean and variance of a weighted sum:

$$E[y] = \sum_{i=1}^{n} a_i E[x_i], \tag{16}$$

$$\text{Var}[y] = \sum_{i=1}^{n} a_i^2 \text{Var}[x_i] + 2 \sum_{i=1}^{n} \sum_{j=i+1}^{n} a_i a_j \text{Covar}[x_i, x_j] \tag{17}$$

These expressions are exact no matter what the distribution over X, provided only that it has a finite mean and covariance matrix. If the distribution over X is a multivariate normal for the weighted sum model, the resulting output distribution will be exactly normal. But even if the inputs are not normal, according to the central limit theorem, the distribution of y will tend to become normal for large n, for any reasonable distributions on the x_i, provided they are independent.

8.3.4. Products of Powers with Log Transform

These results may easily be extended to another important class of models, namely, products of powers of uncertain variables. (This also comprises ratios of powers, which are simply products with negative powers for terms in the denominator.)

$$y = \prod_{i=1}^{n} x_i^{a_i}$$

By applying a log transform to this, the function becomes a weighted sum of the uncertain inputs. The weights are simply the powers of the variables:

$$\ln(y) = \sum_{i=1}^{n} a_i \ln(x_i)$$

Hence, we can obtain expressions for the mean and variance of the log of the output in terms of the mean and variance of the log of the inputs:

$$E\left[\ln(y)\right] = \sum_{i=1}^{n} a_i E\left[\ln(x_i)\right] \tag{18}$$

$$\text{Var}\left[\ln(y)\right] = \sum_{i=1}^{n} a_i^2 \text{Var}\left[\ln(x_i)\right] + 2\sum_{i=1}^{n}\sum_{j=i+1}^{n} a_i a_j \text{Covar}\left[\ln(x_i), \ln(x_j)\right] \tag{19}$$

The mean of the log of a random variable is the same as the log of its geometric mean, and the variance of the log is the same as the log of its geometric variance. By analogy with the weighted sum, these expressions are exact, provided the geometric means and geometric covariance matrix for X are finite. If the distribution over X is multivariate lognormal (i.e., $\ln(X)$ is multinormal), the distribution of y will be exactly lognormal. Similarly, according to the central limit theorem, for any reasonable independent distributions on the x_i, the distribution y will tend to become *lognormal* for large n.

The lognormal approximation for multiplicative models is widely used. For example, in risk assessments that involve evaluating the impact of a pollution release on human health and the environment, the risk is often modeled as the product of the probability of release with the amount of release, the fraction of the release that reaches the receptor location, the amount of exposure realized by the target organisms at the receptor, and the dose-response relationship representing the health or environmental effect. The uncertainties in each component of the release, transport, fate, exposure, and health effect assessments can be combined using the lognormal model.

8.3.5. Products of Powers with Relative Error

It is also possible to apply the Gaussian approximation for direct error propagation in a product-of-powers model. This avoids the effort of having to transform to and from the log space, and allows use of arithmetic means and variances instead of the less familiar geometric means and variances. However, the results are only approximate, and it only works when the uncertainties are small relative to the means of the variables. It leads to a particularly simple formulation in terms of relative error, that is, the ratio of the standard deviation to mean for each variable. This approach is widely used for error propagation in engineering and the physical sciences.

As above, we are interested in error propagation for a product-of-powers model:

$$y = \prod_{i=1}^{n} x_i^{a_i}$$

By applying (14) to the product-of-powers model we estimate the expected value of y as the product of the powers of the means of the x_i:

$$E[y] \approx \prod_{i=1}^{n} E[x_i]^{a_i} \tag{20}$$

In order to apply (15) to estimate the variance, we will first need the partial derivatives:

$$\left[\frac{\partial y}{\partial x_i}\right]_{X^0} = \frac{a_i}{E[x_i]} \times \prod_{j=1}^{n} E[x_j]^{a_j}$$

Using (20) we get

$$\left[\frac{\partial y}{\partial x_i}\right]_{X^0} = \frac{a_i}{E[x_i]} E[y] = \frac{a_i}{x_i^0} y^0$$

Using these partial derivatives in the Gaussian approximation for the variance of y, equation (15), we get:

$$\text{Var}[y] \approx \sum_{i=1}^{n} \text{Var}[x_i] \left(\frac{a_i}{x_i^0} y^0\right)^2$$

Dividing by y^{0^2} we get:

$$\frac{\text{Var}[y]}{y^{0^2}} \approx \sum_{i=1}^{n} a_i^2 \frac{\text{Var}[x_i]}{x_i^{0^2}}$$

This may be looked at in terms of the *relative error* (also known as *relative standard deviation* or *coefficient of variation*), that is, the ratio of standard deviation to the mean for each variable:

$$h(z)^2 \equiv \frac{\text{Var}[z]}{z^{0^2}} \tag{21}$$

Substituting this into the previous expression, we get the following simple and useful formula:

$$h(y)^2 \approx \sum_{i=1}^{n} a_i^2 \, h(x_i)^2 \tag{22}$$

In other words, we can estimate the relative error of a product of powers by the root sum of squares of the relative error of its components, weighted by the squares of their powers.

As an example, consider the following model:

$$z = \frac{r s^2}{t \sqrt{u}}$$

Suppose we are given the accuracy of r, s, t, u as their percent standard deviation (i.e., relative error times 100):

$$h(r) = 1\%, \quad h(s) = 1\%, \quad h(t) = 3\%, \quad h(u) = 2\%$$

What is the accuracy of z? Applying (22), where the a_i are the powers of the four variables, we get,

$$h(z)^2 \approx (1 \times 1)^2 + (2 \times 1)^2 + (-1 \times 3)^2 + (-0.5 \times 2)^2,$$

$$h(z)^2 \approx 15,$$

$$h(z) \approx 4\%.$$

Note that in a simple product of a set of uncertain variables, if the coefficients of variation of two uncertain quantities differ by more than a factor of 3, the smaller relative uncertainty may generally be ignored. Its relative variance will be about an order of magnitude less (actually a factor of 3^2). In this way the propagation process through a cascaded chain of models may often be greatly simplified.

8.3.6. *Higher Order Approximations*

So far we have considered only first order approximations to the general function and treated only the mean and variance of the distributions. These work well for small uncertainties with smooth, well-behaved functions, but may not work so well for large uncertainties that are typical in many areas of policy and risk analysis. One way to improve the accuracy of the approximation is to use higher order terms from the Taylor expansion. Effectively, this allows us to approximate the function by quadratic, cubic, or higher order surfaces, fitted at the nominal scenario.

If the function actually is a quadratic or cubic and so on, this approach can provide exact results. Seiler has developed tables of correction factors that provide better approximations or exact expressions for a variety of common functions (Seiler, 1987). These include products of two, three, and four terms, powers of single terms, and more complex combinations. A very simple example is the exact expression for a weighted sum where, unlike in our earlier analysis, the weights a_i are also uncertain.

$$y = \sum_{i=1}^{n} a_i x_i$$

If we can assume the variables x_i and weights a_i are all independent, the following is the exact expression for the variance:

$$\text{Var}[y] = \sum_{i=1}^{n} (E[a_i])^2 \, \text{Var}[x_i] + (E[x_i])^2 \, \text{Var}[a_i] + \text{Var}[a_i]\text{Var}[x_i] \quad (23)$$

The first two terms are the first order (linear) approximation; the third is the correction term. As Seiler (1987) points out, the correction is always positive, thus increasing the final error. For more complex functions, the propagation may be done in multiple stages.

Unfortunately, the algebraic complexity increases rapidly with the complexity of the function. For example, the exact expression for the product of four normal variables contains twenty-eight terms. So unless the function is one of the simpler cases, this method of moments employing higher order terms can rapidly become intractable.

8.3.7. Finding Derivatives

To employ the method of moments, we need to calculate the partial derivatives of the model. Given a computer implementation of the model, it is often relatively easy to compute this numerically. Conceptually, the simplest way is to take each uncertain input x_i, one at a time, perturb it slightly from the nominal scenario, by Δx_i. The derivative is estimated as the ratio of the change in output to the change in the input:

$$\left[\frac{\partial y}{\partial x_i} \right]_{X^0} \approx \frac{f(x_i^0 + \Delta x_i) - f(x_i^0)}{\Delta x_i}$$

(We assume all inputs other than x_i are left unperturbed.) Higher order derivatives are computed similarly from their standard definitions in terms of small perturbations. Of course, for computation the actual perturbation must be sufficiently large not to get lost in the imprecision (e.g., round off error) of the computation.

In practice, it may be preferable to use larger perturbations, comparable to the range of variation for each input. In this case, we are no longer fitting a hyperplane (or higher order surface) tangential to the actual response surface at the nominal scenario, but rather to intersect more distant points of the response surface. This may actually produce a better fit in many cases when averaged over the domain of the inputs.

This one-input-at-a-time perturbation will require evaluation of the model for the base case, and then once for each uncertain input for a first order approximation, and an additional evaluation for each input and each pair of inputs for a second order approximation. If there are very many uncertain inputs, and the model is expensive to evaluate, the cost may become prohibitive. To mitigate this, one may be able to do some initial screening based on inspection of the model to eliminate some of the uncertain inputs as contributing negligibly to the overall uncertainty. Another approach possibility is to use a factorial design in selecting scenarios for evaluation, which can allow estimation of the low-order derivatives from a smaller number of evaluations.

A way to reduce the computational effort is to perform symbolic differentiation on the model, chaining through it to obtain the partial derivative of the output(s) with respect to each uncertain input. The final step is to evaluate them, using the values for the nominal scenario (generally the means of the inputs). For a simple model this is often not hard to do by hand, but for complex models it can be extremely arduous. For models used in nuclear engineering and safety analysis, this process has required many person-months of analysis (Iman and Helton, 1988). In cases of such complexity, one might also worry about the reliability of the analysis. Would errors necessarily be discovered?

Nowadays another possibility is to perform the symbolic differentiation by computer program (Rall, 1981; Oblow, 1983a). Typically in large engineering applications where there is interest in systematic sensitivity and uncertainty analysis, models have been implemented as large FORTRAN programs. Oblow (1983b) describes a program named GRESS, which takes FORTRAN source code as input, and via symbolic differentiation generates additional code to compute and chain the derivatives through the model. With this extended model, a single additional run will be sufficient to compute the required first order derivatives.

For complex dynamic models that need to be solved by sophisticated iterative techniques, there are a variety of approaches to improving the efficiency for computing their sensitivities. This is the field of *differential sensitivity theory*. Such approaches employ specialized numerical procedures, utilizing knowledge of the model structure, to minimize the computational effort. Techniques include *adjoint methods* (e.g., Koda, Dogru, and Seinfeld, 1979; Cacuci et al., 1980; Cacuci, 1981a, 1981b; Hall, Cacuci, and Schlesinger, 1982) and Green's function methods (e.g., Hwang et al., 1978; Dougherty, Hwang, and Rabitz, 1979). These techniques tend to be rather complex to use and time-consuming to implement, although availability of programs such as GRESS for automatic symbolic differentiation of the model could help significantly. While they may be useful for very large dynamic models, for example in atmospheric modeling, they seem unlikely to be necessary for most applications in policy and risk analysis. Consequently, we will refer the interested reader to the references for more detailed description.

8.3.8. Moments and Other Properties of Distributions

One feature of the method of moments, which is sometimes cited as an advantage, is that it does not require specification of the entire probability distribution of the input parameters, but only the first few moments, typically only the mean and variance. Whether this is really an advantage depends on the form in which the input uncertainties are given. If they are given in the form of mean and standard error, then, of course, it is an advantage, provided no higher moments are wanted. In nuclear power safety studies and other risk analysis for complex engineering systems, failure frequencies are typically given as a median, m, and uncertainty factor, f. To translate these into mean and variance requires some strong assumptions about the shape of the distribution. Commonly, the distributions are assumed lognormal, with median at m and 95th percentile at $m \times f$. Moments can be derived accordingly. However, other distributions that may be fit may have quite different moments, especially if they are symmetrical (Martz et al., 1983). The method of moments cannot avoid this problem any more than other methods.

A related problem, peculiar to the method of moments, is how to obtain percentiles from the moments computed for the outputs. The Tchebychev inequality provides confidence bounds based on the computed variance. Generalizations of this inequality by Markov and Cantelli (Mallows, 1956) allow use of higher moments as well. Such confidence intervals are usually highly conservative (i.e. much wider than necessary), although in a few cases, because of inaccuracies in the method of moments, they may instead be too narrow (Martz et al., 1983). An alternative approach is to fit a distribution to the moments, such as a lognormal, and obtain appropriate percentiles from that. This may give better results but relies on knowledge about what will be an appropriate form for the distribution.

8.3.9. Advantages and Disadvantages of the Analytic Methods

First order or Gaussian approximation is very widely used in engineering and the physical sciences, particularly in the relative error form for products of powers. Higher order approximations, often known as the method of moments, have been applied quite widely to the analysis of complex models. The approach has two important advantages:

- Once the algebraic analysis has been performed, the numerical calculations are usually relatively simple.
- It provides a very clear approach to uncertainty analysis, generally decomposing the variance of each output into the sum of the contributions from each input.

However, it suffers from three disadvantages:

- The complexity of the algebra can increase rapidly with the complexity of the model, particularly if higher order terms will be required.
- Because it primarily produces moments of distributions, usually only the mean and variance, it is hard to obtain reliable estimates for the tails of output distribution.
- It is basically a local approach and will not be accurate if the uncertainties are large, if the model is not smooth (for example the response surface has discontinuities), or if important covarience terms are omitted.

8.4. Discrete Distributions and Decision Analysis

We introduced the use of discrete probability distributions to approximate continuous ones, and their combination into probability trees as a basic idea, in

Section 8.2. This approach is widely used in decision analysis, where probability trees are generalized to *decision trees*, which contain decision nodes as well as uncertain event nodes. Decision analysis uses a variety of techniques for uncertainty propagation and analysis, but with the primary attention on the relative merits of alternative decisions. The degree of merit of decision and outcomes is generally quantified in terms of *utility*, expressing the preferences of the decision maker and attitudes to risk when there is uncertainty. The decision-oriented approach gives a particular focus to sensitivity and uncertainty analysis: The key question is not simply "Can this assumption or this uncertainty affect the results?" but, rather, "Could it change the decision?" In this book we do not attempt a detailed description of the philosophy and techniques of decision analysis except insofar as they impinge on the specific topics at hand. The interested reader is referred to Raiffa, (1968), Howard and Matheson (1984), and Watson and Buede (1987).

One topic addressed briefly is the issue of how best to convert a continuous distribution into a discrete one if we wish to use a probability tree approach. A second topic is the issue of controlling the size of the tree. As already pointed out, the number of end branches in a scenario tree, and therefore a probability tree or a decision tree, grows exponentially with the total number of uncertain variables (and decision variables). If we have, say, n uncertain variables (or decision variables), each discretized to m levels, a symmetric tree will have m^n end nodes, leading rapidly to computational tractability. We will discuss two approaches to mitigate this problem. One attempt is termed the method of *discrete probability distributions*. The other, widely used among decision analysts, is to use sensitivity analysis to identify those, hopefully few, uncertain variables that contribute the lion's share of the uncertainty, and simply to ignore the uncertainty in the rest. Finally, we investigate some of the more sophisticated approaches to uncertainty analysis developed in decision analysis.

8.4.1. Discretizing Continuous Distributions

In practice, most uncertain quantities in policy and risk analysis, such as the cost of a new product, or the environmental concentration of a toxic chemical, are most naturally thought of as continuous rather than discrete. Suppose you have determined that the uncertainty is important by initial sensitivity analysis, and assessed a continuous subjective probability distribution for it, using the methods described in Chapter 7. If you wish to use this distribution in a decision tree, the question arises of how to convert it into a discrete probability distribution. It is usual among decision analysts to approximate continuous distributions by discrete distributions with three to five values. Conventionally, the middle value is chosen equal to the median of the continuous distribution, and the other points are chosen roughly to minimize the total area between the continuous

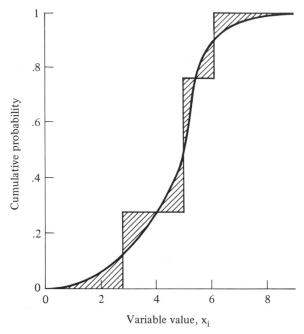

Figure 8.9. Fitting a discrete distribution to a continuous one.

cumulative distribution and the stepwise cumulative function representing the discrete distribution. This area is crosshatched in Figure 8.9.

It has been observed that this approach, minimizing the integral of the absolute difference between the cumulative distributions of the discrete distributions and the continuous one, may not be the best approach. It typically leads to substantially understating the variance, by 15% to 30%, depending on the shape of the underlying distribution. It is usually better to have the side points farther away from the midpoint. Several authors have proposed methods which maintain the first few moments as accurately as possible in the discrete approximation (Keefer and Bodily, 1983; Miller and Rice, 1983). It may not always be worthwhile to go to the effort of finding the optimal approximation, unless one has software that does it automatically. But it is as well to remember that the conventional approach can lead to significant underestimation of the uncertainty.

8.4.2. The Method of Discrete Probability Distributions

In an attempt to moderate the exponential complexity of the probability tree approach to propagating uncertainties, Kaplan proposed an alternative, which he calls the method of *discrete probability distributions* (DPD) (Kaplan, 1981). This was developed for application to uncertainty analysis of fault trees in the risk assessment of nuclear power. We illustrate with an example.

System   Fault tree

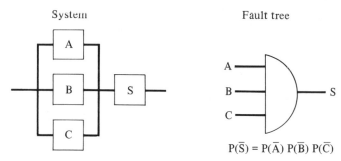

$$P(\overline{S}) = P(\overline{A})\, P(\overline{B})\, P(\overline{C})$$

Figure 8.10. Example of a system with three parallel subsystems.

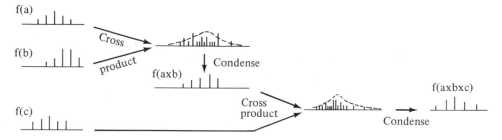

Figure 8.11. Cartoon of the method of discrete probability distributions applied to the system of Figure 8.10. The distributions shown are illustrative and are not a worked-out example.

Consider a simple redundant safety system S consisting of three subsystems, A, B, and C, as in Figure 8.10. These are arranged in parallel so that S fails (is unavailable) only if all three of A, B, and C are unavailable simultaneously. If the unavailability rates of the three subsystems are denoted a, b, and c, respectively, assuming the three subsystems are independent, we can compute the unavailability rate, s, for the entire system as the product $s = a \times b \times c$. Suppose we are given probability distributions over the unavailability rate for each subsystem, and the rates are considered independent. How can we propagate these uncertainties to obtain the probability distribution over the unavailability rate s for the entire system?

The first step of the DPD method is to discretize them, let's say each into a five point discrete distribution, as illustrated in Figure 8.11. Suppose we represent the DPDs for A and B as:

$$([a_1, \alpha_1], [a_2, \alpha_2], [a_3, \alpha_3], [a_4, \alpha_4], [a_5, \alpha_5])$$

$$([b_1, \beta_1], [b_2, \beta_2], [b_3, \beta_3], [b_4, \beta_4], [b_5, \beta_5])$$

where each pair $[a_i, \alpha_i]$ is a value and corresponding probability, so $\alpha_i = Pr(a = a_i)$, and similarly for b. We then obtain a corresponding distribution for $a \times b$

taking the cross products of the values and of the probabilities, obtaining a DPD with $5 \times 5 = 25$ value-probability pairs:

$$[a_i \times b_j, \alpha_i \times \beta_j] \text{ for } i, j = 1 \text{ to } 5$$

This is essentially just the standard approach with probability trees, but the next step is different. The DPD for $a \times b$ is *condensed*, that is, the twenty-five-point distribution is approximated by a five-point distribution. Thus, when using the result of this to obtain the cross product for $a \times b \times c$, the resulting DPD has only twenty-five points, rather than $5 \times 25 = 125$ points. This may itself be condensed before participating in further computations. In this way the potential combinatorial explosion is moderated.

When combining two DPDs, the quantities they represent are assumed to be independent. Information about how combined quantities depend on their components is lost in the process of condensation. Thus, if two quantities, x and y, both depend on a common third quantity, b,

$$x = a \times b, \qquad y = b + c \times d$$

straightforward application of the method to compute $x \times y$ will ignore their correlation and produce incorrect results. Sometimes the order of the calculations can be rearranged to eliminate multiple occurrences of the same parameter in different places, so that each parameter only appears in the expression for a single higher order quantity. But this kind of rearrangement can require considerable ingenuity (Martz et al., 1983), and in some cases it is impossible. In more complex situations, more than three variables may need to be combined without intermediate condensation, and the complexity reduces to the standard combinatorial approach. This puts a severe limitation on the applicability of the method.

Another major deficiency of the DPD method is the difficulty of performing uncertainty analysis with it to compare the contributions of different sources of uncertainty. Because the discrete probability distributions are condensed after each step in the computation, the information about which input scenarios are responsible for which outputs is lost. Thus, it does not provide any simple way to compute the degree to which each input has contributed to the uncertainty in the output.

8.4.3. Decision Analysis and Uncertainty Analysis

Decision analysts most commonly convert continuous uncertain quantities and decisions to discrete quantities so that they can use probability trees and decision trees for uncertainty propagation and analysis. It might seem that the combinatorial difficulties of enumerating scenarios in such trees would severely limit the complexity of the models they can handle. They generally approach the problem by conducting systematic deterministic sensitivity analysis to identify which uncertain inputs and decisions may have significant impact on the results, and which are unlikely to do so. The most commonly used measure of uncertainty importance is nominal range sensitivity, the effect on the output of holding each input from low to high level, holding the rest at nominal values (described in Section 8.2). It usually turns out that only a handful of the variables account for most of the variation in consequence. Only those need to be modeled as uncertain in the probabilistic analysis, and the rest are treated as fixed at their nominal value. In this way a model that may have many dozens of uncertain variables and decisions may be reduced to one that has less then a dozen or so, and therefore become computationally tractable for decision tree programs running on microcomputers.

So far, in our discussion of sensitivity and uncertainty analysis, we have been content to talk of effects on outcomes. Decision analysis, with its emphasis on decision making, provides some important distinctions to sharpen these ideas. For example, suppose you are interested in buying a particular new model of car which is available from two different dealers, one of whom asks for a price which is a thousand dollars less than the other. You may be somewhat uncertain just how good the car will turn out to be, and consequently uncertain about how you will feel about the entire transaction. But, assuming the car and options will be identical from the two dealers, it is obvious that uncertainty about the quality of the car is irrelevant to which dealer you choose. The point is that the importance of an uncertainty depends on how much it could affect the decision, not simply the outcome.

In the terminology of control theory, a measure of sensitivity or uncertainty importance is called *open loop* if it is a measure of how far an assumption or uncertain quantity affects the outcome utility (or other outcome measure) for a fixed decision (Howard, 1971). If, on the other hand, the decision may be adjusted to reoptimize the outcome reflecting the change in assumption or input value, the measure is called *closed loop*. Closed loop sensitivity is generally a more powerful and relevant measure, but often more difficult to compute. Open loop sensitivity is a weaker measure, in that open loop sensitivity in a variable is necessary but not sufficient for closed loop sensitivity. But uncertainty about the car quality exhibits open loop sensitivity, but not closed loop sensitivity. Uncertainty about the relative prices of the two dealers would produce both open and closed loop sensitivity, because it could affect both the outcome and which decision is best.

One closed loop measure of uncertainty importance, well known in decision analysis, is the *expected value of perfect information* (EVPI). The EVPI is a measure of the importance of uncertainty about a quantity in terms of the expected improvement in the decision that might be obtained from knowing the value of the quantity exactly. The measure of improvement is the expected difference in expected value of the outcome (utility) before and after the true value of the quantity becomes known. In the car example, the EVPI for the car quality would be zero with respect to the decision of which dealer to buy from. The EVPI of the relative prices of the two dealers might be quite large if there were significant uncertainty about which would be cheaper. Note that EVPI (and any closed loop measure of uncertainty importance) is specific to a particular decision variable.

Another closed loop measure of uncertainty importance, namely the *expected value of including uncertainty* (EVIU) is discussed in more detail in Chapter 12. The EVIU is a measure of the value of explicitly modeling uncertainty in a quantity instead of assuming some fixed value.

Decision analysts generally tend to use easy-to-compute open loop sensitivity measures, such as range sensitivity, for initial screening of variables to find out which are important. They sometimes go on to examine closed loop sensitivity measures, particularly the EVPI, for a few of the variables explicitly modeled as uncertain. Modelers such as policy and risk analysts from other traditions have generally placed less emphasis on decisions for focusing modeling, and have stayed with simple open loop measures. In practice EVPI is generally computed using discrete decision trees, although analytic approaches derived from Taylor expansions have been developed both for the EVPI (Howard, 1971) and for the EVIU (Henrion, 1982, and Chapter 12). The use of other computational techniques for uncertainty propagation, such as Monte Carlo sampling, for closed loop sensitivity measures does not seem to have been reported hitherto.

8.5. Monte Carlo and Other Sampling Methods

One can view the combinatorial scenarios and probability tree approach as a way of sampling points from the uncertain input domain, that is the subset of the n-dimensional space defined by the ranges of the n uncertain parameters. The combinatorial scenarios define points at all the vertices of a regular rectangular grid in that space. (This is illustrated in Figure 8.5 for a two-dimensional case.) There are many other ways of sampling from that space, of which the best known and simplest is *Monte Carlo simulation*. To avoid having to assess the relative likelihood of different points with the input space, uniform distributions are sometimes used.[2] More often, probability distributions may be assessed for each uncertain parameter, using the kind of techniques described in the previous chapters. In crude Monte Carlo

---

2. We note, and duck, the philosophical arguments about the difference between representing your beliefs by a uniform distribution and using a uniform distribution because you don't know the distribution.

analysis, a value is drawn at random from the distribution for each input. (Techniques for generating values when inputs are probabilistically dependent are discussed in Section 8.5.7.) Together this set of random values, one for each input, defines a scenario, which is used as input to the model, computing the corresponding output value. The entire process is repeated m times producing m independent scenarios with corresponding output values. These m output values constitute a random sample from the probability distribution over the output induced by the probability distribution over the inputs. One advantage of this approach is that the precision of the output distribution may be estimated from this sample of output values using standard statistical techniques.

The issue of the computational complexity of Monte Carlo methods has often engendered confusion, and so we address the question of computational complexity explicitly, and describe in some detail methods for helping to decide how many Monte Carlo runs are necessary to achieve a required degree of accuracy. We also survey some other sampling methods that can improve the accuracy over crude Monte Carlo given a limited number of model runs. Finally, we outline techniques for uncertainty analysis using random sampling approaches.

8.5.1. Monte Carlo Has Linear Complexity

It is important to understand that the output sample from simple Monte Carlo consists of independent random values from the output distribution, irrespective of n, the number of uncertain inputs. For a given output distribution, the accuracy of the estimates of its parameters depends on the sample size m, but not on the number of inputs n. If a model is made more complicated with the addition of more uncertain inputs, there is usually no need to change the number of runs, except perhaps if the changes substantially increase the variance of the output. The number of runs required, m, depends on the relative accuracy required of the output distribution but, for a given degree of uncertainty, is independent of the number of inputs n. The effort to run the model for each scenario is typically proportional to n, the number of uncertain inputs. Thus the appeal of Monte Carlo sampling is that its computational complexity is linear in n, in contrast to discrete probability tree methods whose complexity is generally exponential in n.

Another advantage of Monte Carlo schemes is that there is no need to discretize continuous distributions as there is for standard probability tree approaches, since the values can be generated directly from the continuous distribution. On the other hand, if the uncertain variables and their distributions are inherently discrete, it is equally easy to sample directly from these discrete distributions. It is also possible to apply Monte Carlo techniques to probability trees. Instead of explicitly enumerating all paths through the tree, that is, all the combinatorial scenarios, a program can generate a random sample of scenarios. Each is generated by selecting a branch at each chance node using the specified branch probabilities. Because the accuracy of this approach depends on the number of scenarios sampled, but not the number of possible scenarios they are sampled from, it can be applied to probability trees of arbitrary size. There is no need to construct the entire tree explicitly.

8.5.2. Selecting the Sample Size: Uncertainty about the Mean

How should one choose the sample size m? It should depend both on the cost of each model run, and what one wants the results for. An advantage of Monte Carlo techniques is that one can apply standard statistical techniques to estimate the precision of estimates of the output distribution. This is because the generated sample of values for each output variable is a random sample from the true probability distribution for that variable.

First, suppose the primary interest is in the precision of the mean of the output variable y. Assume we have a random sample of m output values generated by Monte Carlo simulation:

$$(y_1, y_2, y_3, \ldots y_m)$$

We estimate the mean and standard deviation of y in the usual way, as described in Section 5.3.2:

$$\overline{y} = \sum_{i=1}^{m} \frac{y_i}{m}$$

$$s^2 = \sum_{i=1}^{m} \frac{(y_i - \overline{y})^2}{(m-1)}$$

In the same section, equation (4) gives the following as a confidence interval with confidence α, where c is the deviation for the unit normal enclosing probability α:

$$\left(\overline{y} - c\frac{s}{\sqrt{m}}, \overline{y} + c\frac{s}{\sqrt{m}} \right)$$

Suppose we wish to obtain an estimate of the mean of y with an α confidence interval smaller than w units wide. What sample size will we need? We will need to make sure that the width of the interval is less than w:

$$2c\frac{s}{\sqrt{m}} < w$$

We rearrange this in terms of m

$$m > \left(\frac{2cs}{w}\right)^2 \tag{24}$$

To use this, we should first make small Monte Carlo run with, say, ten values to get an initial estimate s^2, the variance. From this, we can then use this expression (24) to estimate how many samples are needed in total to reduce the confidence interval to the requisite width w.

For example, suppose we wish to obtain a 95% confidence interval for the mean that is less than twenty units wide. Suppose your initial sample of ten gives $s = 40$. The deviation c enclosing a probability of 95% is about 2. Substituting these numbers into (24) we get

$$m > \left(\frac{2 \times 2 \times 40}{20}\right)^2 = 8^2 = 64$$

To get a total of sixty-four runs, another fifty-four runs should be done in addition to the ten already done.

8.5.3. *Estimating Confidence Intervals for Fractiles*

Another criterion for selecting sample size is the precision of the estimate of the median and other fractiles, or more generally the precision of the estimated cumulative distribution. In Section 5.3.3 we saw how to obtain a confidence interval for Y_p, the pth fractile of Y. Without loss of generality, we assume the sample m values of y are relabeled so that they are in increasing order,

$$y_1 \leq y_2 \leq \cdots y_m$$

Sample value y_i is an estimate of fractile Y_p, where $p = i/m$.

According to equation (7), the following pair of sample values constitutes the confidence interval with confidence α:

$$(y_i, y_k) \tag{25}$$

where

$$i = \left\lfloor mp - c\sqrt{mp(1-p)} \right\rfloor$$

$$k = \left\lceil mp + c\sqrt{mp(1-p)} \right\rceil \tag{26}$$

and c is the deviation enclosing probability α of the unit normal, and $\lfloor x \rfloor$ means rounding x down and $\lceil x \rceil$ means rounding it up.

Suppose we wish to achieve sufficient precision that the α confidence interval for the pth fractile Y_p is given by (y_i, y_k), where y_i is an estimate of $Y_{p-\Delta p}$ and y_k is an estimate of $Y_{p+\Delta p}$. In other words, we want α confidence of Y_p being between the sample values used as estimates of the $p-\Delta p^{th}$ and $p+\Delta p^{th}$ fractiles. What sample size will we neeed? Ignoring the rounding, we have approximately

$$i = m(p - \Delta p), \qquad k = m(p + \Delta p)$$

So

$$k - i = 2m\Delta p \tag{27}$$

From equations (26) above we have

$$k - i = 2c\sqrt{mp(1 - p)}$$

Equating the two expressions for $k - i$, we obtain

$$2m\Delta p = 2c\sqrt{mp(1 - p)}$$

$$m = p(1 - p) \left(\frac{c}{\Delta p}\right)^2 \tag{28}$$

For example, suppose we want to be 95% confident that the actual 90th percentile, $Y_{.90}$ is between the estimates of 85th and 95th percentiles, $Y_{.85}$ and $Y_{.95}$. So we have $\Delta p = 0.005$, and $c \approx 2$. Substituting the numbers into this expression, we get:

$$m = .90 \times (1 - .90) \times (2/0.05)^2 = 144$$

On the other hand, suppose we want the 95% confidence interval for the least precise estimated percentile (the 50th percentile) to be plus or minus one estimated percentile. Then,

$$m = 0.5 \times (1 - 0.5) \times (2/0.01)^2 = 10,000$$

Note that these results are completely independent of the shape of the distribution. So if one finds this an appropriate way of stating one's requirements for the precision of the estimated distribution, you can determine the sample size before doing *any* runs to see what sort of distribution it may be.

8.5.4. How Many Runs Are Enough?

In typical applications for the uncertainty analysis of reliability models for nuclear power plants, analysts have used very large numbers of Monte Carlo runs, over 18,000 runs in one example (Jackson et al., 1981). As just seen, this allows sufficient accuracy that we can be more than 95% confident that the true percentile of the distribution is between the estimates for its two neighboring percentiles, for instance, $(x_{.49}, x_{.51})$ is a 95% confidence interval for $x_{.50}$. Before either expending all this computer time or giving up in disgust at the prospect of doing so, it is a good idea to consider whether this much precision is really needed. For example, in nuclear safety reliability codes, the input values and uncertainty factors for most of the component failure rates are based largely on expert judgment. The difference between an uncertainty factor of 10 and one of 12 is unlikely to be subjectively discriminable to the expert assessor. In such a case, this degree of precision in the propagation of these uncertainties is probably pointless. The approximation uncertainty contributed by the finite number of runs will be totally dominated by the empirical uncertainty from the input parameters. Thus, in most uncertainty analyses of quantitative policy models, a few hundred or sometimes only a few tens of runs may be quite sufficient.

Where computing costs do turn out to be a significant issue, there may be several ways of reducing them. Sometimes the computation involved in the model itself can be reduced by some reordering of expressions. One example of this is in fault tree analysis, where a fault tree is reduced to its minimal cut-sets. Substantial savings may be obtained by omitting those cut-sets that are shown by initial analysis to make negligible contributions to the top event frequency. It can also pay to look at the Monte Carlo code itself. Early work was much concerned with improving the efficiency of random sampling. But examination of one widely used code, SAMPLE, developed for the Reactor Safety Study (Rasmussen et al., 1975), revealed that most of the effort was consumed in sorting the m output values to produce the cumulative probability distribution. Replacement of the sorting algorithm, which required time of order $O(m \log m)$, by a categorizing algorithm to generate the histogram, requiring time of order $O(m)$, improved overall performance by an order of magnitude or more for an m of thousands (Jackson, 1981).

8.5.5. Variance Reduction Techniques

Another way to reduce the computational effort for sampling schemes is to improve their statistical efficiency by one of a number of variance reduction techniques (Rubinstein, 1982; Johnson, 1987). These techniques use structural knowledge or other information about the model to reduce the variance in estimates of the mean, or other parameters of interest of the output distribution.

The *controlled variate* method may be used if there is a simplified approximation to the full model that is cheaper to run. For example, an analytic model based on a Taylor series expansion (method of moments) might be used. Input scenarios may be computed in the usual random way (or using a stratified approach, as described in the next section). Let the exact model be $y = f(X)$, and the approximate one be $y' = f'(X)$. Each input scenario X_i for $i = 1 \ldots m$ is fed into both complete and approximate models producing outputs $y = f(X_i)$ and $y' = f'(X_i)$. With the simple model it is easy to calculate the approximate mean output $E[y']$. The mean from the complete model can then be calculated in terms of the difference from the approximate model, instead of directly:

$$E[y] = E[y'] + \sum_{i=1}^{m}(y_i - y_i')/m$$

If the approximate model is any good at all the variance of the difference $(y_i - y_i')$ will be less than the variance of y_i alone. Hence, the variance in the sample mean will be less than if it was calculated directly. A given precision should thus be attainable with fewer runs. Analogous techniques may be used for estimating other parameters of the output.

8.5.6. Stratified Sampling and Latin Hypercube Sampling

It is important to understand that the value of Monte Carlo methods is not primarily the randomness of the sampling but the resulting equidistribution properties of the sets of points in the parameter space. Once it is recognized that a primary objective is to produce a more uniform distribution of points in parameter space, then systematic or stratified sampling techniques become appealing. In *stratified sampling* the sample space for an input parameter is divided up into strata, and input values are obtained by sampling separately from within each stratum instead of from the distribution as a whole. One version of this, which is being used increasingly widely, has the impressive name of *Latin hypercube sampling* (LHS) (Iman, Davenport, and Zeigler, 1980). It is more straightforward than it sounds.

To generate m samples using LHS, each input distribution is divided up into m equiprobable intervals. In *standard LHS*, a single value is sampled at random from within each of these intervals, according to the probability distribution. This produces a sample of m values for each input distribution that are more uniformly spread out than for strict random sampling. An alternative, *midpoint LHS*, produces yet more uniform sampling. In this case, we choose the median of each of the m probability intervals. This is repeated for all the probabilistic inputs. A scenario is generated by selecting one value at random from each of the inputs, but without replacement, from the m sample values for each input.

We end up with m scenarios, with each value from each input being used only once.

In Latin hypercube sampling, because the sample scenarios tend to be more evenly spread out over the input domain, the sample from each input will represent the mean, variance, and other parameters of the distribution more accurately than with unstratified random sampling. With midpoint LHS, the mean and variance of the sample will often be almost exact. If the model is roughly linear, the mean of the output will converge more rapidly. The same is true if the uncertainty in the output is dominated by one or two inputs. On the other hand, if there are many uncertain inputs contributing and the model is highly nonlinear, LHS may not be much better than crude Monte Carlo.

If LHS is sometimes much better and never worse than crude Monte Carlo, why should we ever use the latter? One reason is that the statistics may be harder to compute with LHS. With standard LHS, the sample scenarios and hence the outputs are random, but they are not completely independent. Thus statistics for estimating the precision of the results for Monte Carlo, as discussed in preceding paragraphs, will be inaccurate for LHS. Typically they will underestimate the true precision. Of course, if one would rather have higher precision, even if unsure exactly what level of precision, this is not a problem.

In general, midpoint LHS performs considerably better than standard LHS, but it is subject to a rather subtle, if rare, problem. If the model exhibits periodicity with respect to an input with a wavelength comparable to that induced by the m equal probability intervals, midpoint LHS could produce misleading results. As a worst case, consider this model:

$$x \sim \text{Uniform}(0, 100)$$

$$y = \cos(2\pi x)$$

The expectation of y should be zero (averaging over an integral number of cosine wave patterns with amplitude 1.) Suppose we perform midpoint LHS with a sample size of 100. Then x will be divided up into 100 equiprobable intervals, whose midpoints are $(0.5, 1.5, 2.5, \ldots 99.5)$. Evaluating y at each point will give a cosine of an odd number of radians, which yields -1. Hence, it will estimate the mean $E[y]$ as -1. Although it is important that modelers be aware of this danger, such periodic behavior is very unusual in policy and risk analysis models, and should be predictable.

8.5.7. Generating Correlated Input Variables

As mentioned in Section 6.4.6, when two input quantities are judged to be probabilistically dependent, it is often best to try to structure the model to model the dependence explicitly, by adding, if necessary, the common factor that causes the dependence. In this way the need to assess the probabilistic dependence directly is avoided. However, in some cases this may not be practical, and the dependence may be expressed directly as correlations. How can we generate sample values for dependent uncertain inputs with a specified correlation?

It is not hard to generate correlated normal distributions. Suppose we wish to generate random samples for two variables x and y with unit normal distributions and correlation r. We define an auxiliary variable, z. We generate a sample of values for x and z, from independent normal distributions, either in the standard way, or using Latin hypercube sampling. We use these to compute a corresponding sample for y,

$$y := rx + z\sqrt{1 - r^2}$$

where the notation := denotes a replacement statement. The sample for y will also be from a unit normal with the specified correlation to x. If we wish x and y to have mean and standard deviation other than 0 and 1, respectively, say, μ_x, σ_x, μ_y, σ_y, we can transform them appropriately:

$$x := \mu_x + \sigma_x \times x$$

$$y := \mu_y + \sigma_y \times y$$

These transformations will not affect their correlations. Given a $n \times n$ covariance matrix (which must be positive definite), this approach can easily be generalized to generate n correlated normal variates (Scheuer and Stoller, 1962).

If we want to generate correlated continuous random variables with other kinds of marginal distributions, the situation becomes trickier. In fact, it is not generally possible to generate two random variables, each with an arbitrary marginal distribution and with any specified Spearman correlation. But Iman and Conover (1982a) have shown how it *is* possible to generate variables with specified *rank-order correlation*. They describe a method for generating n variables with arbitrary strictly increasing cumulative functions and specified rank order correlation matrix. They start by generating n unit normal variables with the specified correlation matrix. They then transform each input sample from the unit normal to the desired marginal distribution. This transform will not necessarily preserve the Pearson correlations exactly, but any strictly monotonic transform is guaranteed to preserve the rank-order correlations.

Just as the mean or variance of a random sample will not be identical to the exact mean and variance of the parent distribution, so the rank correlation matrix for the results of the generation method just described will not be precisely that specified. Even samples generated from uncorrelated distributions are likely to have nonzero correlation, just because of random noise. Iman and Conover (1982b) describe a technique that, when combining sample values for the inputs to form scenarios, can control the resulting correlations. Thus, it produces results whose correlations are more exactly those specified. This may be used even for variables intended to be uncorrelated, since it can reduce incidental correlation from the sampling process to nearer zero. In effect this increases the uniformity of the sampling process, not simply over each individual input dimension but also over the joint domains of pairs of inputs. This reduces the consequent noise in the simulation process, and increases sampling efficiency.

8.5.8. Importance Sampling

In crude Monte Carlo or standard Latin hypercube sampling, all input values are generated equal, in the sense that the probability of any value being generated is proportional to the probability density at that point. If one is more interested in some parts of the output distribution than others, it is often possible to use *importance sampling* to generate more sample points to illuminate these aspects of special interest, and fewer in other parts (Clark, 1961). For example, in a safety analysis of a reactor vessel, events that could lead to a failure are likely to be of particular interest. To examine this more efficiently, one may artificially inflate the probability of choosing input values that are likely to lead to this, so that even if the prior probability of vessel failure is very small, one can still simulate a significant number of events that lead to failure. Thus, one might adjust the sample generation process so that inputs that lead to higher internal pressure and inputs that lead to lower vessel strength are sampled disproportionately. The adjustment to the probability of each input value is termed its *importance weight*. The importance weight of the corresponding output value is the product of importance weights of all the input values that lead to it. To estimate the true probability distribution for the output value, you must restore the actual probability of each sample that is inversely proportional to its importance weight. This approach, which has seen fairly wide use in scientific applications, has considerable (so far largely unrealized) potential for uncertainty propagation in risk analysis problems with low probability, high consequence risks, where the extreme upper tail of the distribution is often of much greater interest than the rest of it.

8.5.9. Measures of Uncertainty Importance

Monte Carlo and other random sampling techniques have occasionally been criticized for not supporting attribution of uncertainties (e.g., Cox and Baybutt, 1981). But in fact a variety of rather powerful measures of uncertainty importance are available. One useful approach is to compute the correlation between the sample of output values and the corresponding sample of values for each input. Let us consider m samples from the output and a single input, denoted as y_k, x_k, for $k = 1$ to m. We compute the sample correlation as:

$$U_\rho(x, y) = \frac{\sum_{k=1}^{m}(x_k - \overline{x})(y_k - \overline{y})}{\sqrt{\sum_{k=1}^{m}(x_k - \overline{x})^2 \times \sum_{k=1}^{m}(y_k - \overline{y})^2}}$$

The correlation gives an estimate of the linear contribution of each input to the output uncertainty: It is inherently a global measure of uncertainty importance, averaging the effect of each input over the joint probability distribution for all other inputs.

Several related approaches have been demonstrated based on regression analysis of the output samples with respect to the uncertain inputs. Consider a least squares regression model fitted to estimate the output y as a linear function of the inputs x_j. (Note that the index j is over the n inputs, where k was over the m sample values for one input).

$$\hat{y} = b_0 + \sum_{j=1}^{n} b_j x_j$$

The b_j regression coefficients are measures of the linear sensitivity of y to the inputs x_j (Draper and Smith, 1981). They have the disadvantage that they depend on the units or scale of measurement of y and x_j. A more useful measure of uncertainty importance, known as the *standardized regression coefficient* (SRC), may be obtained by multiplying each coefficient by the ratio of the estimated standard deviations of x_j to y:

$$U_{\text{SRC}}(x_j, y) = \frac{b_j \times s_y}{s_j}$$

It is often useful to perform stepwise regression, producing a sequence of linear models consisting of 1, 2, 3, up to n of the input variables respectively. Inputs are added one at a time to maximize the improvement in fit of the model according to R^2 value. The sequence in which they are selected is a useful measure of their uncertainty importance, as is the increment in R^2 they produce. Iman and colleagues (Iman and Conover, 1980; Iman and Helton, 1988) have also suggested the use of partial correlation coefficients. These are measures of the contribution of each uncertain input to the output uncertainty, after removing the effects attributable to the other inputs. They are particularly useful when there are significant correlations between the inputs.

Correlations, whether partial or not, and regression coefficients are a measure of the strength of linear relationship between input and output. They do not necessarily provide a good measure of nonlinear monotonic relationship. If the distributions of input or output are far from normal, particularly if they have one or two long tails, they are liable to distortion from the effect of outliers. One way to avoid this problem is to rank order the sample values for each input and for the output, and examine rank-order correlations. This is a good measure of the strength of monotonic relations, whether linear or not. It may also be useful to examine the effects of squares, products, and higher order combinations of inputs in the regression analysis to see if there are important nonmonotonic and interaction effects.

To understand more about the nature and strength of relationships between inputs and outputs of a model, it is often useful to examine scatter plots of one against the other. These can provide a lot of insight, show nonlinear effects, thresholds, and so on, and may be useful in suggesting relationships to test with regression (Iman and Davenport, 1982). For more details and illustrations of the use of these various measures, see Iman and Conover (1980, 1982a); Iman and Davenport (1982); Iman and Helton (1985, 1988).

8.6. Fourier Amplitude Sensitivity Test

An approach that examines sensitivity to inputs, averaged over the input parameter space (although it does not provide a measure for attribution of probabilistic uncertainty), is the *Fourier Amplitude Sensitivity Test* (FAST), (Cukier et al., 1973; Schaibly and Schuler, 1973; Cukier, Schaibly, and Schuler, 1975; Cukier, Levine, and Schuler, 1978). The essence of this technique is to generate a curve in the parameter space that is a periodic function of each parameter, with a different frequency for each. The problem is to generate inputs x_{ij}, for each parameter x_i, and each model run, $j = 1 \ldots m$:

$$x_{ij} = E[x_i] + v_i \sin(w_i s_j), \qquad i = 1 \ldots n$$

where v_i are positive constants chosen so that the parameter values vary between assigned upper and lower limits: $\{w_i\}$ is a set of integer frequencies chosen so there is no interference (correlation) between the parameters; s_j is a parameter selecting points along the n-dimensional search curve. Equally spaced values, s_j, are chosen to generate the x_{ij}. The relative contribution of each input parameter to the range of the output can be measured by a discrete Fourier analysis of the output. The contribution of each input is measured by the contribution of its characteristic frequency, as specified by w_i, to the outputs.

8.7. Response Surface Methods

For large, computationally expensive models it is sometimes useful to build a simplified *response surface*, which is an approximate version of the full model (Myers, 1971; Downing, Gardner, and Hoffman, 1985). The response surface is generally fitted to a moderate number of model runs. If many model runs are needed for some application, then instead of expensively evaluating the whole model, it is possible to substitute the simplified response surface model and greatly reduce the computational cost. For example, if a large number of Monte Carlo runs are required for uncertainty propagation and analysis, these may be economically carried out using the response surface. This approach may be particularly useful for real time tasks, such as real time control of a complex system, a manufacturing process or aerospace vehicle. A response surface model can be fitted to a large and sophisticated model of the system; but when rapid response is required to predict the effect of control measures in real time, the simple response surface model may be used. This response surface approach has been developed for uncertainty analysis of some very large computer codes for simulation of the liquid metal fast breeder reactor (Vaurio, 1982). Another example involves a regional photochemical air pollution model (Milford, Russell, and McRae, 1988).

There are three key issues in response surface modeling: first, how to select the small sample of scenarios with which to run the large model. Second, how to screen the uncertain inputs and identify which ones need to be modeled explicitly. And third, how best to fit a response surface to these results. In complex engineering models, there may be tens or hundreds of uncertain inputs, and it may initially be unclear which of these are of any significance. Usually, inspection of the model structure and/or judgment from experience may be sufficient to rule out at least some of the inputs as possibly having significant impact on the output uncertainties. Discovering which of the rest are important must rely on examination of the model behavior.

A simple selection approach, perturbing one input at a time, keeping the rest at nominal values, is highly inefficient. It will require at least as many runs as uncertain inputs, and even then is restricted to modeling local behavior around the nominal scenario, ignoring nonlinearities and interactions between inputs. Combinatorial scenarios will cover a larger part of the model behavior, but require far too many model runs in general. Fractional factorial designs (FFD) (Box, Hunter, and Hunter, 1978) have been quite popular. These select a subset of the combinatorial scenarios. There is an extensive statistical literature on FFD, on how best to choose scenarios to be able to estimate higher order behavior with minimal runs. (See Box and Hunter, 1961a, 1961b, for a good expository article on two-level fractional factorials.) Others (e.g., Vaurio, 1982) have used Monte Carlo and related random sampling techniques, which they suggest as a convenient and reliable way to cover the input domain.

The main purpose of the sampling process is to identify those uncertain inputs that contribute most to the output, that is, essentially to perform uncertainty analysis. Usually just a few uncertain inputs are found to contribute the majority of the uncertainty in the output. The simplified response surface need model only the effect of these, and can generally ignore the other inputs. The techniques for uncertainty analysis described in Section 8.5.9 may be used for this task in identifying which variables should be used in the response surface. A variety of correlation and stepwise regression techniques have been used (Vaurio, 1982). Depending on the model, it may be wise to examine quadratic and higher order relations to see if there are significant nonmonotonic relations or interactions. Vaurio (1982) also describes methods to test the significance of possible discontinuities in model behavior.

Once the important parameters are identified, the problem is to construct a response surface model that most accurately reproduces the output values as a function of them. The most common scheme is simple linear and quadratic regression models, fit to the test scenarios (Iman and Helton, 1988). For models with complex behaviors, more sophisticated fitted surfaces may be appropriate. Regionwise quadratics have been found to give good results, using a different quadratic function for different quadrants of the input hyperspace. The inputs and outputs may be transformed before trying to fit them. Of course, the more complex the functions to be used, the better the fit is likely to be, but the more effort and ingenuity is required of the analyst in devising it. The availability of flexible surface–fitting software can make this process much easier (Vaurio, 1980a, 1980b).

One difficulty with response surface methods is obtaining a reliable guide to the accuracy of the results. Statistical measures of goodness of fit of the surface to the selected points, such as R-square, or the maximum residuals, give a lower bound on the likely error. But they depend partly on the degrees of freedom of the surface: If the number of parameters is comparable to the number of points fitted, then a high degree of fit has little significance. If it is important to get a better idea of the accuracy, a small number of independent additional runs of the full model may be performed for validation. These should be chosen for scenarios distinct from the scenarios to which the response surface was originally fit. The response surface may guide selection of points that are expected to generate outcomes in particularly interesting regions.

8.8. Selecting a Method

As we have seen, there exists an almost overwhelming variety of different methods for representing, propagating, and analyzing uncertainties. They have been developed and applied in a wide range of modeling domains, in policy and risk analysis as well as more traditional areas of science and engineering. These include financial investment planning, physics, chemical engineering, nuclear engineering and safety analysis, ecological modeling, and atmospheric modeling, to list but a few. In the beginnings of uncertainty analysis, traditions about which method to use grew up within the shelter of different application areas. This resulted in a degree of isolation and incompatibility of views between analysts even though they were working on methodologically similar kinds of problems. However, in recent years there has been more extensive sharing of ideas between disciplines, which has led to a number of reviews and comparative experiments, applying different techniques to the same problem to identify their relative advantages and disadvantages. At least for some kinds of application, a degree of concensus about the appropriateness of particular techniques now seems to be starting to develop.

This last section of this chapter is intended to distill the findings from our discussion and from other comparative literature to help guide analysts confronted with the need to select a method for a particular problem at hand. After a brief discussion of the criteria for comparison, we examine the pros and cons for some of the key choices. Among those comparative studies we have found particularly useful have been Martz et al. (1983), and Iman and Helton (1985; 1988).

8.8.1. Criteria

As a counter to the natural tendency for one's thinking to be dominated by just one consideration, it is useful to list out the full range of criteria that may be relevant to choice of method. These criteria may be organized into the following four groups:

- *Uncertainty about the model form:* What is the relative importance of uncertainty about the form of the model versus the contributions of parameter uncertainty? If model structure and relationships are disputed or poorly known, extensive evaluation of parameter uncertainty within a specific model may be pointless and misleading. If the model structure is well characterized, parameter uncertainty analysis is typically appropriate.
- *The nature of the model:* How large is it, in terms of the number of uncertain inputs, and the computational cost of a single run? How large are the uncertainties? Is its response surface smooth, monotonic in its inputs, and is it reasonably approximated by simple functional forms? Or does it show complex, nonmonotonic, or discontinuous behavior?
- *The requirements of the analysis:* What is the main purpose of the analysis? Are significant actions to be based directly on its results? Is the uncertainty analysis intended to guide refinement of the model and/or decisions about what additional information to collect? Is the central tendency (mean or median) of the outputs the main interest, or is a solid characterization of the uncertainty also important? How precise an estimate of the full distribution is necessary? Are extreme tails of the output of importance? How much precision is needed in the identification and ranking of the main contributors to the uncertainty?
- *Resources available:* How much time (calendar time and staff time) is available to conduct the analysis? What kinds of skills and experience do the analysts have? What kinds of computing resources, and, in particular, what kind of software is available?

In technical comparisons of methods, it is easy to focus on computation costs, since they are often the simplest to quantify. But as computer resources continue to diminish in cost, for all but the most colossal models they will tend to be dominated by the other costs, particularly human resources. Thus, for models of moderate size (i.e., modest computational cost per run), the most important questions may be about the amount of human effort a method requires, to set up and run the uncertainty analysis, and to interpret the results.

8.8.2. When to Use the Method of Moments

When a model is simple and the uncertainties are small relative to its nonlinearities, the first order method of moments, that is, the Gaussian approximation and particularly its relative error formulation for products of powers, is very useful. In these cases, the application of the approach is straightforward, and lends itself to quick, back-of-the-envelope calculations. It provides a clear basis for uncertainty analysis, by partitioning up the variance of the outputs as the sum of the contributions for each input. This kind of approach is widely used in the physical sciences and deserves to be more widely known and used among policy and risk analysts. It is especially helpful in developing intuitions about how uncertainties combine and propagate.

Having said this, it is important to acknowledge that the uncertainties in policy and risk analysis are often rather large compared to nonlinearities in the models. Hence, first order approximations, representing the response surface as a hyperplane, can be quite inaccurate. Although there have been attempts to develop techniques using higher order approximations (e.g., Seiler, 1987), these get algebraically complicated rapidly as the complexity of the model increases. Moreover, it is hard to discover just how good or bad a given approximation may be to the actual model, and consequently how safe it is to rely on the results. The basic problem is that these schemes are local, looking at perturbations around the nominal scenario, and may not work well globally.

An apparent advantage of the method of moments is that it requires only the first few moments of input distributions, typically the mean and variance, without needing complete specification of the entire distribution. But concomitantly, it provides only these moments for the output distributions. In applications such as nuclear safety analysis, where the tails of the distributions are of particular interest, this can be a serious deficiency.

There has also been considerable research on the development of adjoint methods for differential sensitivity analysis for complex dynamic models. However, analysts who have attempted to use these have reported they can be extremely difficult to implement, often requiring an effort for the uncertainty analysis comparable with the original model development effort (e.g., Iman and Helton, 1988). To remedy the analytic complexity of obtaining partial derivatives in complex models, one may employ automated systems for symbolic differentiation. In contrast, Monte Carlo and other sampling techniques are generally rather easy to apply to existing computer models. It is mainly a matter of putting an outer repetition loop around the program to run it for multiple scenarios.

It is increasingly apparent that quite few sample runs are often sufficient, particularly with more efficient sampling strategies. Therefore, the computational advantages of the method of moments, in requiring fewer model runs, are less obvious. Moreover, for all but the most enormous models, the time the analyst spends implementing the model, and setting up and interpreting the uncertainty analysis, is more important than the computational cost. It is now clear that sampling methods provide measures of uncertainty importance that are at least as useful as differential methods. Finally, the difficulty of estimating the accuracy of the approximation is a major drawback of the method of moments. For all these reasons, it increasingly appears that sampling techniques are the technique of choice over the method of moments for all except simple near-linear models with small uncertainties.

8.8.3. Discrete Probability Tree vs. Monte Carlo

Among practicing decision analysts by far the most common approach to uncertainty analysis is using discrete probability distributions to form probability trees or, more generally, decision trees. Currently, the use of Monte Carlo approaches is considerably less frequent. Among the advantages of the discrete probability tree enumeration schemes are the following:

1. Provided the model is quite small, with not more than three or four uncertain quantities and decisions, the tree can be a clear and appealing representation. It is easy to explain, and the computations can be carried out with pencil and paper or hand calculator.
2. It is generally easier to express probabilistic dependencies among variables as discrete conditional probability distributions, than to express them in terms of correlations between continuous variables.
3. It is generally much easier to apply Bayes' rule to reverse conditioning in discrete probability trees than it is for continuous variables.

On the other hand, Monte Carlo and other sampling methods have some important advantages over tree schemes:

1. If uncertain quantities are continuous, there is no need to discretize them for sampling schemes. (If they are already discrete, this also poses no problems for Monte Carlo.)
2. The imprecision in the propagated distributions and uncertainty measures can be estimated easily by standard statistical methods, and improved simply by taking additional samples. The imprecision due to the discretization for tree-based methods is much harder to estimate.
3. Measures of uncertainty importance are more powerful than those typically used in tree enumeration schemes.
4. The computational effort is essentially linear in the number of quantities represented as uncertain, rather than exponential as it is in tree enumeration schemes.

In summary, tree enumeration schemes are appropriate for models that have a modest number of uncertain inputs. Typically, if there are more than a dozen or so uncertain inputs, they are likely to be computationally intractable. If there are complex probabilistic dependencies to be represented, and especially if Bayesian inference is required, then tree representations have important advantages. If there are not, then Monte Carlo methods may be more appealing. The advantages of its linear computational complexity and easily measurable precision are important, and the wider availability of flexible Monte Carlo software may lead to wider use of the technique for decision analysis.

If there are complex dependencies and Bayesian inference is required, and there are many uncertain quantities, it may be hard to find any tractable scheme. But by careful sensitivity analysis of deterministic models or uncertainty analysis of simplified models, it may be possible to identify a small number of uncertain inputs that dominate the uncertainty in the results. Then the rest of the uncertain inputs can be treated as deterministic, and tree enumeration schemes may be rendered tractable.

8.8.4. What Type of Sampling Scheme to Use?

The various alternatives to crude Monte Carlo sampling, including the controlled variate, Latin hypercube sampling, and importance sampling schemes, all improve convergence rate at little extra cost, other than a slightly more complex program. Given software that provides these alternatives in a form that can be easily applied, there seems little reason not to use one of them. Latin hypercube sampling seems to be particularly valuable. Although it can introduce slight bias in the estimates of moments, in practice this seems negligible. Midpoint LHS is still better than standard LHS, as long as one can be sure the model does not contain any high frequency behavior, which is extremely unlikely in policy and risk models. The Iman and Conover (1982a) scheme for reducing incidental correlation between uncertain inputs to near zero is valuable in further improving the uniformity of sampling. Importance sampling appears to have been little used in policy and risk analysis, but it has considerable potential in cases where particular regions of the model domain are of special interest, as in the upper tails of failure frequencies in nuclear reliability analysis.

8.8.5. When to Use Response Surface Methods

For models that are very expensive to run, response surface methods (RSM) become attractive. The initial effort to develop a good response surface may be significant, but once it is available a wide variety of sensitivity and uncertainty analyses may be performed, provided they stay within the domain of the input space for which the surface was fit. The functional form and coefficients of the surface should themselves give considerable insight to which inputs are contributing most uncertainty and in what ways. The analytical effort in developing a response surface may be greatly eased by the use of flexible software for screening input variables and exploring the fit of different surfaces, such as SCREEN and PROSA-2 (Vaurio, 1980a).

Given an appropriately well-behaved function, moment methods and RSM may in many cases give greater accuracy for similar computational effort (or equivalently the same accuracy for less computational effort) than Monte Carlo. However, with Monte Carlo it is easy to use standard statistical tests to find out just how accurate the output distribution is, in terms of confidence intervals on moments and fractiles. But with the former methods, except in very simple cases it is difficult to find out just how accurate the results are, and whether, in fact, this is one of the cases in which results are poor, at least in certain parts of the domain.

8.8.6. The Importance of Software

In most cases, a major factor in selecting an approach to uncertainty propagation and analysis is the effort spent setting up and conducting the analysis. This can be much affected by the availability of easy-to-use and flexible software to support the approach. Lack of software or computing resources will tend to favor approaches that can be done without special programs, primarily Gaussian approximation or probability trees for small models. Several packages are now available running on microcomputers to perform decision analysis that can support uncertainty analysis using probability trees (three are reviewed in Henrion, 1985). There are also a number of packages to support Monte Carlo analysis, including Latin hypercube sampling and correlational uncertainty analysis. These include IFPS (Execucom, 1983), Demos (Henrion and Morgan, 1985), and packages for Latin hypercube sampling (Iman, Davenport, and Zeigler, 1980; Iman and Shortencarier, 1984; Iman, Shortencarier, and Johnson, 1985). New software products for decision analysis and Monte Carlo simulation are becoming available all the time. Issues in the design and use of computer packages for uncertainty analysis are addressed in more detail in Chapter 10.

References

Ahmed, S., Metcalf, D. R., and Pegram, J. W. (1981). "Uncertainty Propagation in Probabilistic Risk Assessment: A Comparative Study," *Transactions of the American Nuclear Society: 1981 Annual Meeting*, 38:483–484.

Bier, V. M. (1983). "A Measure of Uncertainty Importance in Fault Trees," *Transactions of the American Nuclear Society: 1983 Annual Meeting*, 45:384–395.

Box, G.E.P., and Hunter, J. S. (1961a). "The 2^{K-P} Fractional Factorial Designs," Part I, *Technometrics*, 3, no. 3 (August): 311–351.

Box, G.E.P., and Hunter, J. S. (1961b). "The 2^{K-P} Fractional Factorial Designs," Part II, *Technometrics*, 3, no. 4 (November): 449–458.

Box, G.E.P., Hunter, W. G., and Hunter, J. S. (1978). *Statistics for Experimenters*, Wiley-Interscience, New York.

Cacuci, D. G. (1981a). "Sensitivity Theory for Nonlinear Systems. I. Nonlinear Functional Analysis Approach," *Journal of Mathematical Physics*, 22:2794–2802.

Cacuci, D. G. (1981b). "Sensitivity Theory for Nonlinear Systems. II. Extensions to Additional Classes of Responses," *Journal of Mathematical Physics*, 22:2803–2812.

Cacuci, D. G., Maudlin, P. J., and Parks, C. U. (1983). "Adjoint Sensitivity Analysis of Extremum-Type Responses in Reactor Safety," *Nuclear Science and Engineering*, 83:112–135.

Cacuci, D. G., Weber, C. F., Oblow, E. M., and Marable, J. H. (1980). "Sensitivity Theory for General Systems of Nonlinear Equations," *Nuclear Science and Engineering*, 75:88–110.

Cheney, E. W. (1966). *Introduction to Appoximation Theory*, McGraw-Hill, New York.

Clark, C. E. (1961). "Importance Sampling in Monte Carlo Analyses," *Operations Research*, 9:603–620.

Cox, N. D. (1977). "Comparison of Two Uncertainty Analysis Methods," *Nuclear Science and Engineering*, no. 64:258–265.

Cox, D. C., and Baybutt, P. (1981). "Methods For Uncertainty Analysis: A Comparative Survey," *Risk Analysis*, 1:251–258.

Cukier, R. I., Fortuin, C. M., Schuler, K. E., Petschek, A. G., and Schaibly, J. H. (1973). "Study of the Sensitivity of Coupled Reaction Systems to Uncertainties in Rate Coefficients: I Theory," *Journal of Chemical Physics*, 59:3873–3878.

Cukier, R. I., Schaibly, J. H., and Schuler, K. E. (1975). "Study of the Sensitivity of Coupled Reaction Systems to Uncertainties in Rate Coefficients: III Analysis of the Approximations," *Journal of Chemical Physics*, 63:1140–1149.

Cukier, R. I., Levine, H. B., and Schuler, K. E. (1978). "Nonlinear Sensitivity Analysis of Multiparameter Model Systems," *Journal of Computational Physics*, 26:1–42.

Dougherty, E. P., Hwang, J.-T., and Rabitz, H. (1979). "Further Developments and Applications of the Green's Function Method of Sensitivity Analysis in Chemical Kinetics," *Journal of Chemical Physics*, 71:1794–1808.

Downing, D. J., Gardner, R. H., and Hoffman, F. O. (1985). "Response Surface Methodologies for Uncertainty Analysis in Assessment Model," *Technometrics*, 27, no. 2: 151–163.

Draper, N. R., and Smith, H. (1981). *Applied Regression Analysis*, 2nd ed., Wiley, New York.

Execucom, Inc. (1983). *IFPS Tutorial*, Execucom Systems Co., Austin, Tex.

Fiksel, J. R., Cox, L. A., and Ojha, H. D., (1984, March). "Dealing with Uncertainty in Risk Analysis," Arthur D. Little, Inc., paper partially supported by the National Science Foundation, Division of Policy Research and Analysis, under Grant No. PRA-8303162.

Hall, M.C.G., Cacuci, D. G., and Schlesinger, M. E. (1982). "Sensitivity Analysis of a Radiative-Convective Model by the Adjoint Method," *Journal of the Atmospheric Sciences*, 39:2038–2050.

Henrion, M. (1982). *The Value of Knowing How Little You Know*, Ph.D. diss., School of Urban and Public Affairs, Carnegie Mellon University, Pittsburgh.

Henrion, M. (1985). "Software for Decision Analysis: A Review of Riskcalc, Arborist, and Supertree," in Personal Computing & OR/MS, *OR/MS Today*, 12, no. 5: 24–29.

Henrion, M., and Morgan, M. G. (1985). "A Computer Aid for Policy and Risk Analysis," *Risk Analysis*, 5, no. 3: 195–208.

Howard, R. A. (1971). "Proximal Decision Analysis," *Management Science*, 17, no. 9:507–541.

Howard, R. A., and Matheson, J. (1981). "Influence Diagrams," reprinted in Howard and Matheson (1984).

Howard, R. W., and Matheson, J. (1984). *The Principles and Applications of Decision Analysis*, 2:719–762, Strategic Decisions Group, Menlo Park, Calif.

Humphreys, P., and Berkeley, D., "Handling Uncertainty: Levels of Analysis of Decision Problems," in *Behavioral Decision Making: Theory and Analysis*, ed. G. N. Wright, Plenum, New York.

Hwang, J.-T., Dougherty, E. P., Rabitz, S., and Rabitz, H. (1978). "The Greens Function Method of Sensitivity Analysis in Chemical Kinetics," *Journal of Chemical Physics*, 69:5180–5191.

Iman, R. L., and Conover, W.J. (1980). "Small Sample Sensitivity Analysis Techniques for Computer Models, with an Application to Risk Assessment," *Communications in Statistics*, A17:1749.

Iman, R. L., and Conover, W. J. (1982a). "Sensitivity Analysis Techniques: Self-Teaching Curriculum," NUREG/CR-2350, SAND81-1978, Sandia National Laboratories, Albuquerque, N.M.

Iman, R. L., and Conover, W. J. (1982b). "A Distribution-Free Approach to Inducing Rank Correlation Among Input Variables," *Communications on Statistics: Simulation and Computing*, 11, no. 3:311–334.

Iman, R. L., and Davenport, J. M. (1982). "Rank Correlation Plots for Use With Correlated Input Variables," *Communications on Statistics: Simulation and Computing*, 11, no. 3:335–360.

Iman, R. L., Davenport, J. M., and Zeigler, D. K. (1980, January). *Latin Hypercube Sampling (Program User's Guide)*, prepared by Sandia Laboratories for the U.S. Department of Energy under Contract DE-AC04-76DP00789, SAND79-1473.

Iman, R. L., and Helton, J. C. (1985). *A Comparison of Uncertainty and Sensitivity Analysis Techniques for Computer Models*, NUREG/CR-3904, SAND84-1461, Sandia National Laboratories, Albuquerque, N.M.

Iman, R. L., and Helton, J. C. (1988). "An Investigation of Uncertainty and Sensitivity Analysis Techniques for Computer Models," *Risk Analysis*, 8, no. 1 (March):71–90.

Iman, R. L., and Shortencarier, M. J. (1984). *A FORTRAN 77 Program and User's Guide for the Generation of Latin Hypercube and Random Samples for Use with Computer Models*, NUREG/CR-3624, SAND83-2365, Sandia National Laboratories, Albuquerque, N.M.

Iman, R. L., Shortencarier, M. J., and Johnson, J. D. (1985). *A FORTRAN 77 Program and User's Guide for the Calculation of Partial Correlation and Standardized Regression Coefficients*, NUREG/CR-4122, SAND85-0044, Sandia National Laboratories, Albuquerque, N.M.

Jackson, P. S., Hockenbury, R. W., and Yeater M. L. (1981). "Uncertainty Analysis for System Reliability and Availability Assessment," *Nuclear Engineering and Design*, 68:5–29.

Johnson, M. (1987). *Multivariate Statistical Simulation*, Wiley, New York.

Kaplan, S. (1981). "On the Method of Discrete Probability Distributions – Application to Seismic Risk Assessment," *Risk Analysis*, 1:189–198.

Keefer, D. L., and Bodily, S. E. (1983). "Three-point Approximations for Continuous Random Variables," *Management Science*, 29:595–609.

Koda, M., Dogru, A. H., and Seinfeld, J. H. (1979). "Sensitivity Analysis of Partial Differential Equations with Application to Reaction and Diffusion Processes," *Journal of Computational Physics*, 30:259–282.

Korn, G. A., and Korn, T. M. (1968). *Mathematical Handbook for Scientists and Engineers*, McGraw-Hill, New York.

Lave, L. B., and Epple, D. N. (1985). "Scenario Analysis," pp. 511–528 in *Climate Impact Assessment*, ed. R. W. Kates, J. H. Ausubel, and M. Berberian, Wiley, New York.

Mallows, C. L. (1956). "Generalizations of Tchebycheff's Inequalities," *Journal of the Royal Statistical Society*, Series B, no. 18:139–168.

Martz, H. F., Beckman, A. G., Campbell, K., Whiteman, D. E., and Booker, J. M. (1983, April). *A Comparison of Methods for Uncertainty Analysis of Nuclear Power Plant Safety System Fault Tree Models*, NUREG/CR-3263, LA-9729-MS, Los Alamos National Laboratory, N.M.

Milford, J. B., Russell, A. G., and McRae, G. J. (in press). "Spatial Patterns in Photochemical Pollutant Response to NO_X and ROG Reductions," *Environmental Science and Technology*.

Miller, A. C., and Rice, T. R. (1983). "Discrete Approximations of Continuous Distributions," *Management Science*, 29, no. 3:352–362.

Myers, R. H. (1971). *Response Surface Methodology*, Allyn & Bacon, Newton, Mass.

Oblow, E. M. (1983a, May). *An Automated Procedure for Sensitivity Analysis using Computer Calculus*, ORNL/TM-8776, Oak Ridge National Laboratory, Oak Ridge, Tenn.

Oblow, E. M. (1983b). *GRESS – Gradient Enhanced Software System Version B: User's Guide*, ORNL/TM-8339, Oak Ridge National Laboratory, Oak Ridge, Tenn.

Raiffa, H. (1968). *Decision Analysis: Introductory Lectures on Choice Under Uncertainty*, Addison Wesley, New York.

Rall, L. B. (1981). *Automatic Differentiation: Techniques and Applications*, Springer-Verlag, New York.

Rasmussen, N., et al. (1975). *Reactor Safety Study*, (WASH-1400), U.S. Nuclear Regulatory Commission, Washington, D.C.

Rubinstein, R. Y. (1982). *Simulation and the Monte Carlo Method*, Wiley, New York.

Schaibly, J. H., and Schuler, K. E. (1973). "Study of the Sensitivity of Coupled Reaction Schemes to Uncertainties in Rate Coefficients. II, Applications," *Journal of Chemical Physics*, 59:3879–3888.

Scheuer, E. M., and Stoller, D. S. (1962). "On the Generation of Normal Random Vectors," *Technometrics*, 4:278–281.

Seiler, F. A. (1987). "Error Propagation for Large Errors," *Risk Analysis*, 7, no. 4:509–518.

Springer, M. D. (1979). *The Algebra of Random Variables*, Wiley, New York.

Vaurio, J. K. (1980a). *PROSA2, and Probabilistic Response Surface Analysis and Simulation Code*, Argonne National Laboratory, ANL/RAS-80-26, Argonne, Ill.

Vaurio, J. K. (1980b). "Statistical Determination of Threshold Variables," *Transactions of the American Nuclear Society*, 35:263–264.

Vaurio, J. K., (1982, September). *Statistical Identification of Effective Input Variables, Reactor Analysis and Safety Division*, ANL-82-57, Argonne National Laboratory, Argonne, Ill.

Watson, S. R., and Buede, D. M. (1987). *Decision Synthesis: The Principles and Practice of Decision Analysis*, Cambridge University Press, New York.

Whitfield, R. G., and Newsom, D. E. (1984, April). *A Survey of Methods for Uncertainty Analysis*, report prepared for U.S. Department of Energy, Argonne National Laboratory, Argonne, Ill.

The Graphic Communication of Uncertainty

"The purpose of computing is insight, not numbers."
Richard Hamming

9.1. Introduction

If, to paraphrase Richard Hamming's remark about computing, the goal of policy analysis is insight, not numbers, then clearly one of the most important challenges of policy analysis is to communicate the insights it provides to those who need them. Such insights can include an appreciation of the overall degree of uncertainty about the "bottom line" conclusions, an understanding of which sources of uncertainty and which modeling assumptions are critical to those conclusions and which are not, and an understanding of the extent to which plausible alternative assumptions can change the conclusions that are reached. The insights obtained will ultimately be qualitative in nature, even if the models they derive from are quantitative. This means it is incumbent on the analyst to find ways to present quantitative results in a manner that will most clearly communicate the information they contain and aid users in developing the appropriate qualitative insights. Most experienced analysts believe that graphical techniques play an indispensable role in this process, yet the use of graphics to communicate uncertain information has been the focus of remarkably little attention.[1] This chapter is concerned with exploring some of the alternatives that are available for graphic presentation of uncertain quantitative information, and some of the necessary tradeoffs between simplicity and sophistication, particularly in choosing the dimensionality of information to present. Our hope is that a greater awareness of the range of possible alternatives may lead to more thoughtful choice among them. Although we will discuss results from a study we have done for one-dimensional displays, for the most part, the absence of empirical studies of the relative virtues of alternative displays means that the choice of displays remains largely a matter of personal judgment.

9.2. Displaying One-dimensional Probability Distributions

There are three basic ways of presenting a probability distribution over a one-

---

1. Tufte (1983), and Cleveland and McGill (1985) have done interesting recent work on graphics. However, neither focuses particularly on the problems of using graphics to communicate uncertainty. Although the focus is not on graphics, some interesting graphical ideas related to communicating uncertainty can be found in Tukey (1977).

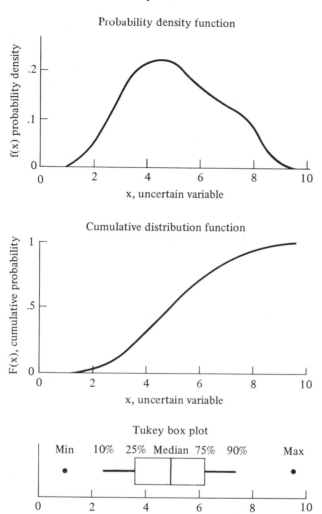

Figure 9.1. Three conventional displays of a probability distribution. Note that none of these conventional displays indicates the location of the mean of the distribution, which in the example shown lies just to the right of the median at $x = 5$.

dimensional uncertain quantity: as a probability density function (PDF), as a cumulative distribution function (CDF), or by displaying selected fractiles, as in a Tukey box plot (Figure 9.1).[2]

---

2. The standard Tukey box plot shows a horizontal line from the 10th to the 90th percentiles, a box from the 25th to the 75th percentiles and a vertical line at the median, and points at the minimum and maximum observed values. Several variants of the box plot are common.

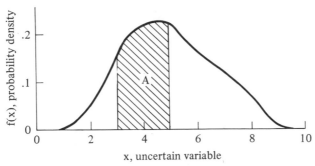

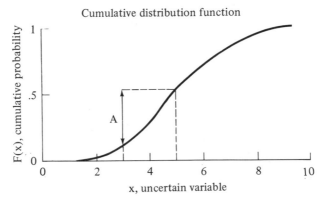

Figure 9.2. The cumulative probability distribution $F(x)$ is the integral of the probability density function. Thus, for example, $\int_3^5 f(x)\,dx = A = F(5) - F(3)$. In the illustration shown, $A = 0.4$.

As indicated in Figure 9.2 the cumulative distribution function is the integral of the probability density function. If the PDF is properly normalized, the CDF will grow monotonically from 0 to 1.

Although the PDF, CDF, and box plot contain similar information, they emphasize rather different aspects of the probability distribution. In Section 9.3 we discuss some empirical comparisons of the performance of these and other distributions in communicating various information. However, some useful and important differences can be identified without experimental studies. The box plot emphasizes confidence intervals and the median. The density function clearly shows the relative probabilities of different values. It also clearly presents the mode(s) as peak(s) in the curve. It is much more difficult to spot multimodal distributions by looking for multiple inflexion points on a cumulative distribution (see Figure 9.3). It is much easier to judge symmetry or skewness, kurtosis, and other features of the shape of the distribution on the density function.

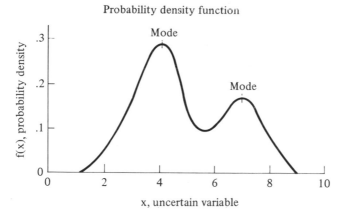

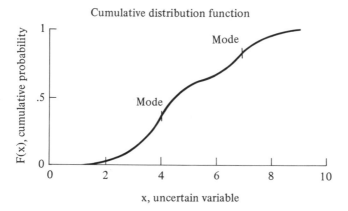

Figure 9.3. Comparison of PDF and CDF for displaying the modes and shape of a distribution.

In general, the density function, being the derivative of the cumulative function, is a much more sensitive indicator of variations in probability density. This may be an advantage if it is important to emphasize small variations, or it may be a disadvantage if, for example, the distribution has been estimated from a Monte Carlo sample, and the small variations are simply random sampling noise of no intrinsic interest. In presenting a sample distribution the density function will look much noisier than the cumulative with equivalent bin sizes (see Figure 9.4).

If the probabilities that the quantity lies in specified intervals is of interest, or if specified fractiles or confidence intervals for the quantity are important, obviously the cumulative form is more useful. If the fractiles or intervals of interest can be restricted to those in the box plot, that simpler representation may be preferable. If two distributions are being compared to determine if one

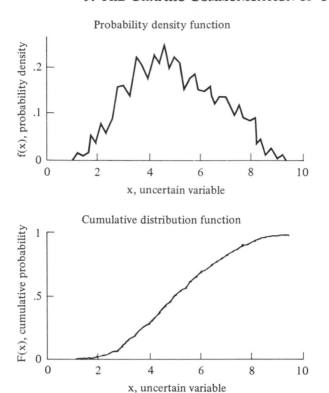

Figure 9.4. The effect of noise is much greater on the probability density function than it is on the cumulative distribution function.

is stochastically dominant over the other, the cumulative representation is best: Stochastic dominance between distributions implies no intersection between their cumulative functions (see Figure 9.5).

Discrete distributions can be shown in a variant of the density form, with vertical lines (or arrows), whose height is proportional to the probability mass (not density) at those points (see Figure 9.6). Mixed distributions, with both continuous and discrete components, can be shown in the density form through the use of delta functions at the locations of the probability masses, as in Figure 9.7. In this instance it is not easy to use the height of the vertical arrow to represent probability, since the vertical dimension is probability density, not probability. The delta functions in the probability density function show up in the cumulative distribution function as vertical steps. An example of a situation in which a mixed distribution is useful in displaying the estimated health impact of a given dose of chemical is when there is a finite probability that the dose may yield no health impact.

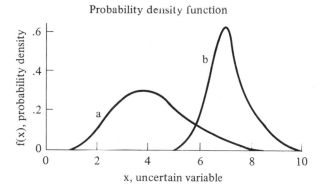

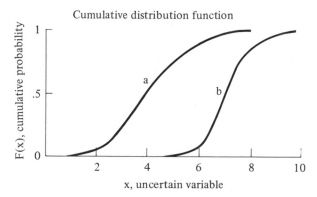

Figure 9.5. Stochastic dominance is most easily seen with the cumulative distribution function. In the example shown, distribution *b* stochastically dominates distribution *a*.

To summarize, we have argued that the density function best displays

- the relative probability of values,
- the most likely values (modes),
- the shape of the distribution (skewness, kurtosis, etc.), and,
- small changes in probability density,

and the cumulative function best displays:

- fractiles, including the median,
- probability of intervals, including confidence intervals,
- stochastic dominance, and
- mixed, continuous and discrete, distributions.

Of course, there is no reason to use only one representation. If, as we suggest below, both the density and cumulative forms are used together, with *x* axes lined up, one gets the advantages of both forms. Moreover, looking at both together can help educate viewers about the meaning and properties of probability distributions.

Probability mass function

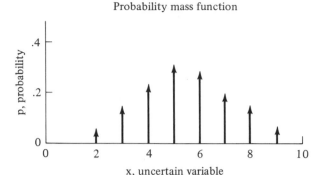

x, uncertain variable

Cumulative distribution function

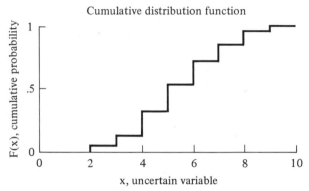

x, uncertain variable

Figure 9.6. Example of a discrete distribution represented in terms of a probability mass function and cumulative distribution function.

9.3. Experimental Findings on Communicating Uncertainty about the Value of a Single Uncertain Quantity

With the exception of some work on the interpretation of probabilistic weather forecasts (Murphy et al., 1980; Murphy, 1986),[3] there have been few evaluations of the effectiveness of alternative means of communicating uncertainty about the value of an uncertain quantity. In collaboration with Harold Ibrekk we have conducted one study that used nine alternative graphical displays for communicating univariate uncertainty. The discussion that follows briefly summarizes this work, which is focused on communication to nontechnical people. Additional details can be found in Ibrekk and Morgan (1987).

9.3.1. Experimental Design

Figure 9.8 shows the nine graphical representations the study used. The simplest (display 1) was a traditional point estimate with an "error bar" that spanned a

3.   The discussion in this section is based on Ibrekk and Morgan (1987).

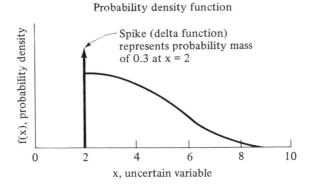

Probability density function

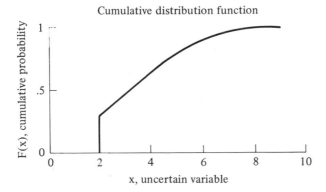

Cumulative distribution function

Figure 9.7. Example of the mixture of a continuous and discrete distribution.

95% confidence interval. Subjects were not told the length of the interval until the second half of the experiment. Six alternative displays of probability density were used because, as Fischhoff and MacGregor (1983) have argued, formally equivalent representations are often not psychologically equivalent. These displays included both a conventional probability density function (display 4) and a discretized version of the density function (display 2), which we thought subjects might find more familiar and less confusing because in this display the concept of probability density is replaced with the concept of the probability that the result lies in a fixed interval. Display 3 was another representation of discretized probability density, which used a pie chart to communicate probability, where the pie sections span equal intervals in the uncertain quantity. We suspected that a common problem with the conventional probability density display would be that subjects would focus on the height of the curve rather than the area under the curve. Display 5 involved a probability density function of half its regular height together with its mirror image. Our intent in this display was to try to focus subjects' attention on the *area* enclosed between

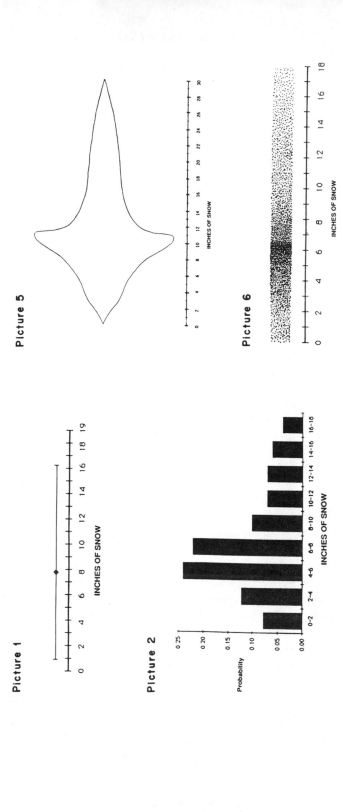

Picture 5

INCHES OF SNOW

Picture 6

INCHES OF SNOW

Picture 1

INCHES OF SNOW

Picture 2

Probability

INCHES OF SNOW

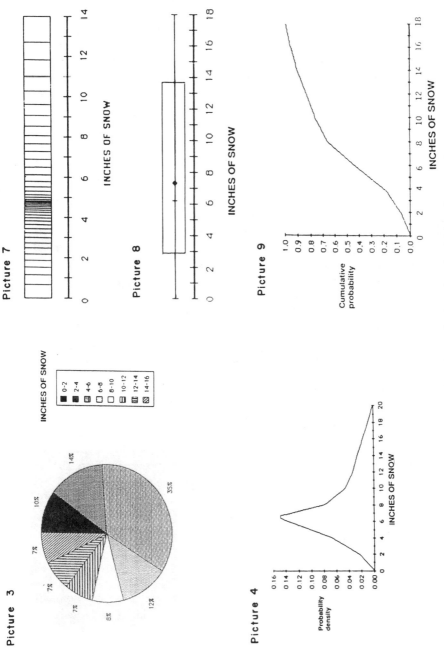

Figure 9.8. Illustrations of the nine displays for communicating uncertain estimates for the value of a single variable used in the experiments by Ibrekk and Morgan (1987).

the curves. In displays 6 and 7 we eliminate variations in the height of the display by using horizontal bars of constant width that have been shaded to display probability density using either dots or vertical lines. Displays of this type would be particularly useful in summary or comparative tables designed to communicate simultaneously information about a number of different quantities. The eighth display was a Tukey box plot modified to exclude the maximum and minimum values and to display the mean with a solid point. The final display was the conventional cumulative distribution function, the integral of the probability density function. All displays were generated with the same computer graphics system, to make their realizations as similar in style and quality as possible.

The questionnaire was divided into two major parts. The first half asked subjects to make a series of judgments without having received any explanation of how to use or interpret the various displays. The second half asked subjects to make similar judgments after having received fairly detailed nontechnical explanations. Questions were posed in terms of predictions about events such as the depth of a predicted snowfall and flood. The forty-nine subjects in the main study were volunteer workers for the Beechwood Farms Nature Reserve in Pittsburgh, Pennsylvania, and their spouses. In order to compare the performance of this sample with a group that had fresh technical training, eighteen questionnaires were administered to an opportunity sample of engineering undergraduates at Carnegie Mellon. Details on the subjects and the experimental design are available in Ibrekk and Morgan (1987).

The same functional form for the probability distribution was used in the experimental tasks throughout each of the two halves of the experiment, but in a number of the displays different numerical scales were used so as not to have the similarity of the distributions become apparent to the subject. The distributions used in the first and second halves of the experiment were similar in shape, the second having a somewhat more pronounced asymmetry. As Figure 9.8 indicates, the distributions used were skewed with a tail to the right. A second set of mirror image distributions with tails to the left were used to examine for possible effects of left–right asymmetry in the responses.

9.3.2. Results

Results were evaluated in a number of ways. Conventional statistical comparisons of the actual to the "correct" responses were performed for each question. In addition, histograms of all the responses for each question were generated, and then normalized to allow comparisons across the displays. In the case of the interval and range questions these allow a simple direct comparison of performance between the displays that contain probability density information and display 1, which does not. The histograms also allow the identification of a number of systematic behaviors by subjects that are not apparent in the conventional statistical analysis. Finally, a variety of correlation studies were run to examine how subjects' responses to some questions (e.g., familiarity with display) are correlated with their response to others (e.g., correctness of response).

Figure 9.9 displays histograms of the responses for questions about the "best estimate" before the provision of an explanation of the displays (left) and after the provision of the explanation (right). Results are reported as the ratio of the estimated to actual means. The closest estimates to the true means result for displays 1 and 8, which explicitly marked the location of the mean. The location of the modes of the displays that subjects saw are indicated with the large triangular marks. The strategy subjects used to produce a "best estimate" for displays 2, 4, and 5 was clearly to select the point where the curve was highest, and the strategy they used for displays 6 and 7 was clearly to select the point of maximum probability density (i.e., densest shading). This conclusion is strengthened by our obtaining "best estimates" that were greater than the mean and corresponded with the mode for the questions that used distributions skewed to the left.

Responses for the pie chart display, and to a lesser extent the histogram display, are confused because we asked subjects to "answer each question with only *one number*," but some provided a range for their best estimate in these cases. When this occurred, we coded the midpoint. There is a weak suggestion that some subjects chose an answer to be close to halfway around the pie chart (the median), but the data do not allow a clear resolution.

To the right of each histogram in Figure 9.9 is a summary of how sure subjects were of their answers ranging from unsure at the left to sure at the right. The displays mark the median response with an open point, the interquartile range with the bar, and the maximum and minimum values with vertical lines. Subjects were most sure about their responses for displays 1 and 2 and least sure about their responses for displays 5 and 9. It is clear from display 2 that people can be quite sure they are correct while producing responses that are incorrect. Intrasubject correlations showed no significant association between how sure a subject was about the correctness of his or her response and the actual correctness of that response.

In descending order, subjects indicated they had seen displays like those in 3 and 2 many times before, displays like 4, 9, and 1 less frequently, and displays like 6, 7, 5, and 8 few or no times before. The fact that very few people claimed to have seen previously the displays we invented provides some indication of the quality of our subjects' responses. There is no apparent relationship between familiarity and how sure people said they were of their responses.

Comparing the responses before and after the provision of explanations shows that the explanations have a weak effect, but in most cases there are more

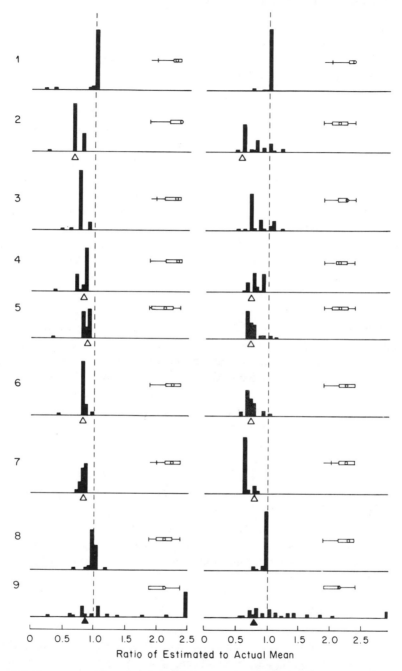

Figure 9.9. Histograms of the ratio of estimated to actual mean for the nine displays of Figure 9.8 obtained when subjects were asked to give their "best estimate" value before (left) and after (right) receiving explanations of the displays. Open triangles mark the location of the mode. Solid triangles on display 9 mark the location of the mean. Small modified box plots report the index of how sure subjects were of their answers ranging from "not at all sure" on the left end of the line to "very sure" on the right end. Vertical marks indicate the highest and lowest response. Open points mark the median response. Boxes span from the 25th to 75th percentile of responses.

responses closer to the true mean, indicating that people are trying to use the explanations.

The results for display 9, the cumulative distribution function, are the most dramatic. Used alone without explanation, CDFs are clearly likely to mislead a significant number of nontechnical people. Twenty-one of the forty-five respondents who provided usable answers produced estimates of the mean that were in excess of the true mean, and seventeen produced estimates that corresponded to the maximum possible value. Very similar performance was observed in the pilot tests run with secretaries. In contrast, none of the engineering undergraduates produced estimates which corresponded to the maximum possible value. Only three out of eighteen estimates given by this group were in excess of the true mean.

The location of the medians in the CDF displays our subjects saw are marked with solid triangles. Given the wide range in responses the mean and median lie too close together in the displays used to allow us to reach firm conclusions about whether some people's "best estimate" values were driven by the median. However, the results are certainly suggestive. Once an explanation was provided, most respondents appear to have tried to estimate the mean correctly, but experienced difficulty in producing a good estimate. After the explanation only four out of forty-five respondents continued to report the maximum possible value. Three of these four also reported the maximum value before explanation (the fourth estimated the lowest value reported before explanation).

Figure 9.10 displays results for estimates of the probability that $x > a$, and Figure 9.11 displays responses for estimates that $b > x > a$. These plots are normalized so that a correct response yields a value of one. Because of variations in the numerical scales employed, the location of the 100 percent point varies across displays and is marked under each display with a short, heavy vertical bar. While noisy, the overall performance on these questions displays only a few systematic biases.

Because it provides no information other than the mean and the 95% confidence interval, display 1 provides a base against which to compare other responses. For the $x > a$ questions only displays 3 and 9 (displays 3, 4, and 9 for the engineering undergraduates) produce results which clearly show more central tendency around the correct response than that obtained in display 1, although performance is degraded for display 3 after explanation. For the $b > x > a$ questions only display 3, before explanation, and display 9, after explanation, clearly show more central tendency than that obtained with display 1 (displays 3, 4, and 9 all showed more central tendency both before and after explanation for the engineering undergraduates). Several of the probability density displays (2, 4, 5, and 6) appear to do slightly better than display 1 after explanation. Displays 2 (the histogram), 3 (the pie chart), and 9 (the CDF) are displays in

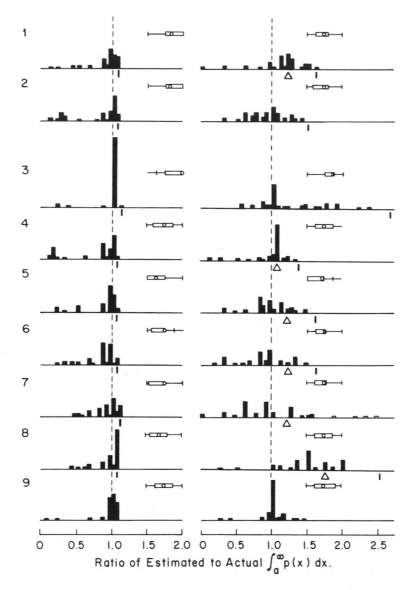

O   0.5   1.0   1.5   2.0   O   0.5   1.0   1.5   2.0   2.5

Ratio of Estimated to Actual $\int_a^\infty p(x)\, dx$.

Figure 9.10. Histograms of the ratio of the estimated to actual probability that the value that occurs will be greater than some stated value (i.e., $x > a$) for the nine displays of Figure 9.8 before (left) and after (right) receiving explanations of the displays. Solid vertical bars mark the 100% point and move because the value falls at different points on the different displays. Open triangles mark the answers that would result if a heuristic of simple linear proportion were employed. Small box plots report the index of how sure subjects were of their answer as in Figure 9.9.

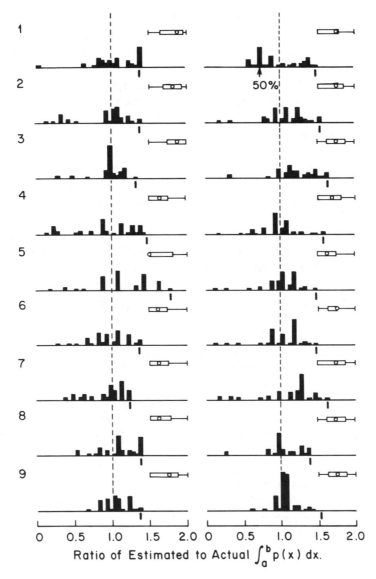

Figure 9.11. Histograms of the ratio of the estimated to actual probability that the value that occurs will lie in some stated interval ($b > x > a$) for the nine displays of Figure 9.8 before (left) and after (right) receiving explanations of the displays. Notations are as in Figure 9.10.

which it is possible to read the answer to the $x > a$ and $b > x > a$ questions with little or no estimation.

Given the very poor performance in producing a "best estimate" value from the CDF, we were surprised that our subjects did very well in estimating both the probability that $x > a$ and the probability that $b > x > a$ from the CDF. The only display for which performance is superior to the CDF is the pie chart, and this only *before* an explanation was provided. Most of our subjects appear to have used the pie chart correctly before explanation (i.e., adding the probabilities), but got confused when we explained it. This together with its poor performance on estimates of mean values suggests to us that the pie chart is not in general a good display to use in communicating to laypersons because there is too great a potential for confusion and misinterpretation.

In the absence of understanding the concept of probability density, or knowing the value of the probability density, the use of a linear proportion heuristic seems likely. The large triangles shown in Figure 9.10 correspond to the responses that would have been obtained if one used linear proportion (i.e., assumed a uniform probability density along the full interval spanned). This is shown only for after-explanation cases, since the correct response and the linear proportion response lie too close together to reliably differentiate in before-explanation cases. It appears that a linear proportion heuristic may have been used in displays 1 and 8 (the error bar and modified box plot). There is some suggestion this may also be happening in the case of display 4 (the PDF), but the separation is not sufficient to allow a clear resolution. It is clearly not being employed for displays 2, 5, 6, and 7.

For questions about $x > a$ before explanations were provided, displays 2 and 4, the two PDF displays, show a small clustering (roughly 20%) of low responses. These correspond very closely to the response one gets from estimating $x < a$ rather than $x > a$. A similar phenomena can be observed in the responses before explanation for questions about $b > x > a$. In this case the low cluster corresponds to the probability that falls outside the interval from a to b. These clusters disappear after explanation. Eight out of eleven respondents who gave low responses for $x > a$ on display 2, and seven out of ten respondents who gave low responses for $x > a$ on display 4, also gave low responses on $b < x < a$. This phenomenon is *not* observed in the estimates given by the undergraduates.

After explanation, subjects could infer that display 1 did not contain the information needed to answer the $b > x > a$ question. It is interesting to note that roughly 20% of the responses were in the cell that corresponds to a response of 50%. It seems possible that this results because subjects associated odds of 50:50 with lack of knowledge, although no clear pattern is apparent when one checks how sure these respondents were that their estimate was "the same as our estimate." Just under 10% of the undergraduates displayed similar behavior.

In the questions after explanation, subjects were asked "What is the 95% confidence interval of the expected flood depth in this town?" and were asked to respond by inserting numbers in the phrase "__ to __ feet." Lower bound estimates were systematically too high, upper bound estimates were

Table 9.1. *Ratio of estimated to actual 95% confidence intervals by display ordered in terms of decreasing performance*

Display	Ratio of estimated to actual 95% confidence interval
1	.97
9	.88
3	.84
5	.81
8	.78
7,4	.76
6	.74
2	.71

Note: Differences between ratios for display 1 and displays 9, 5, and 2 were checked and found to be significant by the Wilcoxon matched-pairs sign-ranked test.

systematically too low. The ratio of the estimated interval to true intervals as a function of display is shown in Table 9.1. The best performance was for display 1, where the error bar gave the correct answer. The next best performance was for the CDF, from which it is possible to read the correct answer directly. The poorest performance is reported for the histogram display, but this result is somewhat misleading. If, instead of evaluating the distance between the upper and lower estimates given, one checks the bin in which the upper and lower values were located, over half the respondents placed the ends in the right bins. A somewhat higher number placed the ends in the right bins for the pie chart, the other discretized display. Of the probability density–based displays, display 5, the mirrored PDF, performed best.

Despite the relatively high level of education of the Beechwood volunteers, analysis of the performance of individual subjects against their previous background and experience suggests that a "rusty knowledge" of statistics, a graduate degree, or use of information about uncertainty on the job, does not significantly improve subject performance.

At the conclusion of both the first and second parts, subjects were shown all of the displays on a pair of facing pages and asked which one display they would prefer to have used. Table 9.2 reports the results. Note the somewhat different preferences of the engineering undergraduates (reported in brackets).

In addition to the differences noted in the preceding discussion, a few other differences between the engineering undergraduates and the nontechnical Beechwood volunteers should be noted. Although the undergraduates' responses on the $x > a$ and $a < x < b$ questions were similar to those of the Beechwood volunteers, in all but one case the distributions of the undergraduates' responses

Table 9.2. *Preferences expressed by the nontechnical subjects when asked to choose one display before and after explanation (preferences expressed by the smaller group of undergraduate engineers are reported in brackets)*

Display	Number of subjects who choose			
	Before explanation		After explanation	
1	2	(1)	2	(–)
2	17	(11)	8	(5)
3	14	(2)	11	(1)
4	3	(1)	2	(1)
5	1	(–)	0	(–)
6	1	(–)	1	(–)
7	1	(1)	6	(1)
8	2	(–)	5	(–)
9	3	(1)	9	(9)

about the true answers were slightly narrower. The exception was display 1, the PDF, for $x > a$ questions.

Given the more homogeneous nature of the undergraduate group, and their higher level of working technical knowledge, especially in probability and statistics, these narrower distributions are not surprising. Indeed, the surprise is that the undergraduates did not perform considerably better than they did. Further, across the full set of questions, students who had taken courses in probability and statistics do not appear to have performed better than those who had not.

9.3.3. Discussion

This study only scratched the surface of a problem that clearly needs more examination with a variety of improved and more focused experimental designs. Nevertheless, several conclusions do emerge.

The performance of a display depends upon the information that a subject is trying to extract. Displays that explicitly contain the information people need (i.e., mark the location of the mean in the case of our displays 1 and 8; contain the answers to questions about $x > a$ and $b > x > a$ in our displays 2 and 9; or provide the 95% confidence interval as in display 1) show the best performance.

Although it was popular (Table 9.2) and performed well under some circumstances, the pie chart (display 3) shows potential for confusion and should be avoided.

In making judgments about the location of the "best estimate" in displays of probability density, people show a tendency to select the mode rather than the mean unless the mean is not explicitly marked.

In making judgments about probability intervals in displays that do not forcefully communicate a sense of probability density, people may show a tendency to use a linear proportion strategy which is equivalent to an assumption of uniform probability density.

The various simplified probability density displays (displays 5, 6, 7) all perform about the same (despite their varying popularity) and so can probably be used interchangeably when one is trying to produce simplified plots to indicate the ranges that variables assume in applications such as summary or comparative tables. A box plot or simple error bar display does a better job if means are the primary attribute being communicated, but less well if one is trying to communicate probability intervals when probability density is not uniform along the horizontal axis. Further work is obviously required to develop a simple horizontal display. Display 5, combined with a solid point on the axis that marks the location of the mean, might be effective at communicating both mean and intervals, but it is not popular (Table 9.2) and it is unclear to us how much the horizontal separation of the mean and the mode in asymmetric distributions will confuse some people. Further study of simple horizontal displays is clearly needed.

For presentations that do not have to be confined to a narrow vertical space it seems likely that the best strategy is to combine displays to obtain the best features of each. Until future experiments suggest otherwise, we recommend the use of a CDF and a PDF plotted directly above each other with the same horizontal scale and with the location of the mean clearly indicated on both curves with a solid point. An example is provided in Figure 9.12. However, the results of this study suggest that one should not depend on *all* users correctly interpreting this or any other display.

We suspect that people may easily confuse the median of a CDF with the mean, particularly if the mean is not marked. This may also be an issue in expert elicitation of probability distributions. We have seen indications during elicitation that some experts associate the median of a CDF with their "best estimate." Our Carnegie Mellon colleague Robyn Dawes (personal communication, 1986) has argued to us that the very different performance of the CDF for estimates of the mean versus estimates of intervals and ranges may not be surprising because, he suggests, very different cognitive procedures are required in the two tasks. He argues that many people find it more straightforward to think of $p(x > a)$ than of probability density and suggests that the common practice of introducing the PDF before the CDF in introductory courses in probability may not be wise. This issue warrants further exploration.

Finally, our results suggest that rusty or limited statistical knowledge does not significantly improve the performance of semitechnical or laypersons in interpreting displays that communicate uncertainty. Results from the comparison with engineering undergraduates indicate that a working knowledge of basic probability and statistics eliminates the most obvious problems of misinterpreta-

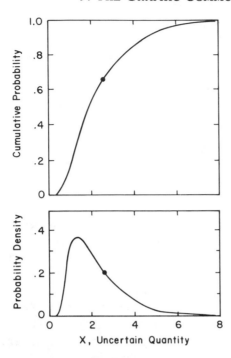

Figure 9.12. Example of the CDF plotted directly above the PDF with the same horizontal scale and with the location of the mean clearly indicated. This is the display the authors recommend until future experiments suggest otherwise.

tion, such as those that arose with the CDF. However, although the performance of the undergraduates on the estimation tasks was better, it was not dramatically better. This suggests that future studies of the problems of communicating uncertainty should not focus just on the problems of communicating to semitechnical and laypersons.

Given the growing importance of communicating uncertainty in the results of quantitative risk analysis, the outputs of automated computer modeling systems such as Demos (see Chapter 10), and a variety of other contexts, we hope that others will begin to undertake empirical work of the sort reported in this paper, both refining issues related to univariate displays and exploring issues that involve multivariate displays, sensitivities, and correlation structures.

9.4. Graphing Two-dimensional Uncertainty

Suppose one wishes to communicate a probability distribution over quantity x_1 conditional on the value of quantity x_2. Perhaps it is easiest to select a few representative values for x_2, say, $x_2 = 1$, $x_2 = 2$, and $x_2 = 3$, and display the probability distributions for x_1 conditional on each of these values,

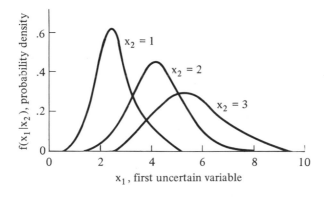

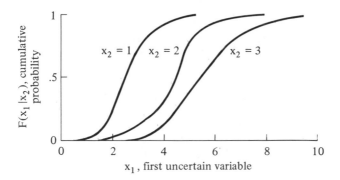

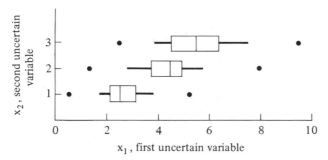

Figure 9.13. Alternative displays for two-dimensional conditional distributions.

$f(x_1| x_2 = 1)$, $f(x_1| x_2 = 2)$, $f(x_1| x_2 = 3)$. As in the single dimensional case, the distributions may be shown as probability density functions, as cumulative probability distributions, or as Tukey box plots (Figure 9.13). The Tukey box plots have the advantage that they can be arranged along the vertical axis, according to the value of x_2. A similar ordering for the cumulative distribution requires the introduction of an additional display dimension. An example of

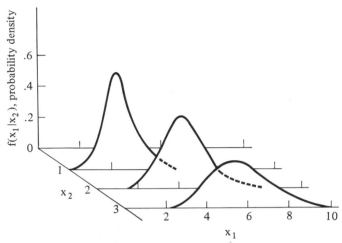

Figure 9.14. Example of a display which orders conditional probability density functions $f(x_1 \mid x_2)$ in order of increasing values of x_2. Note that this is *not* the same surface as $f(x_1, x_2)$.

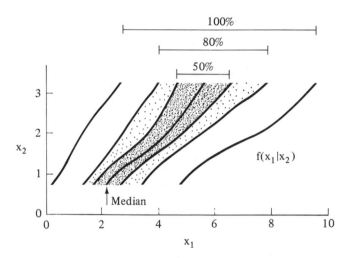

Figure 9.15. Example of a fractile graph for the example distributions shown in Figures 9.14 and 9.13. Since this is a plot of $f(x_1 \mid x_2)$, *not* $f(x_1, x_2)$, the probability distributions make sense only if read horizontally.

such a three-dimensional display for the case of the density function is shown in Figure 9.14, for discrete values of the variable x_2.

By constructing contours at equal height in a display such as that in Figure 9.14, or by joining up the corresponding points in a box plot display of the sort shown at the bottom of Figure 9.15, it is possible to create what we will call a *fractile graph*.

In this representation the curves join up equal fractiles on each conditional distribution. The central line represents the median estimate of how x_1 changes with x_2. The other fractile curves bound *confidence bands* of 50 percent, 80 percent, or any other desired level, around the median curve. The fractile graph shows the shape of the response of x_1 to x_2 and how the uncertainty about x_1 varies with x_2, as shown by the varying width of the confidence bands. It is also easy to see skewness in the distributions as asymmetry in the confidence bands. Because this display shows $f(x_1 \mid x_2)$ it can only be read horizontally. Care must be taken to remind viewers that this display is *not* a two-dimensional contour plot of $f(x_1, x_2)$. Because this distinction may be unclear to semitechnical and nontechnical users, some care should be exercised in the labeling and use of such displays.

In the example shown, the mean and median values lie rather close together. In highly skewed distributions, they may not, in which case it may be desirable to display the mean explicitly.

If the position and number of modes is of particularly interest, the density form is still useful. If precise cumulative probabilities for specified values are of interest, then the cumulative is still useful. But otherwise the fractile graph is probably the clearest and most easily understood form. It is a simple extension of the graph of the deterministic response of x_1 to x_2, rather than a new projection, and for that reason likely to be much easier to understand for the newcomer to uncertainty analysis.

The probability distribution of x_1 conditional on x_2 is a three-dimensional surface, which in Figures 9.13 and 9.15 we have displayed in the two-dimensional plane. The third dimension is either probability or probability density. In the probability density and cumulative probability forms we have discretized x_2 into $x_2 = 1$, $x_2 = 2$, and $x_2 = 3$, to allow projection onto the two-dimensional surface. In contrast, in the box plot and the fractile graph the x_2 axis is represented explicitly, and it is the probability dimension that has been discretized, into 0, 10%, 25%, 50%, 75%, 90%, and 100% values. Because the probabilities usually derive from rather rough subjective assessments, the discretization of the probability dimension typically entails far less loss of useful information than does discretization of other dimensions of a graph. In general, if a choice must be made about which dimension to discretize, this is a good argument for selecting the probability dimension.

9.5. The Abstraction Dilemma

A typical policy model has many sources of uncertainty; it may have dozens of uncertain empirical parameters, several model domain or form parameters, one or more decision variables, and a few value parameters. Each of these contributes a potential dimension for the results of the analysis, to be tabulated or graphed. There are two strategies, at opposite extremes, that can be used in performing analysis and presenting results: We shall call these the *all combinations* strategy, and the *naive decision analysis* strategy.

The *all combinations strategy* is motivated by the desire to investigate and understand the effects and interactions of all the uncertainties and variables in the model. First, select the N most interesting from the uncertain quantities, decision variables, scope variables, value parameters, and so forth. Then select a set of interesting values – perhaps a low, medium, and high – for each of them. Next, evaluate the model for all combinations of these and tabulate the results as an N-dimensional matrix. It may be possible to find ingenious ways to display subsets of these results graphically. Obviously the problem is that the number of scenarios increases exponentially with N. If N is large, the computational effort to evaluate them all may also become prohibitive. Even if the resources are available to compute all the results, the resulting N-dimensional matrix will be indigestible, unless some convenient means can be found for abstracting over this vast bulk of information.

In the opposite strategy, *naive decision analysis*, again one starts by selecting N uncertain variables. Uncertainty about the value of each empirical parameter is expressed in the form of a subjective probability distribution, possibly obtained from a suitable technical expert. These uncertainties can then be propagated through the model, either through a discrete probability tree or using Monte Carlo simulation or a similar sampling technique. One way to look at probabilistic modeling is as a method for combining each separate dimension of uncertainty into a single dimension of uncertainty on the outcome variable.

If the model contains index variables, such as time or space, we need to incorporate aggregation functions to arrive at measures useful for evaluating possible outcomes. For example, in assessing the effects of acid rain, the effects might be summed over geographic regions, suitably weighted, and then total annual effects could be discounted to obtain an aggregate present value effect. The decision maker's values and risk attitudes can be expressed in the form of a single utility function, multi-attribute if necessary, that can express the worth of any probability distribution over possible outcomes in terms of its expected utility. If future decisions must be considered in selecting current decisions, one may assume they will be made so as to maximize expected utility conditional on the information available at that point. This is the *roll-back* assumption.

In these ways each dimension of variation can be aggregated or abstracted over, whether it derives from an empirical parameter, an index variable, a value parameter, or a decision variable. The final result of this naive decision analysis is an expected utility for each primary decision being contemplated. If the primary decision variable is one-dimensional, so is this result. The best decision according to this approach, then, is the one that maximizes the expected utility.

The result of this type of analysis is simple, digestible, and eminently easy to

1. Model dimensions

2. Discrete and continuous
   ranges on those dimensions

3. Model domain

4. Model

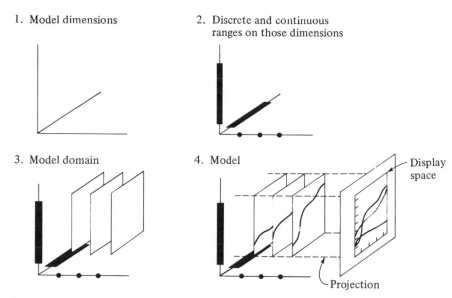

Display space

Projection

Figure 9.16. Illustration of the process of abstraction as a projection from the model space to the display space.

communicate. But by the same token, its drawback is that it provides numbers without insight. It provides no explanation of why that decision is best or insights into the structure of the situation.

Both the "all combinations" and the "naive decision analysis" approaches are, of course, caricatures of the two extremes. We termed the latter *naive* because most practicing decision analysts are well aware of the importance of examining the sensitivity of conclusions to uncertainties and understanding what is and is not important in the decision problem. The point is, of course, to decide which variables to aggregate over, which to assess probability distributions over, and which to vary parametrically. Clearly the number is strictly limited by the computational resources and the difficulties of displaying multidimensional results in comprehensible ways. Only two dimensions can easily be displayed as continuous, or three in perspective graphs. Any others must be discrete. The goal must be to strike the appropriate balance between the simple but uninformative, and the sophisticated but incomprehensible.

9.6. Abstraction as Projection

A model may contain many variables and parameters, each with a possible dimension of variation in output, constituting the *model space*. Graphic representations of the outputs can typically display only a few of these dimensions, which make up the *display space*. The choice of display requires an abstraction of the possible information; it can be seen as a projection from a larger dimensional model space to the smaller dimensional display space (see Figure 9.16). In this projection, some dimensions are eliminated, and some continuous ones may be converted to discrete ones.

The problem in designing displays to communicate the implications of a model is essentially in selecting, out of the many candidates, which dimensions to retain in this projection. If there is an explicit decision variable in the problem, it will always be important to display the effect of changes in this. If there are key value parameters, such as the "value of life" in benefit–cost analysis of motor vehicle safety regulation, these should also be analyzed parametrically. If empirical uncertainty is treated probabilistically, the probability distribution over outcomes takes up an additional dimension in output displays. If the dimensionality is not already overwhelming, a parametric analysis of one or two of the key empirical parameters is likely to generate additional insight, particularly if there is scientific disagreement about their values.

9.7. Multidimensional Examples

In this section we shall look at some examples of multidimensional displays of uncertainty analysis of various models. We do not present these necessarily as ideals to aspire toward. They certainly have their deficiencies. We present them as examples illustrating some issues and demonstrating some possibilities.

Figure 9.17 displays some results of a cost–benefit analysis of various auto safety policies, including the voluntary wearing of seat belts, the compulsory wearing of belts, the use of passive (or automatic) belts, and airbags. The model assumes that these policies are each adopted over the entire United States. The model incorporates probability distributions modeling the effectiveness and usage rates of each restraint system, averaged over the opinions elicited from various experts. The figure displays cumulative probability and annual net benefits ($ billions) as the two continuous dimensions (along the y and x axes). The policies form an inherently discrete set of values along a decision dimension, within each graph. And the three graphs represent three values selected as discrete points ($0.3M, $1M, and $3M) from the continuous value parameter, investment in safety per life saved (sometimes called the "value of life"). Thus, the entire page displays four dimensions.

Figure 9.18 shows the same results with the same four dimensions; however, in this case investment in safety per life saved is displayed as a continuous variable, and uncertainty in net benefits is displayed through the use of error bars. This form allows more direct comparisons between policies and is thus probably the superior display (it was, unfortunately, not the one that appeared in the published paper). The effect of changing the rate of investment in safety per life saved on the relative benefits of each alternative is clear. The relative size of uncertainties about each policy is indicated by the vertical bars that display 80% confidence intervals.

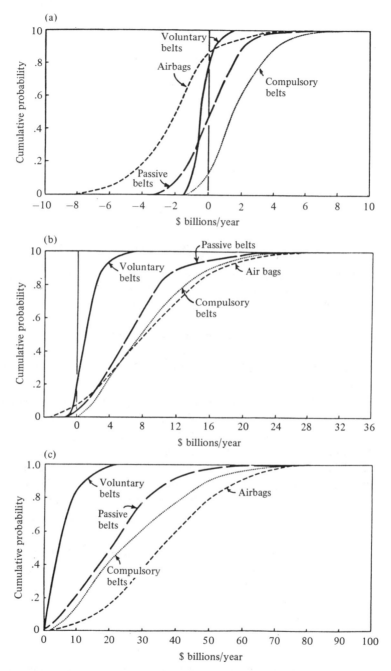

Figure 9.17. Net benefits of policies for auto safety if investment in safety per life saved is (a) $0.3 million (top); (b) $1 million (middle); and (c) $3 million (bottom). From Graham and Henrion (1984).

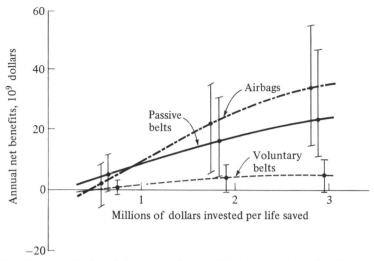

Figure 9.18. Alternative display of the net benefits of policies for auto safety that allows a more direct comparison of the alternative polices than that possible with Figure 9.17. Vertical bars display 80% confidence intervals.

When the width of the confidence bands is not sufficient and the actual shape of the distributions are needed in the comparison of alternative policies, a display such as that shown in Figure 9.19 can be used. Of course, such a display is less feasible if many cross sections are required.

From our analysis of sulfur air pollution from power plants, which has been discussed in several earlier chapters, Figure 9.20 shows perspective graphs of the probability density functions of the fraction of sulfur present as SO_2 and as sulfate in a power plant plume, as a function of downwind flight time from the stack. This figure presents three continuous dimensions: x as concentration, y as probability density, and x_2 as the index variable time. The two graphs together indicate a fourth discrete index parameter, the chemical species, SO_2 and SO_4. One problem with this presentation is that it loses information about mass balance.

A triangle plot can be used to display three dimensions if the quantities are constrained to add to a fixed value. For example, the allocation of a fixed amount of mass among three compartments or categories, m_1, m_2, m_3, can be illustrated in this way. Figure 9.21 shows an example in which 60% of a given mass resides in compartment m_1, 25% resides in compartment m_2, and 15% resides in compartment m_3.

Figure 9.22 shows a triangle plot that reports mass balance at a given flight time of sulfur in the plume of a coal-fired power plant using the subjective judgments of one of the atmospheric science experts we interviewed. In this plot, uncertainty about where the mass balance point should be within the

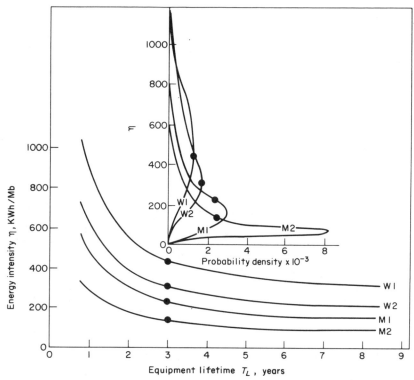

Figure 9.19. Display showing the distributions associated with several continuous curves, each of which represents a different policy option. The actual figure shown is from an analysis of the energy implications of office automation. Explanation of the specifics can be found elsewhere (Nair et al., 1982).

triangle is represented by a two-dimensional probability distribution. The two closed contours on each distribution enclose 50% and 90% of the probability respectively. Thus, the display space here actually contains four dimensions, the three mutually dependent concentration dimensions, and the discretized probability dimension.

Of course, the results of analysis need not be presented in a single display but may be presented from several different perspectives, showing various subsets of the key dimensions of variation, and abstracting or aggregating over the others. Each may provide its own insights. In general, it is wise to present displays in a sequence of increasing dimensionality. The simplest ones should be easily understandable, and can provide a training in the graphical techniques to help decoding of the more complex displays that follow. The sequence of figures displaying atmospheric transport and effects of sulfur oxides is an example of such a sequence.

Figure 9.23 shows a quasi perspective of three triangle plots of the type show

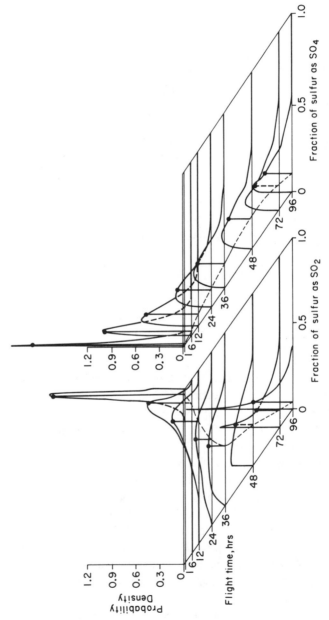

Figure 9.20. Perspecive graphs of the probability density function of the fraction of sulfur present as SO₂ or sulfates, as a function of time downwind. (Morgan et. al., 1984).

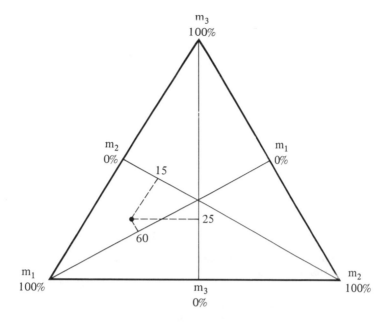

Figure 9.21. A triangle plot can be used to display three variables whose sum is constrained to a fixed quantity. The example shown is for a fractional mass balance in which $m_1 + m_2 + m_3 = 100\%$.

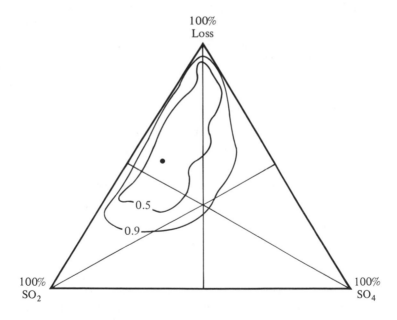

Figure 9.22. Triangle plot of sulfur fate at a fixed downwind range in the plume of a coal-fired power plant.

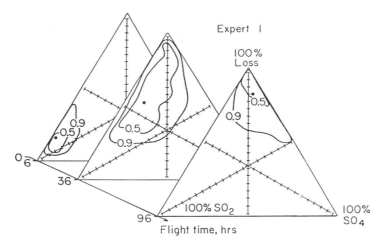

Figure 9.23. A triplet of triangle plots, displaying changes in sulfur mass balance with flight time in the plume of a coal fired power plant.

in Figure 9.22. This adds in the extra discretized index dimension of time downwind from the smokestack emissions.

Figure 9.24 is a multiple display of triplets of triangle plots showing the implications of the probabilistic opinions of each of seven atmospheric experts for the mass balance of sulfur. It combines on one page a six-dimensional display space, including the three dimensions of concentration, the discretized probability dimension, the discretized time dimension, and the discrete dimension indexing over different experts. This may be some kind of record, illustrating the possibilities, and perhaps also the dangers, of high dimensional displays.

9.8. The Importance of Audience

It should be clear from the preceding section that the design of displays to communicate the results of uncertainty analysis involves a number of factors. These include:

- finding a clear, uncluttered graphic style and an easily understood format,
- making decisions about what information to display,
- making decisions about what information to treat in a deterministic form and what to treat in a probabilistic form, and
- making decisions about what kinds of parametric sensitivities will provide the key insights.

The notion of display design as a projection from a many-dimensional model space into smaller-dimensional display spaces, and as selection of a small number of dimensions to display, in continuous or discrete forms, can provide a useful framework in which to think about these decisions in a systematic way.

However, all of these observations must be treated as conditional statements, conditioned by the knowledge of the intended audience. In a recent paper titled "Why a Diagram Is (Sometimes) Worth Ten Thousand Words?" Larkin and Simon (1987) argue that the utility of a graphical representation such as a diagram or picture in communicating information to a user depends critically on the knowledge the observer brings to bear on the problem. For example, in looking at a chess board a novice sees only pieces in certain grid locations, whereas an expert "sees" other features such as the "open files," the sequences of vacant squares running from the player's side of the board to the opponent's side. Framing the problem of graphical communication and problem solving in computational terms, Larkin and Simon argue that the usefulness of a diagram depends on its computational efficiency, which depends on a combination of the data structures, programs, and strategy for attention management that the user applies and on the physical properties of the diagram. They conclude:

The advantage of diagrams, in our view, is computational. That is diagrams can be better representations not because they contain more information, but because the indexing of this information can support extremely useful and efficient computational processes. But this means that diagrams are useful only to those who know the appropriate computational processes for taking advantage of them. (Larkin and Simon, 1987)

This conclusion implies that diagrams intended to be useful in describing policy analyses will effectively convey information about models, their structure, associated uncertainties, and implications – only to the extent that the basic ideas on which they are based (influence networks, functional representation, parametric analysis, probability density, maximization, cost–benefit analysis, etc.) are concepts familiar to and understood by the users. This suggests that specific techniques for graphical communication are likely to be of varying utility when employed by different user populations. Thus, for example, an experienced decision analyst may find a particular representation of model structure very helpful because it succinctly encodes in a very compact way ideas about structure with which the analyst is intimately familiar. In contrast, a technically literate client with no real modeling experience may find the same representation opaque because he or she is not sufficiently familiar with the underlying ideas that it summarizes to decode the content easily and efficiently.

Thus, the suitability of display designs depends much on the training and experience of the intended audience. Many audiences have little understanding of probabilistic information. Of course, this may slowly change as uncertainty analysis becomes more common. When knowledge is limited and rusty, a sequence of displays of related information of increasing sophistication and complexity may enable readers to grasp in successive steps displays they would not grasp if they were presented only in their final form. In general, it is probably unwise to design displays only for the least skilled in the audience; exposure to displays of varying sophistication will help viewers improve their skills in interpreting graphs, and so develop more sophisticated consumers.

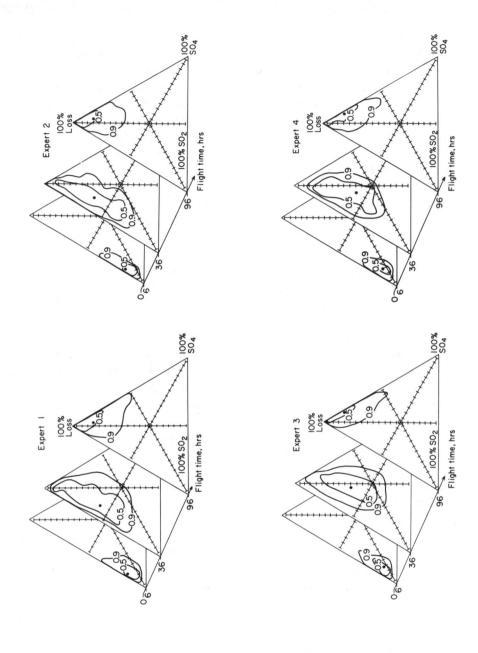

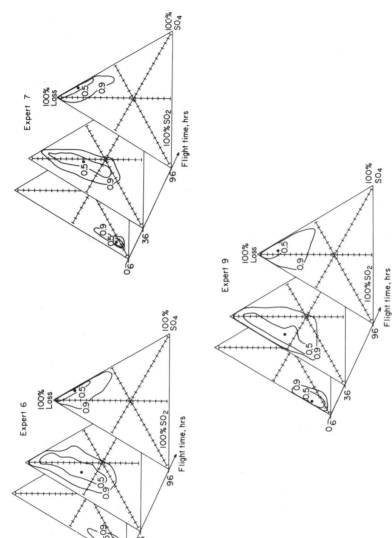

Figure 9.24. Triplets of triangle plots displaying change in mass balance over time downwind, based on models using the different judgments about atmospheric science from seven different experts (Morgan et al., 1984). This figure combines on one page a six-dimensional display space, including the three dimensions of concentration, the discretized probability dimension, the discretized time dimension, and the discrete dimension indexing over different experts.

If the displays are generated on-line on a computer display screen directly from the model outputs, then there is the possibility of interactively selecting and designing displays to suit the skills and special interests of the viewer. If the viewer can be actively involved in the selection of the display projections and choice of graphic forms, the experience is likely to be much more motivating and educational than is possible in more traditional, passive modes of communication.

Most of the suggestions and examples presented in this chapter are based on qualitative insights we have developed from our own experience as practicing analysts. Clearly, many different solutions to the problems of graphical presentation are possible. The increasing availability of sophisticated interactive computer graphics should make it easier to experiment with alternative approaches to a particular problem as a function of audience. Until such research is done, and, indeed, even after it has been, there will remain plenty of scope for judgment and creativity in the design of displays for communicating uncertainty.

References

Cleveland, W. S., and McGill, R. (1985). "Graphical Perception and Graphical Methods for Analyzing Scientific Data," *Science*, 229:828–833.

Fischhoff, B., and MacGregor, D. (1983). "Judged Lethality: How Much People Seem to Know Depends Upon How They Are Asked," *Risk Analysis*, 3:229–235.

Graham, J. D., and Henrion. M. (1984). "A Probabalistic Analysis of the Passive-restraint Question," *Risk Analysis*, 4:25–40.

Henrion, M., and Morgan, M. G. (1985). "A Computer Aid for Risk and Other Policy Analysis," *Risk Analysis*, 5:195–208.

Ibrekk, H., and Morgan, M. G. (1987). "Graphical Communication of Uncertain Quantities to Non-Technical People," *Risk Analysis*, 7, no. 4: 519–529.

Larkin, J. H., and Simon, H. A. (1987). "Why a Diagram Is (Sometimes) Worth Ten Thousand Words," *Cognitive Science*, 11, no. 1: 65–99.

Morgan, M. G., Morris, S. C., Henrion, M., Amaral, D.A.L., and Rish, William R. (1984). "Technical Uncertainty in Quantitative Policy Analysis: A Sulfur Air Pollution Example," *Risk Analysis*, 4 (September): 201–216.

Murphy, A. H. (1986). "Bibliography on Forecast Terminology," Department of Atmospheric Sciences, Oregon State University. Corvallis, Ore.

Murphy, A. H., Lichtenstein, S., Fischhoff, B., and Wenkler, R. L. (1980). "Misinterpretation of Precipitation Probability Events," *Bulletin of the American Meteorological Society*, 61:695–701.

Nair, I., Morgan, M. G., and Henrion, M. (1982). "Office Automation: Assessing Energy Implications," *Telecommunications Policy*, 6, no. 3 (September): 207–222.

Tufte, E. R. (1983). *The Visual Display of Quantitative Information*, Graphics Press, Cheshire, Conn.

Tukey, J. W. (1977). *Exploratory Data Analysis*, Addison-Wesley, New York.

10   Demos: A Case Study in Computer Aids for Modeling Uncertainty

Most of the techniques for propagating uncertainty that were discussed in Chapter 8 require significant computational effort and hence the use of a computer. One reason many of these techniques have seen relatively little use in policy analysis is that until recently, analysts who wanted to make use of them were faced with developing much of the necessary computer software from scratch. Increasingly, this is no longer true.

There are two rather different approaches that can be taken to the problem of providing software support for policy analysis. The more conventional is the development of special purpose packages that perform one or another specific task. Most readers are familiar with packages such as spread sheets, equation solvers, and statistical tool kits. At least one commercial spread-sheet package, "@Risk", marketed by Palisade Corporation, supports substantial treatment of uncertainty through stochastic simulation. Software packages serving the special needs of policy analysts include commercially available tools that support the preparation, averaging out and folding back of discrete decision trees. Other examples include "Arborist," marketed by Texas Instruments; "Supertree," marketed by the Strategic Decision Group; and "Decision – 1 2 Tree," marketed by Riskcalc Associates. An example of a different kind of special package is provided by various systems that fit around an existing deterministic FORTRAN model and allow one to turn it into a Monte Carlo simulation (Gardner, Bojder, and Bergstrom, 1983; Iman and Shortencarier, 1984; Iman, Shortencarier, and Johnson, 1985).

An alternative approach is the development of a general computer environment to support a variety of needs in quantitative policy modeling, including the treatment of uncertainty (Cazalet and Cambell, 1983; Geoffrion, 1987; Goldstein, 1983). Since the late 1970s two of us (Henrion and Morgan) have been involved in the development of such a system, which we call "Demos."

Because software systems are continually changed and updated we will not attempt a detailed review of available systems, which would quickly become obsolete.[1] However, because its development has figured so centrally in the evolution of our views about the treatment of uncertainty in policy analysis, and because so many of the insights we have gained are quite general in nature, in

---

1. For a review of the three decision tree packages Arborist, Supertree, and Decision – 1 2 Tree (formerly Riskcalc), see Henrion (1985). For a review of the spread-sheet system Predict! see Henrion (1987).

Table 10.1. *Design requirements for a computer aid for risk analysis*

A computer aid for risk analysis should provide convenient means for:

- representing uncertain quantities as probability distributions, either discrete or continuous, for propagating probabilistic values through a model, and for displaying the resulting distributions graphically;
- performing various kinds of sensitivity and uncertainty analysis, both deterministic and stochastic;
- representing models in a nonprocedural language with conventional algebraic syntax;
- interactively defining and editing input values and model structure, and supporting management and comparison of alternative model structures;
- supporting progressive refinement and disaggregation of model structure, and allowing mathematical relationships to be specified independently of the dimensionality of the variables; and
- representing documentary and explanatory text in a form that is integrated with the mathematical structure to facilitate communication of the model.

this chapter we provide a brief description of the Demos system and discuss some of the lessons its development and use have provided. We use the example to illustrate a number of key issues in the design of computer aides for quantitative policy analysis, including the modeling of uncertainty, nonprocedural models, array abstraction, and integrated model documentation. We also use the Demos example to examine the thorny question of how to evaluate the contribution of such aids and their effects on the conduct of analysis. Readers interested in a more detailed description of Demos than that provided here are referred to the *Demos Users Manual* (Henrion and Wishbow, 1987).

10.1. Demos: A General Software Environment for Policy Modeling

In designing the Demos environment, we set out to build a system that would both support and encourage policy analysis that meets the attributes of "good" analysis spelled out in Section 3.9. Evaluation studies we have conducted (Henrion et al., 1986) suggest we have been successful in building a tool that can support good analysis. As discussed in the paragraphs that follow, they have also made it clear that this alone is not sufficient to assure good practice.

Table 10.1 lists the specific design objectives we established,[2] which are motivated by considerations outlined in Chapter 3 and elaborated in subsequent chapters. The need to represent and deal with various kinds of uncertainty is discussed in Chapter 4. Sensitivity and uncertainty analysis are discussed at length in Chapter 8.

---

2. Much of the discussion of this section is based directly on Henrion and Morgan (1985).

10.1.1. Nonprocedural Interactive Environment

To achieve a model that is appropriate to the questions at hand usually takes several iterations as each version is successively analyzed to discover its critical sensitivities, and is elaborated or simplified. With a conventional procedural programming language, such as FORTRAN, model development is a cumbersome process, often carried out not by the analyst directly but through a specialist programmer as an intermediary. The iterative refinement loop may take weeks or months for each cycle. This discourages extensive exploration and encourages the analyst to use the first working model that satisfies minimal criteria.

Although there are important exceptions, most models for risk analysis, cost–benefit analysis, engineering economics, and similar policy applications are algorithmically simple. They can easily be expressed as a set of algebraic relationships defining variables in terms of other variables and input values. Such models may most naturally be specified in a modeling language that is *nonprocedural*, in the sense that it states the functional relationships among variables without specifying the flow of control. A nonprocedural language allows the relationships to be specified in standard algebraic syntax in whatever sequence is easiest; the system chooses the sequence of computation according to its own dictates of consistency and efficiency. Thus, the analyst can construct, examine, and modify the model directly without needing major programming expertise. Nonprocedural languages tend to be much easier to use than conventional procedural languages. The declarative style, in which each variable is defined by a mathematical expression in terms of other variables, is closer to the way most models are conceptualized. The variables may be specified in whatever sequence seems most natural, and the question of in what sequence to evaluate them, or how to solve them if they have mutual dependencies, may be selected by the modeling system, according to the dictates of consistency and efficiency.

Nonprocedural languages tend to be substantially more concise. Prywes, Pnueli, and Shastry (1979) have estimated that programs in procedural languages average a factor of five longer in number of statements than equivalent programs in nonprocedural languages. This length difference is vividly illustrated by a comparison of a FORTRAN decision analysis model (the ADEPT acid deposition model) (Balson, Boyd, and North, 1982) with our reimplementation of the same model in Demos (Rubin et al., 1984). The original FORTRAN was 2,734 lines long, of which about 40% were comments. The equivalent Demos model was 553 lines, of which 80% were comments. Thus, the total lines were shrunk by a factor of 5, and the number of actual statements or expressions were shrunk by a factor of 50. The scope of specification errors or bugs is reduced by at least as much, or more, because of the reduced interdependence among statements in a nonprocedural language.

In these comparisons (and those of Prywes et al. [1979]) the improvement due to nonprocedurality is confounded with the effect of "array abstraction," that is, the ability of languages like Demos to specify an operation on all the elements of an array in a single expression without having to iterate explicitly through every element.

10.1.2. Array Abstraction

One of the principal objectives in adopting a top-down process of model development (as illustrated in Figure 3.2) is to identify those parts of the problem that contribute the most uncertainty and so are most likely to be worth refinement or disaggregation (e.g., partitioning the population into sub-populations with different levels of exposure and susceptibility to the risk). In conventional modeling languages, the modeler must specify explicitly how operations on vector or array values should be performed in each relation-ship. Changing the level of aggregation often entails drastic restructuring of the model. In practice, this usually means that the modeler does not use a progressive refinement strategy; instead, he or she decides in advance the level of disaggregation to use based on hunch rather than experiment. Ideally, a modeling language should allow relationships between variables to be speci-fied without reference to irrelevant array dimensions, which may need to be changed.

With these considerations in mind, Demos has been designed with powerful facilities to allow mathematical relationships to be specified independently of the dimensionality of the variables. Of course, the flexibility and power of these facilities means that as their more advanced capabilities are used, their proper application requires knowledge and careful thought.

Array abstraction is a language feature independent of procedurality, and in fact a few procedural languages, notably APL, also provide this capability. The ability of statements in nonprocedural financial planning languages, such as IFPS, to apply implicitly to all columns (time periods), and operations on ranges of cells in spread-sheet software, such as Lotus-123, are also examples of array abstraction, although they are limited to abstraction over one and two dimensions, respectively. Reimann and Waren (1985) identify the difficulty in interacting with higher dimensional information as a major weakness of many mainframe decision support systems and DSS generators.

Languages like APL will happily perform binary operations on multidimen-sional arrays provided they are "conformant" (have similar dimensions), but the modeler must ensure that the operations are appropriate for the interpretation of the dimensions. In Demos, array values "know" what they are indexed by, and so operations on them can automatically be generalized to the appropriate multidimensional form, linking the corresponding dimensions of operands. If the operands have different indices, then it creates the cross product. This turns out to be extremely convenient for joint parametric sensitivity analysis, in which two or more uncertain inputs are given ranges of alternative values. All combinations of inputs are computed together, and the resulting parametric sensitivities may be graphed for direct comparison of joint impacts. It also means that models can be built using scalars, and subsequently elaborated by disaggregating over various dimensions with no need to redefine the initial model, since the defining expressions will work no matter what the dimensionality of the variables to which they refer.

10.1.3. Ease of Examination and Communication

Communicating the model and the results of analysis is a crucial part of the modeling process: The model's authors need to verify its logic and understand its implications; reviewers need to be able to provide external criticism; and policymakers need to understand the basis for the recommendations of the analysts. Currently the use of computer modeling often seems to obstruct communication more than enhance it. Greenberger has written:

The typical policy model is not designed for ease of communication with the decision-maker. Even the model builder may have difficulty comprehending fully the essential workings of the model. Ideally, the model should be presented to the policymaker, not as a "black box" with assumptions and data feeding into the left and results coming out of the right, but as an "open box" whose inner workings are sufficiently simplified, exposed and elucidated to enable the policymaker to trace the chain of causality from input to output on at least an elementary and fundamental level. (Greenberger, 1981)

Of course, computer aids can do little to facilitate the process of communicating and assessing models unless text describing assumptions, sources of information, and documentation is integrated with the computer representation of the model. Incorporation of this material into the computer model enables the automatic preparation of annotated results of analysis and documented descriptions of the model. The system can then help maintain consistency between the documentation and the model as it is iteratively updated. It also enables reviewers to scrutinize the model in "softcopy" form, that is they can interact with the computer model directly rather than being restricted to a hardcopy report. This allows them to examine its assumptions themselves, investigate the reasons for any unexpected behavior, and perform sensitivity analyses on assumptions they find questionable.

Demos is designed to encourage users to supply explanatory text as they build and refine models. Whenever a new variable is defined, the system prompts for a variety of associated explanatory text. Each variable is described by a *name*, or a mnemonic by which it is identified to the system, and a number of other *attributes*. These usually include a brief *title*, which identifies it to the user; its *units* of measurement, if any; a *description* of what it represents with relevant assumptions; and a *definition*. The user may add other attributes to provide further documentation, for example, an *explanation* of why a value, distribution, or relationship was used in the definition, or a *source*, referring to the person who specified it or to external documents.

Here is an illustration:

```
Variable: R_wlm
Title: Risk factor for wlm exposure.
Units: cancers/wlm
Description: Lifetime per capita risk of cancer per
  working level month of exposure to radon and its
  decay products in air at equilibrium.
Definition: lognormal(0.0002,2.5)
Explanation: Since available human epidemiological
  results on the health effects of radon treat dose in
  terms of working level months (w/m) we do so here. This
  measure is then converted to more conventional units
  using the dose conversion factor D-conv. Fractional
  equilibrium is treated by introducing an indoor
  equilibrium factor F_in.
Sources: The distribution represents the subjective judgment
  of the panel members based on the literature review
  provided in Chapter 3 of the 1986 report Scientific Basis
  for Risk Assessment and Management of Uranium Mill
  Tailings, U.S. Research Council, Board on Radioactive
  Waste Management, Washington, D.C.
```

It is possible to build and run Demos models through a general purpose full-screen editor so that modifications to explanatory text can be easily made.

Demos is designed to be used interactively, employing either simple screen displays on terminals or work stations or more complex capabilities that make use of the features of a good high-resolution graphics work station such as a Sun, MicroVAX, or IBM-RT. There is also a version that will run on a free-standing Macintosh II. The system contains a variety of capabilities to produce graphical output, the simplest of which can be used with virtually no instruction. When the user wants to save specific textual, numerical, or graphical results, or portions of interactive sessions, these can be written as files for later analysis or printing on a conventional or laser printer.

To facilitate an iterative approach, users build, modify, and employ models in Demos through the same interactive on-line interface. Variables in a model can be evaluated at any time, even when the model is still under construction. If a variable's definition is incomplete, the system determines this fact and notifies the user.

As models get complex, they become difficult to understand and manage. Hierarchical organization is usually the best strategy for resolving such problems. To make this easy in Demos, facilities exist to support the bundling of groups of variables into submodels and the nesting of submodels into hierarchies.

Comparison between the results of different modified forms of the same model is a centrally important strategy in the iterative approach to model construction and use. To support this behavior, Demos allows the definition of alternative model versions. In addition a variety of special commands, such as the "WhatIf" command, which allows the effects of temporary modifications to be examined, have been developed to facilitate testing of alternatives.

10.1.4. Values and the Representation of Uncertainty

A Demos model consists simply of a set of variables of the types discussed in Chapter 4. The definition of a variable may be a simple number, an array, a probability distribution, or a mathematical expression relating it to other variables. This expression may represent a physical, economic, or logical relationship, or a subjective judgment of influence (Howard and Matheson, 1981, 1984). It is used by the system in computing the value of the variable. It may contain the usual arithmetic and logical operators, using a conventional algebraic syntax. A range of standard mathematical functions, statistical functions, and functions for creating and operating on arrays are also available. Probabilistic values may be specified by standard distributions (uniform, normal, etc.), or by points on an arbitrary cumulative distribution function.

Thus for example to set the variable **x** equal to a lognormal distribution with a geometric mean of 4 and a geometric standard distribution of 2.5 one types

```
x:= lognormal(4,2.5).
```

To change this to a distribution that runs from 1 to 15 and that takes on a value of 5 at a cumulative probability of .2, a value of 7.5 at .4, of 9.2 at .6, and of 11 at .8, one simply types:

```
x:= fractiles[1, 5, 7.5, 9.2, 11, 15]
```

The interval between specified fractiles can be selected by the user.

Each variable has a *mid-value*, which is evaluated deterministically using median values of all the input distributions on which it depends. It may also have a *probabilistic* value, that is, a probability distribution (possibly multivariate), computed by one of several methods of probabilistic simulation. The mid-value is often useful for preliminary verification of the model before embarking on a full-scale probabilistic analysis. In performing stochastic simulations, Demos can use either standard Monte Carlo or simple or random Latin hypercube sampling as discussed in Chapter 8.

```
Welcome to DEMOS (version II, 13-Dec-82)
Do you want to start a new Project? [Yes]: yes

Name of Project? [V2]: TXC                          Ignore default name "V2".
Description: Example risk analysis of air pollutant TXC.
Author: Henrion & Morgan

Project Txc is ready to be defined.
Type "Help" if needed
>Variable Xd                                 ">" prompts the user for a command.
Title: Extra deaths                          Demos prompts for the Attributes of Xd.
Units: d/year
Description: Extra deaths per year attributed to exposure to TXC
Definition: Pop * Conc * H

H is undeclared in the definition of Xd       Demos suggests defining H.
Do you want to declare it? [Yes]:            We accept the default answer "yes".

Declaring Variable H
Title: Health damg. coeff.
Units: /yr-ug/m↑3
Description: Slope of health damage function: Increase in annual death ~
       rate per person exposed per increment in TXC concentration of ~
       1 microgram/cubic meter.
Definition: 10↑-6                                              i.e. 10⁻⁶
```

Figure 10.1. Start of transcript of Demos session to define a risk model of a hypothetical air pollutant called TXC.

10.1.5. An Illustrative Example

The best way to describe the capabilities of Demos is with an example. Of course, the best example is a live demonstration, but because that is not possible in the pages of this book, we offer some printed excerpts from such a session.

Suppose we are concerned with the health effects of some hypothetical air pollutant named TXC. We start with a very simple model of the form:

Xd = Pop * Conc * H

where **Xd** is the annual number of extra deaths due to TXC, **Pop** is the number of people exposed, **Conc** is the annual average concentration of TXC, and **H** is the slope of a linear, no threshold, health damage function. As an example, if **Pop** is 30 million people, **Conc** is 5 $\mu g/m^3$, and **H** is 10^{-6} extra deaths/person $\mu g/m^3$ yr, then **Xd** = 15 deaths/yr. We can begin to implement the model in Demos as shown in Figure 10.1. In this and following dialogs, user input is underlined to distinguish it from text printed by the system. Explanatory comments have been added in *italics*.

We can go on in a similar way to provide definitions of **Pop** and **Conc**. To see the resulting value of **Xd**, we may use the **Why** command. This allows one to explore the structure of a model and the basis on which values were computed:

```
>Why Xd
Xd      :Extra deaths          (d/yr)              =150
Description: Extra deaths per year attributed to exposure
to TXC
Xd = Pop*Conc*H
Pop     :Population            (people)            =30M
Conc    :Concentration         (ug/m^3)            =5
H       :Health damag. coeff.  (/yr-ug/m^3)        =1u
```

Conventional single character suffixes are used as a compact notation for very large and small numbers (e.g., 30M means 30 Million, 10K means 10 thousand (K for Kilo), 5m means 5×10^{-3} (m for milli), and 1u means 10^{-6} (μ for micro)).

Now suppose there is considerable uncertainty about the concentration of TXC and the health damage coefficient. After consulting available empirical data or technical experts, we conclude that the uncertainty about the concentration may be represented by a lognormal distribution with a geometric mean (median) of 5 and a geometric standard deviation or uncertainty factor of 2, i.e., the range (5/2, 5×2) encloses a 68% credible interval. Suppose also that we interview an expert on the health effects of TXC and, using appropriate elicitation procedures (see Chapter 7) we encode his uncertainty about the true value of **H** as a subjective probability distribution. To incorporate these uncertainties in the Demos model we redefine **Conc** and **H** by assigning them these distributions:

```
>Conc:=Lognormal(5,2)
 H:=Fractiles[0, 0, 0, .25, .6, 1, 1.5, 2.2, 3, 5, 10]/1M
```

That **Conc** and **H** are now probabilistic in no way affects the definition of **Xd** which depends on them. The resulting probability distribution induced over the extra deaths, **Xd**, may be displayed as a probability density function by the **PDF** command, as illustrated in Figure 10.2. This rather crude plot may be produced on any alphanumeric terminal; with a suitable output device, a true graphic display may be produced, in color if available. Subsequent figures in this paper show graphs from such a terminal. According to the distributions specified above for **H**, there is a 20% chance of no mortality and, therefore, as shown in the cumulative distribution in Figure 10.3, there is a 20% chance of zero deaths.

Space constraints preclude our carrying this problem further with the same level of detailed discussion. Subsequent figures illustrate segments from a session in which this model is progressively elaborated and explored. We consider levels of control for TXC emissions in terms of costs and benefits, and show how to compute the expected value of perfect information.

In Figure 10.4, we explore the effect of assuming that there is a threshold in exposure concentration below which no deaths occur. Several thresholds are explored simultaneously by defining the threshold, **Th**, as a vector of four

>PDF Xd

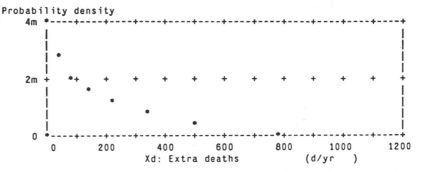

Figure 10.2. Plot of the probability density function for **Xd**, the extra deaths estimated to result from exposure to the hypothetical air pollutant TXC.

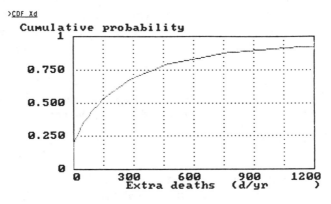

Figure 10.3. Cumulative probability distribution function for extra deaths estimated to result from exposure to the hypothetical air pollutant TXC. The plot is printed from the screen of a graphic display terminal.

alternative values (0, 2.5, 5, 7.5). Variables that depend on **Th** are automatically computed for each value.

In Figure 10.5, we introduce the level of population control as a decision variable, and in Figure 10.6, we add a cost function including both control costs and mortality costs. This provides a marginal cost formulation for investigation of the level of control that will minimize expected total social cost.

Figure 10.7 shows the total cost as a function of the level of control (reductions in TXC emissions). The five curves show five fractiles (quantiles) of the probability distribution, indicating the median (0.5), a 50% interval (0.25 to 0.75), and an 80% interval (0.1 to 0.9) for the predicted cost. Note how the width and skewness (asymmetry around the median) vary with control level. This suggests that the degree of risk aversion will be important.

```
>Xd := Pop*Hdf                                We assign a new definition to Xd.

Hdf is undeclared, in the Definition of Xd
Do you want to declare it? [Yes]:            We accept the default answer "yes"

Declaring Variable Hdf
Title: Health damage fn
Units: /yr
Description: Increment in annual death rate per individual from exposure.
Definition: (Conc - Th)*H*IfPos(Conc - Th)
             "IfPos" is an indicator function, 1 if its argument is positive, otherwise 0
Th is undeclared, in the Definition of Hdf
Do you want to declare it? [Yes]:

Declaring Variable Th
Title: Threshold
Units: ug/m+3
Description: Threshold below which TXC has no effect.
Definition: [0, 2.5, 5, 7.5]
                                        Try a range of alternative values for the threshold.
>Xd                                     These induce a vector of corresponding values on Xd.
Xd          : Extra deaths      (d/yr   ) =
  Th            0 2.500      5 7.500
     [    150     75      0      0]       Deterministic or "mid" values.
>Mean(Xd)                               Means are computed from the entire distribution
  Th            0 2.500      5 7.500    derived from probabilistic simulation. Since the
     [ 314.9 182.5 92.78 45.15]         distributions are skewed, the means are quite
>CDF-Xd                                 different from the mid values.
```

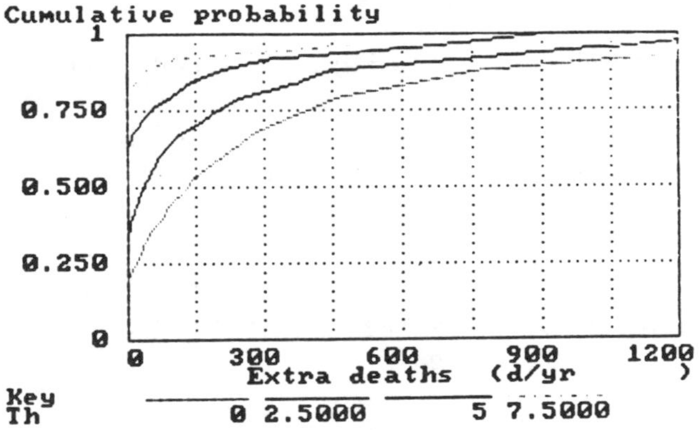

Cumulative probability

```
Key
Th          0 2.5000        5 7.5000
```

Figure 10.4. Segment of an interactive Demos session in which the model is extended to explore four levels of threshold in exposure concentration below which there are no deaths.

In Figure 10.6 we assumed the "value of a life," or, more precisely, the amount of investment deemed appropriate to avert a low probability statistical death from TXC exposure, to be $1 million. Obviously this is a value judgment open to controversy. So in Figure 10.8, we examine the sensitivity of the expected cost curve to values ranging from $0.3 million to $3 million.

The expected value of perfect information (EVPI) is a powerful measure of sensitivity to uncertainty. In Figure 10.9, we define the EVPI for the decision

```
>Th  := Uniform(0,5)                    Replace the multiple threshold levels with a distribution.
>Conc  := BaseConc*(1 - Ctrl)

BaseConc is undeclared, in the Definition of Conc
Do you want to declare it? [Yes]:

Declaring Variable BaseConc
Title: Base concentration
Units: ug/m↑3
Description: Base atmospheric concentration, assuming no emissions control,
Definition: Lognormal(10,2)

Ctrl is undeclared, in the Definition of Conc
Do you want to declare it? [Yes]:

Declaring Variable Ctrl
Title: Control level
Units:
Description: The factor by which the concentration is reduced due to ~
        abatement of TXC emissions,
Definition: [0, .25, .5, .7, .8, .85, .9, .95]            Try several levels.
```

Figure 10.5. Concentration is redefined in terms of **BaseConc**, a base level, and **Ctrl**, the level of emissions control, a decision variable.

on the optimal level of control as the difference between the minimum expected cost and the expected minimum cost. It is automatically evaluated for each value of life, **Vl**.

In Figure 10.10, the *Whyall* command provides one view of the entire model. It lists each of those variables defined in terms of others with its defining relationship and the variables on which it depends. Finally, the model can be saved in the form of a text file. This can be edited, printed, and reloaded into Demos for another session.

In this example, we have tried to illustrate how interactive refinement and exploration could speed the process of developing a model for risk analysis and obtaining quantitative insights about which are the key uncertainties, and understanding their impact on the decision.

10.2. Evaluation of Demos

We have undertaken a variety of formal and informal evaluations of the Demos system.[3] The goal in these evaluations has been to investigate whether use of the system promotes more effective modeling and treatment of uncertainty in quantitative policy analysis. In particular, we wished to test our hypotheses that the use of such a system would encourage analysts to more completely and successfully:

1. represent and analyze variable and parameter uncertainty;
2. engage in sensitivity analysis and iterative model refinement;

---

3. Much of the discussion in this section is based directly on Henrion et al. (1986).

```
>Variable Cost
Title: Total cost
Units: $/yr
Description: Annual total cost to society including control costs and ~
        total Extra deaths times "value of life"
Definition: CtrlCost + Vl * Xd

CtrlCost is undeclared, in the Definition of Cost
Do you want to declare it? [Yes]:

Declaring Variable CtrlCost
Title: Control costs
Units: $/yr
Description: Annualized cost of emissions control technology. ~
        Assumes a log cost function, so that there is a constant factor A. ~
        to reduce emissions by a factor of 10.
Definition: -A*Log(1 - Ctrl)

A is undeclared, in the Definition of CtrlCost
Do you want to declare it? [Yes]:

Declaring Variable A
Title: Control cost coeff.
Units: $/yr
Description: Control cost parameter: Incremental cost to reduce TXC ~
        emissions by a factor of 10.
Definition: Lognormal(100M, 1.5)

Vl is undeclared, in the Definition of Cost
Do you want to declare it? [Yes]:

Declaring Variable Vl
Title: "life value"
Units: $/d
Description: Size of investment deemed appropriate to avert a death from TXC
Definition: 1M
```

Figure 10.6. The total social cost is defined as the sum of the control costs and the social costs. Control costs increase exponentially as the level of control approaches 100%. Social costs are proportional to the deaths.

3. document and record model structures, assumptions, and implications to facilitate communications.

A major purpose in examining these questions has been to identify ways in which the design of Demos, and future systems like it, might be significantly improved.

One problem in evaluating a system like Demos is that it is hard to know what to compare it against. It is probably impossible to devise a formal experimental protocol that could provide unambiguous evaluations of issues as broad and fuzzy as the three listed above. Although rigorous experiments can be devised to address much narrower questions, it is not clear that answers to these would help very much. If providing an integrated set of facilities in a single system exhibits the hoped-for synergy among the facilities, then any reductionist approach that evaluates the performance of each individual facility, in isolation, may miss the

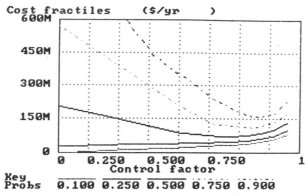

Figure 10.7. Probability distribution for cost as a function of level of control. The distribution at each level of control is indicated by the five fractiles (quantiles) 0.1, 0.25, 0.5, 0.75, 0.9.

```
>Vl := [300K, 1M, 3M]                      Range of values for "value of life".
>Graph Mean(Cost) By Ctrl                  Graph mean cost against Ctrl for each Vl.
```

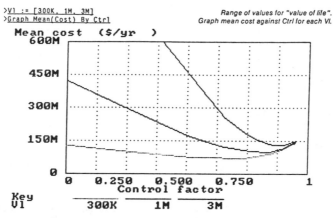

Figure 10.8. The "value of life," **Vl**, so far assumed as $1 million, is likely to be controversial, so we perform a parametric sensitivity analysis to examine the effect of changes over a factor of 10.

```
>Variable Evpi
Title: Exp val perf info
Units: $/yr]
Description: Expected value of perfect information; ~
        The difference in expected cost between the decision that ~
        minimizes expected cost with current information and the optimal ~
        decision given perfect information.
Definition: Min(Mean(Cost), Ctrl) - Mean(Min(Cost, Ctrl))
                              Min(y, x) gives the minimum value of y by selection of x.
>Evpi
Evpi        : Exp val perf info ($/yr     ) =
   Vl        300K    1M    3M
         [ 37.3M 53.4M 67.2M]
```

Figure 10.9. We define the expected value of perfect information for the control decision as the difference between the minum expected cost and the expected minimum cost.

>Whyall

```
Xd              : Extra deaths      (d/yr    ) =     75
     Description: Extra deaths per year attributed to exposure to TXC
     Xd = Pop*Hdf
Pop             : Population        (people  ) =     30M
Hdf             : Health damge fn   (/yr     ) =   2.50u


Conc            : Concentration     (ug/m†3  ) =      5
     Description: Average annual ambient concentration of TXC in atmosphere.
     Conc = BaseConc*(1 - Ctrl)
BaseConc        : Base concentration(ug/m†3  ) =     10
Ctrl            : Control factor    (        ) =   0.500


Hdf             : Health damge fn   (/yr     ) =  2.50u
     Description: Increment in annual death rate per individual from exposure
     Hdf = (Conc - Th)*H*IfPos(Conc - Th)
Conc            : Concentration     (ug/m†3  ) =      5
H               : Health damg. coeff(/yr-ug/m†) =    1u
Th              : Threshold         (ug/m†3  ) =  2.500


Cost            : Total cost        ($/yr    ) = 105.M
     Description: Total cost to society: Control costs plus mortality.
     Cost = CtrlCost + Vl * Xd
Xd              : Extra deaths      (d/yr    ) =     75
Ctrlcost        : Control costs     ($/yr    ) =  30.1M
Vl              : "life value"      ($/d     ) =     1M


Ctrlcost        : Control costs     ($/yr    ) =  30.1M
     Description: Annualized cost of emissions control technology ~
          Assumes cost increment A to reduce emissions by a factor of 10.
     CtrlCost = -A*Log(1 - Ctrl)
Ctrl            : Control factor    (        ) =   0.500
A               : Control cost coeff($/yr    ) =    100M


Evpi            : Exp val perf info ($/yr    ) = Undefined
     Description: Expected value of perfect information: ~
          The difference in expected cost between the decision that ~
          minimizes expected cost with current information and the optimal ~
          decision given perfect information.
     Evpi = Min(Mean(Cost), Ctrl) - Mean(Min(Cost, Ctrl))
Ctrl            : Control factor    (        ) =   0.500
Cost            : Total cost        ($/yr    ) = 105.M
```

Figure 10.10. A summary of the model produced by the *Whyall* command. Only mid-values are given, so EVPI is undefined.

point. On the other hand, holistic examination of the performance of the system tends to be informal and may fall prey to overinfluence by anecdotal evidence of doubtful generality.

In their recent review of software psychology, Curtis et al. (1984) have argued that in undertaking such evaluations, one is well advised to employ a mixed strategy "to provide converging evidence on the phenomena or behaviors under investigation." In addition, they argue that it is important "to design experiments which seek to demonstrate the limitations as well as the advantages" of the particular system or design features being evaluated.

Among the approaches we have used to evaluate Demos are:

- comparison of the system's features with other systems in terms of availability, ease of use, and generality, as described above;
- examination of the reaction of users, as evidenced by desire to use the system, individual comments, formal evaluation questionnaires, and interviews;
- performance of specific experiments with users to examine particular aspects or features of the system; and
- review by expert modelers of projects resulting from use of the system.

In what follows we describe each of these approaches and then examine the results in terms of their bearing on the three hypotheses listed above.

10.2.1. Experimental Use

Static evaluations of the recipe of features that go into a system (Reimann and Waren, 1985) may suggest whether or not it is suitable for particular purposes, but "the proof of the pudding is in the eating." Accordingly, we examined the use of the system in several studies with varying degrees of structure. These included several observational studies with research users as well as a series of three studies of the use of Demos by a group of sixteen first- and second-year graduate students enrolled in the graduate Research Methods course of the Department of Engineering and Public Policy at Carnegie Mellon. These students all held undergraduate degrees in science or engineering but had limited experience in policy modeling and uncertainty analysis.

In the first of the graduate student studies we examined the initial problems of learning to use Demos. Half the subjects had a hardcopy user manual, and the others had access to the same material interactively, in "softcopy" form. Their task was to construct a simple probabilistic model. In the second study, subjects were asked to explore and critique an existing moderate-sized Demos model designed to compare alternative policies for improving motor vehicle crash safety (Graham and Henrion, 1984). The goal was to test the feasibility and usefulness of an interactive approach for reviewing policy models. In the third study, the students were asked to choose a modest-sized, previously published policy model, reimplement it in Demos, and perform a probabilistic uncertainty analysis on it. Subjects submitted a hardcopy report including printouts of the model and Demos outputs describing the results of each task.

In addition to these three tasks specified by the investigators, Demos has been used by choice for about twenty policy modeling projects by researchers and policy analysts both at Carnegie Mellon and elsewhere. Several of these projects have resulted in published reports or articles (Nair, Morgan, and Henrion, 1982;

Amaral, 1983; Dayo, 1983; Moscowitz et al., 1983; Graham and Henrion, 1984; Morgan et al., 1984; Rubin et al., 1984).

All users were required to submit any resulting reports and articles and answer an evaluation questionnaire.

For the three experimental studies and for voluntary users, over the two-year evaluation period, complete traces of user interaction with Demos were collected and comments were solicited automatically at the end of each session. Each user filled in an evaluation questionnaire before and after Demos use. The questionnaire contained questions to establish the user's previous experience in policy modeling and uncertainty analysis and with computer aids, in particular to identify information systems or aids used in previous projects. It also requested a series of ratings for seven modeling activities in terms of the degree to which Demos made each easier or harder, and whether users engaged in that activity more or less, relative to previous comparable modeling projects without Demos. After their use of Demos the sixteen graduate student subjects and most of the other users participated in a thirty-minute debriefing interview with the investigators. In these interviews we sought clarification of answers on the questionnaire, and explored problems in the Demos models created.

It is important to notice that, for a system intended to improve modeling, even positive evaluation of the system by users does not necessarily indicate that it is successful in its goal of improving the quality of modeling. It might just be more convenient or fun to use. For this reason we considered it important to examine the quality of the resulting work. Two of us each carefully reviewed the resulting models and associated analysis, and in the debriefing interviews we sought clarification on modeling strategies and explored apparent deficiencies. Clear-cut objective rating of the quality of modeling is hard to provide, since there remains an important element of taste: The problem is akin to evaluating writing style. However, specific deficiencies, such as improper or skimpy treatment of parametric uncertainty, probabilistic dependence, sensitivity analysis, refinement, and documentation, were relatively easy to identify.

The purpose of this kind of evaluation is not to demonstrate once and for all that a computer aid can significantly improve the quality of policy modeling for engineering–economic analysis. This a very broad and ill-defined question, and a simple yes or no answer would probably be neither possible nor meaningful. However, well-designed evaluation studies can discover the ways in which various features of an information system may improve or hinder performance of the various activities involved, and hence identify important issues and problems to be addressed in the design of better systems. Thus evaluation does not stand as an independent activity, but as part of an ongoing cycle of research and development. Note that by "information system," we should not be restricted narrowly to the computer program, but should consider the entire user environment including system documentation, tutorial, and educational context.

10.2.2. Treatment of Parameter Uncertainty

The evaluation studies yielded overwhelming evidence that Demos promotes the explicit characterization and treatment of parameter uncertainty, primarily through the use of subjective probability distributions.

All of our graduate student subjects, and all of the experienced modelers who answered the question about probabilistic analysis in the evaluation questionnaire, indicated it was easier (20%) or much easier (80%) to deal with parameter uncertainty in Demos than in other environments. All but one of the student subjects who responded, and all of the experienced modelers, indicated they did more such analysis in Demos than when they worked in other environments.

The reimplementations by graduate students of previously published policy studies all involved more explicit characterization of parameter uncertainty than did the original studies. Similarly a study of the user traces and resulting models developed in the new analyses undertaken by Carnegie Mellon graduate students and faculty and by off-campus analysts revealed far more explicit analysis of parameter uncertainty than is found in most contemporary policy studies. Indeed, several of these analysts, including the three major off-site users, employed Demos because they knew they wanted to deal with parameter uncertainty and found the Demos environment the most convenient way to do this.

Although the use of Demos promoted considerably more analysis of uncertainty, careful review of the models the graduate students built revealed a number of problems in the way they handled uncertainties. The problems encountered vary considerably, but they can be roughly divided into two groups. The first are problems arising from a failure to recognize and deal with issues of correlations or stochastic dependence among variables. Such issues can be fairly subtle. The problems appear to arise because the modelers did not systematically look for and think about correlation and stochastic dependence. In all the cases we identified, once we had figured out the problem and explained it to the modeler he or she had no difficulty understanding the concern. Even experienced modelers were occasionally found to experience such problems. However, experienced modelers appear to have learned to be reflective and questioning, and although they may initially make errors in setting up a model they appear to be effective at identifying these problems and getting them fixed.

The second group of problems we encountered involved a failure to distinguish between different classes of quantities when deciding how to deal with parameter uncertainty. Indeed, it was this observation that lead us to develop the arguments about how to treat uncertainty in different types of parameters and variables that we spelled out in Chapter 4 (see Table 4.1).

Thus, with respect to hypothesis one, we conclude that for both experienced and inexperienced modelers, Demos does promote more explicit characterization and treatment of parameter uncertainty. The adequacy of such treatments is excellent among experienced modelers; however, among inexperienced modelers (even those with substantial technical backgrounds) the adequacy of treatment is often mixed because of failures to recognize and deal appropriately with issues of correlation, stochastic dependence, and different variable types. In the words of our hypothesis, while Demos allows more complete treatment of parameter uncertainty it encourages successful treatment primarily in the sense of making it easier for people who already know what they are doing to do the right things. Inexperienced modelers often do not find it natural to do these right things, and may sometimes blunder into incorrect usage.

10.2.3. Sensitivity Analysis and Model Exploration

The split between experienced and inexperienced modelers is even more striking when we looked at our second hypothesis: that Demos would allow and encourage modelers to engage in sensitivity analysis and model refinement more completely and effectively. According to the questionnaire responses, most users appeared to believe that this hypothesis is true: 80% of our student subjects and 90% of our experienced modelers reported that it is easier to do deterministic sensitivity analysis in Demos than in other modeling environments; 70% of the student subjects and 50% of the expert analysts reported they actually did more deterministic sensitivity analysis in Demos. There was less consensus on model revision and elaboration. Only 55% of the student subjects, but all of the experienced modelers, said it was easier to revise and elaborate models in Demos than in other environments in which they had worked. Only 25% of student subjects, but 75% of our experienced modelers, said they actually did more such revision and elaboration in Demos. Since most of our graduate student subjects had relatively limited previous experience, these comparisons reported by the students may be more comparison with their idea of what they think they would normally do than with what they have done in previous modeling.

Despite all these lovely statistics, our interviews and studies of the traces of Demos sessions lead us to conclude that in fact only a few of the most experienced modelers came close to making what we would consider to be adequate use of the capabilities for sensitivity analysis and model revision and elaboration that Demos makes available. From our interviews, we conclude that the primary reason is that most users do not view the process of model building, refinement, and use as an iterative process of exploration and learning whose objective is insight (i.e., Figure 3.2). Rather they see it more as a linear "one-shot" process of building something that produces answers (i.e., Figure 3.1). Experienced modelers who do adopt the approach illustrated in Figure 3.1 clearly recognize the power of the tools that Demos makes available. Most other users see these tools primarily as an easy way to run a few simple sensitivity runs for the sake of completeness once the model has been built.

10.2.4. *Communication of Assumptions and Results*

Our third hypothesis was that Demos would allow and encourage analysts to communicate model structure, behavior, assumptions, and limitations to other analysts and users more completely and effectively. At the simple level of model documentation, about 60% of our student subjects and 90% of our experienced modelers said it was easier to provide documentation in Demos; 80% of our students and 65% of our experienced modelers said they did more documentation in Demos. A couple of students responded that they did not do any more documenting in Demos than they did in FORTRAN or Pascal, although their models appeared to be quite extensively documented as a result of their having responded to requests for information they received from the system as they built the models. When we asked them about this in the interviews, we were amused by their response that they "hadn't really thought of all that as documentation ... it was just stuff you put in because the system asked for it"! It appears that Demos more completely and successfully allows and encourages simple model documentation than is normal in conventional policy-modeling environments.

We have already discussed the considerable reduction in model size and improved modularity from the use of a nonprocedural modeling language, and also from multidimensional array abstraction. This significantly eases the task of model understanding relative to a model in an procedural language, such as FORTRAN. Indeed, it is hard to imagine a source listing of a FORTRAN model being used as the primary representation to help communicate the model structure.

One advantage of Demos over procedural languages that we had not fully anticipated is the considerable reduction in the effort needed for debugging and verifying model correctness, that is, checking correspondence between the conceptual model and computer implementation. Debugging is greatly speeded by incremental compilation and interactive evaluation. The *Why* command displays the definition and value of a variable and those variables on which it depends, and so facilitates stepping through the dependence network to discover the source of any major discrepancies between computed and anticipated numbers.

One goal in the design of Demos was to facilitate interactive, on-line review and exploration of a model in softcopy as an alternative or adjunct to the traditional hardcopy report. Demos maintains the network of dependencies among variables, or *influence diagram*, and provides several commands, including the *Why* and *Tree* commands, to display these relationships and step around through the network, examining the explanatory documentation attached to the variable located at each node. For very simple models, especially models that can be effectively displayed on a single terminal screen, these capabilities work well in supporting model exploration and understanding.

However, in an experiment where subjects were asked to understand and critique a motor vehicle safety model (Graham and Henrion, 1984) involving about fifty variables (requiring about ten 20-line screens to display), subjects tended to get disoriented and complained of getting lost in their written and verbal reports. To alleviate the problem, some subjects spontaneously produced a hardcopy listing and used it as a road map as they navigated around the network structures interactively. Others tried to draw their own influence diagrams by hand, based on the dependencies they discovered. This does not seem to be a problem limited only to relatively inexperienced modelers. Experienced analysts shared the same problems in understanding complex, unfamiliar models. Very similar findings of disorientation when navigating a network of help frames were obtained in the evaluation of the ZOG system (Mantei, 1982). One may also compare approaches to computer "adventure" games: Usually the first thing an experienced player does with a new game is try to draw a network map of the game world.

It became clear that the hierarchical network of dependencies between variables, as revealed in a piecemeal fashion by the available commands, does not by itself provide sufficient organization to allow easy grasping of a complex model. We concluded that a higher level of abstraction provided by dividing up the set of variables into a hierarchy of submodels might help, and that automatically generated graphical maps of the model hierarchy and dependency networks could help users locate parts of the model within their context. We discuss these and related innovations in Section 10.3.

The graduate student subjects were asked not just to understand the model they were given but also to evaluate it critically. Just as they did relatively little sensitivity analysis or model restructuring when developing their own models, so too they engaged in little active evaluation activity of this kind when they were asked to critique an existing model. For example, many accepted key assumptions such as the trade-off between lives saved and dollars spent on safety technology without sensitivity analysis to determine the effect on the conclusions of plausible variations.

10.2.5. Implications of these Evaluations

Demos has proved to be highly successful in the sense that users find it friendly and easy to use, and experienced analysts attach great value to the expanded capabilities that it makes available. However, as the preceding discussion makes clear, it has only partly met our design objectives in promoting more effective policy modeling and uncertainty analysis. And in the hands of unskilled analysts, it can provide easy access to a variety of errors that were previously inaccessible.

From our evaluations we have identified two rather different problems that will require attention if the field is to move closer to realizing the objectives that motivated us to build Demos. Work is needed on:

1. improving the knowledge and analysis skills of the people who perform policy analysis, and on
2. providing analysts with more powerful flexible tools for organizing their thinking and their work as they construct and use policy models.

Our experiences in developing and evaluating Demos have given us many insights that have significantly affected the way we now teach students in policy analysis. Most of these insights have been reflected in earlier chapters of this book. As we and others continue to refine and formalize insights about the practice of policy analysis, it may begin to be possible to automate at least some of them in the form of help- and advice-giving systems associated with general analysis environments such as Demos. At a simpler level, we have concluded that collecting examples of both errors and good solutions in policy modeling can be valuable both in the instruction of new analysts and in supporting the ongoing work of practicing analysts. We have begun some activities in this area but have little to report here.

We have made rather more progress on putting computers to work to address the second problem of helping analysts organize their thinking and their work. In the final sections of this chapter we describe a set of experimental interface facilities that Charlie Wiecha and we have developed to allow a Demos user to build and interact with models in terms of graphical displays of hierarchically organized influence diagrams.

10.3. Demaps: An Experimental Graphics User Interface to Demos

Demaps is a system that provides a graphical interface to Demos.[4] It has been designed to exploit the four mechanisms of abstraction, hierarchical decomposition, multiple views, and connectors between multiple views in order to facilitate model construction and exploration and try to reduce users' disorientation in large Demos models. Figure 10.11 shows a typical Demaps screen display for the top level of a model on the costs and benefits of passive restraints in reducing automobile fatalities. Individual variables are shown as nodes shaped like ovals in the diagram. Each node has two connection points, one below the node for links from variables it depends on, and the other above the node for links to variables it in turn influences. Thus, data flows from the bottom to the top of the diagram in Figure 10.11. The diagram is an abstraction of the concrete model in that only the dependencies between variables are shown graphically. Many different functional forms could be represented by the same set of nodes and links. The detailed way in which each variable depends on others is specified in its algebraic definition. The definition is visible not

---

4. The discussion in this section is based directly upon Wiecha (1986) and Wiecha and Henrion (1987a, 1987b).

directly in the diagram but in the scrolling text and pop-up displays shown in Figure 10.11.

The abstraction of Demaps diagrams is important in understanding and designing models. The lack of an explicit representation for algebraic operators in the diagrams allows models to be read and designed in stages which consider each of the following concerns independently:

- What are the significant variables that should be, or are, included in a model, and which lie outside of its scope?
- What are the qualitative dependencies among the variables included in the model?
- What are the quantitative algebraic definitions which implement the dependencies?

The first two of these involve qualitative choices about significant variables and their interrelationships. Working in Demaps a new variable can be added by using the mouse to pick up and drag an oval variable icon from the left of the diagram to the desired location in the influence diagram. When this is done a blank template of attributes is created in the text display. As links are drawn graphically to other variables, its textual definition is automatically modified to list those variables on which each variable depends. Because the graphical links are an abstraction of the definition, the system cannot automatically specify the actual functional form of the resulting dependencies. Demaps creates a "FunctionOf" relation to represent the abstract dependencies in text form. For example, if links were drawn from a variable X to variables A and B, the definition of X in the text display would be set automatically to: FunctionOf(A, B). Links may be removed between variables graphically by using the dagger icon from the left column. As each link is cut, the FunctionOf definitions are altered to reflect the new set of dependencies.

Demaps does not require understanding and design to proceed in linear sequence from stage to stage. Rather, the abstraction of model structure facilitates each type of consideration without overly constraining the later stages. By focusing attention on different considerations at each stage, the diagrams can be an important aid in structuring debate about alternative model designs. Like the idea graphs of Cognoter (Foster and Stefik, 1986), influence diagrams in Demaps help make model structures transparent and invite others to comment on and revise them.

Models may be decomposed into a hierarchy of submodels that are shown as boxes in Figure 10.12. Submodels have both external and internal views. An external view, for example, of the benefits submodel in Figure 10.12, displays the interface between the submodel and its external context. The external view consists of a box representing the submodel along with connections to variables which are inputs to, or depend on outputs from, the submodel. The internal view of the benefits submodel shown in Figure 10.11 displays the details of the submodel implementation by showing the variables and connections relating the submodel's inputs to its outputs. Submodels are a second form of abstraction

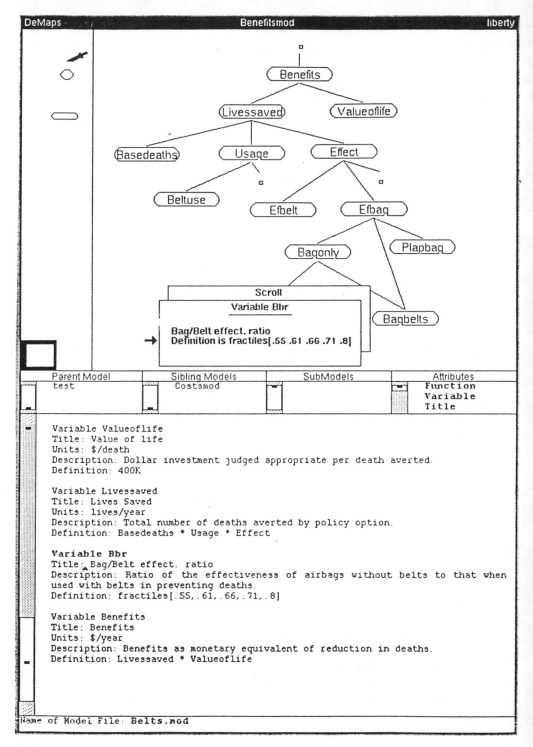

Figure 10.11. Detailed view of benefits portion of automobile restraint model in Demaps. Variables are shown as ovals, and links between them indicate the flow of data. Variables external to a submodel are shown by small square connector nodes. Menus attached to a node give an abbreviated textual description of that variable.

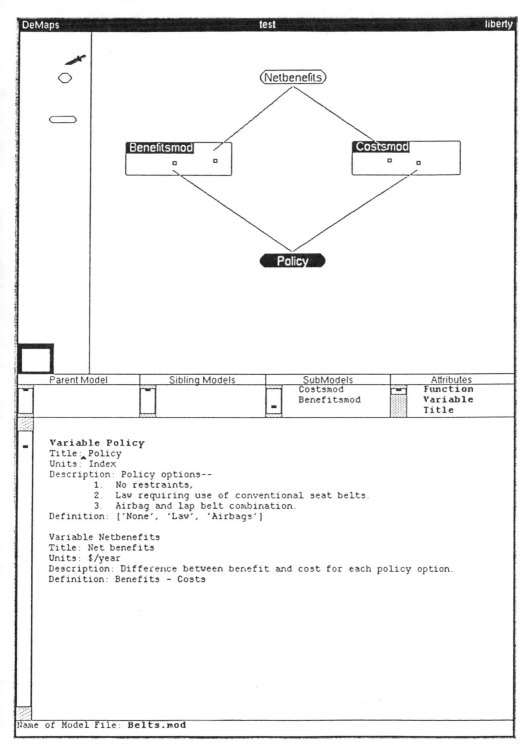

(Netbenefits)

Benefitsmod   Costsmod

Policy

Parent Model	Sibling Models	SubModels	Attributes
		Costsmod	**Function**
		Benefitsmod	**Variable**
			Title

Variable Policy
Title: Policy
Units: Index
Description: Policy options--
       1.   No restraints,
       2.   Law requiring use of conventional seat belts.
       3.   Airbag and lap belt combination.
Definition: ['None', 'Law', 'Airbags']

Variable Netbenefits
Title: Net benefits
Units: $/year
Description: Difference between benefit and cost for each policy option.
Definition: Benefits - Costs

Name of Model File: **Belts.mod**

Figure 10.12. The external view of the model's benefits and costs computations.

in Demaps diagrams, which allow models to be built and viewed by hiding information about components that are not relevant in a given context.

The hierarchical set of submodels is displayed using the control panels at the center of Figure 10.12. Each panel contains the names of the displayed model's parent, sibling, and child submodels. The current model view can be shifted to any of these other submodels by clicking on one of their names, or multiple displays created to view several model diagrams simultaneously.

Linkages between variables in different submodels are represented by offpage connectors, shown as small squares in Figures 10.11 and 10.12. Offpage connectors may link a variable to variables in other models, as in Figure 10.11, or they may link models to each other when the outputs of one model are used directly as inputs to another, as in Figure 10.12. In both cases, menus can be displayed when the mouse is positioned over a connector node that lists the remote variables represented by that connector. The structure of the diagram is thus a form of fish-eye view (Furnas, 1986) in that details of a limited area of the system are selectively augmented with objects at a greater "distance" from the focus of attention that are significant given the current view.

10.4. Evaluations of Demaps

Along with Charlie Wiecha we have conducted a variety of experimental studies to evaluate the Demaps system. The results are reported in detail elsewhere (Wiecha, 1986; Wiecha and Henrion, 1987a, 1987b). Here we briefly summarize.

In our principal series of evaluations we used four subjects who were faculty or postdoctoral fellows from the Department of Engineering and Public Policy at Carnegie Mellon University. All four were accomplished analysts who had had considerable experience in developing and evaluating large scale quantitative policy models. They were each given a separate training session before the study to learn how to use Demaps. Everyone took an informal test before each study session to make sure they were familiar with all commands.

We asked subjects to compare two versions of a benefit–cost analysis model of various policies toward passenger restraints in automobiles (Graham and Henrion, 1984), and to select one policy. The policies considered by each model included no seat belts, a law mandating their use, and combined belts and airbags. In these studies, the same base model version was compared with a different alternative version in two sessions for each subject. Each session lasted somewhat less than an hour. All of our expert subjects spent over half of their time in sensitivity analysis during our study sessions.

In these experiments we arranged for Demaps to display both model versions side by side on the screen, each with a diagram and text window. Because the two versions had different implications, subjects were required to explore and understand them in depth in order to evaluate which, if either, was most appropriate. They were able to conduct "what-if" sensitivity analyses to examine the importance of any assumptions they found suspect. Subjects were also given an explicit list of the variables that differed between the versions.

Each session was recorded on videotape using three cameras, and transcripts of each session were generated and analyzed using standard techniques of verbal protocol analysis (Ericsson and Simon, 1984). Details are available in Wiecha (1986).

To judge the consistency of this coding process, one of the eight transcripts (that judged as most difficult to encode originally) was completely recoded after a delay of three weeks. The recoded transcript was compared with the original coding, and any occurrence of extra, missing, or differing processes counted as an error. The recoded and original transcripts agreed in 91% of 480 elementary processes.

10.4.1. Summary of Findings from Demaps User Studies

It is clear from both the formal and informal studies we have conducted that, by providing hierarchical influence diagrams, Demaps considerably enhances a user's ability to conceptualize and navigate through a Demos model. Further, the system is easy to use. Our subjects proved able to learn to use Demaps effectively in an hour or so. Thus, at this highest level, we view the experimental system as a success.

The results of our studies with expert users have been analyzed both to examine the processes by which experts went about understanding and comparing models, and to understand the operation of various specific features of the interface. We do not yet have formal experimental evidence on the ways in which Demaps affects the construction of new models.

Our studies of aggregate comprehension processes found that subjects adopted two rather different approaches to model understanding and analysis. The more common involved working systematically through the entire model before engaging in What-if sensitivity analysis. However, in three of the eight sessions, three of the four subjects adopted an incremental strategy that deferred examining model documentation until required later on. We call this strategy "test-before-read."

In many cases, subjects using the test-before-read strategy reexamined a model's structure in response to unexpected results from a What-if test. In such cases, the subject has formulated an expectation of the outcome of the test but finds conflicting results from the model. Several successive incorrect hypotheses related to a single variable may be tested before an effort is made to comprehend the model more completely. These results suggest that the test-before-read strategy may be less effective than reading the model more completely from the start.

On the other hand, the read-before-test strategy may not always be feasible. In large models, particularly, there is often too much material to be completely read. The important research question is, how can the test-before-read strategy be made more effective? In small models, the entire structure of the model can be internalized. Meaningful questions can then be asked because information about the interactions between each variable and the rest of the model is accessible directly in the reader's memory. One way large models can be made more understandable is by attaching constraints to the value of each variable. Warnings would be generated automatically whenever a variable violated its constraint. The constraints themselves are a type of documentation that can be used to develop an appropriate understanding of the purpose of each variable. Another approach is to allow users to annotate models with comments about each variable.

Our subjects displayed no preconceived notions of which variables should be questioned in the models. This is perhaps surprising, since a number of variables in the study models are typically controversial, such as the "value of life." Rather, subjects selected each What-if test based on the results of previous tests and on knowledge gained during earlier explorations of the model. This knowledge was summarized by a number of explicit model critiques identifying variables and clusters of variables that had been found to be problematic, or of interest for further exploration.

In three of four subjects, between 80% and 90% of all variables selected for sensitivity analysis had been the focus of a prior critique. Most critiques occur when questioning the model behavior, but a number also occur when generating ideas for sensitivity analysis. Critiques thus emerge as a major organizing factor in model comprehension strategies: They summarize knowledge gained from exploration of the model and suggest ideas for further exploration. Critiques may thus provide a means for improving the effectiveness of the test-before-read strategy, which stresses incremental learning resulting from successive sensitivity analyses.

The central problem with test-before-read was formulating sensible What-if tests without completely understanding a model. One way to gain a better understanding of small parts of large models may be to annotate them with critiques attached to individual variables. Other reviewers could browse through a set of critiques previously attached to a variable while formulating their own ideas for sensitivity analysis. Through exposure to previous comments, reviewers would understand each variable well enough to question it intelligently without having explored the rest of the model. Such annotation may also hold potential for instruction. By students engaging in an ongoing computer-based discussion of models through stored critiques, they may be able to acquire more quickly the iterative evaluation strategies typical of experts.

One very interesting and frequent criticism was that the system lacked sufficient high-level information to properly understand the models even for subjects using the read-before-test strategy. Of course, the Demos model contained detailed information about each variable and submodel of a sort not found in a conventional model. But experts were asking for more general discussion of assumptions and the judgments made in the process of model construction.[5]

The key question here is whether it is appropriate to attach all such information as attributes of variables and submodels, or whether the somewhat different kinds of organization possible in linear text reports have intrinsic advantages. The model-based organization may work better for organizing explanations and criticisms, when there are many modelers and reviewers. Certainly organization around the mathematical model structure makes it clear just what information and explanation are available or lacking for each component, which may not be so clear in a linear text.

In related work on electronic books ("hyper-text") (Brown University, 1986) there is a notion of a web of links among chunks of text. Multiple versions of the webs may be created to allow a given data base to be browsed according to linear or network organizations. Further experimentation on applying these ideas to quantitative decision models seems called for. However, it is relevant to note Borenstein's finding in his study of Help systems, that the quality of the text was much more important than the access mechanism (Borenstein, 1985).

Since our studies of a number of the specific features of Demaps' displays and capabilities are principally of interest to experts in human–computer interaction, we refer readers elsewhere for details (Wiecha 1986, 1987a, 1987b). In summary we found that:

- subjects tend not to make many transitions between the graphical and textual representations of a model as compared to the number of transitions they make within each representation;
- a wider variety of variables is examined in the diagram representation than in the text; and,
- the hierarchically arranged influence diagrams are the primary vehicle by which users navigate through the model. Attention shifts to the text to examine the details of a variable just identified in the diagram, and shifts back to the diagram to continue searching the model for different variables.

Recently many of the ideas developed in Demaps have been incorporated in a new interface system called Hyper-Demos that we have implemented in Hypercard on a Macintosh II. Testing of this system has just begun.

---

5. Such a discussion is in the journal article describing the model the experts were using (Graham and Henrion, 1984). Their critique was that they needed access to this material in order to evaluate the model adequately.

10.5. Conclusions

Demos, and especially Demaps, are experimental systems. Our extended discussion of them has been offered not to "sell" readers on the virtues of these particular software environments but rather to argue, through concrete example, the importance of developing powerful flexible software environments for the construction and use of policy models. The experimental evaluations we have just outlined clearly demonstrate the importance of adopting an empirical approach to the evaluation of such systems. Further work on these and similar computer environments for policy analysis can lead to:

- systems that meet most of the original design goals we outlined for Demos;
- a better understanding of the cognitive processes involved in the construction and use of good policy models and analyses; and,
- systems that significantly facilitate our ability to teach the skills of good policy modeling and analysis.

However, it is important to remember that computer systems, even powerful ones, are not a cure-all. They are not a substitute for knowledge and careful thought. Although they can produce spectacular results with modest effort in the hands of a skilled analyst, they can also produce spectacular garbage of extraordinary complexity in the hands of an incompetent or careless analyst. The saving grace is that if we insist that these systems make it easy to examine, exercise, modify, and critique the models they support, it should be possible to open these models up to a process of critical peer review, which, over time, could revolutionize the field of quantitative policy analysis.

References

Amaral, D.A.L. (1983). "Quantifying Uncertainty in the Health Effects of Respirable Sulfates," Ph.D. diss., Department of Engineering and Public Policy, Carnegie Mellon University, Pittsburgh.

Balson, W. E., Boyd, D., and North, D. W. (1982). *Acid Deposition: Decision Framework. Volume 2: User Guide to the Acid Deposition Decision Tree Program*, Research Report No. RP 2156-1, Electric Power Research Institute, Palo Alto, Calif.

Borenstein, N. (1985). "The Design and Evaluation of On-Line Help Systems," Ph.D. diss., Carngie Mellon University Computer Science Department, Pittsburgh.

Brown University (1986). *Intermedia*, Proceedings of the Conference on Computer Supported Cooperative Work, Austin, Tex.

Cazalet, E. G., and Cambell, G. L. (1983, September). *RML User's Guide – Version 2.0*, Decision Focus Inc., Los Altos, Calif.

Curtis, B., Soloway, E. M., Brooks, R. E., Black, J. B., Ehrlich, K., and Ramsey, H. R. (1986). "Software Psychology: The Need for an Interdisciplinary Program," *Proceedings of the IEEE*, 74, no. 8:1092–1106.

Dayo, F. B. (1983). "Choice Between Alternative Nuclear Energy Systems: A Decision Analytical Model for Less Developed Countries," Ph.D. diss., Carnegie Mellon University, Pittsburgh.

Ericsson, K. A., and Simon, H. A. (1984). *Protocol Analysis: Verbal Reports as Data*, MIT Press, Cambridge, Mass.

Foster, G., and Stefik, M. (1986). "Cognoter, Theory and Practice of a Collaborative Tool," pp. 7–15, in *Conference on Computer-Supported Cooperative Work*, ed. H. Krasner and I. Greif, The Association for Computing Machinery, New York.

Furnas, G. (1986, April). "Generalized Fisheye Views," pp. 16–23, in *Human Factors in Computing Systems*, ed. M. Mantei and P. Orbeton, *CHI'86 Conference Proceedings*, Boston.

Gardner, R. H., Bojder, U. R., and Bergstrom, U. (1983). *PRISM: A Systematic Method for Determining the Effect of Parameter Uncertainties on Model Predictions*, Studsvik Energiteknik AB, Report/NW-83/555, Nykoping, Sweden.

Geoffrion, A. M. (1987). "An Introduction to Structured Modeling," *Management Science*, 33:547–588.

Goldstein, S. (1983). "Software for Explicit Probabilistic Mathematics," paper presented at the Sixth MIT/ONR Workshop on Command, Control and Communications, July 25–29, Cambridge, Mass.

Graham, J. G., and Henrion, M. (1984). "The Passive Restraint Question: A Probabilistic Analysis," *Risk Analysis*, 42, no. 2: 25–40.

Greenberger, M. (1981, October). "Humanizing Policy Analysis: Confronting the Paradox in Energy Modelling," in *Validation and Assessment of Energy Models*, ed. S. Gass, National Bureau of Standards (Special Publication 616).

Henrion, M. (1985). "Software for Decision Analysis," *OR/MS Today*, 12 (October): 24–29.

Henrion, M. (1987). "Predict! Uncertainty Analysis in a Spread Sheet," *Risk Analysis*, 7:539–541.

Henrion, M., and Morgan, M. G. (1985). "A Computer Aid for Risk and Other Policy Analysis," *Risk Analysis*, 5:195–208.

Henrion, M., Morgan, M. G., Nair, I., and Wiecha, C. (1986). "Evaluating an Information System for Policy Modeling and Uncertainty Analysis," *Journal of the American Society for Information Science*, 37, no. 5: 319–330.

Henrion, M., and Wishbow, N. (1987). *Demos User's Manual: Version Three*, Department of Engineering and Public Policy, Carnegie Mellon University, Pittsburgh.

Howard, R. A., and Matheson, J. (1981). "Influence Diagrams," reprinted in Howard and Matheson (1984).

Howard, R. A., and Matheson, J. (1984). *The Principles and Applications of Decision Analysis*, 2, Strategic Decisions Group, Menlo Park, Calif., pp. 719–762.

Iman, R. L., and Shortencarier, M. J. (1984, March). *A Fortran-77 Program and User's Guide for the Generation of Latin Hypercube and Random Samples for Use with Computer Models*, SAND83-2365, Sandia National Laboratory, Albuquerque, N.M.

Iman, R. L., Shortencarier, M. J., and Johnson, J. D. (1985, June). *A Fortran-77 Program and User's Guide for the Calculation of Partial Regression and Standardized Regression Coefficients*, SAND85-0084, Sandia National Laboratory, Albuquerque, N.M.

Mantei, M. (1982). "A Study of Disorientation Behavior in ZOG," Ph.D. diss., University of Southern California, Los Angeles.

Morgan, M. G., Morris, S. C., Henrion, M., Amaral, D.A.L., and Rish, W. B. (1984). "Treating Technical Uncertainty in Policy Analysis: A Sulfur Air Pollution Example," *Risk Analysis*, 4, no. 3: 201–216.

Moscowitz, P. D. et al. (1983). *Health and Environmental Effects Document for Photovoltaic Energy Systems*, Biomedical Assessment Division, Brookhaven National Laboratory, Upton, N.Y.

Nair, I., Morgan, M. G., and Henrion M. (1982). "Office Automation: Assessing Energy Implications," *Telecommunications Policy*, 6, no. 3: 207–222.

Prywes, N., Pnueli, A., and Shastry, S. (1979). "Use of a Nonprocedural Specification Language and Associated Program Generator in Software Development," *ACM Transactions on Programming Languages and Systems*, 1, no. 2: 196–217.

Reimann, B. C., and Waren, A. D. (1985). "User-Oriented Criteria for the Selection of DSS Software," *Communications of the ACM*, 28, no. 2: 166–179.

Rubin, E. S., Hahn, R., Henrion, M., Lave, L., Marnicio, R. J., McRae, G. J., Small, M. J., and
    Talukdar, S. (1984). *A Conceptual Framework for an Integrated Assessment of the Acid
    Deposition Problem*, final report, Center for Energy and Environmental Studies, Carnegie
    Mellon University, Pittsburgh.
Wiecha, C. (1986). "An Empirical Study of How Visual Programming Aids in Comprehending
    Quantitative Policy Models," Ph.D. diss., Department of Engineering and Public Policy,
    Carnegie Mellon University, Pittsburgh.
Wiecha, C., and Henrion, M. (1987a, September). "Linking Multiple Program Views Using a Visual
    Cache," Proceedings of Interact-87, Stuttgart.
Wiecha, C., and Henrion, M. (1987b, December). "An Empirical Study of Strategies for Under-
    standing Quantitative Decision Models," Proceedings of the Eighth International Conference
    on Information Systems, Pittsburgh.

11   Large and Complex Models

"A theory should be as simple as possible, but no simpler."
Albert Einstein

Most of the best policy models are small and simple. At least in their essentials, they can be easily understood and described to others. They present relatively modest computational demands for modern digital computers. These attributes flow directly from the requirements that to be useful, policy models must be understandable and modest enough to be vigorously exercised to explore the implications of alternative assumptions and polices.

Of course, many models are not small and simple. There are some models, especially some science and engineering models, that are large or complex because they need to be. But many more are large or complex because their authors gave too little thought to why and how they were being built and how they would be used.

Policy analysts occasionally find themselves confronted with large and complex models. Sometimes the problem is to use the results or insights gained from a large science or engineering model in a policy analysis. More often the problem involves large and complex models someone wants to use directly in policy analysis. This chapter briefly explores some of the special issues that arise in such situations.

11.1. What Are "Large" and "Complex" Models?

Large models are models requiring large amounts of human, computational, or other resources in their construction and operation. If they are organized so that their structure and their outputs are easy to understand, and so that their solution is straightforward, large models may not be complex.

The definition of complexity has been a topic of interest in a number of fields.[1] Several decades ago, Warren Weaver (1948) defined two kinds of complexity. By "disorganized complexity" he meant "a problem in which the number of variables is very large, and one in which each of the many variables has a behavior which is individually erratic, or perhaps totally unknown." He argued

---

1. In a recent doctoral thesis Richard Henneman (Henneman, 1985; Henneman and Rouse, 1986) reviews the concept of complexity as it has been approached in physical science, general systems theory, computer science, software engineering, psychology, and several other fields. Complexity has been an issue of particular interest in software engineering (McCabe, 1976; Kearney et al., 1986). Although interesting, the details of these discussions are, unfortunately, of only limited use in clarifying the issues of complexity in the context of policy modeling.

that probabilistic techniques have made excellent progress in characterizing the bulk properties of such systems, and cited examples ranging from thermodynamics to the operation of telephone switching centers. In contrast, he argued, "organized complexity" involves problems in which probabilistic approaches cannot cope but in which it is necessary to deal explicitly with a large number of variables. Although Weaver did not say so, it seems apparent that whether a complex system is organized or disorganized in his terminology depends largely on the level at which one is trying to explain its behavior.

Jay Forrester (1969) defines a complex system as a "high-order, multiple loop, nonlinear feedback structure." He places great emphasis on feedback and nonlinearity, arguing that these features are likely to lead to "counter intuitive behavior" in complex systems.

Herbert Simon provides a discussion of these issues that we find particularly useful. He informally defines a complex system as

one made up of a large number of parts that interact in a nonsimple way. In such systems the whole is more than the sum of the parts, not in an ultimate, metaphysical sense but in the important pragmatic sense that, given the properties of the parts and the laws of interaction, it is not a trivial matter to infer the properties of the whole. (Simon, 1982)

He argues:

How complex or simple a structure is depends critically upon the way in which we describe it. Most of the complex structures found in the world are enormously redundant, and we can use this redundancy to simplify their description. But to use it, to achieve the simplification, we must find the right representation. (Simon, 1982)

Simon argues that most, perhaps all, of the world's human and natural systems are hierarchical in structure, that is, they are either "decomposable" into subsystems whose interactions are negligible, or are "nearly decomposable," that is they are decomposable into subsystems "in which the interactions among the subsystems are weak but not negligible."[2] Simon argues that it is unlikely that complex physical, biological, or social systems would evolve that are not hierarchical, since the various subelements of these systems need to have been individually stable long enough for the larger system to be built up or evolve. This has the interesting implication that in trying to understand any particular behavior of a complex hierarchical system, there are some natural limits or boundaries to the detail with which all aspects of the subsystems involved must be understood. To use a physical example, much can be understood about atoms and molecules without paying detailed attention to subatomic particles. Similarly, much can be understood about geology, oceanography, or atmospheric science without paying detailed attention to atoms and molecules. Everything in this world interacts with everything else, but for most behaviors a modest

2. If this is not true of some complex systems, such systems may be very difficult to detect or understand, since it is probably only by understanding the interaction of subelements that we are cognitively capable of building up an understanding of the whole.

subset of those interactions is far more important than all the others. That is, the system is decomposable, or at worst nearly decomposable, into a hierarchical structure.[3] Clearly such a decomposition may be required along several different dimensions. The examples we have cited focus principally on spatial scale but implicitly also suggest the importance of temporal scale. Electric power systems provide a good example of a system often analyzed through decomposition according to time scale. Fault processes can involve time scales of fractions of seconds; voltage and frequency transients can involve periods of seconds to minutes; questions of economic dispatch and load management typically involve time scales of minutes to hours; and expansion planning involves time scales of months to years (Dy Liacco, 1967; Morgan and Talukdar, 1979; Kokotovic et al., 1980; Winkelman et al., 1980).

If we apply Simon's perspective to policy problems, the implication is that the process of policy analysis should be the process of identifying, isolating, and understanding those aspects of the system, and their interactions, that matter for the particular problem of interest.

Complex models need not be large in terms of the amount of computer code they require. In practice, however, they frequently are. They typically require large amounts of human resources in their construction and operation – if for no other reason than that they are difficult to understand. Large need not imply complex and complex need not imply large, but for simplicity in the discussion that follows we will talk only about "large and complex" models.

11.2. Large and Complex Policy Models: Some Examples

The best way to understand why we believe so strongly that (consistent with the requirements of the problem being addressed) policy models should be kept small and simple is to look briefly at a few of the difficulties that have developed when attempts were made to construct and use large and complex models in policy research and analysis.

Our first set of examples are a variety of contemporary policy-motivated models built by groups in places such as the National Laboratories of the U.S. Department of Energy and by or for a number of U.S. federal regulatory agencies such as the Environmental Protection Agency, the Federal Energy Management Agency, and the Nuclear Regulatory Commission. For simplicity we refer to these as "general purpose regulatory models," although not all were constructed in direct support of the needs of specific regulatory agencies.

The second set of examples, which we will examine in somewhat greater

---

3. As we shall see, the extent to which this argument applies is often a function of the time horizon over which system performance is being described. Thus, for example, the farther into the future one tries to predict weather with a general circulation model, the more important the effects of small-scale details become.

detail, are the models of dynamic social, economic, and environmental systems built in the 1960s and 1970s. Although many investigators and modeling techniques were involved, the name of Jay Forrester and the technique of "systems dynamics" are perhaps the best known. For simplicity we will refer to these as the "global systems models," although many of the systems studied were of less than global dimensions.

11.2.1. General Purpose Regulatory Models

In the United States a variety of large and complex policy models have been built in support of the missions of regulatory agencies. Some of these models have involved attempts to couple technical, economic, social, and other aspects of a large sociotechnical system such as the system for energy supply, conversion, and use. Others perform impact assessment tasks such as computing the dispersal and consequences of exposure to chemical pollutants from a set of sources, or computing the transport, uptake, and metabolism of radioactive species and decay products and the doses they contribute to different organs of the body. Still others attempt to perform optimization such as that involved in choosing between alternative strategies for controlling and disposing of toxic and hazardous materials. There are many examples of such models. Most are not clean examples because as well as displaying some or all of the difficulties of large and complex models, they also have positive attributes, or represent honest if less than successful attempts to move in constructive directions. To avoid all the qualifiers and explanations that would be necessary if we used specific examples, our discussion is largely general.

Although some of them are heavily used and cited, these large and complex models are often not very satisfactory and their contribution to the formulation of clear, insightful understanding and policy direction is typically limited. There are several reasons for this. They are often hard to run and poorly documented. They tend to get used in a run-once-for-the-answer mode, with the result that they contribute relatively little insight about possible alternative ways of structuring and thinking about the problem. They rarely contain a satisfactory treatment of uncertainty and they are often not well validated, so that thoughtful users have limited confidence in their outputs. Despite the enormous effort often invested in their construction and use, our overall assessment is that their contribution to the process of developing informed regulatory policy is often modest, and sometimes negative.

In our experience, most of the policy modeling difficulties one might initially ascribe to the large size or complexity of these problems are not inherent to the problems themselves but arise from a failure to adopt good policy analytic practice or to use computer environments that provide appropriate software support. Restating the arguments of previous chapters: Policy models should start out simple, including only things that seem quite likely to be important. It is often very hard to figure out a priori which aspects of a problem matter. So, one should do sensitivity analysis to find them. In doing such analysis, many quick iterations are generally better than a few slow ones. Because all models are only partial representations of reality,[4] the objective should be to get a representation that is good enough across all relevant aspects of the problem to serve the purposes at hand. It should not contain elaboration and detail that are unnecessary for the purpose at hand. Ronald Howard (Howard and Matheson, 1984) has put it well in arguing for a "uniform wince" criterion. In other words, he argues that if one looks critically at any given part of a model, with the model's intended application in mind, one should not "wince" any more than when looking critically at any other part.

There are several reasons why general purpose regulatory models do not adopt this strategy but are designed or grow to be large and complex. Often they are built to be used by many different users who face different problems in different applications. This means they must include mechanisms that allow them to be adapted to a wide variety of specific circumstances. Frequently the result is a model that is really not right for anybody.

When it is possible to build a general purpose model that will adequately serve the needs of a number of different users, difficulties often arise in documentation and interface design. In principal, it should be possible to handle the tailoring of a general purpose model and its assumptions to a specific problem in a clear and transparent way. In practice, the solutions are often cumbersome, complex, and opaque.

In this context it is important to differentiate between single models that are very large and complex and big assemblies of models the individual elements of which are modest in size and complexity. Probably the most powerful tool available to handle complexity is structured hierarchical design. With this approach, large-scale problems can often be successfully treated by breaking them down into subelements, applying the sensitivity–iteration process to the design of each element, and then applying the same process to each assembly of elements up the hierarchy. Unfortunately, when people build large assemblies of models for policy purposes they often neglect to pay adequate attention to this latter step, and a system that could be simple to conceptualize and work with instead grows like Topsy into an impenetrable mess.

The regulatory environment in the United States, which is dominated by a legal, often adversarial, perspective, also contributes to the growth of some

---

4. If they were not just partial representations of reality, they would typically be of no use.

large and complex models. Although courts will review regulatory decisions on procedural grounds, they are often reluctant to examine the substance of a decision's analytical content. Because consideration of all aspects of a problem is one important procedural requirement, there is pressure at least to mention in the record of the decision process everything that may be relevant to the problem. This has led to environmental impact statements consisting of long lists of things that might be affected, with little or no critical discussion of their relative magnitude or of the significance of their impacts. These same forces have led to a tendency on the part of regulatory agencies to build models that include everything, whether it matters to the specific issues under consideration or not.

Good analysts who will adopt a sensitivity driven iterative approach to model development are often difficult to find, especially in regulatory agencies. Thus, if they do not exercise particular care in selecting their analysts, regulatory agencies will usually end up with models built with a linear approach (e.g., Figure 3.1) rather than an iterative approach (e.g., Figure 3.2) to the process of policy analysis. The result can be on the one hand a model that contains many things that are not necessary and, on the other hand, a model that leaves out critically important factors.[5]

Agencies often also adopt a cut-and-paste approach to modeling that involves sticking together various pieces of code originally developed for other reasons. There is, of course, nothing wrong with using existing code that is right for the job. All too often, however, what gets used is not right, and inappropriate or extraneous portions do not get edited out.

Of course, if they set out to find good analysts, agencies can almost always find them, typically in a few leading consulting firms and research universities. But agency management is frequently reluctant to make and justify the critical judgments necessary to hire these people, or is unable to tell the difference between really good analysts and mediocre analysts. Large and complex models certainly look impressive to the poorly informed. Poorly informed managers who do not have experience and self-confidence in selecting models and modelers may even be scared off by the very simplicity and transparency of good policy models – reasoning perhaps that something so clear and simple couldn't possibly be what is needed for such a complex and difficult problem. It takes enormous self-confidence and analytical sophistication to be willing to say in a regulatory environment, "Yes, we do not explicitly include that factor in

---

5. Perhaps the most graphic example of the latter that we have seen is a rail transportation model one of us examined for USEPA which was part of a much larger model to solve hazardous waste disposal problems. The transportation model contained a fancy traffic flow program to dispatch tank cars over alternative rail routes. However, it neglected to worry about how to get the empty cars back from the disposal sites. Thus, effectively, the model used tank cars only once, piling the used ones up at the disposal sites!

our model because we ran the following series of sensitivity studies and found that for this circumstance that factor just doesn't matter given the size of the uncertainties we are dealing with."

The development of large and complex models by agency management is not always inadvertent. Such models can be used to "snow" people with complexity. In some instances agency management has used this as a way of avoiding or masking difficult judgment calls that a decision maker would otherwise have to make, or make explicit.

Finally, because of management decisions, general purpose regulatory models often get built by committee. No single analyst or small group of analysts is put in charge. Rather, groups of different analysts and advisors, all with selected stakes and specialized knowledge, are given partial responsibility for building and evaluating the model. The result is that nobody is able to perform the careful systematic testing and judicious refinement through trimming and elaboration that good modeling requires.

11.2.2. Global systems models

Although today's general purpose regulatory models are often large and complex, their domain is usually more restricted than the domain of the global systems models popular in the 1960s and 1970s.

Because many social, economic, and environmental systems are large and complex, people's understanding of their operation is often limited and incomplete. This makes policy formulation difficult when it involves these systems. Beginning in the 1960s it became popular to argue that such policy problems could be resolved by simulating the entire system with computer models. Proponents argued that by capturing the system's complexity in a model, its behavior under various policy scenarios could be simulated. In the process, they argued, both an improved understanding of the system and more informed policy choices would then become possible.

Forrester argued the importance of such modeling as follows:

Intuition and judgment, generated by a lifetime of experience with the simple systems that surround one's every action, create a network of expectations and perceptions that could hardly be better designed to mislead the unwary when he moves into the realm of complex systems. One's life and mental processes have been conditioned almost exclusively by experience with first-order, negative-feedback loops. Such loops are goal seeking and contain only a single important system level variable ... From all normal personal experience one learns that cause and effect are closely related in time and space ... In complex systems all these facts become fallacies ... But, the complex system is far more devious and diabolical than merely being different from simple systems ... The complex system presents an apparent cause that is close in time and space to the observed symptoms. But the relationship is usually not one of cause and effect. Instead both are coincident symptoms arising from the dynamics of the system structure. Almost all variables in a complex system are highly correlated, but time correlation means little in distinguishing cause from effect ... With a high degree of confidence we can say that the intuitive solutions to the problems of complex social systems will be wrong most of the time. (Forrester, 1969)

We believe that Forrester has exaggerated his case. Human intuitions and conventional social science wisdom about human systems are not "wrong most of the time." The subsystems in many human and natural systems are often more loosely coupled than Forrester's argument implies. Indeed, if they were not, they might not have evolved. But he is clearly correct in pointing out that such systems can display "counterintuitive" behavior.

Practitioners of large-scale modeling approaches began cautiously. For example, in the introductory chapter of his book *Urban Dynamics*, Jay Forrester (1969) wrote:

Although this book is presented as a method of analysis rather than as policy recommendations, it is probably unavoidable that many will take these results and act on them without further examination of the underlying assumptions. Doing so is unjustified unless the pertinence of the model itself is first evaluated against the requirements of the particular situation. The approach presented in this book is suggested as a method that can be used for evaluation of urban policies once the proposed dynamic model or a modification of it has been accepted as adequate.

But over time, the caution displayed in this early work began to fade. By the time of his book *World Dynamics*, Forrester was writing:

In spite of the tentative nature of the world model described here, various conclusions are drawn from it. Man acts at all times on the models he has available. Mental images are models. We are now using those mental models as a basis for action. Anyone who proposes a policy, law, or course of action is doing so on the basis of the model in which he, at that time, has greatest confidence. Having defined with care the model contained [in this book] and having examined its dynamic behavior and implications, I have greater confidence in this world system model than in others that I now have available. Therefore, this is the model I should use for recommending actions. Those others who find this model more persuasive than the one they now are using presumably will wish to employ it until a better model becomes available. (Forrester, 1971)

Forrester's work in *World Dynamics* led to the Forrester–Meadows Club of Rome global model, which was widely popularized in the book *The Limits to Growth*. In the introduction to this book we find the following:

In spite of the preliminary state of our work, we believe it is important to publish the model and our findings now. Decisions are being made every day, in every part of the world, that will affect the physical, economic and social conditions of the world system for decades to come. These decisions cannot wait for perfect models and total understanding. They will be made on the basis of some model, mental or written, in any case. We feel that the model described here is already sufficiently developed to be of some use to decision makers. Furthermore the basic behavior modes we have already observed in this model appear to be so fundamental and general that we do not expect our broad conclusions to be substantially altered by further revisions. (Meadows et al., 1974)

This evolution from a cautious research orientation to aggressive policy advocacy is the central element in understanding the global modeling movement of the 1970s, and the vigorous conflicts that it generated.

A number of ther global modeling projects were undertaken in the decade that followed the publication of *The Limits to Growth.* Many of them[6] are succinctly summarized in Meadows, Richardson, and Bruckman (1982).

At about this same time the NSF Division of Environmental Systems and Resources, as part of the RANN program, funded a series of large national and regional models for resource and environmental simulation. Between 1970 and 1977 this division invested a significant fraction of its $20 million grant budget in eighteen large interdisciplinary computer modeling projects (Mar, 1977). These models ranged from large scale dynamic models not unlike the earlier Forrester–Meadows models to data management-oriented geographic information systems. This same period also saw a growth of modeling in the fields of international relations and diplomacy (Guetzkow, 1963; Guetzkow and Valadez, 1981), in military strategic studies (Brewer and Shubik, 1979), macroeconomics, and a variety of other fields.

11.2.3. Insights from Experiences with Global Systems Models

Despite the enthusiasm of the time, there is consensus today that most of the global systems and similar policy-oriented models built in the 1960s and 1970s fell short of their original expectations. The reasons have not yet been subjected to adequate examination and vary considerably from one field to another. In some cases, particularly for the more research oriented modeling efforts, they involve things like disciplinary myopia. But for the more policy-focused efforts we believe that five shortcomings figured importantly in contributing to the limited policy utility of these efforts: (1) inadequate and incomplete understanding of the systems being modeled and a concomitant lack of attention to model verification; (2) failure to be sufficiently specific about the objectives of the modeling project; (3) failure to examine carefully the implications of uncertainty in input variables and model time constants; (4) inability to deal with the stochastic elements in the systems being modeled; and (5) difficulties arising from the ideological perspectives of the analysts. Not surprisingly, the relative importance of these factors varies considerably across different areas of application.

That insufficient understanding of the systems being modeled was a major problem should be no surprise. It was because of this insufficient understanding that many of these projects got launched. Often the argument was that what had been missed in earlier work was a treatment of the dynamics of the system. For example, in the context of urban systems Forrester (1969) argued categorically that "when structure is properly represented, parameter values are of secondary importance. Parameter values must not be crucial because cities have much the

---

6. The Forrester–Meadows model; the Mesarovic–Pestel model; Bariloche model; MOIRA model; SARU model; FUGI model; and UN world model.

same character and life cycle regardless of the era and the society within which they exist."[7]

However, what much of the work actually demonstrated was that while the broad form of the dynamics is often important, so too in many systems are the details and the specific parameter values.[8] Robert Ayres (1984) has argued that, since results by Smale (1976,1980) have shown that models involving four or more multicomponent first order nonlinear differential equations can display any dynamical behavior, "it follows that the model is likely to be extremely sensitive to subjective assumptions on the part of the modeler." Ayres observes:

An example in point is the original five-variable nonlinear model of Forrester (1971). Forrester tried to argue ... that the pessimistic conclusions of his [world dynamics] model were essentially due to its *form* and were independent of parametric assumptions, thus justifying his lack of concern with empirical data. It was shown quite convincingly by Boyd (1972), however, that the model can be modified to yield *optimistic* results ... by the addition of one more dependent variable ("technology") and some plausible assumptions about the parametric relationship between technology and capital investment, quality of life, birthrate, natural resource base, and so on. In short, the parametric details really do matter more than the form – a fact that probably will not surprise many people who have worked with models. (Ayres, 1984)

Many of the "global models" were not actually very big or complex; but they involved systems that are not well understood and whose operations are not easily subjected to empirical examination. The same problems were often true of more complex models. In a review of the RANN resource and environmental models Mar (1974) observed that "many modelers consider models validated when all variables they feel are important are included and none of the relationships between variables are incorrect by the modeler's standards." Without an empirically based approach to validation, problems are inevitable. When the systems are as large, complex, and poorly understood as many of those that were being modeled, validation becomes an almost impossible task. We would argue that in such circumstances the need for empirical validation of any given model becomes secondary to a more general need for a coherent program of basic research. Indeed, Donella Meadows has written, "I personally believe that human understanding of human socioeconomic systems is still so faulty that the basic research function of computer modelling is by far the most important" (Meadows et al., 1982).

It is hard to disagree with this view. Unfortunately many "global systems" modeling projects were *not* undertaken with research as the primary objective. Often the promotion of a specific world view and set of policy recommendations were the primary objectives. This limited significantly the opportunity for

---

7. The urban historian Joel Tarr has pointed out to us in a private communication that many urban specialists would take strong exception to the assertion that "cities have much the same character and life cycle regardless of the era and the society within which they exist."

8. Further, both the model's structural details and the parameter values may change over time.

serious research contributions and has probably impeded the kind of model-aided social system research that Forrester called for in his early writings. In the case of macroeconomic modeling the concern has often been with producing a business forecast rather than advancing fundamental understanding of the economy. In this case the impact has been less serious, giving rise principally to "a needless acrimonious debate" (Kmenta and Ramsey, 1981).

Finally there is the problem that the systems that were being modeled in this work contain significant stochastic components that place serious limitations on the level of predictability that is possible. This problem is not unique to the "global systems" modelers.

11.3. Limits Imposed by Stochastic Processes

Stochastic elements of two kinds play an important role in many systems. On the one hand there is the problem of variability, which occurs on a scale finer than the temporal or spatial sampling of the model. This problem is particularly apparent in physical models such as weather and climate models, in which fine-scale structure must be handled parametrically (Thompson, 1957). Land and Schneider (1987) argue that the limits to predictability that have been demonstrated in physical systems probably also apply in many social systems. They argue:

Suppose . . . that we grant social scientists (economists, demographers, political scientists, sociologists, etc.) full knowledge of all future exogenous events that may impact on social systems (e.g. wars, earthquakes, volcanic eruptions, cartels, technological innovations). Suppose that we also grant them consummate skill in finding correct parametric representations of the relevant behavioral function for whatever phenomena it is they are modeling. But suppose that these phenomena contain certain processes that are governed by nonlinear mechanisms that do not average out and "forget" initial "small events" (i.e. are non-ergodic). And suppose that the parametric models – whether computer-based or not – are of finite size and hence of finite resolution, so that there are real-world micro-events that lie beneath their notice. Then the inherent potential amplification of these unnoticeable small events may create a region of uncertain (i.e. non-predictable, non-forecastable) outcomes in the solution space of the model.

In brief even under these most favorable circumstances, a parametric model that forecasts accurately with certainty is an impossibility. This result depends critically on the assumption that the model possesses nonlinearity, non-ergodic parametric mechanisms. (Land and Schneider, 1987)

These arguments begin to approach classical philosophical arguments about human free will. Indeed, Ayres (1984) has discussed the problem essentially at that level, terming it the "Seldon paradox." [9] "If we believe," Ayres argues, "that leaders do occasionally lead, that history would have been different if Napoleon or Hitler had never been born, that policy is not a sham, that policy-makers do

---

9. Named after the hero of a series of science fiction novels by Isaac Asimov about a modeling expert named Hari Seldon.

exist – both as individuals and as institutions – then macro-indeterminacy cannot be ignored in models." While Ayres focuses on leaders, Land and Schneider's argument is actually broader, arguing effectively that the actions of many free agents, and the operation of many social institutions, may all contribute over time to macro-indeterminacy.

If we do not grant Land and Schneider's assumptions of full predictability of events such as wars and earthquakes, we come to the other kind of stochastic element that can have important effects on large systems: major changes in the operating environment (what a statistician would call "nonstationarity"). The impact of the Arab oil crisis on energy forecasts made in the early 1960s is an excellent illustration of the importance of such events (which economists call "shocks"). Unfortunately, although a good model of the system may tell you how it will respond to any hypothetical set of events or changes in the operating environment, predicting such events is generally impossible. An excellent illustration of the problem is provided by macroeconomic models. In evaluating a large number of these models, Meltzer has concluded that:

> forecast errors for [economic] output growth are so large relative to quarterly changes that it is generally not possible to distinguish consistently between a boom and a recession either in the current quarter or a year in advance. The data on which I have relied to reach this conclusion are not new, and they are not unusual. The same conclusion applies to other periods. It is a general implication of many studies of forecasting accuracy using different methods and models.
>
> Many of these forecast errors for growth of real output or for inflation that I have considered fall within a relatively small range. No single technique or model seems capable of substantially reducing the size of forecast errors. A plausible inference ... is that the forecast errors we observe are close to the minimum we are likely to find with current forecasting techniques and models under current policy procedures. Remaining errors appear to be mainly random variation caused by myriad unanticipated real shocks, changes in expectations, foreign influences, and actual, perceived or anticipated changes in government policy action.
>
> These findings and interpretations, if correct, reinforce doubts about the possibility of using forecasts to guide discretionary policy action to reduce fluctuations. They do not imply that variability cannot be reduced. The size of forecast errors depends on policy rules. Alternatives to discretionary policy based on judgments and forecasts are available. More stable, predictable policies may be more successful in reducing fluctuations than well-intended activism. (Meltzer, 1987)

The discussions that ensue lead one to the conclusion that in building policy models of large complex social and physical systems, the objective should not be prediction but, rather, insight that can guide the development of heuristic policy strategies. For several decades climatologists have used climate models (Schneider, 1987) to argue that the best strategy for dealing with possible human impacts on the climate is to try to operate human activities so as to minimize those impacts on the grounds that the system is too complex to allow accurate predictions. System ecologists have advanced similar arguments in the context of complex ecological systems such as in the control of the spruce bud worm and in other pest control problems (Holling et al., 1979; Clark, Jones, and Holling, 1979). Drawing on ideas from these and other fields, especially evolutionary biology, Clark (1980) has argued for an "adaptive" approach in the design of policy, calling for policies that "adapt themselves to the developing situation and, in so doing, cultivate the will necessary for their adoption and continued pursuit." Of course, adaptive strategies are successful only so long as the world remains reasonably benign. Sufficiently dramatic and rapid changes can undo any such strategy. Ayres (1984) has argued that "models may have more utility in conveying to decision makers the extreme sensitivity of outcomes to small changes in the choice of control variables when they are in certain critical ranges." Thus, he argues, "it seems imperative for modelers to give more attention to the range of uncertainty, *with emphasis on uncertainty arising from decisions and policy choices not yet made.*"

11.4. Legitimate Reasons for Building Large and Complex Models

There are legitimate reasons for building large and complex models. Such models are justified when the details of the system are well understood *and* the inclusion of these details in the model is essential to the insight or answer that is sought. Such conditions are usually met *only* in physical science and engineering. In these fields, in which the fundamental principles and interactions involved in many problems are understood in great detail, large complex models are routinely built for a wide variety of applications ranging from tracing the trajectories of particles through accelerators to the design of large chemical reactors, the design of aircraft structural elements, or the layout of VLSI circuits.

Large complex models also play an important role in research on problems where many details are *not* completely understood. Studies of regional air pollution, weather, and regional and global climate[10] provide good examples. Modeling any of these problems involves complex systems of coupled differential equations and large amounts of data to establish initial conditions. These models cannot be used to produce precise predictions like those of engineering design models. Rather they provide a vehicle for research on systems we do not yet fully understand. They offer a strategy for summarizing our current understanding and subjecting it to critical empirical evaluation. The same is true in many other fields, some of which – systems ecology and certain problems in social science such as demography and macroeconomics – involve even less complete understanding than weather and climate. So long as these models remain research and documentation tools, they can often be justified.

---

10. In this case the models involve not just the atmosphere but also the dynamics of the oceans and land surfaces including the cryosphere.

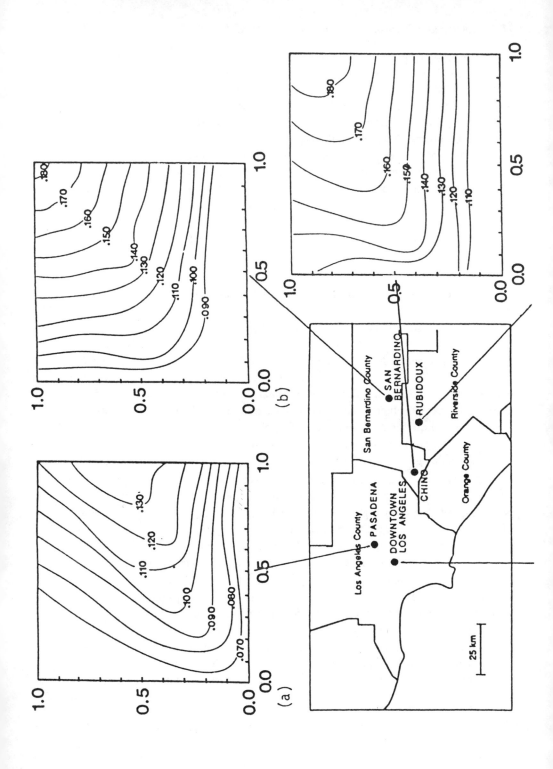

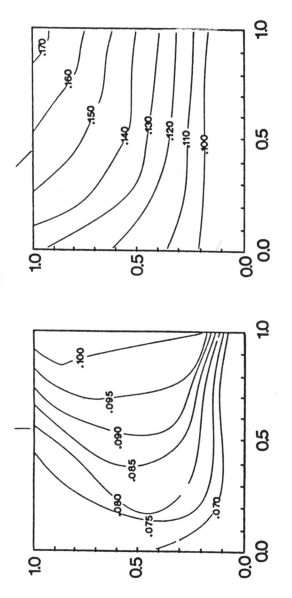

Figure 11.1. Response surfaces showing predicted response of peak ozone concentrations in parts per million at locations across the Los Angeles basin to reductions in emissions in oxides of nitrogen (vertical axes) and of reactive organic gases (horizontal axes). The upper right-hand corner of each diagram corresponds to the base case with no reductions (Milford et al. 1989).

11.5. Simplifying Large Research Models for Policy Applications

It is inevitable that policy analysts will occasionally want to make use of large and complex models developed for engineering design, or as part of scientific research. These models are typically not well suited for policy applications. They are unwieldy, frequently incomplete, expensive to run, and usually not suitable for use in the kind off iterative probing approach to analysis summarized in Figure 3.2.

Using techniques discussed in Chapter 8 it is often possible to do more uncertainty analysis on such models than is typically done. But although these techniques can be extremely useful, they will not turn a large complex scientific research model into a flexible, easily exercised policy model.

In our view, if one has to, the appropriate way to use large scientific models in the policy process is to abstract and simplify from their structure and outputs. In some cases this can be done directly to produce a response surface over the relevant model domain (ranges of important variables) which can be used in policy studies. A good example of this is a large atmospheric pollution model of the Los Angeles basin (Milford, Russell, and McRae, 1989; Stockwell et al., 1988). Milford, Russell, and McRae have repeatedly simulated this model in a series of CRAY-XMP runs to produce a number of response surfaces that display its complex nonlinear performance. Some examples of these response surfaces are shown in Figure 11.1.

Another strategy that may be possible once a big research model has been built and empirically validated is to abstract from it simplified analytical models that provide satisfactory results over those model domains (ranges of important variables) of interest to the policy process. These simplified models can then be exercised repeatedly to explore various policy alternatives. Simplistic models of complex systems that have been built without empirical validation can be useless or dangerous. In contrast, a simple model that abstracts the relevant empirically validated insights from a complex scientific model for use in a specific policy problem can be a powerful and valuable tool.

In circumstances where neither a response surface nor a simplified abstracted model are feasible, experts may be able to use insights from selected runs of their large models together with a number of smaller models to construct bounding, scaling, and other arguments. Using these and professional judgment they may be able to offer useful advice and guidance for policy purposes. Except when standard well validated engineering design models are being used, the one thing it is almost never appropriate to do is to run a big research model and then adopt its output as policy gospel.

The key point to remember is that without thorough and systematic modeling and analysis of the uncertainty of the problem, we can not be sure that the results of a model, especially a very large and complex one, mean anything at all.

References

Ayres, R. U. (1984). "Limits and Possibilities of Large-Scale Long Range Societal Models," *Technology Forecasting and Social Change*, 25:297–308.

Boyd, R. (1972). "World Dynamics: A Note," *Science*, 177:516–519.

Brewer, G. D., and Shubik, M. (1979). *The War Game: A Critique of Military Problem Solving*, Cambridge University Press, New York.

Clark, W. C. (1980). "Witches, Floods and Wonder Drugs: Historical Perspectives on Risk Management," in *Societal Risk Assessment; How Safe is Safe Enough?*, ed. Richard C. Schwing, and Walter A. Albers, pp. 287–313, Plenum Press, New York.

Clark, W. C., Jones, D. D., and Holling, C. S. (1979). "Lessons for Ecological Policy Design: A Case Study in Ecosystem Management," *Ecological Modeling*, 7:1–53.

Dy Liacco, T. E. (1967). "The Adaptive Reliability Control System," *IEEE Transactions on Power Apparatus and Systems*, PAS-86:577–530.

Forrester, J. W. (1969). *Urban Dynamics*, MIT Press, Cambridge, Mass.

Forrester, J. W. (1971). *World Dynamics*, Wright-Allen Press, Cambridge, Mass.

Guetzkow, H. S. (1963). *Simulation in International Relations: Developments for Research and Teaching*, Prentice-Hall, Englewood Cliffs, N.J.

Guetzkow, H. S., and Valadez, J. J., eds. (1981). *Simulated International Processes: Theories and Research in Global Modeling*, Sage Publications, Beverly Hills, Calif.

Henneman, R. L. (1985). *Human Problem Solving in Complex Hierarchical Large Scale Systems*, Report 85-1, Center for Human-Machine Systems Research, Georgia Institute of Technology, Atlanta.

Henneman, R. L., and Rouse, W. B. (1986). "On Measuring the Complexity of Monitoring and Controlling Large-Scale Systems," *IEEE Transactions on Systems, Man, and Cybernetics*, 16 (March-April): 193–207. This paper also contains an extensive bibliography.

Holling, C. S., Dantzig, G. B., Clark, W. C., Jones, D. D., Baskerville, G., and Peterman, R. M. (1979). "Quantitative Evaluation of Pest Management Options: The Spruce Budworm Case Study," in *Current Topics in Forest Entomology*, ed. W. E. Waters, U.S. Forest Service General Technical Report, WO-8.

Howard, R., and Matheson, J. E. (1984). *The Principles and Applications of Decision Analysis*, Strategic Decisions Group, Menlo Park, Calif.

Kearney, J. K., Sedlmeyer, R. L., Thompson, W. B., Gray, M. A., and Adler, M. A. (1986). "Software Complexity Measurement," *Proceedings of the ACM*, 29:1044–1050.

Kmenta, J., and Ramsey, J. B. (1981). *Large Scale Macro-Econometric Models*, North Holland, Amsterdam.

Kokotovic, P. V., Allemong, J. J., Winkelman, J. R., and Chow, J. H. (1980). "Singular Perturbation and Iterative Separation of Time Scales," *Automatica*, 16:23–33.

Land, K. C., and Schneider, S. H. (1987). "Forecasting in the Social and Natural Sciences: An Overview and Analysis of Isomorphisms," in *Forecasting in the Social and Natural Sciences*, eds. K. C. Land and S. H. Schneider, pp. 7–31, Reidel, Dordrecht.

Mar, B. W. (1974). "Problems Encountered in Multi-disciplinary Resources and Environmental Simulation Models Development," *Journal of Environmental Management*, 2:83–100.

Mar, B. W. (1977). *Regional Environmental Systems: Assessment of RANN Projects*, Department of Civil Engineering, University of Washington, Seattle.

McCabe, T. J. (1976). "A Complexity Measure," *IEEE Transactions on Software Engineering*, SE-2: 308–320.

Meadows, D. H., Meadows, D. L., Randers, J., and Behrens, W. W. III (1974). *The Limits to Growth*, 2d ed., Universe Books, New York.

Meadows, D. H., Richardson, J., and Bruckmann, G. (1982). *Groping in the Dark: The First Decade of Global Modeling*, Wiley, New York.

Meltzer, A. H. (1987). "Limits of Short-Run Stabilization Policy," *Economic Inquiry*, 25:1–14.

Milford, J. B., Russell, A. G., and McRae, G. J. (1989). "Spatial Patterns in Photochemical Pollutant Response to NO$_x$ and ROG Reductions," *Environmental Science and Technology*, 23:1290–1301.

Morgan, M. G., and Talukdar, S. N. (1979). "Electric Power Load Management: Some Technical, Economic Regulatory and Social Issues," *Proceedings of the IEEE*, 67:241–312.

Schneider, S. H. (1987). "Climate Modeling," *Scientific American*, (May): 72–78.

Simon, H. A. (1982). *Sciences of the Artificial*, 2d ed., MIT Press, Cambridge, Mass.

Smale, S. (1967). "Differentiable Dynamical Systems," *Bulletin of the American Mathematical Society*, 73:747. Reprinted in S. Smale, (1980), *Mathematics of Time*, Springer-Verlag, New York.

Smale, S. (1976). "On the Differential Equations of Species in Competition," *Journal of Mathematics and Biology*, 3:5.

Stockwell, W. R., Milford, J. B., McRae G. J., Middleton, P., and Chang, J. S. (1988). "Non Linear Coupling in the NO$_x$-SO$_x$-reactive Organic System," manuscript, Department of Engineering and Public Policy, Carnegie Mellon University, Pittsburgh.

Thompson (1957). "Uncertainty of Initial State as a Factor in the Predictability of Large Atmospheric Flow Patterns," *Tellus*, 9:275–295.

Weaver, W. (1948). "Science and Complexity," *American Scientist*, 36:536–544.

Winkelman, J. R., Chow, H., Allemong, J. J., and Kokotovic, P. V. (1980). "Multi-Time-Scale Analysis of Power Systems," *Automatica*, 16:35–43.

"As for me, all I know is I know nothing."
Socrates, *Phaedrus*, sec. 235

An awareness of the limitations of one's knowledge has long been recognized as an important aspect of wisdom. Socrates went so far as to maintain that his wisdom consisted solely in his recognition of the extent of human ignorance in his attempt to explain why the Delphic oracle had pronounced him wisest among men. While it may be easy to admit the virtue of this "Socratic wisdom," it seems less easy to maintain a full consciousness of it when engaged in practical decision-making.

As discussed in Section 4.2, the development of the personalistic or Bayesian theory of probability (Savage, 1954; de Finetti, 1974) provides a way for us to conceptualize some kinds of ignorance by characterizing our degrees of uncertainty in terms of subjective probabilities. Bayesian decision theory builds on this to provide a conceptual framework for explicitly incorporating our uncertainties about our information in the process of making decisions. The art of decision analysis that has sprung from this theoretical work offers a range of techniques intended to make these developments applicable for practical decision-making, at least for those decisions worth systematic attention. To the extent that we can capture our opinions of the limitations of our knowledge by subjective probability distributions over the quantities we are uncertain about, decision analysis appears to provide a way of operationalizing this Socratic precept.

In Chapter 3 we presented a number of arguments for why we consider the characterization and treatment of uncertainty to be important in quantitative policy analysis. Perhaps the most compelling of these arguments are organizational and behavioral in nature, but we also outlined several arguments within the more narrow context of decision theory. This chapter[1] develops some of these ideas in more depth. It takes a decision theoretic approach to quantify the advantages of a probabilistic treatment of uncertainty in policy modeling in terms of expected value, relative to decision methods that ignore uncertainty. It introduces the notion of the *expected value of including uncertainty* (EVIU), as a measure of the effect of considering uncertainty in the context of a specific decision problem. It then compares it to the more familiar concepts of risk premium and the expected value of perfect information (EVPI), develops a

---

1. This chapter is largely based on Henrion (1982, 1989). Here we present the key ideas but omit proofs and detailed derivations.

general approximation to the EVIU, and illustrates its application to various classes of decision problem to explore when ignoring uncertainty is likely to be harmless or dangerous. Finally it discusses some limitations in the measure and recaps some of the more qualitative reasons outlined in Chapter 3 for considering uncertainty that may not be captured in the EVIU.

12.1. The Expected Value of Including Uncertainty (EVIU)

It is generally easier to ignore quantitative analysis and treat all continuous uncertain quantities as fixed at some central, nominal value. This obviates having to assess probability distributions and greatly simplifies calculation. If, on the other hand, you *do* consider the uncertainty explicitly, you may make better decisions. The question we wish to examine is how much better you will do, in expected value terms, if you include the uncertainty in your analysis. The notion of the *expected value of including uncertainty* (EVIU) quantifies this as the expected difference in value of a decision based on a probabilistic analysis and a decision that ignores uncertainty.

The EVIU depends on what decision you are considering, which quantity (or quantities) whose uncertainty you are concerned about modeling, and the loss function (or utility function) you will use to evaluate the eventual decision and outcome of the uncertain quantity. Suppose you are a decision maker facing a decision problem, where

$d \in \mathbf{D}$ is your decision chosen from space $\mathbf{D}$,
$x \in \mathbf{X}$ is an uncertain empirical variable in space $\mathbf{X}$,
$L(d, x)$ is your loss as a function of decision, d, and state x,
$f(x)$ is your prior subjective probability density (SPD) on x,
$\mathrm{E}[L(d, x)] \equiv \int_{\mathbf{X}} L(d, x) f(x) \, dx$
              is your prior expectation over x of the loss for decision d, and
$d_y \equiv \mathrm{Min}_d^{-1} \mathrm{E}[L(d, x)]$ (29)
              is a decision that minimizes the expected loss over your prior, i.e.,
              your *Bayes' decision*.[2]

If you decide to ignore uncertainty you will use some "best estimate" for x, which presumably will be some central value of the subjective probability distribution (SPD) you might otherwise have assessed for x. It is not clear whether, in practice, this "best estimate" will be the mean, mode, median, or some other central point on this hypothetical SPD. For the moment let us assume it is the mean:

$x_{iu} = \mathrm{E}[x]$ is the value of x you assume when ignoring uncertainty,
$d_{iu} \equiv \mathrm{Min}_d^{-1} L(d, x_{iu})$ (30)
              is the deterministic optimum decision that minimizes your loss
              ignoring uncertainty.

---

2.   The notation $d_* = \mathrm{Min}_d^{-1} f(d)$ means d_* is a value of d such that $f(d)$ is a minimum.

Definition 1: Your *expected value of including uncertainty* is your expectation of the difference in loss between an optimal decision ignoring uncertainty, d_{iu}, and your Bayes' decision, d_y:

$$EVIU \equiv \int_{\mathbf{X}} \left[L(d_{iu}, x) - L(d_y, x) \right] f(x) \, dx$$

$$= \mathrm{E}\left[L(d_{iu}, x) \right] - \mathrm{E}\left[L(d_y, x) \right] \tag{31}$$

By the definition of d_y

$$\mathrm{E}\left[L(d_y, x) \right] \leq \mathrm{E}\left[L(d_{iu}, x) \right] \qquad \forall d_{iu}$$

$$\text{and so, } EVIU \geq 0 \qquad \forall x_{iu} \tag{32}$$

Thus the explicit inclusion of uncertainty in your analysis should at least not make you worse off in terms of expected value (neglecting the extra effort involved in the analysis). This should not be surprising, since your uncertain prior on x contains potentially useful information that is lost if you treat x as certain. If you consider uncertainty, you are effectively using more information than if you ignore it, and the EVIU is the expected value of this additional information.

12.2. The EVIU and the EVPI

Since the EVIU is a measure of the value of a kind of information, it may be useful to contrast it with the more familiar measure, the *expected value of perfect information* (EVPI):

$$EVPI \equiv \mathrm{Min}_d \mathrm{E}[L(d, x)] - \mathrm{E}[\mathrm{Min}_d L(d, x)]$$

$$= \mathrm{E}[L(d_y, x)] - \mathrm{E}[L(d_{pi}(x), x)] \tag{33}$$

$$\text{where } d_{pi}(x) \equiv \mathrm{Min}_d^{-1} L(d, x) \tag{34}$$

is a decision strategy that minimizes loss given perfect information x.

Both EVIU and EVPI compare the expected value of the Bayes' decision d_y with another decision made without uncertainty. For the EVIU this other decision, d_{iu}, is made when the uncertainty is *ignored*, although it is there; and for the EVPI this other decision, d_{pi}, is made after the uncertainty is *removed* by obtaining perfect information on x. The EVPI is the expected cost of begin uncertain about x, whereas the EVIU is the additional expected cost of pretending you are not uncertain.

The EVIU, like the EVPI, gives expected value in terms of the units of the loss function, (dollars, lives, utilities or whatever), and it depends on the degree of uncertainty in the priors. Here we are more interested in examining the effects of the *structure* of the loss function on the benefits of considering uncertainty in relative terms, so that we can find some general conclusions about classes of loss function. Thus, it is useful to consider the ratio of the two terms, which is a dimensionless index of the relative severity of the expected effect of ignoring uncertainty about x:

Definition 2: We define the ratio of the EVIU to the EVPI as the *Socratic ratio*:

$$S_{iu} \equiv \frac{EVIU}{EVPI} \tag{35}$$

It is a prior measure of the expected benefits of Socratic wisdom (i.e., admitting one's uncertainty) relative to the expected benefits of perfect wisdom (i.e., knowing the truth).

12.3. The EVIU and Risk Premium

Perhaps the most obvious reason for considering uncertainty in the outcome value is that most people seem to be risk averse and not interested simply in maximizing expected monetary gain (or other numeraire). If you subscribe to the von Neumann–Morgenstern axioms, your preferences should be consistent with having a utility function $U(v)$ over value v, such that, for all probability distributions over v, you should wish to maximize expected utility, $E[U(v)]$. For any lottery, characterized by your subjective probability distribution $f(v)$, there should be a *certainty equivalent* $\tilde{v}$ such that you are indifferent between playing the lottery and getting $\tilde{v}$ for sure:

$$U(\tilde{v}) = E\big[U(v)\big|\, f\big]$$

If you are risk averse, the certain equivalent will be less than the expected loss, and the difference between them is known as the *risk premium*:

$$r = E[v] - \tilde{v} \tag{36}$$

The risk premium is conventionally interpreted as the price you are willing to pay to avoid uncertainty. Suppose you have an investment whose current value to you, v, is uncertain, and you have an offer to sell it for c. You should be willing to sell it if $c > \tilde{v}$, netting an increase in equivalent expected value of $c - \tilde{v}$. But if you ignored uncertainty, and assumed $v = E[v]$, then you wouldn't be willing to sell unless $c > E[v]$ and so could lose an amount $c - \tilde{v}$ in expected value, which cannot be greater than the risk premium. So in this situation the risk premium provides an upper bound on the EVIU for uncertainty in v, depending on the value of c.

For a risk-neutral decision maker, utility is linear in value (or loss), but, depending on the decision model, its value may not be linear in the uncertain quantities. In that case, there may still be good reason to consider uncertainty, because the expected value may not be the value computed deterministically using the means of the uncertain state variables. In the remainder of this chapter we do not go into risk preferences explicitly in the analysis, although one could consider the loss functions (as negative utility functions) to embody them implicitly.

12.4. When Ignoring Uncertainty Doesn't Matter

To gain more insight into when it may be important to include uncertainty in your analysis and when it may not matter, we shall look at a variety of common classes of loss function. We start out with the linear and quadratic loss functions. In each case we assume that the value of x ignoring uncertainty is equal to its mean

$$x_{iu} = \mathrm{E}[x]$$

First let us consider a general linear loss function, where the decision space is discrete

$$d \in \{d_1, d_2, \ldots d_n\}$$

and the loss function is

$$L(d, x) = \begin{cases} a_1 + b_1 x & \text{if } d = d_1 \\ a_2 + b_2 x & \text{if } d = d_2 \\ \ldots & \ldots \\ a_n + b_n x & \text{if } d = d_n \end{cases}$$

where the a_i and b_i are constants.

Since $L(d, x)$ is linear in x, the expected loss for any decision d, is equal to the loss assuming x is fixed at its mean, that is its value ignoring uncertainty:

$$\mathrm{E}[L(d, x)] = L(d, \mathrm{E}[x]) = L(d, x_{iu})$$

By definition, the Bayes' decision minimizes the expected loss, and therefore is the same as the decision that minimizes loss assuming x is fixed at its mean, that is the decision ignoring uncertainty:

$$d_y \equiv \mathrm{Min}_d^{-1} \mathrm{E}[L(d, x)] = \mathrm{Min}_d^{-1} L(d, x_{iu}) = d_{iu}$$

Since the Bayes' decision turns out to be the same as the decision ignoring uncertainty, the expected loss is the same in either case:

$$EVIU \equiv \mathrm{E}[L(d_{iu}, x)] - \mathrm{E}[L(d_y, x)] = \mathrm{E}[L(d_{iu}, x)] - \mathrm{E}[L(d_{iu}, x)] = 0$$

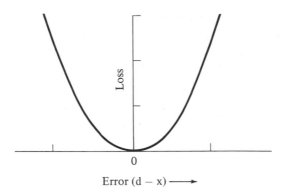

Figure 12.1. Quadratic error loss function.

So considering uncertainty makes no difference to the decision, and hence to the outcome in the case of a linear loss function.

Now let us look at the quadratic loss function, with the form

$$L(d, x) = k\,(d - x)^2$$

where k is a positive constant. This is illustrated in Figure 12.1. The expected loss is

$$E[L(d, x)] = k\,(d^2 - 2d\,E[x] + E[x^2])$$

To find the Bayes' decision, we minimize the expected loss by setting its derivitive to zero:

$$\frac{\partial E[L(d, x)]}{\partial d} = k\,(2d - 2E[x]) = 0$$

Hence

$$d_y = E[x]$$

If we ignore uncertainty, assuming x is fixed at its mean, we act as if the loss is:

$$L(d, E[x]) = k\,(d^2 - 2d\,E[x] + E[x]^2)$$

To find the optimal decision ignoring uncertainty, we minimize this expression, setting its derivitive to zero:

$$\frac{\partial L(d, E[x])}{\partial d} = k\,(2d - 2E[x]) = 0$$

So

$$D_{iu} = E[x]$$

We find that the Bayes' decision is the same as the decision ignoring uncertainty, for the quadratic loss function just as for the linear loss function. As so, considering uncertainty makes no difference to the decision and, therefore, nor to the outcome. Thus, for what are probably the two most commonly used loss fuctions, the EVIU is zero.

The squared error loss function, as well as being mathematically convenient, has been suggested as a reasonable approximation to smooth, non-negative loss functions for parameter estimation, on the grounds of fitting the Taylor expansion up to second order terms (e.g., Degroot, 1970). The widespread use of loss functions that are linear in the uncertain variables in practical decision problems, and the pervasiveness of quadratic loss functions for continuous parameter estimation, may have contributed to the not uncommon impression that explicit treatment of uncertainty doesn't make much difference.

12.5. Cubic Error Loss

Since we find that the conventional squared error loss has zero EVIU, let us go one better and consider loss functions that are cubic in the error.

$$L(d, x) = r\,(d - x)^2 + s\,(d - x)^3, \qquad r > 0$$

The case where $s > 0$, is graphed in Figure 12.2. The "J-shaped" part of the curve in Figure 12.2 should be a reasonable approximation for a wide variety of asymmetric, smooth functions where loss is nondecreasing in absolute error. One important class of examples in which such loss functions arise is capacity planning decisions, such as building a road, airport, or power plant, where the decision maker wants to match the size to the uncertain future demand. Overcapacity leads to unnecessary capital expense being shared by too few users; undercapacity leads to traffic jams, overcrowding, blackouts, or substituting expensive alternatives. Typically, costs increase faster with underestimation error than with overestimation, and the loss function is smooth but asymmetric.

Suppose we confine out interest to the "J-shaped" part of the curve, where loss increases monotonically with absolute error. Thus we assume the Bayes' decision under uncertainty is constrained to be in this range, $(d_y - x) > e_{\min}$. We assume, as before, that the decision ignoring uncertainty is to match the mean value of the uncertain quantity.

$$d_{iu} = \mathrm{E}[x]$$

It can be shown (Henrion, 1989) that in the case with a cubic loss function the Socratic ratio cannot be greater than one-third:

$$S_{iu} = \frac{EVIU}{EVPI} \le \frac{1}{3}$$

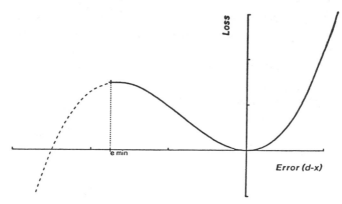

Figure 12.2. Cubic error loss function.

This result is interesting because it indicates there is a limit to how large the EVIU can be relative to the EVPI. Even including uncertainty in the analysis where it matters the most, it is still less than a third as important as obtaining better information about the uncertain quantity.

12.6. The Bilinear or "Newsboy" Loss Function

Since we have seen that the EVIU is zero or relatively small for smooth loss functions, let us consider a simple asymmetric loss function with a discontinuity function:

$$L(d, x) = \begin{cases} a\,(d - x) & \text{if } d \geq x \\ b\,(x - d) & \text{if } d < x \end{cases} \qquad \text{where } a, b > 0$$

This is sometimes known as the *newsboy problem*, Figure 12.3: A newsboy is trying to decide how many newspapers to order, d, so as to match the uncertain demand, x. He loses a cents per excess newspaper if he orders too many, and forgoes b cents per newspaper in lost profit if he orders too few. This kind of loss function has important application to a variety of stock-ordering and plant-sizing decisions where there is a hard maximum producing a discontinuity in slope.

For analytic convenience we assume a uniform prior on x, with mean $\bar{x}$ and width w:

$$f(x) = \begin{cases} 1/w & \text{if } \bar{x} - w/2 \leq x \leq \bar{x} + w/2 \\ 0 & \text{otherwise} \end{cases} \qquad \text{where } w > 0 \qquad (37)$$

This is illustrated in Figure 12.4. Again the decision ignoring uncertainty is simply the mean:

$$d_{iu} = \bar{x}$$

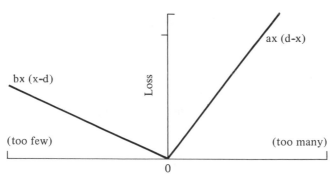

Figure 12.3. Bilinear or "newsboy" loss function.

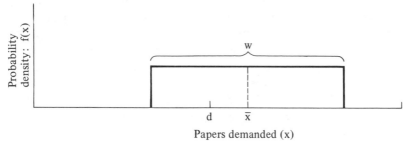

Figure 12.4. Uniform prior on x for "newsboy" problem.

We can then derive the following results.[3]

$$EVPI = \frac{wab}{2(a+b)}, \qquad EVIU = \frac{w(a-b)}{8(a+b)}$$

$$S_{iu} = \frac{EVIU}{EVPI} = \frac{(a-b)^2}{4ab}$$

Notice that in this case the Socratic ratio, S_{iu}, is *independent* of the uncertainty, w, that is, the EVIU does not increase with uncertainty relative to the EVPI. However, it becomes infinite as $a/b \to 0$ or as $b/a \to 0$. The EVIU depends on the ratio of the two slopes a/b, and increases without limit as this ratio departs from unity in either direction. There is no bound to the size of the EVIU relative to the EVPI: For very asymmetric loss functions, the expected loss from ignoring uncertainty may be much greater than the loss due to uncertainty; that is, considering uncertainty may be vastly more important than getting better information.

Although the uniform prior may not be appropriate for many situations, similar results apply to situations with other priors.

3. For the derivation, see Henrion (1982).

12.7. The Catastrophic or "Plane-catching" Problem

We have seen that the EVIU is zero for the symmetric quadratic loss function, relatively small for the asymmetric cubic loss function, but can be large for a strongly asymmetric bilinear loss function. The catastrophic loss function may be viewed as a limiting case of the bilinear. Loss increases linearly with the error on one side, and there is a step function giving a large sudden loss for even small errors on the other side. This describes situations where you are trying to attain a target value, and, provided you undershoot, your loss decreases linearly the closer you get to the target; but the slightest overshooting of the target leads to catastrophe.

A simple example is a busy person trying to catch a plane. The decision is how long to allow for the trip to the airport. You want to balance the cost of time wasted from leaving too early against the risk of major loss from missing the plane if you leave too late. This is the interpretation we use to illustrate the problem. But in addition to similar situations when trying to catch buses, trains, boats, and the like, it arises with great frequency in many critical aspects of engineering design. Examples include deciding how thick or strong to make some structural element of a bridge or aircraft, or the wall of a reactor vessel. Thinner and weaker elements will be cheaper, but their capacity is more likely to be exceeded by the uncertain peak stress and so result in catastrophic failure.

The loss function may be formulated as

$$L(d, x) = k(d - x) + \begin{cases} 0 & \text{if } d > x \\ M & \text{if } d < x \end{cases}$$

Here, d is the decision, how long to allow for the trip to the airport in the plane-catching illustration; x is the uncertain quantity, how long it will actually take to get to the airport; k is the marginal cost to you per minute of leaving earlier; M is the loss to you of missing the plane. If we measure the loss in minutes, then we can set $k = 1$, and assess the equivalent time lost from missing the plane. Figure 12.5 graphs an example, showing loss in minutes as a function of the decision d, assuming that the loss from missing the plane is five hours (300 minutes).

We assume that the constants k and M are positive, and that

$$M > k(d - x) \text{ for all } d, x$$

which implies you would never want to deliberately miss the plane if you knew x. If you did know x, the optimal decision with perfect information is, of course, to allow exactly the time it will take, that is,

$$d_{pi} = x$$

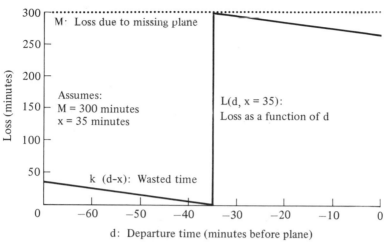

Figure 12.5. Catastrophic or "plane-catching" loss function.

Suppose you are uncertain about x, and your opinion is represented by a subjective probability density function, $f(x)$. Then your Bayes' decision, d_y, that is, the decision minimizing your expected loss, has the following property:

$$f(d_y) = \frac{k}{M}$$

In other words, the Bayes' decision is to allow an amount of time for the trip whose probability density is equal to the ration k/M. Assuming that the density function $f(x)$ is unimodal, and has a maximum density greater than k/M, there will be two points satisfying this. The Bayes' decision is at the point with the larger value.

Suppose you entirely ignore uncertainty in x and assume it is fixed at its median value $x_{0.5}$. The optimal decision ignoring uncertainty is then to allow exactly this median time for the trip:

$$d_{iu} = x_{0.5}$$

Since, by definition of the median, the actual time required will be greater than this value exactly half the time, this decision ignoring uncertainty will lead you to miss the plane half the time – not a very appealing strategy.

By definition, the expected value of including uncertainty is the difference between the expected loss with a decision ignoring uncertainty and the expected loss with the Bayes' decision:

$$EVIU = \mathrm{E}[L(d_{iu}, x)] - \mathrm{E}[L(d_y, x)]$$

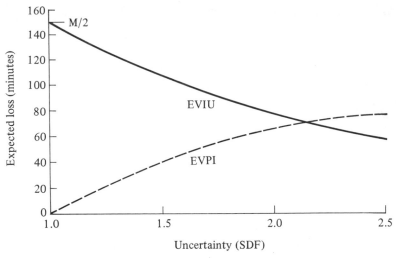

Figure 12.6. EVIU and EVPI as a function of uncertainty for "plane-catching" loss function.

Since the loss function is defined so that the loss is zero for the optimal decision, the expected loss for the Bayes' decision is equal to the expected value of perfect information, or

$$EVPI = \mathrm{E}[L(d_y, x)]$$

It is interesting to look at the EVPI and EVIU as a function of the uncertainty about x. As an example, suppose we model your opinion about x as a lognormal distribution with median 30 minutes, and a geometric standard deviation (GSD), s. The GSD has a similar role for a lognormal that the standard deviation has for the normal distribution. For a distribution with median m and GSD s there is a 68% probability that the true value of x is in the range $[m/s, m \times s]$. Thus, complete certainty is represented by $s = 1$. $s = 2$ means there is a 68% probability the value is within a factor of 2 of the median.

Figure 12.6 plots the EVPI and EVIU in minutes as functions of the uncertainty factor from 1 to 2.5. As one might expect, the EVPI increases monotonically with increasing uncertainty. The greater the uncertainty, the greater the value of eliminating the unceratinty. Perhaps less intuitively, the EVIU *decreases* monotonically with increasing uncertainty. In other words the penalty for ignoring uncertainty is largest when the uncertainty is smallest. The reason for this is that when ignoring uncertainty, you miss the plane exactly half the time, and the expected loss is $M/2 = 150$ minutes. But the relative improvement from considering uncertainty is largest when the Bayes' risk (the same as the EVPI in this case) is smallest. Since the Bayes' risk (and EVPI) *does* increase with uncertainty, this is when the uncertainty is smallest.

In this case, the Socratic ratio $S_{iu} = EVIU/EVPI$, tends to infinity as the uncertainty tends to zero (i.e., $s \rightarrow 1$). But it decreases monotonically with increasing uncertainty, with the value of unity at about $s = 2.2$. This is a very large degree of uncertainty, corresponding to a 95% confidence interval of $(61, 145)$ minutes. So in this problem, the analysis supports what may be clear intuitively, that it is an extremely poor idea to ignore the uncertainty in this class of decision problem. On the other hand, perhaps counterintuitively, it turns out that the expected loss from ignoring uncertainty decreases as the uncertainty becomes larger.

12.8. What Is the "Best Estimate," Ignoring Uncertainty?

So far we have been assuming that the best estimate, x_{iu}, that you would use if you ignore the uncertainty in x, is equal to the mean of the subjective probability density function (SPD) that you would have assessed for x if you had considered its uncertainty explicitly. It is not immediately obvious whether the central values people use are likely to be nearest the mean, median, mode, or some other measure of central tendency. The question deserves empirical investigation but has not yet been examined. Of course, if the SPD on x is roughly symmetric and unimodal, it won't much matter, since all measures will be roughly the same. But there are many policy relevant cases in which SPDs tend to be strongly skewed, and the difference is significant.

Two important examples in risk analysis are the failure frequency for components of a nuclear power plant used in fault tree analysis, and the carcinogenic potency of a chemical under consideration for regulation. Both kinds of quantity are typically non-negative, have a large probability of being very small, and have a long tail on the higher side. In both cases, lognormal distributions are often used (Rasmussen et al., 1975; Crouch and Wilson, 1981). Typically the uncertainties are large, generally expressed as geometric standard deviations (GSDs), uncertainty factors or error factors. These latter terms denote a concept similar to the GSD discussed above, but the range enclosed by the factor (ration to product) represents a 90% or 95% credible interval.

The ratio of the mean to the median is plotted as a function of the 90% uncertainty factor for a lognormal in Figure 12.7. The fact that the mean for such distributions may be many times greater than the median comes as a surprise to many assessors. It seems likely that the central value they would assume when ignoring uncertainty would be nearer the median. A Bayesian decision maker should be concerned with the expected frequency of system failure or the expected health impact (perhaps modified by risk attitude). In such situations he or she would make a very different decision based only on the medians, ignoring uncertainty. Hence, the expected value of including uncertainty (EVIU) might be very large in these cases.

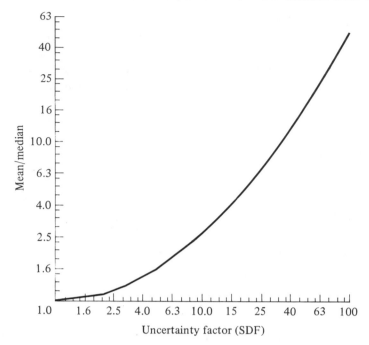

Figure 12.7. Ratio of mean/median for lognormal as a function of the uncertainty (standard deviation).

Even in cases where there is little difference between measures of central value, because the SPD is symmetric, there is the possibility that thinking systematically about the uncertainties may often significantly change one's opinion about its central values, particularly if the probability elicitation includes, as it should, focused consideration of extreme scenarios that might lead to surprising outcomes. For example, in assessing the cost of a large construction project, detailed attention to all the factors that might increase preliminary cost estimates – inflation, delays in material supplies, poor weather, accidents, labor disputes, and so on – may well lead to increasing the assessed mean. Thus, the probability assessment process may be valuable in producing better estimates of the central value, even if the subsequent formal analysis ignores the uncertainties.

12.9. The Duality of Asymmetry in Loss Function and Probability Distribution

We have seen how the effect of including uncertainty may be large when either the loss function is strongly asymmetric or the subjective probability distribution on an uncertain quantity is strongly asymmetric. It is interesting to note that these two conditions are actually dual to each other. For certain problems the condition pertaining may be one or the other, depending on how the uncertain variable is parameterized within the loss function. For example, consider a loss function that is linear in x and where x is lognormally distributed.

$$L(d, x) = f(d) + g(d)x, \qquad x \sim \text{Lognormal}(\mu, \sigma)$$

where $f(d)$ and $g(d)$ are functions of d independent of x. This may be appropriate for risk problems, where x is the frequency of core-melt for a nuclear reactor, or the human carcinogenicity of a chemical agent. In this case the loss function is linear in x, but the probability distribution is asymmetric. An alternative view is to consider y, where $x = e^y$, as the uncertain parameter, and assess y as normally distributed:

$$L(d, x) = f(d) + g(d)e^y, \qquad y \sim \text{Normal}(\mu, \sigma)$$

In this formulation, the uncertainty quantity y is symmetrically distributed, but the loss is an asymmetric function of y. Clearly these two formulations are equivalent. It is a matter of choice whether we view the loss function or the distribution as asymmetric. But either way the asymmetry gives rise to a non-zero, and possible large, EVIU.

12.10. The Use of the EVIU

At first it seems paradoxical to suggest that the EVIU should be used to help decide whether to include uncertainty in an analysis. To compute the EVIU itself requires a probabilistic analysis complete with probabilistic assessment of uncertain quantities. So of what use can it be if the task of computing it is equivalent to the task whose worth it is supposed to evaluate? One use for the EVIU is in the role explored above, as a theoretical tool to produce general insights.

Another way to use it is for sensitivity analysis to guide the process of model construction. Before going to the trouble of eliciting detailed probability distributions from experts for each uncertain quantity, analysts may make their own preliminary rough assessments for initial evaluations of the EVIU for each to test whether more elaborate assessments are likely to be worthwhile. They will still need to formulate and analyze the decision model in probabilistic terms, but this preliminary analysis can avoid unnecessary elicitations of probability. Given the availability of a convenient probabilistic decision modeling system and/or appropriate approximation techniques, the net saving on the elicitations may be considerable.

This role for the EVIU in sensitivity analysis, to guide model construction by identifying those uncertainties most critical to the decision, may be compared to the similar use of the EVPI. The construction of more elaborate models of uncertain quantities will often help to reduce uncertainty about them. In some of these cases the EVPI can be adapted as a sensitivity measure to estimate the maximum expected value of such modeling and suggest which parts may be worth detailing (Tani, 1978; Nickerson and Boyd, 1980). But in other cases, such as the health effects of respirable sulfate particulates or the price of oil in ten years' time, the uncertainty may be largely unresolvable by *any* modeling or information gathering in the time scale of the current analysis. All one can do is to gather the best expert opinions. The question then is how much effort to spend in assessing and representing the probability distributions: How many experts should be interviewed? What measures are worthwhile to reduce biases or improve calibration? And in how much detail should they be modeled? To answer such questions the EVIU is more appropriate than the EVPI as a guide to the analyst.

12.11. When to Consider Uncertainty and When to Use the EVIU

Under what circumstances is it important to include uncertainty explicitly in one's analysis? First consider three situations, much studied by decision theorists: When risk attitude is important; when uncertain information from different sources must be combined (e.g., from the opinions of different experts or data samples); and when a decision is to be made about whether to buy new information. In these three situations there is no real question about whether to consider uncertainty: Formal analysis can hardly proceed without it, and computing the EVIU would usually be superfluous. The EVIU can be of more use for illuminating situations where the answer is less obvious. It has shown us how considering uncertainty has no *direct* benefit in improving the decision when the loss function is linear or quadratic in the uncertain quantities. It can become very important for error functions that are highly asymmetric. It is also likely to be important for highly asymmetric probability distributions, if, as seems likely, the analysts will not use expected value for their "best estimate."

Even if a decision problem, once it is formally structured, has zero or negligible EVIU for the key uncertain quantities, there may turn out to be large *indirect* benefits for considering uncertainty. One, just discussed, is that a thorough examination of uncertainty is likely to change the "best estimate." Another is the use of uncertainty as a guide for development of the decision model in the most productive directions (Tani, 1978; Nickerson and Boyd, 1980). It is also important to consider the broader context within which the formal analysis takes place. For example, although the analyst may be nominally hired to recommend an immediate action, consideration of the uncertainty may show the expected value of better information to be so large that the best decision is to delay immediate action and seek better information. A single quantitative analysis is seldom either the first or the last word on a decision. The decision maker will usually wish to integrate the analytic results with opinions and recommendations from other sources. For such purposes it will be extremely helpful to have a quantitative statement of the uncertainty inherent in the analytic results so that the decision maker can weight them appropriately in combining them.

Furthermore, there is a strong argument that policy analysts have an ethical responsibility to be clear about the limitations of the services they provide. In most policy problems there are not only major technical and scientific uncertainties, but also disagreements on issues of value. If one avoids explicitness about the degree of technical uncertainty, it becomes all too easy to smuggle in personal or institutional value predilection by assuming the numbers that fit them best from within the ranges of reasonable uncertainty. This is misleading, and also serves to divert controversy from the underlying questions of value that are really at issue to the technical and scientific questions, which thereby become unnecessarily confused. In the longer term this can do considerable damage to the credibility of the analyst's profession, although it must be acknowledged that in the short term there may be strong personal and professional rewards in pretending to a spurious degree of certainty, both from reducing cognitive stress and from impressing others with one's expertise.

12.12. Summary

As we have seen in the other chapters of this book, treating uncertainty explicitly involves indentifying sources of uncertainty, expressing them in the form of probability distributions, choosing appropriate computational methods for propagating uncertainty through the model to analyze its effects, and devising clear ways to communicate the results. As such, it may entail substantial effort. In this chapter and elsewhere, we have explored a variety of circumstances of the problem and its analysis that may make this effort wortwhile. These include:

1. The decision maker has significant risk-aversion.
2. Uncertain information from several sources must be combined.
3. Decisions about whether to buy additional information to reduce uncertainty must be made.
4. The loss function is highly asymmetric in an uncertain quantity.
5. Some important uncertain quantity has a highly asymmetric distribution.
6. Thorough examination of the uncertainty about a quantity may change the "best estimate."
7. Consideration of uncertainties can be used as a guide for model refinement.
8. There is need to assess the reliability of the analysis to help decision makers know how much weight to give it.
9. The policy analysts feel an ethical responsibility to be clear about the limitations of their analysis.

It is hard to imagine an important quantitative policy analysis in which none of these apply. Taken together, they provide a compelling argument as to why the effort of treating the uncertainty explicitly is generally worth the candle.

References

Crouch, E., and Wilson, R. (1981). "Regulation of Carcinogens," *Risk Analysis*, 1, no. 1: 47–66.

de Finetti, B. (1974). *Theory of Probability* (2 vols.), Wiley, New York, (translated from the Italian).

DeGroot, M. H. (1970). *Optimal Statistical Decisions*, McGraw-Hill, New York.

Henrion, M. (1982). "The Value of Knowing How Little You Know: The Advantages of a Probabilistic Treatment of Uncertainty in Policy Analysis," Ph.D. diss., Carnegie Mellon University, Pittsburgh.

Henrion, M. (1989). "The Value of Knowing How Little You Know: Part I," manuscript, Department of Engineering and Public Policy, Carnegie Mellon University, Pittsburgh.

Howard, R. A. (1971). "Proximal Decision Analysis," *Management Science*, 17, no. 9: 507–541.

Nickerson, R. C., and Boyd, D. (1980). "The Use and Value of Models in Decision Analysis," *Operations Research* (April).

Rasmussen, N., et al. (1975). *Reactor Safety Study*, NUREG-75/0145 (WASH-1400), Nuclear Regulatory Commission, Washington, D.C.

Savage, L. J. (1954). *The Foundations of Statistics*, Wiley, New York.

Tani, S. N. (1978). "Perspective on Modeling in Decision Analysis," *Management Science*, 24, no. 14 (October).

"God created the World in 4028 B.C. on the ninth
of September at nine o'clock in the morning."
Archbishop Ussher of Ireland, A.D. 1658

Index

abstraction as projection, 245
abstraction dilemma, 243
Adams, Douglas, 141
adaptive strategies, 28, 301
adjoint methods, 190
African countries, number of, 106
air pollution, 9–14, 66, 146, 248–52, 304
Amaral, Deborah, 151–4
American Petroleum Institute, 10
American Physical Society Reactor Study, 7–8
analytic methods for propagating uncertainty, 183–92
  advantages and disadvantages of, 192
anchoring and adjustment heuristic, 106–7, 135, 149
anonymity, 161–2
approximation uncertainty, 55, 67
array abstraction, 260
assumptions, importance of identifying, 38
atmospheric scientists, 66, 146–52
automobile safety, 70, 246–8
availability heuristic, 103–5, 129, 144
axioms of probability, 49
Ayres, Robert U., 298

base rate information, 106
Bayes' decision, 308
Bayes' theorem, 84, 122
Bayesian estimation, 83
Bayesian prior, 84
Bayesian probability, 49, 73, 108, 307
benefit–cost analysis, 21, 25, 56, 246, 282
Bernoulli distribution, 98
best available technology, 28
"best case" scenario, 178
"best estimate," 238, 308
beta distribution, 97, 99, 115
betting, 124–6
bias
  cognitive, 103–7
  statistical, 79, 80
bilinear loss function, 314–15
Biller, William, 10
binomial distribution, 82, 98

bisection elicitation method, 114
botulism, 104
boundaries of analysis, 30
bounded cost, 25
Box–Muller method, 87–8
Brier score, 109
"butterfly effect," 64

calibration, 109, 110–12, 117, 167
  training for, 120–2
calibration curve, 110–12
calibration function, 167
carcinogenic potency, 59, 319
catastrophic loss function, 316–19
CDF, see cumulative distribution function
central limit theorem, 80, 186–7
certainty, absolute, 52
certainty equivalent, 310
chance nodes, 51–2
chance quantities, 50
chance variables, 51–2
chi-squared test, 100
chlorofluorocarbons, 11–14
Cicero, 6
clairvoyant, 50, 143
clarification of values, 54
clarity test, 50, 52, 60–2, 143
Clark, William, 28, 301
classical decision analysis, 69
classical policy analysis, 71
classical probability, 48, 73
Clean Air Act, U.S., 9
closed loop sensitivity, 197
coal-fired power plants, 66, 146
coefficient of variation, 188
cognitive bias, 103–7
coherence of probability judgments, 108
combinatorial explosion, 181, 196
combinatorial scenarios, 178
combining expert opinions, 65–6, 164
complexity, 163, 289–304
computational costs, 212, 304
computer aids, 257–85
computer modeling, 257–85, 289–304